NEW PANCHAYATI RAJ IN TAMIL NADU

(With Act in Original)

About the Author

Ganapathy Palanithurai, Professor in Rajiv Gandhi Chair, Gandhigram Rural Institute is an academic activist working with the people in rural areas for building the capacity of the leaders and people to reinvent sustainable grassroots democracy. He is heading the Department of Political Science and Development Administration, in Gandhigram Rural University, Tamil Nadu. His policy advocacy role at the governmental level is increasingly felt at present in all the three levels, namely, sub-regional, regional and national as he does more field work than theorization. He has been associating himself with State Planning Commission of Tamil Nadu, Centre Planning Commission Population Foundation of India, Rajiv Gandhi Foundation, CAPART, Ministry of Rural Areas and Employment and DANIDA (Danish-Indo Development Agency) in specific areas of activities in connection with empowerment of people. He is in the network of the Non-Governmental Organisations for Panchayat activities. He involves himself in capacity building exercise for local body leaders. He has evolved training module and manual for local body leaders. He has to his credit twenty-nine books, seventy-five articles in reputed journals, ten working papers, seven monographs, seven review articles on three major areas, namely, Legislative Behaviour, Ethnicity and Panchayati Raj System. He was a recipient of Fellowship from Sastri Indo-Canadian Institute, New Delhi and World Academy of Art and Science, USA. He has visited the US and Canada, on academic assignments. He was a visiting fellow in the MiGill University, Canada in 1989. He is a life member of Indian Institute of Public Administration, Indian Association of Public Administration, Indian Association of Political Science, Indian Association of American Studies, and Indian Association of Canadian Studies. He is a member of the expert committee constituted by the Government of Tamil Nadu, to monitor the training programme for local body leaders.

NEW PANCHAYATI RAJ
IN
TAMIL NADU
(With Act in Original)

G. PALANITHURAI
Professor and Head,
Department of Political Science and Development Administration
Gandhigram Rural Institute — Deemed University
Gandhigram-624 302
Tamil Nadu

CONCEPT PUBLISHING COMPANY, NEW DELHI-110059

ISBN 81-8069-031-8

First Published 2003

Published and Printed by
Ashok Kumar Mittal
Concept Publishing Company
A/15-16, Commercial Block, Mohan Garden,
NEW DELHI-110059 (India)

Phone : 25351460, 25351794
Fax : 091-11-25357103
E-mail : publishing@conceptpub.com

THE DIVINE MOTHER'S GRACE

We trust the people
We have faith in the people
It is the people who must
determine their own destinies
and the destiny of the Nation
To the people of India, let us
ensure maximum democracy and
maximum devolution. Let the
people be empowered.

— ***Rajiv Gandhi***

PREFACE

(In India) one should begin with the old panchayat system in the villages and the work upto the top. The panchayat system and the guilds are more representative and they have a living contact with people, they are the parts of the people's ideas.

— Sri Aurobindo

New Panchayati Raj System a much popularised and deeply discussed word and concept in the recent years among the public and politicians. Yet ambiguity persists at every level in perceiving the concept in the context. From the level of the perception of the leaders who had involved in the process of evolving and enacting the New Panchayat Act by amending the Constitution of India to the perception of the common man who is considered as a beneficiary or development participant, one can anticipate a variety of problems. In a country like India with multitude of variations in the socio-political institutions, one would expect such problems. The concept, its relevance, and its implications are to be perceived properly by all those who are involved in the process of operationalising the concept in the real life otherwise it will be very difficult to realise the objectives of the concept. But contrary to expectation, in India, people at different levels perceive the concept differently and operationalise the concept according to their own understanding and need where one would come across problems. In Indian setting we have been witnessing different levels of institutions in terms of their functioning. The levels of functioning vary due to the perception of the individuals who are at the helm of affairs in operationalising the concept. Assessing the performance of these institutions is not so easy. Hence case studies have been made. Details regarding the powers conferred on Gram Panchayats, Block Panchayats and District Panchayats and handling of those powers and responsibilities by the leaders of the different tiers have been analysed in those case studies. Critical areas like capacity building and creating support structure for empowerment of women have been probed in these cases. Problems have been brought out from the cases. With regard to empowerment of women variety of cases have been selected and analysed and in the same way cases have been selected to analyse the functioning of a Gram Panchayat, Block Panchayat and District Panchayat. General overview of Tamil Nadu panchayat has been given. A report of the capacity building exercise has been incorporated to enrich the understanding of the functioning of panchayats in Tamil Nadu. This handy volume would provide a birds eye view of the new panchayats of Tamil Nadu.

This work is the result of a field work done by a team in Rajiv Gandhi Chair. I express my heartfelt thanks to all my colleagues (Dr. V. Ragupathy, M.A. Thirunavukkarasu, M.Gurusamy, S.Devaraj, A.Thangathurai, G.Umashankar and S.P. Ramesh) individuals who have assisted me in preparing this document for publication. Equally I owe a lot to the respondents (the leaders) who have spared valuable their time and energy to meet our queries for this work. They deserve my appreciation and remembrance. I thank them for their valuable contributions to this work. My family members who have deep devotion in their work by performing their role and function without disturbing my role and function. As they have role clarity, they have allowed me to do this kind of works and for which I have to express my sincere appreciation to my wife Mrs. Mala and kids Senthil Vadivu and Aurobindh. Last not the least my secretarial staff who have deep devotion and attachments towards my work and hence they have been always at my disposal. They are to be thanked. Finally I express my sincere thanks to all those individuals who have helped me directly and indirectiy for the completion of this work.

30.06.2002
Gandhigram

G. Palanithurai

CONTENTS

LIST OF TABLES

ABBREVIATIONS

ABDO	—	Additional Block Development Officer
AD	—	Adi Dravida
ACP	—	Affective, Cognitive and Psycho Motor
AEO	—	Assistant Educational Officer
AIR	—	All India Radio
AIADMK	—	All India Anna Dravida Munnetra Kazhakam
AIDS	—	Acquired Immune Deficiencies
AMT	—	Anna Marumalarchi Thittam
ASI	—	Assistant Statistical Inspector
ASSEFA	—	Association of Serva Seva Farms
BC	—	Backward Community
BDO	—	Block Development Officer
CAPART	—	Council for Advancement of Peoples Action and Rural Technology
CPI(M)	—	Communist Party of India (Marxist)
CRSP	—	Central Rural Sanitation Programme
DANIDA	—	Danish International Development Assistance
DDO	—	District Development Officer
DMK	—	Dravida Munnetra Kazhakam
DRDA	—	District Rural Development Agency
DRD	—	Director of Rural Development
DWCRA	—	Development of Women and Children in Rural Areas
EAS	—	Employment Assurance Scheme
EB	—	Electricity Board
ED	—	Engineering Department
GLR	—	Ground Level Reservior
ICDP	—	Integrated Child Development Programme
IFAD	—	International Fund for Agriculture Development
IMR	—	Infant Mortality Rate
IRDP	—	Integrated Rural Development
JGSY	—	Jawahar Gram Samridhi Yojana
JRY	—	Jawahar Rozgar Yojana
JVVT	—	Jawahar Velai Vaaippu Thittam
MBC	—	Most Backward Community
MCH	—	Maternity and Child Health
MDMK	—	Marumalarchi Dravida Munnetra Kazhakam
M.N.Cs	—	Multi National Companies

MSSRF	—	M.S.Swaminathan Research Foundation
NGO	—	Non-Governmental Organisation
NMR	—	National Mortality Rate
NNT	—	Namakku Naame Thittam
NMP	—	Nutritional Meals Programme
OHT	—	Over Head Tank
OHP	—	Over Head Projector
OBC	—	Other Backward Community
PDS	—	Public Distribution System
PHC	—	Primary Helath Centre
PPS	—	Post-Pregnancy Sterilization
PRA	—	Participatory Rural Appraisal
PWD	—	Public Work Department
RD	—	Rural Development
SC/ST	—	Scheduled Castes and Scheduled Tribes
SW	—	Social Welfare
SEO	—	Social Extension Officer
SHG	—	Self-Help Group
SIRD	—	State Institute of Rural Development
STD	—	Sexually Transmitted Diseases
THADCO	—	Tamil Nadu Housing and Adi-Dravida Development Corporation
TOT	—	Training of Trainers
TV	—	Television
TMC	—	Tamil Manila Congress
TWAD	—	Tamil Nadu Water Supply and Drainage
TNEB	—	Tamil Nadu Electricity Board
TANWA	—	Tamil Nadu Women in Agriculture
TNADP	—	Tamil Nadu Agriculture Development Project
TINP	—	Tamil Nadu Integrative Nutrition Project
UNICEF	—	United Nations International Childrens Education Fund
UE	—	Union Engineer
VAO	—	Village Administrative Officer
VHM	—	Village Head Munisif
WRO	—	Water Resource Operation

1

NEW PANCHAYATI RAJ SYSTEM IN TAMIL NADU

The village Republic will be managed by a panchayat which will be living political force and entity. Panchayats will be united in a free and voluntary association by ever widening circle of village republics. It will not be an "apex sustained by the bottom but an oceanic circle where centre will be the individual always ready to perish for the village, the latter ready to perish for the circle of villages and so on, sharing the majesty of the oceanic circle which they are parts".

— ***Mahatma Gandhi***

Introduction

In the recent decades, central governments in the world have started decentralizing political, financial and administrative responsibilities to lower level governments/institutions and even to the extent of private sectors. Decentralization is more specific and intensive in developing countries as they face a number of problems. But it is ultimately due to the extreme political pressure on the central system of governance with an expectations of proper delivery of services, effective mobilization of resources and allocations, and stability in the macro economic system along with equity.

Variety of experiences have been gained by nations in the whole process of decentralization of power. There are ups and downs in the experiments and a stage has come not to argue or debate on whether decentralization is "good" or "bad" is unproductive since decentralization is a political reality through out the world. Against this background India had made a historical and significant attempt through 73rd Constitutional Amendment to decentralize powers to local bodies. This write up provides a descriptive narration of the whole process of decentralization of powers from the initiative of introducing 73rd Constitutional Amendment Act to the functioning of grassroots level institutions in Tamil Nadu in the backdrop of the conceptual framework.

Multiplicity of Concepts

For the concept "decentralization of power" a variety of concepts have been used by the academics and administrators and yet meanings of the concepts are not the same. Using the concepts such as Local Self Government, Local Government, Grassroots democracy, Grassroots institutions, Panchayat Raj, Panchayati Raj System, New Panchayati Raj System, Local Body Institutions, Empowering people, Small Government Approach and Decentralized Governance interchangeably to connote the same meaning of devolving powers and responsibilities from higher level governing institutions to lower level governing institutions. Of course all the concepts are not the same and semantic differences are among the concepts.

Some of the concepts are western in origin and many of them are in indigenous in origin. The concepts have contextual meanings also. Academics and administrators have been using those concepts interchangeably to connote a broader meaning that the problems of the people at the community level are being tackled through service facilities rendered by legitimately created institutions.

At present "Decentralization of Power" is mostly an accepted concept all over the world and hence it is being used everywhere. But at the same time some of the concepts are used as rehtreics such as empowering people and grassroots democracy.

Background of the New Initiative

It is essential to look at the emergence of the new institutional mechanism to perform certain duties and responsibilities in the backdrop of the context. All over the world countries have introspected their development path and initiated the corrective mechanism in the light of the reforms introduced on the domain of economy of the developed countries. The new developments in India is the outcome of an introspection which resulted in the introduction of new policy initiatives which are quiet opposite to the path ways of prosperity which India have followed so far.

At present the three forces State market and society are at loggerhead because of the increased mark oriented economic activities and its resultant activities of controlling over the power of the State and the society. State cannot abdicate its responsibilities as the people for participation in the development process has been increased since the influence of the democratic institutions has been expanded. Stats is not able to control over the influence of the market and hence a parallel organisational set-up is needed to contain the activities of the market when they are exploitative in character. To maintain equilibrium in the system it was thought of empowering the people through an organisational mechanism.

Basic Objectives of Decentralization of Power

Objectives vary from country to country depending on their needs and conditions. In India the objectives are broader and more deeper as they have to create a far reaching results in the attitude, behaviour, performance and life style of the people who live in the rural areas.The objectives are:

a) *Deepening of Democracy* : The confined democracy within the framework of the parliament and state legislatures has to be broadered to percolate in to the society to the level of the last rung of the society. Collectivities who have been hitherto marginalised and deprived have to be brought into the fold of democracy. More numbers from the women and Dalit have to be brought in the system of governance. This should be an affirmative action by which the marginalised and depressed have been given an exclusive space through reservation of seats in the local bodies. Thus it is a process by which democracy is being widened and deepened.

b) *Ensuring and Enlisting Peoples Participation* : Peoples participation is *sinquo non* for development. Development initiatives are to come from the people. People are the initiators and government is a facilitator. To make the government as facilitator from the role of a provider, people have to take initiative. Their participation in the development activities will bring accountability on the part of the government. People have to assess their requirement and chalk out schemes and programmes according to their needs. They should be people's programmes and government has to participate in the programmes by facilitating the people to carry out their programmes on their own.

c) *More Responsibilities to the People* : In the past fifty years all the responsibilities of the people and the community have been taken away and vested with government departments. Communities had enormous responsibilities to manage their affairs on their own and they have their own management system. In the name of nation-state, governments have expanded their departments. The expansion of the government has increased only the management cost not the efficiency in delivery. Hence development works could be allowed to be done with the involvement of the people. Gradually responsibilities should be given to the peoples group.

d) *Reduction of Government Structure* : It is roughly estimated that to deliver one rupee to the people government takes six rupees as delivery cost or management cost. Many of the countries in the world are facing crisis as a result of the expansion of the Departments of governments. Bigness of Government is a burden on the society. It will pave way for the disintegration of the nations. The unwildly expansion of Government departments becomes a threat to elected representatives. Moreover people are terrorised by the government through its procedures, rules and regulations. Larger the size of the government lesser the contact with the people. Hence there will be a gap between the people and the government. In order to avoid this complication of the bigness of the government it was felt that the structure of the government could be reduced to the minimum level and this could be possible only by giving more responsibilities to the people through the institutions created legitimately.

e) *Harnessing the Human Energy* : It is a truism that the way in which the human energy is being utilised development could be achieved accordingly. Human energy has different forms and different levels. The state should find a way to raise the level of the energy of the people and more particularly the state should workout a detailed mechanism through which the energy of the people could be utilised. The developed nations have demonstrated to the world that how best the energy level of the people could be enhanced and how best the enhanced energy could be utilised for activities to accelerate economic growth. To utilise the energy of the people, space could be created approximately. It was thought of an institutional arrangement to utilise the energy of the people.

f) *Administering Development and Social Justice* : It is a well known fact that countries are in the process of decentralizing powers have different objectives. But in India, it was a conscious decision of the central government that panchayati institutions have to work for administering development and social justice by evolving their own plan of action. Traditionally Panchayati Raj has been looked at as an institution meant for providing services and facilities. But in the new context it is meant for not only services and facilities but also growth with equity.

g) *Planning from the Below* : So far planning exercise had been done at the central level which resulted in large scale demands of the people unmet. In the fifty two years of governance, the centralized planning has achieved tremendous results in macro economics of this country and yet the rural realities have not been changed drastically. Still people are living in sub-human living conditions. In order to provide basic facilities, to convert the facilities to growth and to bring economic activities planning exercise has to be done at the micro level. This exercise had been thought of many times in independent India. Now this concept gained currency and this exercise would provide all necessary basic facilities to the people.

h) *Building the Capacity of the People* : It is imperative that people should take more responsibilities and to discharge the responsibilities, the capacity of the people have to be increased. Till date people have developed an attitude that government would provide everything and people have to receive the same. Now the role has been reversed. People have to govern on the peoples programme. Therefore the new system envisages a new task of building the capacity of the leaders and the people.

Establishing the Principle of Subsidiarity

The whole exercise has to revolve around the principle of subsudiarity. Activities that could be carried out at the lower level could be allowed to carry out at that level and things that could not be carried out at that level could be allowed to carry out at the next higher level and likewise activities are carried out at the appropriate levels depending on the capacity of the people. Based on the above principle devolution of power has to be effected.

It should be Pro-Nature

Activities of the people should be oriented towards protecting the environment and maintaining the natural order. While taking decisions at the micro level and implementing schemes and programmes for rural development enough care should be taken to protect the flora and fauna. All the ponds, wells, tanks, channels and lanes are to be protected and maintained properly. All the commons are to be well secured and managed.

It should be Pro-Poor

All the activities are to be decided on the basis of maintaining social equity. While taking decision and fixing priorities for rural development, panchayat has to decide whether the benefits would reach the poor. Consideration has to start from the poor. Unto the last has to be the policy of the panchayat. Poorest of the poor has to be given priority in deciding benefits. In each activity of the panchayats a component of benefit should be there to the poor.

It should be Pro-Women

This is yet another important sector which needs care and attention. Panchayats activities have to be carefully designed so as to provide enough scope for women both in terms of participation and benefits. Hitherto the neglected section of the society women, who could be integrated into the mainstream of economic and political activities. Further, of the problems faced by the rural society 70 to 80 per cent of them are being faced directly by the women as the absence of basic amenities, facilities and services, women are the mostly affected segment. Hence the decentralized political institutions nearer to the people should have resilience to accommodate women folk in their activities.

With the above posited objectives an amendment has been introduced in the parliament to amend the constitution so as to create systematic structure at the lowest level of the social system. The following are the characteristics of the 73rd Constitutional Amendment Act.

Characteristics of the 73rd Constitutional Amendment

73rd Amendment to the Constitution of India is a guideline and a basic framework evolved to guide the state government to take initiative of organising grassroot democracy as a system of governance to administer development and social justice. It opens up a new chapter in the modern political history of India. It has certain key characteristics which cannot be set a side by the state governments. They are:

a) Constitutional Entity : The New Panchayati System came into being as institution of governance with the approval of the Constitution and it is placed in the third stratum of the hierarchy of the institutions of governance. It enjoys the status as enjoyed by the parliament and state legislature in terms of its existence and conduct of election. It is a permanent institution with earmarked role and responsibilities to be discharged by the newly created institution.

b) A New Phenomenon in Federalism : In a federal structure there should be two constituent units maintain their relationship in administering development and peace through the institutional mechanism. There shall be division of powers between the central government and the provincial governments. Likewise, there shall be sharing of resources between the central and state government. But, now there is a third institution which has come into being as institution of self governance with distinct and categorical political, financial and administrative powers to administer development and social justice. Now the concept of federalism brings a new meaning which explains the relationship among the three institutions, namely federal, regional and local. Hence, 73rd Constitutional Amendment brought a new phenomenon in federation.

c) From Representative Democracy to Peoples Democracy : Indian Democracy has the character of a representative form of government and the decision-making has been based on the representations made by the representatives of the people both in the National Parliament and State Legislatures. It is an irony that hundred crore people are being represented by around four thousand and seven hundred representatives of the people through State Legislatures and National Parliament. It is natural that a representative cannot represent millions of people. Hence, even after fifty years of Independence, basic facilities and amenities have not been provided to the people. Now the concept of representation has been changed to direct participation of people in the governing process and thereby an institutional mechanism, namely Gram Sabha was created to enable the people to participate in the development process. Gram Sabha is the basic institution created for the benefit of the people to participate and administer development. To make the people to associate themselves with the community to discuss about the problems of the community and to find out solutions to the problems. It should be out and out an organisation of the people. This body will nurtures democratic principles in the community. Gram Sabha is giving meaning to the concept "Empowerment of People".

d) Three Tier Structure : The new system envisages a three tier structure namely gram panchayat block and district panchayat. The entire panchayati system is operating in the area of a district. To administer development the entire development administration is being divided into three units. All the three units are independent in certain respects and inter dependent in certain respects. Gram panchayat will function at the lowest level and block panchayat will function at the block level and district level and district panchayat will function at the district level. Roles and responsibilities, powers and duties for each tier will be clearly democrated and they have to function as per the powers conferred upon them. Development activities have to be carried out by lower level units and planning, coordination, monitoring and supervision activities have been carried out by the district level body, namely district panchayats.

e) 11th Schedule and Earmarked 29 Subjects : The New Panchayati System is grounded perfectly in the domain of governance authoritatively only through the 11th Schedule conferring 29 subjects to the rural local bodies. As indicated in the Constitution the state subjects, central subjects, panchayat subjects have been indicated 29 items of work. Of the 29 subjects, which of the subjects are to be allocated to gram panchayat and other tiers could be spelt out by the state government through legislation. The role of the state government is to allocate appropriate duties and responsibilities to each tier of the panchayats. 73rd Constitutional Amendment has indicated the suggestive items. It is not an exhaustive list. If the state government wants to give more powers to the local bodies there is no bar. It is more appropriate if the 11th Schedule is given in the fourth list as central list, state list, concurrent list and panchayat list.

f) Reservation of Seats for Women : Reservation of seats for women in all the tiers of local bodies is a new plieno governance. When Rajiv Gandhi brought the 64th Amendment bill it was only 25 per cent of the seats have been earmarked. The one -third reservation of seats for women has been the contribution of P.V. Narasimha Rao.The one-third reservation of seats for women has propelled the whole nation to moot out another demand of the same proportion of reservation of seats for women in the State Legislatures and National Parliament. It is a moot question as to why the reservation of seats in the local bodies has been to women? It is unequivocal from the reply given by many in the authoritative bodies that in the absence of basic facilities the worst sufferers are the women. The tredhery of women is not felt by the policy makers since they are mostly men. By giving the opportunity of taking decision to the women they would reduce the burden of the women.

g) Reservation of Seats for Daliths : Reservation of seats for Daliths in the State Legislatures and National Parliament is not so difficult as these institutions are for away from the communities. Hurdles are not so high for them to function as members of legislative institutions.They are always looked at from the party perspective and not on caste perspective. But it is very difficult for the Daliths to emerge as they are seen by the society from the caste perspective. The whole of human rights violations, discriminations, social injustice are the frequent occurance at the grassroots level. Voices are raised vociferously from the marginalised. Both centre and state governments have not fulfilled the allowed objective of administrating social justice. Hence it is felt that the responsibilities of administrating social justice could be handed over to lower level institution of governance and thereby it has been handed over to local bodies. This process starts from providing reservation of seats to the Daliths in the local bodies as it has been done to women, proportionate to their population. By creating this clause in the Constitutional Amendment, the marginalised has been properly given adequate representation. This is yet another revolutionary step taken by the government knowing fully well that the caste ridden Indian society has to pass through the social conflict for sometime.

h) Creation of Finance Commission : It is a well known fact that the panchayats had been crippled in the past only by reducing the financial allocation as that power was vested with the state government. In order to overcome this eventuality the amendment has incorporated a provision and by which a Finance Commission has to be constituted in every state to suggest the ways and means to share the resources between the local bodies and the state government and in the same way how local body finance could be strengthened. By creating this provision in the amendment act, financial flow to local bodies has been ensured regularly and this provision enables the local body institutions to keep themselves on a permanent footing.

i) Creation of Election Commission : To elect near about 4,700 representatives for State Legislatures and National Parliament, on independent election commission has been created and now they all functions in all the states. As per the new provision, representatives to the tune of 30 millions have to be elected and for which a massive machinery needed. Against this backdrop a permanent election commission has been created.Conducting the election to the local bodies in the main earmarked function of the State Election Commission.

j) District Planning Committee : Though planning is a much loaded concept and publicised word among the people since the days of Jawaharlal Nehru, the Planning Commission at the Centre and the state are not the constitutional entities. But the District Planning Committee is the constitutional creation.This District Planning Committee has come to stay with a specific purpose of altering the planning process. As per the new dispensation planning exercise has to be initiated from the below.For the development of the whole district, the planning committee has to prepare a perspective development plan. Thus the central concept planning has been recognized at all the three levels as institutions of governance functions at all the three levels to administer development.

Ensuring Regular Election to Panchayati Raj System

Election to Local Bodies was the will and pleasure of the state governments. That is why election was not conducted for Local Bodies for about fifteen years in the past. Any number of reasons could be projected for postponing the election. But through the new dispensation election has been ensured as it has been ensured to parliament and state legislatures. The provision which is applicable to Lok Sabha and state legislature election is applicable to New Panchayati Raj System. Hence now Panchayati Raj System becames a permanent entity. No state government can with hold election beyond six months. The above stated features are the key characteristics of the 73rd Constitutional Amendment Act and the spirit of the above act has to be carried out by enacting a suitable conformity act at the provincial level.

Enacting a Conformity Act in Tamil Nadu

In 1994 the state was ruled by the AIADMK under the leadership of J.Jayalalitha. Despite repeated reminders from the central government, state government had not taken any step to move forward in enacting an act to replace the old act. Finally to meet the dead line for enacting a new act as per the direction of the central government, a bill was prepared with haste and presented in the legislative assembly and without any detailed debate, it was adopted. To fulfill the constitutional obligation an act was enacted and it has large number of drawbacks which will work against the basic principles of decentralization of power. The defects are :

a) Absence of Organic Linkages : Even though the principle of subsidiarily is the basis of the New Panchayati Raj System, panchayats institutions within the district should have organic linkages among themselves. As per the newly enacted Act there is no such linkages. This kind of non-linkages have ultimately created a conflict course among the three tiers of panchayats. This conflicting course enabled the officials to establish their supremacy over the panchayats and the elected leaders.

b) Absence of Original Functions : 243(G) of the 73rd Amendment Act says that panchayats have to plan their activities to bring economic development and administer social justice, whereas the panchayats as per the new Act of Tamil Nadu have to perform only agency function. The panchayati functions are to be mentioned in the main body of the Act itself as they have mentioned in the 1958 Act of Madras.

Weak Position of District Planning Committee

District Planning Committee is the integral part of the new panchayat act as a development agency to plan for the development of entire district and to allocate, coordinate and supervise the development activities of the panchayats. Moreover it is a constitutional entity. But in the Tamil Nadu Act, it has been weakened and sidelined by putting the District Collector as the Chairperson of the District Planning Committee.

Powers of the Bureaucracy

District Collector has been designated as the Inspector of Panchayats and the District Collector has got the power to take direct action against the Gram Panchayati Presidents.

District Rural Development Agency (DRDA) has got rural development schemes and programmes and hence the central government has insisted that it should be merged with the district panchayats. As per the new Act, DRDA has to function entirely under the control of the District Collector.

No Linkages between the Revenue Department and Development Administration

As panchayats are being created as institutions of governance they require the linkages between the revenue and development departments for administering development and social justice. At present there is no linkage between the two. The linkages are to be brought through legislation. But the new Act does not provide any clause to establish linkage between the two departments.

Panchayats and CPR Management

Panchayats can be made independent only when they mobilise resources on their own. Common properties are the life line of panchayats and they were taken away from the communities and vested with various government departments. Now panchayats are asked to augment resources without basic bases of resources. Moreover, panchayats can be stabilized and strengthened only through the Land Reform and it has not even been mentioned in the act. Thus the Tamil Nadu Panchayats Act has a variety of weaknesses. The party in power in 1994 was responsible for enacting an Act but it did not put in action by conducting the election to local bodies. It was only the DMK which gave life to the local bodies in Tamil Nadu by conducting the election.

Conditions for Evolution of Panchayats

Act is all the more essential to make the panchayats effective and efficient. But the will of the leader is much more important than of that the Act by itself. Because functioning of local bodies does not rely on the will of the Minister for Local Bodies. To devolve powers to local bodies, powers have to be shared by the Ministers of education, agriculture, health, public works department, village industries and a number of other departments which could be properly coordinated only by the Chief

Minister and not by the Minister for Local Bodies. Further the officials who are working in the Development Departments should have proper orientation and mind set to work with people and their representatives at the local level. They should have proper understanding of the new dispensation. In the same way the elected panchayati leaders should have clear role perception and expected commitment with sincerity and rectitude. Apart from all those things, people must have awareness about the importance of the New Panchayati Raj System. Thus the new system would emerge as a movement not as a scheme and programme of the government.

The Issue

What we witness t-day in the functioning of grassroot institutions is the result of the misconception of the concept by many at different levels in authoritative bodies. Conflicting interest is also working in the local bodies covertly and overtly. Drawbacks in the acts, misguidance and non-guidance of the leaders by the officials, non-cooperation of the officials with elected leaders, exploitation of the ignorance of the elected leaders, non-cooperation of the local MLAs and MPs towards the local body leaders, and big brother attitude of the state government contribute substantially for the stagnation of the Panchayati Raj System in Tamil Nadu. How these issues are operating in the Panchayati Raj institutions? will be explained in this chapter.

The Framework

For the analysis of any issue one should have proper framework and with the backdrop of the framework issues have to be analyzed and explained. This new panchayati system so far has been seen from the backdrop of Gandhian ideals, administrative theories, good governance, decentralization of power, and small government approach. Perspectives vary from individual to individual. For a realistic analysis one should look at things in a given environment. In a state dominated political system, most of the activities of the society relating to the development of society could be carried out only through the government. Moreover even people would look at from the perspective of the government. With regard to New Panchayati Raj System, from enactment of law to allocation of resources and evaluation of programmes State is being the dominant factor. Government is the guiding spirit. Officials of the government are the

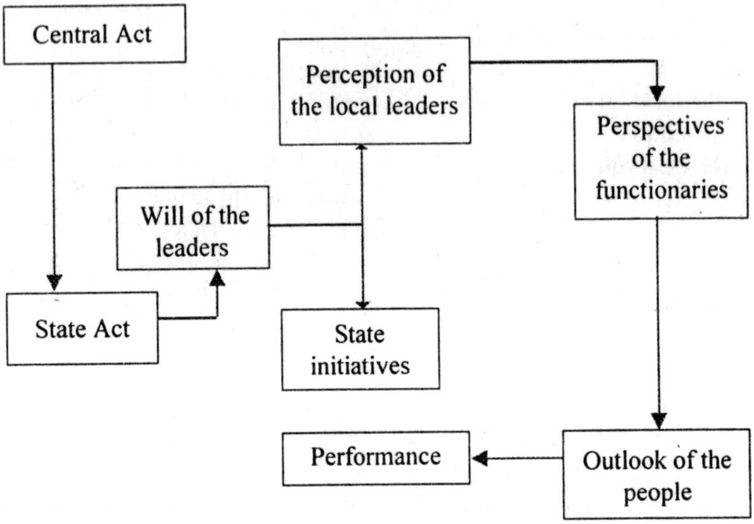

A Simple Framework for Analysis

implementing agents in the process of decentralization of powers. Representatives of the people are the real participants of development. Every segment is important in proper placement of New Panchayati Raj System in Indian polity.

Central Act is the basis and on which the State Act has to be enacted. Even for the Central Act there should be some basis. This new Central Act was enacted in a context where a number of new policies have been enacted to change the framework and approach of development. New Economic Policy, Liberalization and Structural Adjustment are some of the policy options introduced and along with them the decentralization of powers has been introduced. 73rd Constitutional Amendment Act has to be visualised from the wider backdrop of the policy options of the federal government. Following the enactment of the 73rd Constitutional Amendment Act, the state governments have enacted new state laws to reflect the basic spirit of the 73rd Constitutional Amendment Act. Basic analysis should be woven around the linkages between the federal law and the state law. The provisions of the state law has to reflect the spirit of the federal law. The enactment does not stop with it and it is the beginning of the whole process of decentralization of powers.

The federal government has to see that all the state governments not only enacting new legislations in line with the federal act but also taking steps to devolve powers to grassroot institutions from the state down to gram panchayats. State governments should have the necessary will power to strengthen the local bodies by devolving adequate powers along with the needed resources. There are a variety of complications one would expect in the new system when it is being operationalised. All these complications have to be driven out by the decisions of the state government. The functionaries who work in the local bodies have to understand the full implications of the new system. By keeping the functionaries aware of the new system, mind set of them could be changed. It is not only the mind set of the functionaries, even the local body leaders have the same mind set as the functionaries.

From top to bottom, all responsible leaders, and functionaries have to change the mind set. Hence one has to visualise the functioning of the institution from the backdrop of the intentions and interventions of the federal government and the state government, the interface between the functionaries and the elected local body leaders, the perception of the local body leaders and the expectations of the people over local bodies. Thus the analysis of the local bodies need not necessarily be from legalistic perspective or from historical perspective and mostly it should be from the development perspective. It needs broader understanding about the New Panchayati Raj System.

Panchayats at Work

The New Panchayati Raj System came in to being in Tamil Nadu after enacting a new law for local body institutions in the year 1994. Till the arrival of the DMK party to power, it was only an Act beyond that local body institutions have not taken any shape in reality. The DMK came to power and it has decided to conduct the election as per its promise to the people given at the time of election and it did conduct the election simultaneously to all the tiers of the rural local bodies along with the urban local bodies. The conduct of election to local bodies has given life to grassroot democracy. Yet the ills attached to the act still continue in the functioning of local bodies. Some of the provisions have been changed subsequently.

The salient features of the new Act are as follows :

a) a three tier system;
b) Gram Sabha;
c) Establishment of Election Commission;

d) Constitution of Finance Commission;
e) Reservation of seats for SC/ST proportionate to their population;
f) One-third reservation of seats for women; and
g) Constitution of District Planning Committee.

Gram Sabha

Gram Sabha is the nucleus of the New Panchayati Raj System. All the registered voters are the members of the Gram Sabha of that Village Panchayat. As per the Act it has to meet thrice a year and atleast once in six months. President of Gram Panchayat is the presiding officer of the meetings of Gram Sabha. Gram Sabha has to give approval to the budget proposal and annual plan of the village panchayat. Further it has to give approval to the annual audited statement on the expenditure of the Village Panchayat. One-third forms the quorum to transact the business of the Gram Sabha as per the Act. In Tamil Nadu Gram Sabha is a neglected subject and unit in the local body arrangement as both elected leaders and the officials have not shown any interest in it due to many reasons. As per the Government orders, even beneficiaries for many government schemes are to be selected only in the Gram Sabha. But in reality it does not happen. Beneficiaries are selected not in Gram Sabha but in Panchayat Council which is violative of the provision of the Local Body Act of Tamil Nadu. It is a government approved unconstitutional activity. Government of Tamil Nadu emphasizes the transparent activities in all government's programmes and schemes but there is no way to execute it as Gram Sabha is made defunct. It is a night mare to many who have been enjoying power and resources all along. In order to strengthen the Gram Sabha recently government passed an order that all Gram Panchayats have to convene Gram Sabha meeting four times in a year on 15th August, 2nd October, 26th January and 1st May and transact the activities as per the provisions available in the Act. Further quorum of Gram Sabha has been reduced from one-third to one-tenth. Officials from all the Government offices akin to development will also participate in the Gram Sabha meeting as observer of the meeting and he/she will report the proceedings to the inspector of panchayat.

Village Panchayat

A Village Panchayat or Gram Panchayat is constituted for a minimum of five hundred population. Village Panchayat has got members ranging from minimum of five to maximum of fifteen. For Village Panchayat the ward members and the president, are to be elected directly by the voters. Vice-President of the Village Panchayat is elected indirectly among the elected ward members of the Village Panchayat. Village Panchayat has to look after the following subjects :

a) Construction, repair and maintenance of village panchayat roads;
b) Lighting of public roads and public places;
c) Providing drainage facilities;
d) Cleaning of streets;
e) Providing public latrines;
f) Providing burial and burning grounds;
g) Providing water for washing and bathing purposes; and
h) Such other duties notified by the Government then and there.

To enable the Village Panchayat to perform its functions the following decisions have been taken and notified through Government orders:

a) All Village Panchayats will get financial resources from the Government directly without any intermediary. Panchayati Union or Block Panchayat will not interfere in the process;
b) Gram Panchayat Presidents have been designated as Executive Heads and they have been entrusted with powers and responsibilities;
c) Village Panchayat roads can be taken up for works with the resolution of the Panchayats;
d) Facilities like street light, water supply can be maintained and attended to if there is any disrepair;
e) Part time clerks can be appointed by the Panchayat President;
f) House construction plan approval has to be given by the village panchayats;
g) Beneficiaries for the central government schemes and programmes have to be selected by the Gram Panchayat in the Gram Sabha;
h) New Library and information centre in the villages has to be established by the village panchayat.

Panchayati Union

For each development block a panchayat union is formed. Each panchayati union has a Chairperson and a Vice-Chairperson elected in directly by the members of the panchayat council. Union Council Members are elected directly by the people. For every 5,000 population, one union council member will be elected by the people. Members of Parliament and Legislative Assembly elected from that area are *ex-officio* members of the panchayat union council.

Panchayati union has the following duties and responsibilities:

a) Construction, repair and maintenance of public roads;
b) Establishment and maintenance of dispensaries;
c) Construction and maintenance of elementary schools;
d) Preventive and remedial measures connected with any epidemic;
e) Conduct of fairs and festivals;
f) Vetenary relief;
g) Opening and maintenance of Panchayat Union markets;
h) Extension of village sites and regulation of buildings;
i) Maintenance of statistics related to births and deaths;
j) Improvement of agriculture and agriculture stock;
k) Promotion and encouragement of cottage industries; and
i) Other duties and responsibilities entrusted to Panchayati Union by the Government through Government notification.

To enable the panchayat union to perform its duties and the Government of Tamil Nadu has issued notification to take up the following activities :

a) Construction and maintaining Panchayat Union roads, irrigation tanks, and lakes, initiating family welfare activities, executing noon meal schemes and implementing schemes for Adi Dravidas;
b) Works have to be identified from Employment Assurance schemes and they are to be executed;
c) Draught relief works have to be identified and executed;
d) M.P. and M.L.A area development schemes akin to union have to be executed;
e) Panchayat union buildings have to be maintained by the union itself;
f) Panchayat union can supervise the activities in the domain of public health, primary education, drinking water supply, roads, small culverts, khadi and village industries works, technical training education, libraries, rural electricity and non-conventional energy.

Panchayat union administrative arrangement has been modified by which works have been classified in to two divisions and entrusted to Block Development Officer and Assistant Block Development Officer. Two sections work independently with their supporting staff. Infrastructural facilities have also been divided and attached to two divisions.

District Panchayat

District Panchayat is constituted with the directly elected members for every 50,000 population and indirectly elected Chairperson and Vice-Chairperson among the council members. Members of Parliament and State Legislative Assembly of that area are the *ex-officio* members of the District Panchayat Council. District Panchayat will have to perform the following functions :

a) Advise the government in all matters concerning Panchayati Raj institutions particularly on services and development programmes;
b) Watching the progress of the measures undertaken by the government, village panchayats and panchayat union councils in the districts as under the administrative control of the districts;
c) Classification of markets, fairs and public roads in Panchayati Raj institutions, and
d) Collection of data, publication of statistics, demanding any information from village panchayats and panchayati union councils.

To enable the district panchayat to perform the earmarked functions, an administrative change has been effected and by which the Divisional Development Office which is nearer to the district head quarters will supervise the district panchayat activities. Yet another office which is away from the head quarters will look after auditing of the district panchayat activities and the third one will be attached to district panchayat.

District Planning Committee

Government of Tamil Nadu shall constitute in every district a District Planning Committee to consolidate the plans prepared by the district panchayat, panchayat union councils, village panchayats, municipal councils, and municipal corporations in the district and to prepare a draft development plan for the district as a whole. The committee shall consist of the Collector of the district, members of the House of people who represent whole or part of the district, members of the council of states, Members of Legislative Assembly whose constituencies lie within the district, Mayor of the city municipal corporation and all Chairpersons of the municipalities of the district, Chairperson of the district panchayat, one-fifth of the total number of Chairpersons of town panchayats and panchayati union notified by the government every year by rotation, and such number of persons not less than four-fifth of the total number of the committee as specified by the government elected from among the members of district panchayat, town panchayats, municipal councils and corporations in the district in proportion to the ratio between the population of the rural areas and of the urban areas. The District Collector is the Chairperson, district panchayat president is the Vice-Chairperson and Chief Executive Officer of the district panchayat is the secretary of the District Planning Committee. The Committee shall allocate funds to various schemes to the panchayats and panchayat union and shall monitor the implementation of schemes. Now the Government have changed the Chairmanship of District Planning Committee from the Collector to the President of District Panchayat.

Reservation

One-third of positions at all levels of the bodies are reserved for women. SC and ST gets reservation of positions at all levels of the bodies in proportion to their population.

Election and Finance Commissions

An Election Commission headed by the State Election Commissioner appointed by the Governor to conduct the local body elections is mandatory. The Election Commissioner enjoys powers and privileges and status of a judge of the High Court. The tenure of office of the Election Commissioner is two years. However, the Commissioner can be given extension for four more years. In Tamil Nadu elections are conducted on party lines for district panchayats and panchayat union. Elections for village panchayats are not on party lines.

There will be a Finance Commission constituted for every five year to review financial positions of the panchayats and to make recommendations to the Governor as to fix the principles to govern the distribution between the state and panchayats of the net proceeds of the taxes, duties, tolls and fees leviable by the Government. Further to identify the logistics for making grants in aid to the panchayats from the consolidated fund of the state and the measures needed to improve the financial position of the panchayats. The Finance Commission shall consist of a Chairman and four other members. In Tamil Nadu the Finance Commission has recommended only 7% of total revenue to the panchayats with an increase of 1% every year. The Government have given already 8% of the total revenue to local bodies. Government of Tamil Nadu have constituted the Second Finance Commission.

STRUCTURE OF PANCHAYATI RAJ DEPARTMENT IN TAMIL NADU

From State Level to District Level

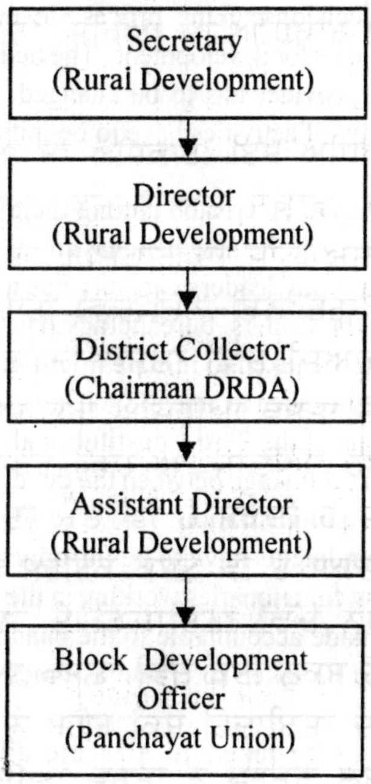

The Secretary Rural Development is in charge of the panchayati raj administration at state level. The Director Rural Development is heading the panchayati raj administration at department level. At district level panchayati raj administration is under the District Collector. He is also the Chairman of the District Rural Development Agency and President of the District Planning Committee. As the inspector of the village panchayats, the District Collector regulates the administration of the village panchayats. He is assisted by personal assistant (Panchayat Development) in administering panchayats. In addition Assistant Director (Rural Development) is functioning under district collector and supervise the working of panchayat unions. At block level, Block Development Officer is administering the panchayats.

Conclusion

Panchayats are for prosperity, social equity, social justice and peoples participation. Economic activities have to be generated. Social justice has to be administered. Women folk has to be emancipated. Planning process has to be initiated from the below. Peoples participation has to be ensured from planning and decision-making process to evaluation of schemes, programmes and activities for development. The belief system of the people that government is a provider has to be changed. To perform all those responsibilities an array of activities have to be initiated. They are:

a) Awareness has to be created among the mass about the role and responsibilities of the new panchayati raj system.
b) Elected local body leaders capacity has to be enhanced.
c) Mind set of the leaders, bureaucracy has to be changed.
d) Steps have to be taken to initiate micro level planning.
e) Steps should be taken to amend such laws which are contradicting the provisions of the 73rd Constitutional Amendment.
f) Establish direct linkage between the development administration and revenue administration.
g) Needed amendments have to be introduced in the state acts.
h) Development functionaries working in the panchayati institutions have to be made accountable to the panchayats.
i) Steps should be taken to create avenues to mobilise resources locally.
j) Steps should be taken to allocate adequate resources to panchayats.
k) Unnecessary interferences of the MPs and MLAs in the local bodies have to be avoided.

Table 1.1 : Reservation of Seats in Each District

OFFICES : District Panchayat Ward Members/Panchayat Union Ward Members/Village Panchayat President

DISTRICT	TOTAL OFFICES			NUMBER OF OFFICES BY RESERVATION																	
				ST-General			ST-Women			SC-General			SC-Women			Women			General		
	1	2	3	1	2	3	1	2	3	1	2	3	1	2	3	1	2	3	1	2	3
Kancheepuram	27	271	648	0	0	2	0	0	0	6	55	157	3	36	80	6	59	133	12	121	276
Vellore	40	400	753	0	3	7	0	2	3	6	51	108	3	33	60	11	105	186	20	206	389
Thiruvannamalai	34	341	860	1	5	10	0	3	4	4	42	121	3	30	72	9	87	217	17	174	436
Cuddalore	29	286	681	0	0	0	0	0	0	6	54	151	3	34	82	7	62	146	13	136	302
Villupuram	47	476	1104	1	3	9	0	2	8	8	84	204	5	46	105	11	114	260	22	227	518
Dharmapuri	41	412	588	0	3	6	0	1	3	4	28	48	2	22	28	12	118	167	23	240	336
Salem	28	282	376	1	6	10	0	2	4	2	28	38	2	13	22	8	84	103	15	149	199
Erode	25	248	340	0	1	1	0	0	0	3	25	35	2	15	23	7	74	96	13	133	185
Coimbatore	27	267	388	0	1	0	0	0	0	3	28	45	2	16	30	7	80	104	15	142	209
Nilgiris	3	34	27	0	0	0	0	0	0	0	4	3	0	2	2	1	11	8	2	17	14
Thanjore	28	276	589	0	0	0	0	0	0	4	32	81	2	22	45	8	75	153	14	147	310
Trichy	24	243	407	0	2	6	0	0	4	2	25	43	2	18	27	6	68	108	14	130	219
Pudukottai	22	226	498	0	0	0	0	0	0	2	18	49	1	14	32	7	66	137	12	128	280
Madurai	23	226	431	0	0	0	0	0	0	2	22	47	2	16	30	6	65	117	13	123	237
Dindigul	23	236	306	0	0	0	0	0	0	2	26	35	2	19	23	6	62	82	13	125	166
Ramanathapuram	18	175	443	0	0	0	0	0	0	2	20	61	1	14	35	5	48	117	10	93	230
Sivaganga	16	156	431	0	0	0	0	0	0	2	16	46	1	9	29	5	47	119	8	84	237
Virudunagar	20	200	450	0	0	0	0	0	0	2	24	61	2	17	38	5	53	112	11	106	239
Tirunelveli	26	266	425	0	0	1	0	0	0	3	29	56	2	17	36	7	77	109	14	134	223
Tuticorin	18	186	408	0	0	0	0	0	0	2	20	55	1	17	30	5	51	107	10	98	216
Kanayakumari	8	84	88	0	0	0	0	0	0	0	2	3	0	0	2	3	32	31	5	50	52
Karur	12	117	158	0	0	0	0	0	0	1	13	19	1	10	16	3	32	37	7	62	86
Perambulur	19	189	322	0	0	0	0	0	0	2	24	49	2	17	27	5	49	81	10	99	165
Thiruvallur	24	245	539	0	0	5	0	0	0	4	46	109	3	28	58	5	58	125	12	113	142
Namakkal	17	175	331	0	6	9	0	3	6	2	17	45	1	16	28	5	44	78	9	89	165
Thiruvarur	18	176	430	0	0	0	0	0	0	4	35	95	2	22	52	4	39	90	8	80	193
Theni	10	98	130	0	0	0	0	0	0	1	11	15	1	7	10	3	30	35	5	50	70
TOTAL	648	6499	12584	3	30	66	0	13	32	83	820	1873	54	537	1075	171	1736	3150	337	3363	6388

(1) — District Panchayat Ward Members, (2) — Panchayat Union Ward Members, (3) — Village Panchayat President.
Source : Computed.

l) Steps have to be taken for strong tie up between the panchayats and NGOs.

To explain and elaborate the points which have been presented in the preceding pages, case studies have been conducted extensively and they will be presented in the following chapters.

It is true that there are very many weaknesses in the Act itself and a variety of existing acts do not permit the state to devolve powers. The capacity of the leaders are not so high to handle all the subjects earmarked for Panchayati Raj and yet leaders are alert and optimistic at present that Panchayat System is the only solution to solve most of the problems in the rural areas. Steps are on to rectify the defects. Local body leaders are putting a one point demand to the state government to devolve adequate powers and resources to the local bodies. Expected pressure has come from the people for devolution of powers and the leaders of local bodies have come to a stage to take powers from the state government on their own in the event of denial of powers to the local bodies.

Notes and References

1. Sarasvathi. *The Madras Panchayat System Vol-I A Historial Survey.* Delhi : Impex India, 1973.
2. Dharampal. *The Madras Panchayat System Vol-II A General Assessment.* New Delhi: Impex India, 1972.
3. Palanithurai G., *Empowering People for Prosperity: A study in New Panchayati Raj System.* New Delhi : Kanishka Publications, 1994.
4. Palanithurai G.,(Ed) *New Panchayati Raj System Status and Prospects.* New Delhi: Kanishka Publications, 1996.
5. Palanithurai G.,(Ed) *Empowering People: Issues and Solutions.* New Delhi : Kanishka Publications, 1996.
6. Palanithurai G., Dwaraki B.R. and Narayanasamy S., (Eds) *Major Issues in New Panchayati Raj System.* New Delhi: Kanishka Publications, 1997.
7. Palanithurai G., *New Panchayati Raj System at Work: An Evaluation.* New Delhi : Concept Publications, 1999.
8. Rajiv Gandhi Foundation, *Voices from Below: Summary proceedings of Sub-Regional workshops on panchayats: Issues and Recommendations,* New Delhi: RGF, 1994.
9. Government of Tamil Nadu, *Democratic Decentralisation: Powers entrusted to Panchayati Raj Institutions.* Chennai : Rural Development Department. 1999.
10. State Planning Commission, Report of the Working Group on Decentralised Planning and Panchayati Raj, Chennai : SPC, 1997.
11. V.B.Athreya & K.S.Rajeswari, *Women's Participation in Panchayati Raj : A Case Study from Tamil Nadu.* Chennai: MSSRF, 1999
12. R. Rukmani, *Panchayati Raj Institutions in Tamil Nadu: A Historical Review.* Chennai : Madras Institute of Development Studies. 1996.
13. State Planning Commission. *Report on the Entrustment of Powers to Panchayats.* Chennai : State Planning Commission, 1997.

14. Rajiv Gandhi Foundation, *Proceedings of the National Seminar on Panchayts.* New Delhi : RGF, 1997.
15. Rajiv Gandhi Foundation, *Proceedings of the National Seminar on Panchayts.* New Delhi : RGF, 1993.
16. State Finance Commission, *Summary of Recommendations of the State Finance Commission for Local Bodies.* Chennai : SFC, 1966
17. Rajiv Gandhi Foundation. *Dialogue on Panchayat : Summary proceedings of four Regional Tripartile Interface Interactive workshops.* New Delhi : RGF, 1999.
18. G. Palanithurai, *Grassroot Democracy in Indian Society.* New Delhi: Concept, 1997.
19. Rajiv Gandhi Foundation, *Revitalisation of Panchayati Raj in India.* New Delhi : RGF, 1999.
20. Government of India, *Renewing Local Self Government in Rural India.* New Delhi : Ministry of Rural Development, 1994.
21. Government of India, *Powers and Functions of Panchayati Raj Institutions — A Framework* New Delhi : Ministry of Rural Development, 1994.
22. Jennie Litvack, Junaid Ahmed and Richard Bird, *Rethinking Decentralization in Developing Countries.* Washington D.C. : The World Bank, 1998.
23. Dennis A. Rondinelli , John R.Nellis and G.Shabbir Cheema, *Decentralization in Developing Countries — A Review of Recent Experience* Washington D.C. : The World Bank, Management and Development Services, 1999.
24. Government of Tamil Nadu, *Highpower Committee Report on Entrustment of Powers to three tier Local Bodies in Tamil Nadu,* Chennai : Rural Development Department, 1999.
25. The Hunger Project, *Women and Panchayati Raj — The Pathway to Social Transformation and a New Future for India.* Bombay : Hunger Project, 1999.
26. Siddartha, Sivaramakrishnan, *Panchayati Raj Institutions in India–A Society Study for the World Bank* Washington D.C. : World Bank, 1999.
27. Siddartha, Sivaramakrishnan, *Discussion : Challenges and Opportunities for Panchayati Raj.* New Delhi : World Bank, 1999.
28. Rural Development Department, *Democratic Decentralisation : Panchayati Raj System in Tamil Nadu.* Chennai : Rural Development Department, 1999.

2

DESIGNING AND MANAGING DISTRICT PANCHAYATS

Introduction

District panchayats have become a bone of contention in Tamil Nadu Politics as the Government of Tamil Nadu have explicitly expressed its reservations over the effectiveness of the District panchayats in administering development and social justice as envisioned in the 73rd Amendment to the Constitution of India.Yet, District Panchayats have constituted, responsibilities have been earmarked, resources have been devolved and they have been performing the assigned functions despite ambiguity in shaping the institution in the overall framework of the Panchayati system. An attempt is made in this write up to evaluate its placement in the panchayat framework and performance from the perspective of the assigned task. To do the above posited objective a case study has been undertaken in Thiruchirapalli district. Before moving into the area of logic of District panchayat one has to understand the fundamental concept of Decentralisation of Power.

Decentralisation of Power

Decentralisation of power refers to the process and practice of devolving powers from the central (federal) government to the grassroots level institutions. This process can include the devolution not only powers but also its antecedents, namely, finance and functionaries. It is not an isolated event or process. It is an integral process operates in a system as a package. But operationalisation of the concept varies from society to society or even country to country. With varying objectives countries have adopted the concept "Decentralisation of Power".[1] One would find a variety of experiences within a country.

Decentralisation of power in the context of globalisation of economy seems to be a paradoxical event and yet it gains currency among the intellectual discourses.[2] Steps are being taken to theorise the process of decentralisation of power. Conceptualisation of devolution of power becomes problematic due to varying degree of cognition among the societies about the concept and its implication. The process gets complicated confused as the concept 'Decentralisation of Power' is perceived differently. In popular term 'Decentralisation of Power' indicates a shift in the notion of governance and institutions inevolved in governance. The efficiency and effectiveness of this process largely depends on how well the whole framework of Decentralisation of Power is being designed and how best the designed institutions and activities are managed by the personnels who are involved in the process of decentralisation.

Decentralisation is conceived and perceived by countries not in one direction. It has been perceived and visualised in different perspectives according to their requirements and local conditions. The concept has its own historical progression.[3] Connotation of the concept varies from era to era. But in the present context, Decentralisation of Power refers to a mass movement marching towards deciding the destiny of the people on their own by participating in the development process.[4] In India the central government has given a concrete shape to decentralisation of power through two constitutional amendments. By these two amendments institutional arrangements have been recognised constitutionally as institutions of governance with earmarked responsibilities. The two amendments are being operationalised through the state confirmity acts especially for urban and rural local bodies. The efficacy and efficiency of the institutions depend on the importance given to these institutions by the state government and its bureaucracy along with the capacity of the leaders who are elected by the people.[5] In Tamil Nadu conformity legislations have been enacted to both urban and rural local bodies and they are put into practice.

Context

Before moving into the actual provisions of the state act on the constitution of district panchayats and their powers, one has to look at the basic approach of the state government towards the decentralisation of powers. 73rd Constitutional Amendment Act is only a framework and it can only guide. How best these guidelines are put into practice, depends on the basic approach of the state government. At present, in India, there are two contending approaches in decentralisation of power.[6] They are namely, Technology driven development and Participatory development. There are a few states who have affirmed their commitment on participatory development and thereby they took steps to activate grassroots democracy.[7] They have both Marxian and Gandhian ideology. There are a few states who have committed in technology driven development and thereby they took steps to upgrade the technology and they go in for high-tech also. Tamil Nadu is in the second category but it has not explicitly stated. The view expressed by the Government of Tamil Nadu on District Panchayats indicates the confusion of the policy makers towards decentralisation of powers. The three tier panchayat brings a framework to decentralization powers as institution of self governance but the two tier panchayats connote that the institutions are only implementing agencies which can implement the schemes and programmes of the governments both centre and the state. The leaders have a mindset that the panchayati institutions have to be perceived only an implementing agency not an institutions of self governance. Remembering the old Panchayati Raj System will not help the society to impure the quality of life in the rural areas. The objectives of the old panchayats mere different from that of the new. Hence the District Panchayati System is in a fix. It moves one step forward and two steps backward[8]. Any how steps are being taken to operationalise the provisions of the 73rd Constitutional amendment through the grassroots institutions. Normally for a realistic evaluation of the performance of the grassroots institutions one has to visualise the following dimensions namely, the political will of the state leader (Chief Minister and his executive), state bureaucracy, capacity of the elected leaders and the awareness of the people about the political system.

Process of Devolution of Powers

To workout the modalities and principles the government of Tamil Nadu has constituted a committee under the leadership of L.C. Jain. The committee had gone into the full details of the process and submitted its report which was considered as one of the best reports available in India for devolution of powers[9]. The L.C. Jain Committee has adopted the following as the approach for devolution of powers :

1. The principle to be applied for bifurcation of functions between State Departments and Panchayats should be that what can be done by the Panchayats and where the panchayats have greater stake and better access to requisite local information and knowledge necessary for development, that matter be assigned to the Panchayats. Similarly, as between the three tiers of the Panchayati Raj Institutions, the functions to be allocated to each tier should be assigned on the

basis of what it can best do and where it is better placed; and only that which it cannot do be assigned to the higher tier, *i.e.,* Panchayat Union and/ or District Panchayat.

2. The scheme of devolution should avoid dual control on the one hand and result in streamlining and speeding of decision-making in respect of development planning and implementation. It should also empower/enable local representative bodies to determine priorities and integrate schemes at the operational level and accordingly deploy, re-deploy available resources to the best possible advantage.
3. Given a wide range of subjects to be assigned to the panchayats, to recommend a phased programme of decentralisation to ensure its success. For this purpose, to identify activities which could be entrusted to the panchayats immediately, *i.e.*, within the first year; activities, which may be entrusted to the panchayats in the next two to three years. Steadily, more and substantive powers should be entrusted by Government to Panchayati Raj Institutions for shaping development and for implementation. This, while placing more responsibilities on the Panchayats, would lighten the burden on the State Government.

For each of the 29 items, the L.C. Jain Committee first examined the existing arrangements and schemes relating to each of the 29 items and applying the above approach determined which of the functions and activities are to be transferred by Government agencies to Panchayat Raj bodies. Next it determined a rational *inter se* distribution of functions and activities between three tier of Panchayat Raj –(Village Panchayats, Panchayat Union Councils and District Panchayats). In order to indicate clearly the responsibilities of village panchayat, panchayat union and district panchayat with regard to implementation of schemes, programmes and projects assigned to them, the Committee identified the relevant institutional linkages.

The report was placed before the cabinet and a number of recommendations had been accepted. Yet the demand for adequate powers for Local Bodies had been continuing. Hence another High Level Committee comprising of representatives of the political parties under the Chairmanship of the Minister for Rural Development and Local Administration had been constituted. This Committee had also submitted its report[10]. Based on the recommendations decision have been taken to devolve more powers to local bodies. The powers given to local bodies are in the form of Action taken report[11].

Constitution of District Panchayats

As per the Tamil Nadu Panchayats Act of 1994, the district panchayat is constituted with the directly elected members for every 50,000 population and indirectly elected Chairperson and Vice-Chairperson among the council members. Members of Parliament and State Legislative Assembly of that area are the *ex-officio* members of the District Panchayat Council[12]. District will have to perform the following functions[13].

Powers and Functions of District Panchayats (The Tamil Nadu Panchayats Act, 1994)

Functions

1. Advise the government on all matters concerning the activities of village panchayats, panchayat union councils in the district as well as the development of the economic resources of the district and the service maintained therein for promoting the culture and welfare of the inhabitants of the district.
2. a) Advise the government on all matters relating to the services maintained by and all development schemes undertaken by all village panchayats and panchayat union councils in the district as well as those agencies in the district, which are under the administrative control of the government.
   b) Watching the progress of the measures undertaken by the government, village panchayats, panchayat union councils and departmental agencies in respect of the services and development schemes aforesaid.
   c) Advising the Government on matters concerning the implementation of any provision of law or any order specifically referred to by the government to the district panchayat such as—
      i) classification of markets as village panchayat markets and panchayat union markets and fixing rates of contribution payable by one authority to the other;
      ii) classification of fairs and festivals as village panchayat fairs, village panchayat festivals and panchayat union fairs and panchayat union festivals;
      iii) classification of public roads (other than roads classified

by the Government as National Highways, State Highways and major district roads) as panchayat union roads and panchayat village roads;

d) advising the government on all matters relating to development or road transport.

Powers

a) Undertaking such measures as it deems necessary;
b) Collecting such data as it deems necessary;
c) Publishing statistics or other information relating to the various aspects of the village regulation or development of the activities of panchayat union councils and village panchayats in the district;
d) Requiring any panchayat union council or village panchayats to furnish such information as may be required by it in relation to the measures undertaken by that panchayat union council or village panchayat for the regulation or development of its activities and such other matters as may be prescribed.

Powers Exercisable by Rural Local Bodies as per the Rules Issued Under the Tamil Nadu Panchayats Act, 1994

1. District Panchayat is competent to accord administrative sanction in respect of the original works costing upto rupees ten lakh. The authorities competent to give technical sanction upto Rs.10,00,000 — are as given below :

Value of Estimate	*Authority to accord Technical Sanction*
(1)	(2)
a) Upto Rs.50,000/-	Block Engineer or Assistant Engineer (Rural Development)
b) Rs.50,000/- to Rs.3,00,000/-	Assistant Executive Engineer (Rural Development)

c) Rs.3,00,000/- to Rs.10,00,000/-	Executive Engineer (Rural Development)

2. District Panchayat is competent to accord administrative sanction in respect of the following nature of maintenance works with the technical sanction of the authorities noted against them :

Value of Estimate	*Authority to accord Technical Sanction*
(1)	(2)
a) Upto Rs.10,000/-	Block Engineer or Assistant Engineer (Rural Development)
b) Rs.10,000/- to Rs.50,000/-	Assistant Executive Engineer (Rural Development)
c) Rs.50,000/- to Rs.2,00,000/-	Executive Engineer (Rural Development)
d) More than Rs.2,00,000/-	Superintending Engineer (Rural Development)

3. District Panchayat is competent to accord administrative sanction in respect of the following nature of electrical works with the technical sanction of the authority noted against them :

Value of Estimate	*Authority to accord Technical Sanction*
(1)	(2)
a) Upto Rs.10,000/-	Block Engineer or Assistant Engineer (Rural Development)

b) Rs.10,000/- to Rs.25,000/-	Assistant Executive Engineer (Rural Development)
c) Rs.25,000/- to Rs.50,000/-	Executive Engineer (Rural Development)
d) More than Rs.50,000/-	Superintending Engineer (Rural Development)

Powers, Functions and Responsibilities entrusted on General Subjects

1. Regular, exclusive and full time Secretary has been positioned for each District Panchayat.
2. All the District Panchayats have been provided with one Ambassador Car with Driver for the use of the District Panchayats.
3. Rules have been issued prescribing the procedure for conduct of District Panchayat Meetings, not exceeding 60 days between two meetings, agenda to be served before 10 effective days, the meeting to be conducted with a quorum of 1/3 of the members.
4. All the officers and staff of the District Panchayats are considered as government servants. The accounts of the District Panchayats are audited by the Department of Local Fund Audit.
5. The District Panchayat Secretary in the rank of Assistant Director of Rural Development also functions as District Planning Officer.
6. Formation of five Standing Committees in District Panchayats. Functions in the following areas
   a) Food and Agriculture,
   b) Industries and Labourers,
   c) Public Works,
   d) Education, and
   e) Health and Welfare including prohibition.
7. The District Panchayat Chairperson is included as one of the Members of the District Purchase Committee.
8. Orders have been issued under the Tamil Nadu Panchayats Act, 1994 and the Constitution of India for the preparation of Annual Development Plan for Village Panchayats, Panchayat Unions and District Panchayats and urban local bodies and place the same before the District Planning Committee.
9. The District Planning Committee is empowered to approve and

monitor the progress of the works under the Decentralised District Plan Scheme.

10. The District Collector has already been nominated as the Inspector of the Panchayats. In order to render necessary assistance to inspect panchayats, various officials of different cadres have been nominated.
11. Sanction powers to incur expenditure from the surplus funds of the District panchayats and Village Panchayats limit refixed by the government.

a) *Village Panchayats*

i) individual work not exceeding Rs.One lakh	: Village Panchayats
ii) individual work more than Rs.One lakh	: Inspector

b) *Panchayats Unions* :

i) individual work not exceeding Rs. 5 lakhs	: Panchayat Union Councils
ii) individual work not exceeding Rs. 10 lakhs	: Inspector of Panchayats
iii) individual work not exceeding with Rs.1 Crore	: Director of Rural Development
iv) individual work exceeding Rs. 1 Crore	: Government

c) *District Panchayats*

i) individual work not exceeding Rs. 10 lakhs	: District Panchayats
ii) individual work more than Rs. 10 lakhs	: Inspector
iii) individual work Rs. 25 lakhs to Rs.1 Crore	: Director of Rural Development
iv) individual work more than Rs. 1 Crore	: Government

12. Erection and maintenance of statues by the Village Panchayats, Panchayats Unions and District Panchayats : hitherto, for erection of new statue will be the responsibility of those who install it and the maintenance of the statues already installed will rest with those who installed it.
13. Under clause (1) Section 2 of the Tamil Nadu Right to Information Act, 1997 (Tamil Nadu Act 24 of 1997), the Governor of Tamil Nadu empowered certain officers specified in column (3) of the table shown in the G.O. in respect of the Organisation or Institution in the corresponding entries in column (2) thereof, to be competent

authorities within their respective jurisdiction, for the purpose of the said Act.

14. It is the normal practice to remove the Chairman through non-confidence motion where such Chairman is indirectly elected by the members of the body. This provision is available in the Urban Local Bodies. Since there is no provision for removing the Panchayat Union Chairperson and District Panchayat Chairperson through no-confidence motion by its respective members in the Tamil Nadu Panchayats Act, 1994, necessary amendments to the Panchayats Act, 1994 have been carried through.
15. Power to accord technical sanction has been enhanced wide G.O.Ms No.286, R.D. Dept., Dt 31.12.98 and Special Rules have been framed for taking up works in panchayat institutions. Rule (5) specified Rs.50,000/- per individual work as the limit for Union Engineers, Rs.3.00 lakhs as the limit for Assistant Executive Engineers and Rs.10.00 lakhs as the limit for Divisional Engineers/Executive Engineers for preparing and according sanction of estimates.
16. Actions will be taken to computerise the Village Panchayat, Panchayat union and District Panchayat accounts, funds, registers and reports, and the Management Information System will be introduced.

Powers, Functions and Responsibilities Entrusted to the Rural Local Bodies on 29 Subjects

1. Agriculture, including Agriculture Extension

1. Advise about the Agricultural Development and Planning.
2. Advise on the Integrated cereals (rice) development programme.
3. Planning and integration for the multiplication and distribution of paddy, millet, pulses, oil seeds, cotton etc.
4. Integration and advise on the procurement and distribution of vegetables seeds.
5. Exercise powers for the implementation of Community Thrashing Floor.
6. Planning and integration of special programme on Waste Land Development.
7. Powers to plan for the execution of development of local manorial resources by utilizing sewage/sullage.
8. Undertake planning in setting up of compost pits.
9. Co-ordination and advise on the Drought Prone Area Programme.

10. Co-ordination and advise on the Integrated Dry Land Development Scheme.
11. Advise about the Integrated Watershed Development Programme.
12. Advise on the National Watershed Development Programme.
13. Advise on the Comprehensive Watershed Development Programme.
14. Advising powers may be entrusted to the District Panchayats for drafting the Agricultural Development Plan for the District with the aim of increasing the agricultural production.
15. In co-ordination with the Agricultural Procedures Groups, the needs of the farmers of the district may be ascertained periodically and suitable suggestions may be given to the Director of Agriculture, Director of Horticulture and the Chief Engineer, Agriculture Engineering for taking suitable actions.
16. The District Panchayats can plan and assist to conduct district level workshops for the Agricultural Scientists and the representatives of the framers to generate new ideas in agriculture technology, transfer of the latest technology from the labs to the land.
17. The District Panchayats can advice and supervise the works relating to minimizing the wastage, storage and preservation of food grains. They can entrust various items of said works to the respective tiers to advice the implementation. All the programmes in respect of agricultural development in the district may be advised by the District Panchayat and offer suggestion. They can also supervise and advice to ensure the availability of agricultural inputs, seeds, pesticides etc. in the appropriate time.
18. To ensure that only certified quality seeds are sold by the private firms and government seed farms. They can advice to the Department of Seed Certification on the seed quality problems.
19. As the apex organisation at the district level, the District Panchayats should consult the peoples representatives of the Panchayat Unions, Village Panchayats on the requirement of agricultural inputs and discuss the matter with the respective officers of the Agriculture Department and advice various measures to the Department of Agriculture.

2. Land Improvement, Implementation of Land Reforms and Land Consolidation and Soil Conservation

1. Supervision of the distribution and development of surplus land and implementation of land ceiling.

2. Supervision of updating the land records.
3. Supervision of the implementation of other Land Reform Acts.

3. A. Minor Irrigation

1. District Panchayats can maintaining the macro level details on the irrigation channels, tanks, supply channels after collecting the information from the Village Panchayats through Panchayat Unions in order to prepare District Plans for improving the water resources in the District.
2. A perspective plan may be drafted for improving the water potential in the district and share the same with the Panchayat Unions and Village Panchayats.
3. The District Panchayats should help the Village Panchayat Unions in providing advice to take up works related to desisting of tanks, with less than 100 acres ayacut, repairs in supply channels and other such works.
4. District Panchayat should undertake review and supervision of all the schemes implemented in the district with regard to construction and maintenance of minor irrigation tanks with an ayacut less than 100 acres.

B. Water Management

1. The District Panchayat can prepare District Plans by collecting and compiling data on ground water potential, quality of water from the Geologist for optimum use of water resources in the District.
2. Maintenance of District level data on soil types and texture, watershed area and preparing perspective plans, sharing of information, experiences gained from the Watershed Management Programmes to Panchayat Unions and Village Panchayats.

4. Animal Husbandry, Dairying and Poultry

1. Supervision and review of livestock sub-centres/hospitals.
2. Review of artificial insemination in sub-centres.
3. Supervision and review of frozen semen scheme under IRDP.
4. Implementation and review of conducting Livestock and Poultry Exhibition at Village and District Levels.
5. Supervision and review of maintenance of slaughter houses.

6. Supervision and review of financial assistance to small and marginal farmers for goat rearing.
7. Supervision and review of Piggery Rearing Scheme.
8. Supervision and review of distribution of birds and animals.
9. Supervision and review of quinquennial livestock census.
10. Supervision and review of financial assistance for rabbit and poultry rearing.
11. Supervision of financial assistance to grass area development.
12. Review of Co-operative Milk Producers Societies.
13. Review of Integrated Dairy Development Scheme.
14. Review of distribution of high breed milching animals.
15. Review of Tribal Area Development Scheme.
16. Review of Western Goat Development Scheme.
17. District Panchayats can arrange for Annual Farmer's Fair, to improve veterinary health care and to communicate research findings of TANVAS to boost cattle development taking into account local condition.
18. Quarterly review by the Standing Committee on Agriculture of the various programmes implemented for livestock development along with Joint Director/Assistant Director (Animal Husbandry).
19. Supervision of Special Area and Integrated Tribal Development Programmes. District Panchayat may also supervise other externally aided schemes.

5. Fisheries

1. Planning, review and supervision of development of inland fish culture through Fish Farmers Development Agency.
2. Planning and review of exploitation of fisheries in inland water and marketing.
3. Planning and review establishment of fresh water prawn factory.
4. Planning and review of establishment of induced prawn culture.
5. Planning and review of establishment of Brackish Water Fish Development Agencies.
6. Review of development of landing facilities in coastal areas.
7. Planning and review of development of infra-structure in the coastal villages.
8. Planning and review of assistance for acquisition for land for developing fishing villages.
9. Planning and review of raining of fisherman in latest fishing

technology and stipend to fishermen.

10. Planning and assistance for financial assistance to the Fisheries Co-operatives.
11. Planning and assistance for the establishment of aquarium.
12. Review of assistance to fisherman for the purchase of hygienic containers and tricycles.
13. Review of the chemical treatment of catamarans belonging to Fishermen.
14. Planning and review for the prevention of Sea Erosion Scheme.
15. Planning and review of Fishermen Group Insurance Scheme.
16. Planning and review of Fishermen Small Savings Scheme.
17. Assist the Department in preparing plans for overall fishery development including welfare of fisher folk in the district.

6. Social Forestry and Farm Forestry

1. District Panchayats with the assistance of forest department can assess the District potentialities promotion of social forestry and farm forestry.
2. District Panchayats with the assistance of forest department can prepare plans and projects for implementation of social forestry schemes through voluntary organisations and Heads of Departments.
3. District Panchayats can consolidate and draft the Action Plan for Social Forestry in tune with the approved financial provision with the assistance of Forest Department.
4. District Panchayats may undertake the implementation and assist in planning Community Wasteland Development Programme.
5. The District Panchayats can review through Standing Committee on Agriculture with the prior permission of forest department, once in three months all the social forestry and farm forestry programmes and inspect the Establishment of Bamboo Estates, Community Wasteland Development Programme, Soft wood and Timber Plantation, Raising of Plantation in Tribal areas, Construction of School buildings/Formation of forest roads in tribal areas.
6. District Panchayats may send proposals to Government about the issues and suggestions on the problems and prospects of social and farm forestry in the District.

7. Minor Forest Produce

1. District Panchayats can conduct Annual Conferences of Officers, Users, and Organizers interested promotion, collection and processing of minor forest produce and to promote the activities of the users, and advise Government on the measures to be adopted for promoting minor forest produce.
2. District Panchayats can organise credit linkages needed for promotion, procurement, processing and marketing of minor forest produce and advise government on the measures to be adopted for promoting minor forest produce.
3. District Panchayats can supervise regulate, plan and review of the programme to increase the plantation areas to improve production of minor forest produce like honey, barks, tamarind, cardamom, bamboo, medicinal plants etc.

8. Small Scale Industries, Including Food Processing

1. Planning and review of the formation of industrial estates and growth centres.
2. Advise and assist the Entrepreneurs Development Programme.
3. Advise and assist the setting up industries in backward areas.
4. Assist in the establishment of common facilities for the small scale industries.
5. Preparation of a plan on the feasibility of starting of industries in the District and to conduct conference on industrial development.
6. At the time of constitution of District Level Standing Committee on Industries and Labour, the General Manager, District Industries Centre may be included as a member of this Committee.

9. Khadi, Village and Cottage Industries

1. District level planning and identification of appropriate training centres for Khadi Silk, Village and Cottage Industries Handicrafts Development.
2. District Panchayats may draw up district plan for development of Khadi, Handicrafts, Sericulture, Cottage and village industries.
3. District Panchayats can identify the Training Centres and Institutes suitable to impart appropriate technological training and disseminate such details to the Panchayat Unions and Village Panchayats.

4. District Panchayats may advise the Khadi and Village Industries Board about the infrastructures needed for exploiting available potentialities in the district.
5. District Panchayats may plan and suggest the implementation of schemes like modernization of looms for Khadi weaving, supply of Beehives to the Adi-dravidar and Tribals, Schemes for Jacquard provision to Khadi silk weavers, fresh supply of tool kits to tappers, scheme for village industries promotion under western ghat development project and promotion for village industries Beekeeping in the Nilgris.

10. Rural Housing

1. Planning and review of allocation of house sites to SCs and STs.
2. Planning and review of Tamil Nadu Rural Housing Scheme.
3. Planning and review of improvement of residential surroundings in rural areas.
4. Planning and review of Indira Awaas Yojana.
5. Planning and review of Housing Schemes for SC and ST.
6. Planning and review of Housing Schemes for BCs and MBCs.
7. Formulation of schemes by taking into account the future for housing needs in the district, formulating integrated housing schemes with an eye to provide houses for all houseless persons in the district and its implementation through appropriate institutions, seeking technical advice from the Building Centres for construction of houses under rural housing schemes and providing technical guidance/ assistance to Village Panchayats/Panchayat Unions etc.
8. Review the progress of implementation of various housing schemes and rendering advice for their proper implementation.

11. Drinking Water

1. Identification and planning of major drinking water schemes.
2. Supervise the implementation of water supply schemes and monitoring the comprehensive water supply schemes within the district.
3. Plan, advice and supervise the implementation of rural water supply schemes for the uncovered habitations under self-sufficiency scheme.
4. Advise and supervise the provision of drinking water supply in the drought-affected areas.

5. Render advice and supervise the comprehensive water supply schemes in fluoride affected areas.
6. Advise and supervise the supply of safe drinking water to habitations affected with high salinity and brackishness.
7. Plan, advise and supervise the supply of desalinated water in the salinity-affected areas.
8. Supervise special water supply scheme and other Accelerated Rural Water Supply Programme in the rural areas.

12. Fuel and Fodder

1. District Panchayats can plan for various development schemes implemented by the Forest Department on rural fuel and firewood plantation.
2. The fodder production can be improved by growing trees in the wastelands in the District for which planning may be done by District Panchayats.
3. District Panchayats may inspect and take follow up action in regard to the TNADP implemented by the Director of Animal Husbandry for increasing fodder production.
4. Planning, execution and supervision of schemes on fodder plant and sapling distribution.
5. Rural Development Department is executing the Non-Conventional Energy Scheme for Bio-gas and Solar Cookers. District Panchayat may be empowered to plan and inspect these programmes.

13. Roads,Culverts, Bridges, Waterways and other means of Communication

1. Planning for the development of roads in the district.
2. Inspection of progress of all the road development projects in the district.
3. Preparation of plans and review of road works executed in local body roads under Jawahar Velai Vaaipu Thittam, Innovative, Jawahar Velai Vaaipu Thittam, M.P. Local Area Development and M.L.A. Constituency Development Schemes, Hill Area Development Programme and works undertaken with external aided projects.

14. Rural Electrification, Including Distribution of Electricity

1. Review of the implementation of all schemes to the rural

electrification taken up in the district.

2. In order to get regular and uniform power supply District Panchayats may collect the data on electricity requirement, availability, new installations required etc., and furnish consolidated district data to Tamil Nadu Electricity Board.
3. The District Panchayat will collect information on the requirement under 'one hut one light scheme' prepare the District Plan and coordinate with TNEB for the implementation.
4. On the basis of information furnished by the Village Panchayats and Panchayat Unions, the District Panchayat will recommended to Tamil Nadu Electrify Board, for proper distribution of power supply to agricultural pump sets.
5. The District Panchayat may be empowered to review and monitor the schemes implemented by Tamil Nadu Electricity Board and suggest ways to improve the power supply on distribution.

15. Non-Conventional Energy Sources

1. Identification of suitable sources for implementing the non-conventional energy sources in District and advise the government.
2. District level interface workshop with users and manufactures of non-conventional energy devices and take follow up action with the concerned authorities.
3. Review of all the related schemes implemented in the District.
4. The District Panchayats may undertake planning and coordination of the development of these schemes. It may also assist in design a master plan at the district level for biogas, wind mills, solar cookers and heaters.
5. The District Panchayats will take action for the identification of potentialities for non-conventional energy sources more specially for solar energy, wind energy and biogas. It will take necessary action to extend this scheme through out the District.

16. Poverty Alleviation Programme

1. District Panchayats can prepare plan for Poverty Alleviation Programmes at District level.
2. District Panchayats may assist in extending technical assistance for planning at Village Panchayat and Panchayat Union level.
3. District Panchayats may supervise and review Poverty Alleviation

Programmes.

4. District Panchayats may review schemes implemented in drought prone areas.
5. District Panchayats may supervise and review Development of Women and Children in Rural Areas.
6. District Decentralised Planning may be arranged by the District Panchayats in active cooperation of Panchayat Unions and District Planning Committee.
7. Review and supervision of schemes implemented under the grants recommended by the Tenth Finance Commission for local bodies.
8. District Panchayat may review integrated Rural Sanitation and Water Supply Scheme implemented in Cuddalore and Villupuram District with the DANIDA assistance.
9. As per the new guidelines of Government of India, District Panchayat may implement and supervise Employment Assurance Scheme.
10. District Panchayats may undertake review of Central Rural Sanitation Programme.
11. District Panchayats may plan and review schemes under which Bio-gas plants to be set up for individuals and community.
12. District Panchayats may undertake Planning and review of smokeless chulahs scheme and National Project on improved chulahs.

17. Education, Including Primary and Secondary Schools

1. Inspection and sending reports to Assistant Educational Officers about the maintenance and repairs of school building, latrines and provision of drinking water facilities, supervision of schools.
2. Exercise powers to start libraries in the district.
3. Review of the improvement of Primary Education and take appropriate action on the same.
4. Since teachers are appointed by the government, the complaints against them may be sent to the officers of the Education Department, who will take action against them.

18. Technical Training and Vocational Education

1. Undertake planning on technical manpower and crafts required for different industrial and other establishments existing in the district.
2. Review the functioning of the government and private industrial technical institutes, polytechnics existing in the district.
3. Plan for establishment of vocational training centres with help of technical experts.

4. Identify suitable locations and recommended starting of vocational schools for women. To supervise such schools and advice for efficient functioning.
5. Plan for starting of new vocations for the benefit of the people.

19. Adult and Non-formal Education

1. Prepare plans and supervise the Non-formal education schemes and Adult Education Schemes, Supervision over staff will be the responsibility of the Government. District Panchayats may send their advice to the officials of the Non-formal Education Department.

20. Libraries

1. Advising the local library authorities for planning new libraries in rural areas.
2. Selection and nomination of one elected member of District Panchayats to the District Library Committee.
3. Preparation of an intensive plan to encourage reading habits in library.
4. Reading habits among the people, integrating rural works with other schemes, arranging general facilities to the libraries, organising financing for libraries will be the responsibility of the District Panchayats, Management of District Libraries and the like under the control of the government.

21. Cultural Activities

1. Planning, review and extend assistance to Karandhai Tamil Sangam.
2. Review and assist Jawahar Bala Bhavan.
3. Establish and review the plans for the District Art Galaries and Art Councils.
4. Establish Music Schools and identify students and undertake review.
5. District Panchayats will organise at district level competitions in art, music, and drama sports training camps in games, exhibitions, and arrange festivals with the help of various Art Schools, cultural troops and sports development authority.
6. District Panchayats will honour artists, craftsmen, sportsmen and compile and maintain details of artists in music, drama and traditional folk arts and update the same once in five years utilizing the assistance of the Regional Assistant Directors of the Department of

Art and Culture.

7. District Panchayats will provide basic infrastructural facilities to improve the standards of games and sports in rural areas.
8. District Panchayats will recommend to government the details of artists living below poverty line for financial assistance.
9. District Panchayats will encourage new art schools and identify best artists in such schools to enable them to improve their talents.
10. District Panchayats will organise special coaching camps and rewards best players and sportsmen so as to encourage track and field events and in other locally popular games.

22. Markets and Fairs

1. Advise and review of the functioning of public markets.
2. Advise and review the private markets.
3. Advise about the functioning of regulated market.
4. Advise and review the primary co-operative market.
5. District Panchayats can plan and construct income generating shopping and marketing complexes in the accessible areas and lease. These shops are to be maintained and kept in good condition, it is duty of the District Panchayats to levy rents for the shops and impose penalty to the defaulters.
6. District Panchayats can take appropriate action for the revival and maintenance of the markets and shops which are in bad conditions.
7. District Panchayat can identify the popular markets/shandies and popular market complexes and declare as the special items and to inform the government.

23. Helath and Saniatations

1. Planning and review of schemes for District/Taluk Headquarter Hospitals.
2. Supervision of schemes implemented for eradication of Tuberculosis, Malaria, Dreaded diseases, Aids, Leprosy like National Health Programmes.
3. Planning and review of establishment of dispensaries in tribal areas.
4. Planning and review of financial help for mobile medical units in remote localities.
5. Planning and review to promote public participation in prevention and control and diseases and identification of beneficiaries.

6. Planning and review to promote Siddha/Ayurvedha/Unani Medicines at District level.
7. Review the safe disposal of hospital westages.
8. Planning and review programmes for involvement of NGOs in conducting Eye and Family Welfare Camps.
9. Planning and review of construction and maintenance of Primary Health Centres and Maternity Centres.
10. Assistance for creating awareness among public about the importance of health environment and control diseases.
11. Planning and review of financial assistance for conducting training for Multi-purpose Health Workers in Primary Health Centres.
12. Supervision and planning of immunization programme for Diphtheria and Polio for school going children.
13. Planning and review of School Health schemes.
14. Planning and review of Birth and Death registration activities.
15. Planning and review of sanitation activities.
16. Prepare annual status reports on the implementation of health care schemes in the district and compare it with other districts and the state to ascertain the relative position of the district.
17. Conduct review meeting with officials of health and development department staff once in 4 months and improve the health services in the panchayat unions and prepare annual report.
18. Conduct macro and micro level assessment of disease control measures and advise the government by sending reports.
19. Supervise and ensure supply of drugs and medical equipments and instruments to all hospitals.
20. Assist the District Planning Committee and Medical and Health Department to prepare and execute local level plans.
21. Prepare Human Resource Development/quality of life index at the district level.
22. Collect data on birth and death rates, NMR, IMR, Still Birth Rate, from the Panchayati Unions prepare a report and make district level data available to the state government.
23. Monitor and review the functioning of school health programme and maintenance of school health cards in primary, secondary schools and provide feedback to government and advise the Panchayat Unions and Village Panchayats for better implementation of the programme.
24. Assist Panchayat Unions and Village Panchayats in creating awareness on health and nutrition among public by organising seminars and discussions.

25. Assist selection and appointment of the medical and health staff and give suggestion to the government about the deployment, transfer and deputation of the Health department.
26. Review the functioning of food analysis laboratories in the district and give suggestions to the regarding remedial measures to be taken to prevent food adulteration.
27. Encourage services provided under traditional system of medicines like Siddha, Ayurvedha and Unani to benefit the people.
28. Supervise supply of drugs and equipment to district level hospitals and Panchayati union dispensaries.
29. Assist in safe disposal of hazardous wastes from all hospitals.

24. Family Welfare

1. Planning and review and supervision of the establishment and maintenance of family welfare centres.
2. Review and supervision of establishment of Block/District Family Welfare Training Centres.
3. Management, maintenance and review of involvement of local bodies and NGOs in family welfare schemes.
4. Review of Family Welfare Training to workers.
5. Review of the schemes for Financial assistance for educating public about Family Welfare Schemes including vasectomy.
6. Proposals for District Family Welfare Programme proposal may be formulated and sent to Director of Family Welfare at State level.
7. The defects and difficulties in the implementation of the programme may be identified by the District Panchayat and with the support of village panchayats and efforts taken with the help of Village Panchayats and Panchayat Unions to overcome the difficulties and ensure effective implementation of family schemes.
8. Efforts for economic development may be taken by the mobilising resources through government, Departments NGOs and Charitable Trusts and facilities in Village panchayats, Panchayat Unions may be improved.
9. Co-ordinate the activities relating to implementation of family welfare programme and arrange for the social audit of activities with the help of elected women representatives.
10. Prepare reports on the maternity services in the district and improve the management information system.
11. Assess the implementation of family welfare programme by the

Panchayat Unions, find out the difficulties and suggest measuring to overcome the same.

12. Arrange for storing sufficient stock of medicines for the respective areas including provision of space for safe storage of medicines and recommend measures to government for cold storage.
13. Involve the private medical practioners and private hospitals in the implementation of family welfare programme and coordinate their efforts for providing better medical facilities to all the people in the area.
14. Organise and conduct seminars, discussions and workshops at district level to improve the performance under Family Welfare Programme.

25. Women and Child Development

1. Review of schemes on the establishment, management and supervision of Nutritious Meal Centre.
2. Review of integrated Child Development Schemes/Sub Nutritious schemes.
3. Review and supervision on implementation of Nutrition noon meal schemes in schools and ICDP centres.
4. Review of the schemes for assistance in formation pre-school and creches.
5. Assist in construction of Child Welfare Centres under Swedish assisted ICDP.
6. Review of scheme on prvention of female infanticide and development of girl children of destitute women.
7. Review and supervision of working women's hostel and production units intended for women.
8. Review of various women welfare schemes such as vocational training, poor widows children and daughters marriage assistance and orphanages.
9. Review of service homes for women.
10. Review of schemes on women groups and its economic activities.
11. Review of creches of children of working and diseased women.
12. Review of women industrial co-operative societies.
13. Review of functioning of orphanages.
14. Review of functioning of all welfare schemes intended for women.
15. Review of schemes for financial assistance to pregnant women who are below poverty line.
16. Review the schemes for the marriage assistance to women who are

below the poverty line.

17. Review the schemes for the financial assistance to Female Children Welfare Scheme.
18. Review of schemes on sewing machines providing to destitute and deserted women.
19. Review of schemes on financial advance to poor widow's daughter's marriage.
20. Review the externally aided project for the women welfare development under IFAD review.
21. Review the functioning of home for the aged.
22. Preparation of reports on nutritional status of women and children, social status of children, socio-economic condition of women based on the statistics obtained from panchayat unions. Compare the reports so prepared in statistics/reports of other districts in Tamil Nadu and with other states and assist in plan preparation by comparing reports.
23. To supervise the guidance bureau units functioning at district level.
24. To supervise the schemes meant for welfare of women and children at district level and offer advise for improvement.
25. To supervise the performance of the Panchayati Union and Village Panchayats with regard to nutrition related activities and render necessary advise.
26. To co-ordinate and to supervise the activities of the Panchayat unions in creating awareness on Family welfare, education, water supply and Rural Development schemes and to integrate the services rendered.
27. To collect information regarding social evils such as child labour, female infanticide, from the Panchayat Unions and render necessary assistance to eradicate them.
28. To assist to remove the hurdles which come in the way to schemes such as self employment schemes for women meant for enhancing their income and loan assistance for starting industries etc.

26. Social Welfare Including Welfare of the Handicapped and Mentally Retarded

1. Review of functioning of the blind and handicapped rehabilitation centres.
2. Review and supervision of the schools and hostels for the physically handicapped.

3. Review the distribution of scholarship to students of handicapped schools.
4. Review the implementation of reservation policy in educational institution and government departments.
5. Review the implementation of integrated Polio establishment of schemes.
6. Review the NGOs activities the rehabilitation of and mentally disabled children.
7. Review the establishment of schools for deaf, dumb and handicapped.
8. Review the employment opportunities for blind registered in Employment Exchanges.
9. Review the implementation of scribe assistance to the blind students.
10. Review the state scheme of the scholarship to handicapped children.
11. Review of scheme on training of juvenile delinquent discharges from approved schools.
12. Planning and review the schemes for prevention and control juvenile problems in the society.
13. Planning and review of the schemes for functioning of correctional homes, vigilance institutions and government approved schools.
14. To prepare reports on the basis of the informations received from Panchayat Unions on census, births and deaths, child labour, street children, aged people, beggars, alcoholics and drug addicts, exploited women etc.
15. To supervise the welfare schemes, rehabilitation schemes, Social defence programmes implemented in the districts with the elected women representative and provide necessary assistance to remove the bottlenecks with the help of concerned departments.
16. To supervise and ensure that the old age pension, free sarees, dhotis distributed by the government etc., are properly reaching the beneficiaries and to sort out the problems.
17. To assist the judiciary and the police department and with their help take all necessary action for initiating stringent action against the persons who instigate drug abuse and those who are involved in the business of drugs and eradicate it completely.
18. To create awareness among the public on the causes for disablility and treat the mentally retarded as a part of the society and to help the implementation of the schemes.
19. To conduct necessary research on the basis of the data furnished by Panchayat Union on rehabilitation, child labour and street children and to assist in the improvement of the programmes.

20. To collect and compile the information village wise on the aged people's programmes through Panchayat Unions and maintain it at district level.
21. To monitor the reservations made for the disabled persons in the educational institutions and government departments and conduct necessary with the respective department officers.
22. To assist in the efforts made by the Panchayats and Panchyat Union increasing awareness among public especially youths on the evils of drug abuse and other social evils which endanger officers.
23. To assist the Panchyat Union and Social Welfare department in popularising small family norms and social defence through family welfare centres. To assist the panchayats, judiciary and police departments to take action against the persons who deliberately engage in begging and avoid engaging themselves in physical labour.

27. Welfare of the Weaker Sections, in Particular, of the Scheduled Castes and the Scheduled Tribes

1. Planning and review of the schemes being implemented by others for the welfare of SC/ST.
2. Review the provision of pathways to burial grounds and burning ghats.
3. Electrification of ST and Adi-Dravida & Tribal houses – Planning and review.
4. Planning and review of the assistance scheme for inter-caste marriages implemented by Social Welfare Department.
5. Planning and review of schemes for assistance to petty traders.
6. Planning and supervision of educational concessions extended to the school going children of SC/ST (books, uniforms, scholarships etc.)
7. Planning and supervision of the construction of Community Halls, Dhobikhanas, etc.
8. Planning and supervision for enforcement of the Civil Rights Protection Act, 1995.
9. Planning and supervision of propagating the evils of untouchability to the public.
10. Planning and supervision of training programmes and special coaching for SC/ST.

28. Public Distribution System

1. Chairman of the District Panchayat and the ward members may inspect the ration shop and send reports to the District Level Committee if any problem noticed.

29. Maintenance of Community Assets

1. Supervision of the activities relating to the identification, registration and recovery of charges from public users of the social assets.
2. Review and supervision of the sale, lease and transfer of public assets.
3. Review and supervision of social assets and ensure protection, encroachment, damages, losses etc.
4. To plan for eliciting support from NGOs in maintenance of public assets.
5. Buildings, lands and other assets of erstwhile District Board were handed over to the Panchayat Unions and Government. The Government will consider case by case to retrieve and hand over those to District Panchayats for its maintenance.
6. District Panchayats may fix and collect tax, rent and user's fee from their commercial and other assets.
7. District Panchayat may lease out its assets and collect lease amount.
8. District Panchayat may be vigilant in protecting its assets from misuse, encroachment and loss and take necessary legal action in this regard.
9. District Panchayat are permitted to receive donations from NGOs and the public to protect and maintain its assets under Section 124 of the Tamil Nadu Panchayat Act, 1994.

A Case Analysis of Thiruchirapalli District Panchayat

Methodology

This study employs the case study method to evaluate the performance of the District Panchayat. For evaluation one should have a clear cut evaluation criteria. Sofar there is no standard scale for evaluation of the performance of the institutions. A simple exercise has been undertaken to see whether the assigned duties and responsibilities have been properly perceived and discharged. What has been done here is, to what extent the

District Panchayat has performed the responsibilities assigned to them? It is only a historical narration of what the District Panchayat has achieved in the past four years.

Thiruchirappalli District Panchayat has been chosen for this study. The reason for selecting this panchayat is that the president of the District Panchayat is championing the cause of the District Panchayat as the leader of Tamil Nadu Association of District Panchayat Presidents and President of the All India Zilla Parishad. Against this background it is decided to undertake this study in Thiruchirapalli district. While studying the performance of a District Panchayat one has to touch upon a number of aspects starting from the perception of the leaders to the performance of the entire District Panchayat council[14]. How they perceive the institution?, matters much with regard to their functioning. From the description of the panchayats by the intellectuals and media in the initial stages, District Panchayat had been perceived as a very strong administrative unit parallel to the district administration. They gained the perception from the argument that DRDA will be merged with District Panchayats and the District Planning Committee will be under the Chairmanship of the District Panchayati President as in other progressive states[15]. With the above stated understanding they moved into the District Panchayat. There is yet another problem, the elected leaders that they have perceived the panchayat institutions as political outfits rather than development institutions. They have started their functioning with a negative note that they are not given due powers and recognition. Further, after hearing from the views of the state government about the position of District Panchayat, they have also lost their interest and developed antagonism towards the state government. Yet they are in position and performing their duties and carrying out the responsibilities. Before analyzing the activities the composition of the panchayats will be presented here.

Table 2.1 : Thiruchirappalli District Panchayati Composition

S. No.	Category	No. of Members
1.	S.C.	2
2.	S.C.(W)	2
3.	Women	6
4.	General	14
	Total	24

Source : Computed.

With regard to functioning, their activities in the council have to be analyzed. At the primary level the details regarding the number of meetings they have conducted and the items covered in each year and attendance are to be assessed. All the above details are given in Table 2.2.

Table 2.2 : Meetings and Attendance

S. No.	Year	No. of meetings	% of attendance	No.of items in the Agendas	Meeting	Duration
1.	1996-1997	6	93.75	30	Ordinary 6 months	Approx. 3 Hrs.
2.	1997-1998	13	95.73	108		
3.	1998-1999	23	99.56	113		
4.	1999-2000 upto Feb	16	100	31		

Women Members Attendance

1.	1996-1997	98%
2.	1997-1998	96.2%
3.	1998-1999	99%
4.	1999-2000	100%

Source : Computed.

Table 2.3 : Budget

Rs.in Lakhs

		Income				Expenditure		
S. No.	Year	Tenth Finance Commission	State Finance Commission	Panchayat Fund	Total Fund	Develop-ment	Administra-tion	Total
1.	1996-97	100	—	—	100	80	20	100
2.	1997-98	50	86.63	—	136.63	126.63	10	136.63
3.	1998-99	25	121.92	25.10	172.02	154.05	17.97	172.02
				Total	408.65		Total	408.65

Source : Computed.

Table 2.4 : Works undertaken during 1997-98 and 1998-99 and works to be undertaken during 1999-2000

(Rs.in Lakhs)

S. No.	Works	1997-98				1998-99				1999-2000	
		TFC		SFC		TFC		SFC		TFC	TFC
		No. of works taken	Cost	No. of works taken	Cost	No. of works taken	Cost	No. of works taken	Cost	No. of works taken	No. of works taken
1.	Passenger Shed	6	1.95	18	6.30	7	1.62	16	4.32	2	—
2.	Drinking Water facility (OHT. LHT Bore wells)	75	28.23	7	52.15	2	2.50	36	28.35	5	11
3.	Road facilities	1	0.30	3	2.75	5	19.16	9	23.78	6	11
4.	Small bridges	6	4.60	12	9.10	2	0.90	10	6.60	6	7
5.	Fair price shop	5	6.29	4	4.80	2	2.87	7	10.42	3	6
6.	Noon meal centre Kitchen	—	—	2	0.45	5	2.05	4	1.64	4	2
7.	Schools	—	—	5	2.80	3	2.55	4	2.10	2	2
8.	Threshing floor	5	2.65	3	1.70	1	0.30	7	4.10	2	1
9.	Street lights	—	—	—	—	—	—	—	3.07	—	—
10.	Cooperative milk society buildings	—	—	1	2.00	—	—	2	3.40	2	1
11.	School toilet facilities	2	2.04	3	2.00	—	—	1	0.70	4	4
12.	Drainage facilities	3	2.20	16	7.56	16	17.15	6	6.65	4	2
13.	Approach road to burial ground	1	0.30	—	—	—	—	—	—	3	2

Source : Computed

It is inferred that they have conducted meetings range between 13 to 23 times in each year for the past four years. Attendance has reached even cent percent. Equally women also participated in the meeting.

Budget and programmes would project their activities in the field. Table 2 and 3 highlight the budget capacity of the district panchayat and the activities carried out in the villages with the grant given by the state government through the Tenth Finance Commission and State Finance Commission awards.

They are fixed and the District Panchayat can recommend certain works within the amount. Beyond this budget they cannot do anything. In the given context, they is no planning exercise to be undertaken by the District Panchayats. In the financial allocations made to District Panchayats. The District Panchayat has to utilize the money for providing facilities to the people which are not being met by the Gram Panchayats and Panchayat Unions. It is a general complaint that the earmarked amount is being shared among the individual ward members and the ward members select the works according to their own rational. It is being criticised by all. But in Thiruchirappalli, District Panchayat has taken an overall view of the development works that take place in different villages with the help of Gram Panchayats and Panchayat Unions, allocations have been made for various activities which are left out in the allocation of the Panchayati Union and Gram Panchayats. The total outlay of Rs. 408 lakhs has been spent on thirteen items of works. Where it is clearly indicated that the amount has to be spent well within the items of works mentioned in the list[16]. Here, there is no opportunity to evaluate the prudent and innovative spending of money for development activities. There is yet another area where one can evaluate the performance of the elected leaders. It is not the quantum of money spent but how the amount is being spent. Whether all these activities are well designed, planned and carried out with the active participation of the people concerned for administering development and social justice that matters. The planning role has been given a status only now by making the District Panchayati President as the Chairperson of District Planning Committee. For initiating multi level planning steps are being taken now. The coordinating and supervisory roles assigned to the District Panchayats have to be performed by the District Panchayat. This aspect has to be verified.

What is unique in Thiruchirappalli District Panchayat? Though the president does not enjoy the majority, he managed with opposition in a very balanced way. All the resolutions have been passed unanimously.

Further, he along with the council members used to participate in all public function. They also constituted standing committees and the committees have performed their role. In the sameway the supervisory powers assigned to the District Panchayats have been effectively utilized and recommendations have been made on various service activities done by the government. Thiruchirappalli District Panchayat has chalked out a perspective plan for the development of the district. For all the development schemes and programmes the district panchayat mobilised the people. Yet another significance is that the District Panchayat is working with district administration hand in hand. District administration lauded the efforts of the District Panchayats[17].

Analysis

District Panchayats have been entrusted with some responsibilities. They are supervisely and advisory in nature. Since most of the powers are supervisory and advisory, the leaders have no capacity to supervise many of the Departments which are not developmental but sectoral. In many districts the district panchayats are not performing their role. But in Tiruchirapalli the powers given to them have been used as the leaders of the panchayati is so effective and he is conscious of his roles and responsibilities. The allocated amount for District Panchayat is also limited. Even in the allocated amount through awards of Tenth Finance Commission and State Finance Commission, much of discretion has not been given to the district panchayat. It is obvious that if the District Panchayati Presidents are capable, they can disturb the day to day administration of many of the departments through supervision and evaluation. Most of the presidents are not able to perceive the details and responsibilities properly and hence they have not involved themselves in inspection and evaluation. But the president of Tiruchirapalli District Panchayat has perceived the assigned role properly and carried out his activities in his office with the active support of the Inspector of Panchayat, other officials and the district ward members. Perhaps this may be due to constant training, the District Panchayat President has undergone for the past three years. Of all the presidents of district panchayats of Tamil Nadu, Tiruchirapalli District Panchayat, President is the only leader who met the higher officials and the ministers inconnection with the devolution of powers to local bodies by maintaining a cordial relationship with all. He is a model for all panchayat leaders. He has organised three massive training programmes for the grassroots level leaders with the help of intellectuals. He prepared a training manual and module and circulated to all the leaders who have attended the training programmes. He consulted his fellow leaders and submitted periodical report to the High Power Committee constituted for devolution of powers. Though he belongs to a political party, he is able to get the support of all the representatives belonging to difficult political parties for panchayat activities because of his moderate approach in dealing with issues akin to Panchayati Raj System. He has proved that however the powers are limited, the district panchayat presidents have space to work and carryout activities.

Conclusion

It is unequivocal that the District Panchayats are not strengthened sofar. Since the Government of Tamil Nadu has openly expressed its reservation on district panchayat, and functionaries are not active in their activities. All the roles assigned to them are supervisory, recommendatory and advisory in nature. Even monetary allocations are made with the condition that they have to spend the amount only on the items which are included in the list identified by the government. Real decision making power and planning power have not been given to the District Panchayats. The assigned functions are considered supervisory in nature which cannot be done since most of the departments are sectoral which cannot be supervised by the District Panchayats. Developmental activities could be done at the district level but these functions are not assigned to them. They concentrate only on carrying out centrally sponsored programmes from both the governments.

Notes and References

1. Jennie Litvack, Junaid Ahmed and Richard Bird, *Rethinking Decentralisation in Developing Countries,* Washington D.C. : World Bank Sector Studies Series, 1998.
2. Jame Manor, *The Political Economy of Democratic Decentralisation,* Washington DC : World Bank Report, 1999.
3. Dennis A. Rondinelli, John R. Nellis and G. Sabbir Cheema, *Decentralisation in Developing Countries : A review of Recent Experience.* Washington DC : World Bank Management and Development Services, 1983.
4. George Mathew, *Panchayati Raj : From Legislation to Movement.* New Delhi : Concept Publishing Company, 1996.
5. G.Palanithurai, *New Panchayati Raj System at Work : An Evaluation,* New Delhi: Concept Publishing Company, 1999.
6. It is called Dilemma of Development and for more details see Rajesh Harsh and C. Srinivas, "Andhra Pradesh : Dilemmas of Development" *Economic and Political*

Weekly, Vol. xxxv No.23 (June 3, 2000).

7. For more details see, T.M. Thomas Isaac and Richard W. Franke, *Local Democracy and Development : People's Campaign for Decentralised Planning in Kerala*. New Delhi : Left Word Books, 2000.
8. G. Palanithurai, How many Tiers for Panchayats, *Gram Rajyam* (11.08.2000)
9. L.C. Jain, *Report on the Entrustment of Powers to Panchayats*, Chennai : State Planning Commission, 1997.
10. Ko.Ci.Mani. *Report of the High Level Committee on Devolution of Powers to Local Bodies*. Chennai : Rural Development Department, 1999.
11. Government of Tamil Nadu., *Democratic Decentralisation : Power Entrusted to Panchayati Raj Institutions*, Chennai : Rural Development Department, 1999.
12. Government of Tamil Nadu, *Tamil Nadu Rural Local Bodies Act, 1994*, Chennai : Publication Division, 1995.
13. *Ibid.*
14. G. Palanithurai, *Perception of Grassroots Democracy and Political Performance*, New Delhi : MD Publications, 1998.
15. Even the L.C. Jain Committee has recommended that DRDA has to be merged with District Panchayats. See K.V. Palanidurai, "Democratic Decentralisation in Tamil Nadu – A status paper" presented in the International Conference on Democratic Decentralisation organised by State Planning Board Kerala at Thiruvananthapuram from 23rd to 27th May, 2000.
16. Annual Report of Thiruchirappalli District Panchayat 1996-1997, 1997-1998, 1998-1999.
17. Observation of the Inspector of Panchayats on the Annual Report of the District Panchayat.

3

DESIGNING AND MANAGING BLOCK PANCHAYATS

(Powers Exercisable by Rural Local Bodies as per the Rules Issued Under the Tamil Nadu Panchayats Act, 1994)

Panchayat Union

1. Panchayat Union Council is competent to accord administrative sanction in respect of the original works costing upto rupees five lakh.
2. Panchayat Union Council is competent to accord administrative sanction in respect of the following nature of maintenance works with the technical sanction of the authorities noted against them.

Nature of Estimate	*Authority to accord Technical Sanction*
(1)	(2)
a) Estimate costing not more than rupees ten thousand	Block Engineer or Assistant Engineer (Rural Development)
b) Estimate costing more than ten thousand but not more than rupees fifty thousand	Assistant Executive Engineer (Rural Development)
c) Estimate costing more than fifty thousand but not more than rupees two lakhs	Executive Engineer (Rural Development)
d) Estimate costing more than rupees two lakhs	Superintending Engineer (Rural Development)

3. Panchayat Union Council is competent to accord administrative

sanction in respect of the following nature of electrical works with the technical sanction of the authority noted against them :

Nature of Estimate	*Authority to accord Technical Sanction*
(1)	(2)
a) Estimate costing not more than rupees ten thousand	Block Engineer or Assistant Engineer (Rural Development)
b) Estimate costing more than ten thousand but not more than rupees twenty five thousand	Assistant Executive Engineer (Rural Development)
c) Estimate costing more than twenty five thousand but not more than rupees fifty thousand	Executive Engineer (Rural Development)
d) Estimate costing more than rupees fifty thousand	Superintending Engineer (Rural Development)

4. Panchayat Union shall grant/license/lease for taking any fish from the water sources lying in their areas.

Powers, Functions and Responsibilities entrusted on General Subjects

1. The government have directed that the surplus funds available with the Panchayat Union can be utilized for undertaking water supply related activities/maintenance of school building including the additional building, development of Village Panchayat, Panchayat Union roads, minor bridges, culverts, water retaining structures and development of minor irrigation tanks/ponds.
2. The government have requested the General Managers of Telephones of the area concerned to issue necessary instructions to provide telephone connection both at office and residence for all the Chairpersons of the Panchayat Union.
3. Provision of space for the Member of Legislative Assembly at the Panchayat Union Office, for the purpose of meeting people in regard

to know and discuss their grievances.

4. Purchase of spares and consumables for street lights maintained by the Panchayat Union and the quality standards and price have been prescribed and permitted.
5. Orders have already been passed to rapidly the Rural Welfare Officers for the field works.
6. In all the Panchayat Unions within the radius of 32 kms from city of Chennai 'City rate system' will be adopted in the preparation of estimates for the works, in accordance with the schedule of rates of Highways and Public Works Departments.
7. For conducting Government function expenditure level has been enhanced to Rs. 2000.
8. The Panchayat Union have been permitted to organize Volleyball, Kabhadi, Football and other sports activities at the Panchayat Union level and to award prizes of Rs.100/- to the winner.

Powers, Functions and Responsibilities entrusted on 29 Subjects as per Schedule IV of the Tamil Nadu Panchayats

Panchayat Unions

1. Agriculture, Including Agricultural Extension

1. Assist in procurement of vegetable seeds and identification of beneficiaries for distribution.
2. Planning for construction of community thrashing floor.
3. Assist in implementation of Waste Land Development Programme.
4. Assist in implementation of natural manure development scheme by utilizing the agricultural waste and planning for setting up of organic manure pits.
5. Assist in implementation of distribution of saplings under horticulture development schemes.
6. Offer suitable advice in integrating of the Drought Prone Area Programme.
7. Advise the integration of the Waste Land Development Programme.
8. Advise in the implementation of Integrated Watershed Development Programme.
9. Advise in the implementation of Integrated Watershed Development Programme in the rain-fed areas.
10. Advise in the implementation of the Comprehensive Watershed

Development Programme.

11. Panchayat Union can encourage farmers to utlize the seeds, pesticides, fungicides, fertilizers and other agricultural inputs distributed under integrated Cereals Development Programme. This activity may be done by the Panchayat Unions through the Agricultural Extension Centres located in the Panchayat Union Office complex.
12. Similar to Integrated Cereal Development Programme, Panchayat Union can assist the Agriculture Department in the identification of beneficiaries under Intensive Production Programme for minor millets, cotton and oil seeds Production Programmes. The activities may be coordinated by local bodies and implemented through the Agricultural Extension Centres.
13. Panchayat Union may advise to create the required production and market infrastructure for the cultivation of soya, beans etc., as single crop or as inter-crop and market the produce.
14. Panchayat Union can select suitable Village Panchayats and tie up with primary Agricultural Coop societies render advice for crop loans and for the construction of rural godowns to facilitate the storage of produce and to provide temporary advance.
15. Panchayat Union can take steps to enhance the horticulture production by making assessment on the requirement of free seedlings in the area, which are distributed by the Horticulture Department free of cost or at subsidized rates. The private nurseries can also be encouraged by the Panchayat Union.
16. The Panchayat Union may monitor the programmes implemented in the Panchayat Union by Agriculture Department. They can co-ordinate with various Departments and Agencies along with Village Panchayats to integrate their efforts and advise the implementation to increase the agricultural productions.
17. In the period of distress when agricultural production is affected due to natural calamities, Panchayat Union can play assisting role of carrying out relief measures and providing crop insurance relief to small and marginal farmers on the basis of Village Panchayats recommendations. They can also advise in the distribution of free fertilizers on the recommendation of the Village Panchayats to small and marginal farmers.
18. Panchayat Union can assess the requirements of agricultural inputs season-wise and assist for stocking adequate quantity to distribute to the farmers without any storage.

19. Panchayat Union can assist the farmers to fully utilize the services of the Agricultural Extension Officers by keeping in coordination with them and advise in respect of imparting training to the farmers.
20. To conserve the important natural resources, like land and water which Agriculture Engineering is implementing, the Panchayat Union can disseminate the information on the values of water to the people for conservation.
21. Basic data like total area, area sown, crop wise/land wise cultivation details, source of water, required quantity and availability are required for proper planning. The Panchayat Union can help in collecting these informations.
22. Panchayat Union can advise in the distribution of crop loans, fertilizers, and pesticides in appropriate time to the farmers through banks. Detailed plans may be drawn in this regard in consultation with the Village Panchayats.
23. The Panchayat Union can advice by contacting the regulated markets in their area for construction of godowns to store and process the produce by following scientific methods and also setting up of cold storage facilities for storing vegetables and fruits. Panchayat Union can advise the process of supply of these goods to the cooperative outlets, other markets for sales. Required training can be planned and imparted to the staff and farmers. The services of voluntary organisation may be availed in planning for creating such infrastructures for storage and preservation of agricultural produce.

2. Land Improvement, Implementation of Land Reforms, Land Conslidation and Soil Conservation

1. Supervision of the distribution and development of surplus lands and implementation of land ceiling.
2. Supervision of updating the land records.
3. Supervision of the implementation of other Land Reforms Acts.
4. Assisting the Revenue Authorities in general without interfering in the individual cases in regulation of Tenancy Act, mode of cultivation and its implementation.
5. Assisting the Revenue authorities in general without interfering in the selection of individual cases in integrating the fragmented lands.

3.A. Minor Irrigation

1. Each Panchayat Union consists of large number of Village Panchayats. Various minor irrigation projects are implemented in Panchayat Union areas. Necessary actions may be taken to ascertain the details on water distribution methods, repairs of supply channels, for the tanks with an ayacut of less than 100 acres, irrigation system, drip irrigation methods categories and priorities the activities. Such details may be recommended to the concerned officials for taking remedial measures.
2. The information on minor irrigation activities should be collected and maintained in the Panchayat Union. The suggestion of the technical personnel such as Geologists and others may be obtained and sent to the District Panchayats for necessary action.
3. Action should be initiated at the Panchayat Union level for collection of information on the tanks with ayacut less than 100 acres situated in the Village Panchayat areas and to take appropriate steps to increase the water storage capacity by undertaking repairs and desilting works during summer season. Solving the problems if any, between the Village Panchayats in sharing of water from the tanks, by regulating the system have been entrusted to Panchayat Unions.
4. Panchayat Union can assist the concerned Departments by co-ordinating with various Village Panchayats in identification of beneficiaries under the scheme like sinking of bore wells, repairing of supply channels.
5. Panchayat Union may offer suggestion for the implementation of Western Ghat Development Programme.

3.B. Water Management

1. By getting the details of ground water potential and other informations from the Geologists, the Panchayat Union may initiate appropriate action.
2. The Panchayat Union may initiate actions in sinking of bore wells in the agricultural lands for enhancing the irrigation potential.
3. The Panchayat Union may assist the concerned officials by co-ordinating various programmes implemented through various departments by drafting suitable plans at Panchayat Union level.

3.C. Watershed Development

1. Panchayat Union may prepare Action Plan for implementing the Watershed Programmes in their respective areas by co-ordinating various services available with the line Departments.
2. The Panchayat Union can assist the respective officials in forming (a) Water Users Groups, (b) Nursery Growers Groups for implementing the Watershed Development Programme.
3. For proper use of land and water, the Panchayat Union can assist in drafting the Action Plan at their levels. The Panchayat Union may also arrange for training the farmers and group members on soil conservation and watershed techniques.
4. Assisting in the implementation of the Integrated Watershed Programmes and review the implementation.
5. Assisting the officers of the Agriculture Department and the beneficiaries in Soil Health Card Programme.

4. Animal Husbandry, Dairying and Poultry

1. Review and supervision of livestock sub-centres and veterinary hospitals.
2. Implementation, review and supervision of artificial insemination sub-centres.
3. Implementation of frozen semen scheme under Integrated Rural Development Programme.
4. Supervision of conducting livestock and poultry exhibition at village and district levels.
5. Implementation of Slaughter Houses Maintenance Scheme.
6. Implementing the Goat Rearing Scheme for small and marginal farmers and agricultural labourers.
7. Implementation of piggery scheme.
8. Implementation and supervision of distribution of birds and animals scheme.
9. Implementation of rabbit rearing and poultry schemes.
10. Implementation of Fodder Development scheme.
11. Review of functioning of Co-operative Milk Producers societies.
12. Review of Integrated Dairy Development Scheme under Integrated Rural Development Programme.
13. Review of high breed milch animals distribution scheme under Integrated Rural Development Programme.

14. Supervision and review of schemes under Hill Area Development Programme.
15. Supervision and review of schemes under Western Ghat Area Development Programme.
16. New Veterinary dispensaries may be opened depending on local needs to carryout veterinary service as per the guidelines of the National Agricultural Council in consultation with the Department of Veterinary Services.
17. Proper maintenance of the existing veterinary dispensaries.
18. Distribution of quality animals to beneficiaries under various programmes.
19. Dissemination of information among the public regarding High Yielding livestock varieties.
20. Supervising the livestock development activities entrusted with Panchayat Union.
21. Steps may be taken for prevention of spread of epidemics relating to cattle in the Panchayat Union.
22. Imparting training to poultry farms and also assist in the supply of poultry feed.

5. Fisheries

1. Identification of beneficiaries and implementation of schemes for augmenting inland water fishing through Fish Farmers Development Agency.
2. Identification of beneficiaries and advise on the schemes for inland water fishing and marketing.
3. Advise for the establishment of fresh water prawn culture.
4. Advise for the establishment of induced prawn culture.
5. Identification of beneficiaries and establishment of salt water prawn culture.
6. Implementation of basic infrastructure improvement scheme for handling fish in the coastal areas.
7. Implementation of basic infrastructure for improvement of the fishermen villages.
8. Assist in the acquisition of land for fishing harbour improvement scheme.
9. Implementation of supply of clean containers and tricycles to the fishermen.
10. Planning for the sea erosion prevention scheme.

11. Implementation of Fishermen Group Insurance Scheme.
12. Implementation of Fishermen Small Savings Scheme.
13. The officials of the Fisheries Department will consult the respective Panchayat Union while preparing the overall fishery development plan including measures for welfare of fishermen.
14. Panchayat Union Chairman may render assistance in the selection of sites for marine and brackish water aquaculture. Instructions will also be issued to the officials of the fishery department to take the assistance of the Panchayat Union for formation of fishermen co-operative and location of fish landing platforms, drying yards, cyclone shelters, guide lights etc.
15. Through Fisheries Department, fishermen can be trained in fish cold storage, processing, packaging and preservation.
16. The Assistance Director of Fisheries, or Officer of FFDA/BFDA/ TNDFC having jurisdiction will attend the Panchayat Union Council Review Meeting.

6. Social Forestry and Farm Forestry

1. Development of Social and Farm Forestry for improving ecology and environment, propagating social and farm forestry messages can be done with the assistance of Forest Department.
2. Degraded community wastelands can be identified and the schemes can be formulated along with the works assigned by the Government and District Rural Development Agency. If necessary, the technical assistance from Forest Department may be obtained.
3. Panchayat Unions are authorised to arrange to promote firewood, fodder and timber producing plants and arrange for extension besides arranging for the sale. They may disseminate the information on planting and growing of seedlings through the forest extension centre. They can also sell the seedlings.
4. Panchayat Union may obtaining technical assistance from the Forest Department for supply of seedlings to the public and for the establishment of nurseries.
5. Panchayat Union with the assistance of the Forest Department may create awareness among public on social forestry component of Tamil Nadu Agro-Forestry Development Project for improving the ecology and environment and for preserving rare and endangered species.
6. Panchayat Union may supervise and review Community Wasteland

Development Scheme and Community Nursery Programme.

7. Minor Forest Produce

1. Panchayat Union can arrange for forming minor forest produce plantations, improve the existing forests, improve the standard of the products for processing and sale of minor forest produce except in the areas of Reserve Forests, Wild Life Sanctuaries and National Parks.
2. Panchayat Union can assist the collectors of minor forest produce to get collection charges except in the areas of Reserve Forests.
3. Panchayat Union may assist for collection of minor forest produce, sale and for assisting Forest Department and other Departments like Village and Handicrafts in implementing the schemes.
4. Panchayat Union may implement Plan and Non-Plan schemes of minor forest produce.
5. Panchayat Union may regulate collection of minor forest produce like honey, barks, tamarind, cardamom, bamboo etc., in areas outside reserve forests.
6. Panchayat Union can assist the Forest Department and supervise the implementation of Tribal Welfare and Adi-Dravida Welfare Sub-Plan for promotion of minor forest produce.

8. Small Scale Indsutries, Including Food Processing Industries

1. Advise and assist in the formation of industrial estates and development centres.
2. Advise and assist in entrepreneurs development programmes.
3. Advise and assist in setting up industries in backward areas.
4. Advise and assist in the issue of loans to groups controlled by Director of Industries.
5. Assist in the establishment of common facilities.
6. Identification of the industries that can be started at the union level and providing basic requirements.

9. Khadi, Village and Cottage Industries

1. Formation of new training and trade centres or improving the existing centres for upgrading the skills of rural artisans and to impart technical skills.

2. Assist in the marketing of the products through co-operative societies.
3. Assist in the issues of loan for rural artisans.
4. Assist the Village Panchayats in selection of beneficiaries for technical training and development schemes.
5. Panchayat Union may take action for integrating the schemes of other agencies for formulating schemes to handicraftsman and others engaged in Khadi and Rural Small Industries and supervise the schemes.
6. Panchayat Union can assist the village people engaged in various production units, trades and other works by enlightening them about technology.
7. Panchayat Union can assist for infrastructure development such as construction of common work places workshop, market complexes.
8. Panchayat Union can make necessary arrangements and supervise to avail loans and financial assistance for their establishment of rural industries.
9. Panchayat Union can supervise whether rebate has been allowed on sale of Khadi cloth produced in the Panchayat Union.
10. Panchayat Union can supervise the implementation of schemes for modernization of looms for khadi weaving.
11. Panchayat Union can formulate new schemes for Khadi development and to supervise the scheme.
12. Panchayat Union can formulate the schemes to supply of beehives to the Adi-Dravidar and Schedule Tribes and to get the income increased.
13. Panchayat Union can formulate the schemes to supply palm tree climbing device for Palmyra tappers and to monitor and supervise the schemes.
14. Panchayat Union can implement and supervise the schemes for providing free books, notebooks and stationery items to the children of Palmyra tappers.

10. Rural Housing

1. Identification of beneficiaries, supervision and review of the schemes in the allocation of house sites to Scheduled Castes and Scheduled Tribes.
2. Supervision and review of Tamil Nadu Rural Housing Scheme.
3. Supervision and review of scheme for improvement of residential areas in rural areas.

4. Supervision and review of Indira Awaas Yojana Scheme.
5. Supervision and review of housing schemes for Scheduled Castes and Scheduled Tribes.
6. Supervision and review of housing schemes for Backward Classes and Most Backward Classes.
7. Identification of suitable house sites for the construction of houses to the hosueless and assist concerned department in its acquisition and distribution.
8. Provide guidance/technical assistance to Village Panchayats, under rural housing schemes, and assist in the distribution of building materials for construction of house under various schemes, constituting Review Committee to review the implementations of rural housing projects.
9. Review, monitoring and supervision of rural housing schemes and supervise the quality of works and materials used for the implementation of various schemes relating to housing.

11. Drinking Water

1. Identification of schemes for Rural Drinking Water Schemes on priority.
2. Management of quality and improvement of schemes.
3. Maintenance of Water Supply Schemes in Panchayat Union and collection of water charges wherever possible.
4. Formulation and undertaking of the drinking water supply projects depending upon their own fund position.
5. Monitoring and maintenance of comprehensive water supply schemes covering less than 5 village panchayats entrusted with joint village committee for its maintenance.
6. Supervision of the water supply schemes implemented in drought affected areas within the limits of Panchayat Union.
7. Supervision of comprehensive piped water supply schemes in fluoride affected areas.
8. Supervision and monitoring the rural water supply schemes implemented for the uncovered rural habitations under self-sufficiency programme.
9. Supervision of the implementation of safe drinking water supply to habitations affected by high salinity and brackishness under minimum needs programme.
10. Supervision of the implementation of desalination projects for the

supply of protected water in the Panchayat Union areas.

11. Supervision of special water supply scheme in rural areas.
12. Supervision of implementation of Accelerated Rural Water Supply Scheme.

12. Fuel and Fodder

1. Considering the importance of fuel, special attention can be given to increase the fuel tree production in the lands belonging to the Panchayat Union.
2. Considering the importance of fodder production, with the guidance of Regional Joint Directors and the Assistant Directors, the Government lands under the control of Panchayat Union may be identified and earmarked for increasing fodder production.
3. Steps may be taken for creating awareness among the public on the benefits of fuel saving stoves and solar cookers.
4. With the assistance of the Joint Directors and the Assistant Directors of Animal Husbandry Department, officials of Forest Department review may be undertaken for identifying suitable fodder trees, undertaking plantation works and to carryout inspections.
5. Execution and supervision of planting of fodder trees in the community waste lands.
6. Panchayat Union can execute, supervise, and render advice on the National Development Scheme on bio-gas and chulah, fuel and fodder development schemes.

13. Roads, Culvert Bridges, Waterways and Other Means of Communication

1. Maintenance and improvement of Panchayat Union roads.
2. Preparation of plans, according permission, supervising the maintenance of roads handed over to the Panchayat Union, monitoring of the quality of the road improvement works.
3. Raising of nurseries, planting and maintenance of saplings on the roadsides.
4. Eviction of encroachments and collection of penalty.
5. Execution of Union roads and link road works, formation of roads under Hill Area Development Programme Jawahar Velai Vaaipu Thittam, Innovative Jawahar Velai Vaaipu Thittam, M.P. Local Area Development and M.L.A. Constituency Development Scheme and

works undertaken with externally aided projects.

14. Rural Electrification Including Distribution of Electricity

1. Supervision and review of the schemes under rural electrification implemented by the TNEB and the Government, particularly electrification of pump sets, power supply connection to the Adi-Dravida housing colonies in Panchayat Union areas.
2. The Panchayat Union may be entrusted with the powers to monitor and review : (a) the erection of electrical pump sets for agriculture and water supply, (b) Provision of street lights , and (c) One hut one light point scheme. The concerned Assistant Engineer/Junior Engineer will attend the Panchayat Union Council meeting pertaining to electricity subjects.

15. Non-Conventional Energy Sources

1. Preparation of plans for utilizing of non-conventional energy sources in Panchayat Union areas.
2. Implementation of schemes like windmills and bio-gas plants.
3. Dissemination and development of conservation of non-conventional energy sources.
4. The Panchayat Union can review the schemes presently implemented by the Department.
5. The Panchayat Union will identify the non-conventional energy sources such as solar, wind mills and bio-gas plants and its extensions and take appropriate action to develop the schemes. The Panchayat Union will propagate the importance and the benefits of non-conventional energy sources through media.
6. The Panchayat Union will arrange for giving proper training for the users.
7. The Panchayat Union will have powers to implement the schemes on the non-conventional energy sources like solar cooker, wind mills pumps, and solar water heaters etc. TEDA may use the concerned Panchayat Union as implementing agencies.
8. The Panchayat Union may have the powers to install the bio-gas plants and educate the public on the importance and use of the plants to implement the Integrated Rural Energy Programme. The Village Panchayats may send the list of identified beneficiaries to the Panchayat Union.

16. Poverty Alleviation Programmes

1. Assist the Village Panchayats in providing technical and managerial assistance for implementation of schemes.
2. Implementation of the schemes entrusted to Panchayat Union.
3. Collection and distribution of data regarding development and management at the District level.
4. Assist in the evaluation of schemes.
5. Preparation of plan at the block level under Swarna Jayanthi Swarozgar Yojana for filling up gap in technological tie-up, training, strengthening infrastructure and market facilities. Also assist village panchayats in organising self-help group and implementing cluster strategies.
6. To review the plans prepared by the Village Panchayats and accord technical approval assistance.
7. To draw action plan and get the technical approval and fund allocation under Land Development Scheme.
8. With the help of Village Panchayats, Panchayat Unions can implement the schemes and integrate other programmes with the Poverty Alleviation Schemes.
9. To assist in supervision of works under District Decentralised Plan and to furnish particulars to the District Panchayat.
10. Planning and implementation of infrastructure development by the rural local bodies.
11. Planning and implementation of Integrated Rural Sanitation and Water Supply Scheme implemented in Cuddalore and Villupuram Districts with the DANIDA assistance.
12. Planning and implementation of Water Supply Schemes executed through the Panchayat Union.
13. Arrange practical demonstration under smokeless chulahs scheme and National Project on Improved Chulahs.

17. Educational, Including Primary and Secondary Schools

1. Supervision of the works related to maintenance and repairs of school building, latrines and provision of drinking water facilities, visiting schools and sending reports to Assist Educational Officers.
2. Opening of libraries.
3. Conducting awareness campaign for full enrolment of children.
4. The Panchayat Union may recommend about the proper running of

schools.

5. Panchayat Union may undertake construction of buildings and provision of facilities in schools.
6. In case Educational Committee is formed by Panchayat Union for watching the activities of the schools and complaints and problems are reported by the Panchayat Union, action will be taken by the officers of the Education Department.

18. Technical Training and Vocational Education

1. Estimation and recommendation of needs for the establishment of new technical institutes and technical education schools.
2. Assist in establishing Industrial Schools for rural youths to get technical training along with their normal education, establishment of technical centres for technical training.
3. Assist in the admission of eligible rural youth in the technical training courses.
4. Prepare plan for the improvement of trained technical manpower through various industrial establishments.
5. Assist in the identification of location for vocational schools and vocational training.
6. Identify the trades and vocational education in and around high schools so as to meet the needs of small scale industries in these areas.
7. Plan for the effective functioning of the vocational training schools with the assistance of the experts.
8. Identify suitable locations and recommend for starting the vocational schools for women.

19. Adult and Non-Formal Education

1. Establishment, supervision and creating necessary non-formal education centres.
2. To supervise and advise the functioning of non-formal education centres.

20. Libraries

1. Assist the Local Library Authority for planning in rural areas.
2. Technical and financial assistance for construction of buildings for

the libraries in rural areas.

3. With regard to Panchayat Union, it will be responsibility to inform the concerned officers about library procedures, arranging books for libraries, to increase the number of readers.

21. Cultural Activities

1. Review the scheme for providing financial assistance to the skilled artists who need help.
2. Management and maintenance of new school of arts.
3. Assist the Sports Development Authority in setting up of play grounds and identification of the youth for coaching them in sports activities.
5. Panchayat Union will arrange for local festivals with the help of Village Panchayats.
6. Panchayat Union will establish, sports complex, drama theatres etc., with the help of experts in the respective Government Departments.

22. Markets and Fairs

1. Planning, identification of beneficiaries, implementation and supervision of the functioning of public markets.
2. Planning, identification of beneficiaries, implementation of private markets.
3. Assist and co-ordinate regulated market.
4. Co-ordinate and advise in functioning of primary co-operative marketing societies.
5. Panchayat Union can open and run daily and weekly markets in the Panchayat Union area. Panchayat Union can license such markets and levy and collect fees therefrom. The Panchayat Union can take up the responsibility of maintaining such markets. The Panchayat Union can take steps to protect the environment from getting polluted for better public health by such markets and at the same time to maintain the law and order.
6. Panchayat Union can identify daily and weekly markets which are popular and notable to declare them as special markets and take steps for their improvement.
7. Panchayat Union can assist the Village Panchayats in implementing the markets and shandies.
8. Panchayat Union can assist the Village Panchayats in maintaining law and order during the fairs and community festivals taking place

at the Village Panchayats and also to provide all sanitary measures.

23. Health and Sanitation, Including Hospitals, Primary Health Centres, and Dispensaries

1. Supervision and review of District/Taluk headquarter hospitals.
2. Implementation, supervision, and review like eradication of tuberculosis, malaria, AIDs, leprosy etc.
3. Implementation, supervision and review of establishing dispensaries in tribal areas.
4. Implementation, supervision and review of mobile medical units in remote localities.
5. Implementation and co-ordination in organising the local people to involve in prevention, and control of diseases.
6. Management and co-ordination of NGOs in conducting eye and family welfare camps.
7. Implementation and supervision of construction, and maintenance of primary health centres and maternity centres.
8. Assist and supervise the schemes of creating awareness among public on the importance of health environment and control of diseases.
9. Providing financial assistance for conducting training of multi-purpose health workers in primary health centres.
10. Assist and implementation and review of immunization for diptheria and polio for school going children.
11. Assist, supervision and advise on the functioning of maternity and child health centres.
12. Implementation and supervision of school health scheme.
13. Implementation and improvement of the status of the birth and death registration.
14. Assist and supervise the sanitation activities.
15. Assess the impact of diseases control measures taken at the village level and report the same to Village Panchayats and District Panchayats.
16. Assist the Village Panchayats in effective implementation of ante-natal and post-natal services to the mothers and also child care.
17. Organise training to Traditional Birth Attendant, Medical Officers and Village level workers to enable them to perform better.
18. Assist the field staff, health staff to create awareness among adolescent school girls on physiological changes and other related issues.

19. Ascertain the medical and health services offered by voluntary organisations and create a link between them and the Village Panchayats for better co-ordination.
20. Ensure conduct of periodical immunization programmes through Village Panchayat and supervise the field staff working in Sub-Centres/Primary Health Centres and hospitals and dispensaries and report to higher officials of concerned departments on the difficulties if any experienced.
21. Monitor the implementation of schemes and programmes funded by the Central and State Governments and report to higher officials of concerned department regarding the implementation of the schemes and call for report on the follow up action.
22. Collect reports on the implementation of Maternal and Child Health care activities at Village Panchayat level and suggest measures to the hospitals and Village Panchayats concerned to improve the services .
23. Assist Village Panchayats in organising health awareness camps.
24. Supervise and monitor periodically the proper implementation of schemes relating to maternal and child health care and immunization.
25. Examine reports obtained from Village Panchayats on health status of school children and epidemics and data derived from surveys conducts at Panchayat Union level and send the same to the District Panchayats with remarks. Supervise and ensure that the immunization and vaccination are done properly against epidemics and killer diseases.
26. Supervise and ensure proper attendance of medical officers and paramedical staff and others working in Primary Health Centres and Health Sub-Centres.
27. Monitor enforcement of the provisions of the Prevention of Food Adulteration Act, 1954.
28. Assist the Village Panchayats financially and technically in the construction and maintenance of works like drainage, public conveniences etc. and supervise periodical solid waste disposal and supervise the implementation.
29. Ensure provision and availability of drugs and equipment in Government hospitals and Panchayat Union dispensaries.

24. Family Welfare

1. Implementation, supervision and assist in the establishment and

maintenance of Family Welfare Centres.

2. Establishment and maintenance of Block/District Family Welfare Training Centres.
3. Administration, maintenance and review of the involvement of local bodies and BDOs in family welfare schemes.
4. Implementation and review of training imparted to Family Welfare Workers.
5. Implementation and review of the schemes for educating public on Family Welfare Schemes.
6. Maintain the statistics on the information related to family welfare collected compiled by Village Panchayats. The Panchayat Union should furnish all the statistics and information about family welfare to the District Panchayats and extend assistance to them for better planning.
7. Supervise the schemes relating to family health at village level, and assist them to remove the difficulties in the implementation of the programme.
8. Establish Maternity and Child Welfare Centres, promote surgical faciiities for small sterilization, establish and maintain Health Sub-Centres and Primary Health Centres.
9. Assist the hospitals engaged in implementing family welfare scheme to get medical equipment by contacting the concerned officials of the Family Welfare Department.

25. Women and Child Development

1. Establishment, administration and supervision of Nutritious Meal Centre.
2. Supervision and review of the Integrated Child Development Schemes and Sub-Nutritious Scheme.
3. Implementation and supervision of the functioning of the Nutrition Schemes in Schools and ICDP Centres.
4. Assit in the creation of pre-school and creches.
5. Assist in the construction of Child Welfare Centres under Swedish assisted ICDP.
6. Assit, supervise and evaluate the nutrition meal scheme.
7. Assist in the prevention of female infanticide and development of children of destitute women.
8. Assist in the supervision of working women hostels and production units.

9. Assist in the supervision of various Women Welfare Schemes such as vocational training, poor widow's children and daughter's marriage and assistance to orphanages.
10. Assist in the women economic development activities.
11. Supervise the creches for children of working and diseased women.
12. Supervise all the women welfare schemes.
13. Supervise the Women Industrial Co-operative Societies.
14. Supervise the functioning of orphanages.
15. Assist in providing financial assistance to pregnant women who are below poverty line.
16. Assist in providing marriage assistance to women who are below poverty line.
17. Assist in getting financial assistance to Female Children Welfare Schemes.
18. Assist in providing sewing machines to destitute and deserted women.
19. Assist in payment of advance to poor widow's daughter's marriage.
20. Assist in women welfare development under IFAD.
21. Supervise the functioning of home for the aged.
22. Assist in identification of eligible beneficiaries under various welfare programmes implemented in the Panchayat Union areas for mal-nutritioned women, children and expectant mothers.
23. Supervise the implementation of the Nutritious Meal Programme in the Village Panchayats.
24. Collect the relevant statistics and information about nutrition related schemes, from panchayats and to prepare the plan on that basis and send the same to District Panchayats.
25. The Panchayat Union may assist the Village Panchayats in implementing schemes like homes for children, pre-school activities and child welfare activities.
26. The Panchayat Union may assist the Village Panchayats in identification of sites for construction of buildings for Child Welfare Centres, in providing technical support in construction of buildings, water supply, sport articles in them.
27. Assist the Village Panchayats in creating awareness on nutrition, health education through mass media, preparation of hand bills, wall posters, songs, folk arts.
28. Involve the educational institutions and hospitals in preparation of evaluation reports regarding implementation of schemes in respect of child welfare and education.
29. Collection of statistics related to child labourers from Village

Panchayats, consolidating and forward the same to District Panchayats.

30. Assist the Social Welfare Department Officials, Non-governmental Organisations and Village Panchayats in running of creche, day care centres, orphanages, homes for destitute children.
31. Assist the Village Panchayats in giving wide publicity about women welfare schemes.
32. Assist the Village Panchayats and non-governmental organisation in identification of eligible women to get technical training, financial assistance for starting and identification of employment avenues for women.
33. Assist the government and non-governmental organisations in the efforts of eradication of social evils like dowry, gender bias, atrocities against women etc.
34. Assist and advise the village panchayats and non-governmental organisations in the conduct of family counselling centres for giving necessary advice and counselling.

26. Social Welfare, Including Welfare of the Handicapped and Mentally Retarded

1. Supervise the Blind and Handicapped Rehabilitation Centres.
2. Supervise the schools and hostels of handicapped.
3. Assist in getting scholarship to students of handicapped schools.
4. Assist in getting financial helps in Integrated Polio Eradication Scheme.
5. Co-ordinate the services of the NGO's for rehabilitation of handicapped and mentally disabled children.
6. Establishment of schools for deaf and dumb for handicapped.
7. Creating employment opportunities to blind who are registered in Employment Exchange.
8. Assist in sanctioning of scholarships to Handicapped Children.
9. Village Panchayats should collect data on weaker sections and transfer such data to District Panchayats for various programme implementation.
10. Integrating the efforts of departments concerned and Village Panchayats in implementing the welfare schemes, nutrition schemes and schemes for welfare of the disabled.
11. To assist in establishing special schools for physically handicapped and mentally retarded.
12. To assist in providing non-formal equation, vocational training with

required infrastructure facilities.

13. To assist physically handicapped and mentally retarded to get aids/ appliances such as hearing aids, artificial limbs and other associated devices.
14. To take appropriate actions to identify bottlenecks in implementing these schemes and assist to remove such hurdles.
15. To compile required data from Village Panchayats regarding street children and maintain registers at Panchayat Union level.
16. To get the data on persons who are above sixty years from Village Panchayats and maintain a registers at Panchayat Union level and send consolidated statistics to District Panchayats.
17. Panchayat Union to assist the Village Panchayats in their endeavour to implement for the important schemes for old age persons and create awareness on drug abuse prevention and rehabilitation of the disabled.
18. In order to rehabilitate the physically handicapped employment assistance is given by State Government. Assistance of non-governmental organisations should be taken to provide vocational training, register in employment exchanges and also to get loan assistance. To enter assistance to officials concerned to implement the various provisions in Persons with Disabilities Act, 1995 (Equal Opportunities, Protection of Rights and Full Participation).
19. To assist the Village Panchayats to co-ordinate the programmes offered by the NGOs for the rehabilitation of street children.
20. To assist the Village Panchayats in their efforts to provide old age pension to the persons above sixty years under the social security schemes.
21. To supplement the efforts taken by Village Panchayats in creating awareness on drug abuse prevention evils caused by this to individual and society. To assist Village Panchayats and social workers in their efforts regarding drug abuse prevention educating on evils of drug addiction. Assisting NGOs in their efforts to help those women who are affected by alcoholism.
22. To help educate children, prevent them from committing offences and mobilise overall community support with the help of non-governmental organisations.
23. To help the officials and Village Panchayats in order to bring the discharged Juvenile delinquents into main stream of the societies and to create awareness among the general public.
24. To visit and help the Observation Homes, Protective Homes, Vigilance

Homes, After Care Homes and Rehabilitation Homes for effective functioning. To help the officials and non-governmental organisations to eliminate bottlenecks in implementing the schemes for Juvenile delinquents and the women in distress.

27. Welfare of Weaker Sections, and in Particular, of the Scheduled Castes and the Scheduled Tribes

1. Review of the schemes being implemented for the welfare of SC/ST.
2. Implementation of the scheme for provision of pathways to burial grounds and burning ghats.
3. Review of the schemes for construction of houses, provision of house sties under various schemes and house improvement.
4. Review of the inter caste marriages schemes implemented by Social Welfare Department.
5. Review the financial assistance to petty traders.
6. Review of the construction of Community Halls, Dhobikhanas.
7. Review of the enforcement of the Civil Rights Protection Act, 1995.
8. Review of the spreading of messages to the public on evils of untouchability.
9. Identification of bonded labourers for their rehabilitation.
10. Implementation of the schemes for rehabilitation of the scavengers and their dependants.
11. Assist and review the training programmes and special coaching for the Adi-Dravidas and Tribals.
12. Implementation and review of the schemes for providing drinking water to the habitations of SC and ST.
13. Collection of reports on the literacy and educational status of Adi-Dravidas and ST from Village Panchayats, consolidate and forward it to District Panchayats.
14. Assist in the distribution of textbooks, uniforms, stipend at the appropriate time to the students.
15. Confirming the basic amenities and infra-structural availability with Government schools and hostels. Conducting of review meeting periodically to overcome the problems and give appropriate advice to improve the conditions.
16. Assisting in the construction of houses on the Government acquired sites distributed to them and integrating the various welfare schemes implemented by various departments for distribution of house sites, provisions of basic amenities and other facilities.

17. Supervise and ensure that the economic development programmes and credit assistance schemes are implemented properly and also assist in the integration of self employment programme to benefit tribal at block level.
18. Planning of infra-structural development programme for tribal development and supervision of the utilization of funds on self employment, wage employment and rural sanitation programmes.
19. Conduct periodical review meeting and remove the bottlenecks in implementation.
20. Assist in imparting training, special training to Adi-Dravidas and STs at Panchayat Union level and conduct review meeting on the evaluation of scheme impact.
21. Helping police for the eradicating untouchability and atrocities against Adi-Dravidas and STs.
22. The Panchayat Union may ensure the organisation of 'Week of Human Love and Affection' every year during January 24th to January 30th. Further, organising awareness camps on the Prevention of Atrocities against the Adi-Dravidas ST Act, 1989 and the Protection of Civii Rights Act, 1955.
23. Assisting deserving people to get free legal aid.
24. Prorogation of rights given to Adi-Dravidas/STs given under Protection of Civil Rights Act, 1955 and Prevention of Atrocities Act, 1989.
25. Conducting survey on bonded labour and sending report to District Panchayats.
26. Follow-up the implementation of Bonded Labourers Abolition Act, 1976.
27. Collection of report on bonded labourers and sending to District Panchayats and supervision of implementation of Bonded Labourers Abolition, 1976.
28. Supervision and evaluation of the rehabilitation of scavengers and their dependants at Village Panchayats level.
29. Conduct of frequent review meetings to enable the above persons to get maximum benefits without any constraints.
30. Supervision of special incentive schemes implemented to improve the educational standard of children studying between 3rd and 6th standard.
31. To ensure that the students are aware of the Chief Ministers Award for continuing their College Education and explain to them in detail.
32. Review of the schemes where assistance is given for providing technical training to the beneficiaries.

28. Public Distribution System

1. Review and reporting to the State and Divisional Level Committee on the issues noticed during the inspection at the ration shop, by the Chairperson of the Panchayat Union and its members.

29. Maintenance of Community Assets

1. Supervise the activities relating to the identification, registration and recovery of charges from public users of the social assets.
2. Review and supervision of the sale, lease and transfer of public assets.
3. Review and supervision of social assets and ensure protection, against the encroachments, damages, losses etc.
4. Planning for eliciting support from NGOs in the maintenance of public assets.
5. State Finance Commission grants devolved can be used for the maintenance of assets of the Panchayat Union.
6. As per Section 186 of the Tamil Nadu Panchayats Act, 1994 the Panchayat Unions are empowered to collect rents etc. from the commercial and other assets.
7. Panchayat Union income generating assets can be leased out. Panchayat Union have powers to fix the lease rent of the assets. Necessary provision for this purpose are available in the Tamil Nadu Panchayats Act, 1994 and the orders issued thereunder.
8. Panchayat Union can take necessary legal action against encroachments, misuse and loss of its assets.
9. Panchayat Union can receive donations from NGOs, and charitable endowments and trusts to maintain community assets.

PLANNING BY THE RURAL LOCAL BODIES

Planning for Panchayat Unions

Sl. No.	Subject	Department	Officers responsible for Planning at Village Panchayat Level
(Preparation of Annual and Five Year Plans incorporating all the Projects and Schemes)			
1.	Crop Production Protection	Agriculture and Horticulture Departments	Asssitant Agriculture Development Officer

2.	Soil and Water	Agriculture and Forest Conservation	District Forest Officer
3.	Animal Husbandry	Animal Husbandry	Assistnat Director
4.	Dairy Development	Dairy Development Department	Dy. Registrar, Diary Development
5.	Fisheries	Fisheries Department	Assistant Director
6.	Social Forestry	Forest Department (Social Forestry)	District Forest Officer (Social Forestry)
7.	Co-operation	Co-operation Department	Dy. Registrar of Co-op. Societies
8.	Rural Development	Rural Development Department	Block Development Officer
9.	Land Reforms	Revenue Department	Tehsildar
10.	Social Welfare	Social Welfare & Nutrition Department	Extension Officer (Social Welfare)
11.	Minor Irrigation	Public Works Department	Revenue Instpector and Assistant Executive Engineer (WRO)
12.	Irrigation Development	Agricultural Engineering Department	Assistant Executive Engineer (WRO)
13.	General Education	Education Department	District Edcuational Officer (SW)
14.	Youth and Sports Activities	Education Department	Extension Officer (SW) Extension Officer (SEO)
15.	Arts and Cultural Programmes	Tamil Development and Culture Department	Extension Officer (SEO) Extension Officer (SW)
16.	Medical	Public Health & Family Welfare Department	Health Inspector, Primary Health Centre
17.	Public Health	Public Health & Family Welfare Department	Medical Officer, (Primary Health Centre)
18.	Water Supply & Sanitation	Rural Development Department	Health Inspector and Union Engineer

Sl. No.	Subject	Department	Officers responsible for Planning at Village Panchayat Level
19.	Housing	Housing and Urban Development Department	Assistant Director Co-operation Housing
20.	Adi-Dravida/ Backward Class Welfare/Tribal Welfare	Adi-Dravida and Tribal Welfare	Special Tehsildar, Adi-Draivda Welfare
21.	Nutritious Meal	Social Welfare Department	TNIP Nutrition Officer
22.	Other Social Welfare Schemes	Social Welfare Department	Extention Officer (Social Welfare)
23.	Energy	Energy Department	Commissioner (Bio-gas)
24.	Non-Conventional Energy	Rural Development Department	Block Development Officer
25.	Rural and Cottage Industries	Small Industries Department	Block Development Officer
26.	Ports, Light Houses and Ship Transport	Highways Department	Assistant Divisional Engineer
27.	Roads and Bridges	Highways Department	Assistant Executive Engineer
28.	Road and Inland Water ways	Highways Department	Assistant Divisional Engineer
29.	Tourism	Information and Tourism Department	Tourist Officer
30.	Economic Development & Statistics	Economic and Statistics Department	Block Statistical Officer (A.S.I)
31.	Civil Supplies	Food and Co-operation Department	Taluk Supply Officer

A CASE ANALYSIS OF THE PATTUKKOTTAI PANCHAYAT UNION

Introduction

Members of Pattukkottai Block Panchayat Council assumed office on 25th October, 1996 after the election based on the New Panchayati Raj System. There are 14 members including the Chairman. As the election to the union wards were held on party basis, the council members are drawn from different political parties. There is no independent councillor in this block panchayat. Details of their political affiliations are given in Table 3.1:

Table 3.1 : Party Affiliation of the Council Members

	Male	Female	Total
DMK	8	6	14
TMC	3	1	4
MDMK	1	—	1
Total	12	7	19

Source : Computed.

There are 43 village panchayats under the jurisdiction of Pattukottai Panchayat Union in administering development.

Panchayat Union Administration

Under the New Panchayati Raj System the middle tier panchayat union administration has a new face.

BDO (Block) and BDO (Panchayat) are the officials heading two wings one deals with the union council and its entire subjects and the other BDO (Panchayat) deals with the village panchayats and its subjects.

The staffing pattern is as follows:

Dy BDO
EO (SS) (ADW) (SW) (AH) (P)
Block Engineer
Additional Engineer
Union Overseer

Road Inspector	3 Nos
RWO grade I	3
RWO grade II	3
RWO women	2

Office Establishment

EO Administration	
EO RLEGP	
EO Noon meal	
Accountant	
Block-level accountant (scheme)	
Assistants	4 Nos
Jr.Assistants	4 Nos
Typist	2
OA	1
Cashier	1
Night Watchman	1
Pump fitter	4
Tailoring instructress	2
Maternity Ayah	2
Dolgate Staff	2
Gang Musthoor	7
Jeep Driver	2

Rural Medical Centre

Medical Officer	2
Pharmacist	2
Nursing Staff	2
Sweeper	2

(There are two rural medical centres in Pattukottai Panchayat Union. The salary of the staff of the centre is met by the Union Administration.)

Council Meeting

As per the G.O., meetings of the council are conducted regularly once in sixty days, without any break since its inception. Sofar, 35 meetings were held and 724 resolutions were passed. The attendance was cent per cent in all the meetings.

It was told that transactions in the council meetings were smooth and cordial as Chairman conducted himself as a non-party leader though he belongs to the DMK party. Problems of each ward are frankly discussed before finalising any scheme and taking any decision. Moreover the ground reality of the areas is thoroughly known to the Chairman. The Chairman used to visit villages periodically, interact with the panchayat presidents, and village level leaders of all political parties about their problems in the rural areas.

Standing Committees in Panchayat Union

There are three committees formed for specific purposes, namely:
1. Appointment Committee,
2. Education Committee, and
3. Public Purpose Committee.

For Appointment Committee, only one member is selected for a period of one year. Since 1996, four times the committee was constituted and four members have been nominated and they served in this committee. A member can serve only one year in the committee.

The Education committee is a standing one for the whole tenure of the union council. The total membership in this committee is three. Out of three, there are two women councillors selected for this committee.

Public Affairs committee is constituted to undertake any activities related to the public on behalf of panchayat union. It is also a standing committee for the whole tenure with three members and out of them one was a women councillor.

All the above mentioned three committees of Pattukottai Panchayat union were formed without any problem. Even though the contest is permitted in the selection of committee members, all members of the three committee were elected unanimously. There was apprehension during the time of committee formation that there would be contest. But it was avoided. It was told that the members understood that they could not get any benefit out of the way as the union Chairman was ensuring always transparency in administration and provides no scope for corruption.

It was told that the members of the Education Committee were evincing keen interest in their assignment. The Education Committee members are periodically visiting panchayat union primary schools and noon-meal centres, submit their reports and their suggestions for maintenance and improvement of infrastructure facilities in the schools for allocating necessary fund. Here one has to notice the active participation of the women member in the activities of the education committee.

Meeting Deliberations

It was told that the members had shared their ward problems freely. Public issues like paddy procurement, irrigation, natural calamities, problems in availing schemes in agriculture and other departments are also discussed in the meetings.

It is reported that on an average, two to three village panchayats are in one union ward and so the members expected more allocation of funds to meet the demands of all three village panchayats. It is the general practice that the allocation of funds will be equal among the wards. It is understood that there is no ward approach and it is only area approach they have adopted for implementing programmes. Village is still considered as independent unit. Hence, the necessity of union ward is not required according to the perceptions of the Gram Panchayat presidents and Chairman of the Block panchayat. It was found that the line department officials like AEO, Agriculture Officer, EB Assistant Engineer and TWAD (Power Pump) officials used to attend panchayat union council meeting in Pattukottai union. Here it is noticed that the officials of the line department have been attending the meetings of the block panchayat council. Normally, they won't attend the meetings of the panchayat councils.

Achievement

Under the New Panchayati Raj System the steps to streamline the financial allocation was carried out as per the recommendation of the state finance commission. Due to this exercise the grant to the union has been enhanced and more number of schemes have been routed through union which resulted into the development of rural area in various sectors. An analysis of various kinds allocation of funds for a number of schemes would help us to identify the areas which have been opted as primary areas.

Specifically provision of drinking water supply, road, street lights and other necessary facilities like community hall, bathing ghat, retaining wall and culvert have been seriously attended by the union council. The following are the details of the activities.

Table 3.2 : Water Supply

Nature of Works	As on 1996	1996 to 2001	Difference
India Mark II Hand Pump	172	216	44
OHI	101	196	95
Public Tap	1815	3337	1522
Street Lights Ordinary	760	1308	548
Tube Light	1620	3656	2336
Sodium	4	239	235
Mercury	2	5	3

Source : Computed.

Table 3.3 : Road
(During the past four year period)

Nature of Work	No. of Work	Kilometre	Amount Rs.in Lakhs
Gravel	199	57.615	71.14
Metal	36	17.150	39.44
Block Top	62	23.100	100.63
Cement Concrete Road	51	2.800	24.42
Improvement of Road	4	1.800	3.65
Formation of Road	1	0.800	0.42
Burial Ground Road	1	0.300	0.40

Source : Computed.

Table 3.4: Other Works Carried out

Sl. No.	Item	Number	Amount Rs.in Lakhs
1.	Group Houses	403	117.58
2.	Culvert	51	7.50
3.	T.V. Room	94	12.59
4.	Retaining Wall	18	4.51
5.	Bathing Ghat	4	1.10
6.	Bus shelter	5	1.29
7.	Community Wall Repair	4	1.00
8.	Drainage	1	0.25

Source : Computed.

Activities under Various Other Schemes

A large number of welfare schemes of State and Central Government are implemented by the union administration. Moreover special schemes like Anna Marumalarchi Thittam, Namakku Naame Thittam, Samathuvapuram, Muvalur Ramamirtham Ammaiyar Memorial Marriage Assistance scheme etc. are implemented by the union administration.

1. Anna Marumalarchi Thittam was undertaken in two villages (Thamaraikottai and T.Vadakadu). Thirteen works at the cost of Rs.19.46 lakhs have been executed in Thamaraikottai south and twenty three number of works at the cost of Rs.25.00 lakhs have been undertaken in T.Vadakadu.
2. Namakku Naame Thittam is considered as a very successful scheme in which the felt needs of the people are properly met by mobilising people's contribution. Year by year the demand for NNT has been increased.

Table 3.5 : Works Carriedout by the Block

Sl. No.	Year	Total Work	Amount Spent (Rs. in Lakhs)
1.	97/98	8	1.530
2.	98/99	27	24.350
3.	99/2000	16	10.000
4.	2000/2001	47	50.88
	Total	98	86.76

Source : Computed.

The major items of works undertaken in Namakku Naame are Auditorium, deepening of tanks, construction of culverts, bathing ghats and block topping of roads.

It was told that as the works undertaken were completed in time and the quality was ensured by the administration of the block, the DRDA, Tanjavur sanctioned all the proposal for the year 2000/2001 submitted by the Pattukottai block panchayat. And the total fund earmarked for Pattukottai union is 45% of the total fund allotted for the whole district. The prime reason for increasing allocation to Pattukottai Block panchayat is that the contribution of people towards the NNT. For an example, works like providing compound wall, fencing work at high schools are not generally permitted in JGSY and whereas under NNT one would find such flexibility to attend the felt needs. But under NNT the flexibility helps the panchayats to attend to the felt needs. Moreover the peoples contribution is one of the welcoming features of this new programme. The compound walls for high school in Karambium, Naduvankottai,

Palanchur and Athirumpattinam were provided in NNT. A special permission was accorded to the scheme by considering the situation of the school site and traffic insecurity.

CRSP

Motivating people for maintaining environmental sanitation seems to be a tough assignment. In Pattukottai Panchayat union, the block officials personally visited and contacted eligible families for CRSP scheme and convinced them to use this scheme and now it as a successful one. Since 1996/97 the demand for CRSP has been steadily increased. The following table shows the achievements in this regard.

Table 3.6 : Implementation of CRSP Scheme

Sl. No.	Year	Subsidy Amount/Unit	Total No.of Beneficiaries	Amount of Subsidy
1.	96/97	Rs. 2000/-	153	3.06
2.	97/98	Rs. 2000/-	179	3.58
3.	98/99	Rs. 2000/-	344	6.88
4.	99/2000	Rs. 500/-	393	1.97
5.	2000/2001	Rs. 500/-	218	1.09

Source : Computed.

So far 1287 individual household latrines were constructed under CRSP. It was told that the union ward members, panchayati president and panchayat ward members seriously associated with the block officials in educating the eligible families and in ensuring the 100% utility.

Programmes like Million well, EAS were also undertaken, 87 poor farmers have availed subsidy amount of Rs. 30.43 lakhs and improved the irrigation potentials for their land. Rs. 14 lakhs have been spent for desilting of tanks.

Construction of Group Houses

Implementation of group housing scheme is a challenging task as a lot of works like site selection, site development and proper planning have to be done in time. In Pattukottai Panchayat union, 403 houses have been constructed from 1996 to 2001. Also repair works have been carried out in 139 old houses. Under katcha house scheme 62 poor got assistance of Rs.6.20 lakhs to convert their hut into fire-proof roof houses.

IRDP

Individual loan cum subsidy was provided to 1539 families. 5 groups are also availed benefits of the IRDP from 1996 to 2001. The block officials and representatives have joined with the bank officials in the recovery camps. Contrary to expectation recovery has been achieved.

Social Welfare Programmes

Marriage assistance to educated girl of poor families @ Rs.10,000 per women was availed through union administration from 1996 to 2000. 863 families benefit have gained by this scheme. It was told that 372 applications were submitted in the year 2001. Marriage assistance to widows' daughter was availed by 25 families. Only one widow availed the benefit of Rs.7000 under Dr.Dharmambal Ammaiyar widow remarriage assistance. Inter caste marriage assistance was given to 15 couple under Annai Anchugam Ammaiyar Memorial Assistance.

The assistance for protecting girl children in poor families was given to 221 poor under Sivakami Ammaiyar Memorial Girl Children Protection Assistance of Rs.1500 per girl child provided the mother has undergone PPS (for birth control). The amount is deposited in fixed terms and after 18 years the matured amount of Rs. 30,000 is given to the girl. Tailoring machine to 4 poor women who know tailoring was given. Preference was given to widows' in this scheme named after Sathiavani Muthu Ammaiyar.

To encourage the poor girl students atleast one in each poor widow family, an assistance of providing books and notebooks free of cost was carried out. 176 girl students belonging to poor widow families got benefits in this scheme. Twenty nine public distribution shops were newly constructed at the estimate of Rs.1.70 lakh per shop.

Samathuvapuram

Samathuvapuram buildings have been constructed in Aladikkumoolai village panchayat. 100 pucca houses with the cost of @ Rs. 50000 per unit were constructed in which the beneficiary's contribution of Rs. 15000 is included.

It was informed that as the site of Samathuvapuram need pile foundation for construction, it was permitted. Hence, within a short period of time, the work was successfully completed and all the houses are occupied. The site is locaed in a tail end of the panchayat as it is located near to Pattukottai in Tanjavur road.

Small Savings

For the past four years Pattukkottai block panchayat has been in the 2nd position in the district in small saving drive. Best noon meal organiser award achieved by Pattukottai union during 2000/2001.

Medical Camp

Twenty Värummun Kappom camps were organised in which 20,546 cases were treated. 25 cases were referred to for heart treatment. The District medical authorities gave the meritorious certificate to the Pattukottai Panchayat Union for organising the camps very effectively and successfully.

Computerisation in the Administration

Two computers are available in the union office. Four staff members have received adequate training in computer operation. It was informed that the profile of village panchayats, programme implementation details, maintenance of various accounts are fed in the computer. It was told that for the effective utilisation of computer, a full-time staff is needed exclusively for computer.

Table 3.7 : Grant Received by the Union

(Rs. in Lakhs)

Sl. No.	Items of the Grant	96/97	97/98	98/99	99/2000
1.	Local cess	0.65	—	—	—
2.	Training deposit interest	0.75	5.88	1.10	0.40
3.	Local surcharge matching grant	16.51	—	0.78	—
4.	Jeep fuel	0.17	0.10	0.08	—
	Jeep fuel maintenance	0.15	0.02	0.02	—
5.	Local Road Maintenance	7.22	—	—	—
6.	2/3 matching grant	1.12	0.97	0.94	0.51
7.	Women and Child Welfare	0.13	0.13	0.13	0.13
8.	10th Finance Commission	10.00	10.00	6.65	—
9.	Flood Relief	6.20	1.80	1.75	—
10.	Rural Water Supply	1.19	0.61	—	—

Contd. ...

Contd. ...

(Rs. in Lakhs)

Sl. No.	Items of the grant	96/97	97/98	98/99	99/2000
11.	State Finance Commission	—	35.57	43.59	43.26
12.	Dispensary Grant	—	0.054	—	0.108
13.	MLA Fund	—	6.42	20.29	22.34
14.	EAS	—	8.20	25.30	54.81
15.	MP Fund	—	3.50	—	11.66
16.	Equalisation Fund	—	4.00	—	—
17.	District Panchayat Fund	—	4.80	4.29	6.14

Source : Computed

Case Study on the Union Chairman

Sri.Vedarathinam, aged 47, with an educational background of matriculation, is hailing from the village head man family in Maravakkadu village. The position of VHM was performed by his grand father and father. After his father's demise, the position was transferred to the respondent. But the VHM post was abolished during the year 1984.

The experience he had gained as VHM shaped the respondent to understand the problems of his village and the people and he tried his level best to serve them better than anybody else. In the year 1986 when election to the village panchayat was announced, people of his village advised him to utilize this opportunity. As people of the village exerted pressure, on him he had agreed and he was unanimously elected as the president of Maravakkadu, a small village situated at the coastal area of Pattukottai union. The respondent tried to catch the Vice-Chairman position in the union but was defeated.

The allocations for the panchayat was very meagre hence basic facilities of the villages were not attended properly. The period between 1986 and 1991 passed without any major achievement. But the respondent got experience in politics as well as administration at the block level at a later stage. Hence, the respondent availed the opportunity and became the president of co-operative society. His honesty helped him to attain the position of the president of the co-operative society without any opposition. As the co-operatives were brought under the officials within six months duration of the inception, the respondent paid his attention in the functioning of "Sardar Vedarathinam salt unit". He served as the honorary president in the salt unit labour association in Maravakkadu.

Political Affiliation

His father was an active congress member. At the time of his father's demise, the respondent was very young and he did not have any knowledge in politics. But during emergency he was drawn towards the DMK as it championed the cause of democracy. Due to this incident, the respondent gave respect to the DMK and involved in DMK party activities.

Election under New Panchayati Raj System

The respondent contested in the union ward, representing two villages and won the election. As the election to the union chairman was indirect, most of the councillors recommended the name of the respondent for the position of Chairperson. And he was unanimously elected as the Chairman of the Pattukottai block panchayat.

Union Administration

As the respondent had already acquainted with the system of union administration and understood the dimensions of the various problem in villages, he decided to do his best to all concerned.

His 19 years service in public life helped him in understanding the people and officials. He is very co-operative, easily accessible and apolitical though he belonged a party. Moreover he was very serious in maintaining his honesty and to save his family reputation. He ensured corruption-free administration at his level atleast.

35 borewells under Jeevandhara scheme to 35 poor SC families were provided and all of them are using the water for agricultural operation. He claims that it is an achievement.

The respondent informed that under New Panchayati Raj System, the fund allocation was properly ensured and so the basic problem in drinking water provision, street light extension, road formation and block topping of metal roads were solved in many villages. Infrastructure facilities were also attended. Additional building to school, new building to ration shop, community halls, panchayat office building, drainage, and cement concrete road for streets were provided. The respondent recollected the earlier period 1986-91 in which only two metal roads have been formed in the panchayat union.

His Development Perspective

The respondent has development perspective. He visualized that infrastructure development should be the precondition for economic development. Better road facilities are very much essential in rural and remote localities. Hence, he felt that almost all villages must be linked with the main roads, all hamlet villages must be linked with main village roads.

His second priority for development is empowering of rural poor mass. He felt that the IRDP was misused inspite of its goodness in conception. He explained that the fisherman who availed IRDP loan for purchasing high quality net failed to use it properly. Hence, the group concept is a welcoming one, he observed. He was very positive in the scope of SHG as women are evincing keen interest and efforts in improving the family status. But he suggested the facilitating services like skiil training, marketing assistance and appropriate technological assistance must be properly coordinated for the effectiveness of the SHG.

He quoted the functioning of Gram Sabha in rural area. Traditionally in all most all villages people accustomed to meet and plan their common activities, for village development. Hence, the SHGs if properly organised would result in achieving development initiatives. He states that the level of awareness of the people is increasing and as a result participation of people in development activities would be increased. Gram Sabha is slowly picking up. People have started participating in the Gram Sabha meeting.

Several elderly wise-men are attending Gram Sabha and they contribute their ideas and practices in augmentation of additional income to village panchayats. The villagers have suggestions to reduce the expenses towards electricity, motor pump maintenance and on a number of areas. People are aware of the administration of New Panchayati Raj System and its implications. Now people have started realising the necessity of peoples contribution towards development activities. Earlier the villagers did not pay their attention on these areas. He emphasised that capacity building is very much needed to the elected representatives in planning, community mobilisation and leadership as the New Panchayati Raj System is expecting a lot from the leaders of the panchayat institutions.

The respondent suggested innovative ideas for augmenting village panchayat income :

1. A marginal share from total paddy procurement to the village panchayat.
2. Cess from the natural resources like salt, sand and mines.
3. A marginal share from the income of prawn culture to the panchayat.

Any agro based business if initiated can be used for income generation and the income from the same may be given to the village panchayat as the village panchayat has to maintain the ecology and environment.

He has a clear understanding on the devolution of power. He opined that those activities that could be carried out by the local people must be given to the panchayat and adequate fund allocation for the same activities could be ensured in plan proposal. He regrets for the delay in actual implementation of government orders in 29 subject earmarked in the 11th schedule. He recalled the successful days of earlier local bodies which had the power in rural high ways, health, education etc.

He suggested that holding of workshops and meetings to disseminate the concept of peoples participation and decentralization of power is an imperative need. He has faith in mobilisation of villagers for development activities. As an example he stated that the PWD is responsible for the present irrigation system. Officials did not ready to understand the problems of villagers. People need a bridge to bring the agricultural products across the small river/stream. This was not approved by the officials. But people have joined themselves and constructed a bridge under NNT.

Another example he outlined that the establishment of Samathuvapuram was earlier with the department of Backward Community along with the Kattida maiyam. After considering the functional efficiency of the union administration, that arrangement was given to union and it becomes a successful one.

The respondent told that the concept of peoples participation, women empowerment, micro economic activities, skill updating, perspective plan, protection of environment and ecology are getting into the mind of the common man during the period of New Panchayati Raj System.

He expressed that the behaviour and attitude of government officials are also changing. The power and authoritativeness and independent functioning of the officials are getting diluted after the introduction of New Panchayati Raj System. The village panchayat presidents are efficiently dealing water supply problems, street lights and provision of public distribution system. The process is picking up but what needed is strengthening of Gram Sabha and capacity building to the president and a speedy disbursement of fund to the local bodies.

It is inferred that the Chairman of the Pattukkottai Block Panchayat hailed from a decent, affluent, and traditional family and he imbibed the good qualities of a leader. He is sincere, honest and hard working gentle man. He has a clearcut perception his role and responsibilities to be discharged by him in the new institutional arrangement.

4

DESIGNING AND MANAGING GRAM PANCHAYATS

Powers Exercisable by Rural Local Bodies as per the Rules Issued Under the Tamil Nadu Panchayats Act, 1994

Gram Sabha

1. Approval of the village plan;
2. Approval of village budget for the year;
3. Approval of audit report on the village panchayat accounts of the previous year;
4. Review of the progress of all the schemes entrusted to the village panchayats. (Section 3 of the Tamil Nadu Panchayats Act, 1994);
5. Approval of the beneficiaries selected and location of institutions and community facilities identified by the village panchayat;
6. Review of the completed works executed in the previous year by the village panchayat and scrutiny of the list of works undertaken in the year by the village panchayat of by any Government Department and agency;
7. Promotion of communal and social harmony among the various scraps of people in the village panchayat;
8. Mobilisation of voluntary labour, contribution in cash and kind for community welfare and development programmes; and
9. Examining annual statement of accounts and audit report of the village panchayat.

Village Panchayat

1. Executive Authority/President of the Village Panchayat shall approve the layouts for construction of residential buildings with the previous approval of the Director of Town and Country Planning or his authorised Joint Director/Deputy Director of Town and Country Planning.
2. Executive Authority/President shall approve the application of buildings and huts in the site situated in the Panchayat areas.

3. President of the Village Panchayat is empowered to prepare estimates with the help of the panchayat assistant to get the approval of the panchayat and execute works upto a limit of Rs. 2000 at a time and not exceeding five thousand in a year in respect of works executed out of Village Panchayat funds.
4. Village Panchayat is competent to accord administrative sanction of the original works consisting upto rupees one lakh.
5. Village Panchayat is competent to accord administrative sanction of the following nature of maintenance works with the sanction of the authorities noted against them.

Nature of Estimate	*Authority to accord Technical Sanction*
(1)	(2)
a) Estimate costing not more than rupees ten thousand	Block Engineer or Assistant Engineer (Rural Development)
b) Estimate costing more than ten thousand but not more than rupees fifty thousand	Assistant Executive Engineer (Rural Development)
c) Estimate costing more than fifty thousand but not more than rupees two lakhs	Executive Engineer (Rural Development)
d) Estimate costing more than rupees two lakhs	Superintending Engineer (Rural Development)

6. Village Panchayat is competent to accord administrative sanction in respect of the following nature electrical works with the technical sanction of the authority noted against them :-

Nature of Estimate	*Authority to accord Technical Sanction*
(1)	(2)
a) Estimate costing not more than rupees ten thousand	Block Engineer or Assistant Engineer (Rural Development)

b) Estimate costing more than ten thousand but not more than rupees twenty five thousand	Assistant Engineer (Rural Development)
c) Estimate costing more than twenty five thousand but not more than rupees fifty thousand	Executive Engineer (Rural Development)
d) Estimate costing more than rupees fifty thousand	Superintending Engineer (Rural Development)

7. The Executive Authority/President of the Village Panchayat is empowered to enter any building or place or land where (i) Tanning of hides and skins, (ii) manufacturing and storing of gun powder, (iii) brewing and manufacture of arrack or other spirit, and (iv) explosive and storing of combustible materials are carried out for the purpose of satisfying himself whether any law, rules, bye-laws or regulations are being contravened.
8. Executive Authority/President shall grant license for erection of pandal or temporary structure on public roads.
9. Village Panchayats are empowered to regulate or prohibit washing animals, clothes or other articles, fishing in any public or tanks or water course and set apart any such places for drinking or for bathing or washing any animals etc.
10. Village Panchayat shall have power to engage on its behalf the counsel and sanction fee payable to them.
11. Village Panchayats shall grant license/lease for taking any fish from the water sources lying in their areas.
12. Village Panchayats are empowered to constitute the following committees to delegate their functions so as to enable them to discharge their functions effectively :

    a) Appointment Committee,
    b) Welfare Committee,
    c) Health, Water and Sanitation Committee,
    d) Public Distribution System Committee,
    e) Agriculture Production Committee,
    f) Works Committee, and
    g) Education Committee.

13. Village Panchayats are empowered to frame bye-laws on matters enumerated below for implementing the provisions of the Tamil Nadu Panchayats, Act 1994 or any other Law:
    a) All matters required or allowed by the Act to be provided in by-law;
    b) The regulation of the time and mode of collection of taxes under this Act;
    c) Use of public tanks, wells, conduits and other places or works for drinking water supply;
    d) The protection of avenues, trees, grass and other appurtenances of public street;
    e) Planting of trees by private persons in public lands on which the village panchayat has powers of control, protection and management and granting licenses for the same;
    f) The inspection of public and private markets and staff and other places therein, including the regulation of their use and the control of their sanitary conditions;
    g) Licensing and controlling brokers, commission agents, weighmen and measure practicing their calling in markets, other than markets coming under regulated market committee;
    h) Prescribing the method of sale of articles whether by measure, weight, bale or piece;
    i) The enumeration of inhabitants of the village panchayat area;
    j) Letting out of public place and buildings like kalyanamandapam, community hall, for public use;
    k) Procedure for getting licenses for encroachments made for putting up temporary structure during the times of fairs, ceremonies and seasonal covering and other purposes;
    l) Conditions to be prescribed while calling for tender works or for supply of goods, materials and other than those prescribed under the rules; and
    m) Terms and conditions to be laid down while auctioning leases of rights of enjoyment of panchayat properties and collection of fees for various purposes.

14. Executive Authority/President is the licensing authority for dogs of the private persons in their houses.
15. Executive Authority/President is the licensing authority for erection of hoarding purposes.
16. Village panchayat is empowered to fix the yearly advertisement tax

within the minimum and maximum limits as stated below :

Sl. No.	Areas	Minimum (per square meter) Rs.	Maximum Rs.
a)	If the village panchayat lies within 3 km radius from any Municipal Corporation	20	250
b)	If the village panchayat lies within 10 km radius from a municipality	15	200
c)	Other village panchayats	10	150

17. Village panchayat is empowered to levy any fee from all registered holders of land served by any irrigation work at such rate per acre as the Collector of the revenue district may from time to time determine having regard to the nature of Kudimaramat work executed or proposed to be executed by the panchayat.
18. Village panchayat shall provide at its cost, places to be used as burial or burning -grounds and may charge rents and fees for the use thereof.

Powers, Functions and Responsibilities Entrusted to the Rural Local Bodies in Tamil Nadu

(A) General Subjects

Village Panchayats

1. Gram Sabha is a constitutional body constituted as a grassroots level democratic institution. This Government have already amended the Act to enable the Gram Sabha to function vibrantly. Gram Sabha through its collective wisdom, guide the panchayat to plan and execute apart from monitoring the implementation of various schemes including schemes of line departments. Therefore by strengthening the Gram Sabha public participation in the scheme of implementation will increase and will pave for the social auditing in due course of time. Therefore government of Tamil Nadu have instructed to

conduct the Gram Sabha at least 4 times in a year, namely January 26th, May 1st, August 15th and October 2nd. Government is taking steps for strengthening the Gram Sabha functioning.

2. The President of Village Panchayat will act as the "Executive Authority" of the Village Panchayats to execute the powers and functions of the village panchayat.
3. Powers have been delegated to the Village Panchayat Presidents for purchase of the spares with regard to maintenance of power pumps and hand pumps by (i) following the rates fixed by the District Purchase Committee every year, (ii) Calling for tenders with sample spares and to compare with the price list of the TWAD Board, as per the G.O.Ms.No.75, Finance Department, Dated: 19.02.97, (iii) The District Purchase Committee will communicate the list and qualitys to all the panchayat unions and village panchayats, (iv) The village panchayats to follow the rates approved by the District Purchase Committee, and (iv) Not to invest huge amount for maintenance.
4. All the village panchayats have been permitted to open a savings bank account in the near by nationalised bank or cooperative bank or in the post office as per the order of priority given in the Government latter.
5. Considering the increased work load due to additional duties and responsibilities entrusted to the village panchayats, only Grade-I panchayats with their own income exceeding Rs. 3.0 lakhs will be permitted for appointing full time panchayat clerk on consolidated pay in lieu of part time Panchayat Assistant/Clerk, where the expenses on salary and other allowances shall not exceed 10% of its own income. The government can fix the upper limit of the consolidated pay.
6. Makkal Nala Paniyalargal are assisting the village panchayats in carrying out important and essential functions for the village panchayats.
7. Rules for the formation of committees in village panchayats for entrusting the power to such standing committees on (i) Taxes, finance, accounts and planning; (ii) Education and health; (iii) Welfare schemes and public distribution system have been framed.
8. Village panchayats have been permitted to extend house service water tap connections to individual houses in their respective area, and can collect non-refundable deposit of Rs.1,000/- in one instalment and Rs.30/- as monthly water charges for house service connection.
9. Village panchayats are empowered to complain to the concerned

officer of T.N.E.B. if anybody uses more than one light under "one light for one hut programme".

10. As the village panchayats have power to evict encroachments in the panchayat vested properties, the police and revenue officials will assist the village panchayats, when their help is sought.
11. The village panchayats can be given priority for taking government lands for construction of libraries, community centres, school buildings and cattle/animal sheds.
12. professional tax is being levied as per the provisions in the new rules from all income earning members including Central Government employees and collected/animal sheds.
13. Village Panchayats can set apart and utilize at least 20% of house tax amount on the drinking water and related works.
14. Village Panchayats have been empowered to levy advertisement tax for which necessary amendment was made to the Tamil Nadu Panchayat Act.
15. For erecting street light poles, the Electricity Board normally do not take prior permission from Village Panchayats. However, when there is a necessity for shifting of poles for taking up certain development works, like widening of roads, electricity board has accepted to collect the actual cost of expenditure (cost of additional materials and labour charges) and then to execute the work immediately.
16. Government have authorised that the ownership certificate for house service electricity connection may be issued either by the Village Administrative Officer or Village Panchayats President and based on that certificate house service connection may be given by T.N.E.B.
17. The powers to collect license fee on the dangerous and offensive trades by the Village Panchayats instead of panchayat unions will be entrusted by suitable amendment to Section 159 of Tamil Nadu Panchayats Act, 1994.
18. The responsibility of maintenance of sand, quarries, clay as per the Tamil Nadu Minor Mineral Act of 1995. Addition and deletion of the quarries from the list maintained by the District Collector, situated with in the Village Panchayats limits, and collection of levy and remitting it to the General Funds of the Village Panchayats. Monitoring and confiscating of the vehicles used for unauthorized transit of the minor minerals. Issue of permits to the vehicles for transporting the minor minerals from the Village Panchayats areas. Visiting the minor quarries and inspecting the accounts maintained by them.

19. The Village Panchayats have been permitted to organise Volley Ball, Kabhadi, Football and other sports activities at the Village Panchayats level and to award prizes to the winners to the tune of Rs. 50/-

Powers, Functions and Responsibilities Entrusted to the Rural Local Bodies on 29 Subjects

Village Panchayats

1. Agriculture, Including Agricultural Extension

1. Assist in identification of beneficiaries in procurement and distribution of vegetable seeds.
2. Assist in identification of beneficiaries for implementation of community thrashing floor.
3. Assist in identification of beneficiaries for distribution of paddy, green manure and blue green algae under subsidy scheme.
4. Assist in the implementation of special programme on Waste Land Development.
5. Assist in identification of beneficiaries for the development of organic manure resources by utilizing sewage/sullage.
6. Assist in identification of beneficiaries under the schemes for distribution of mini kits, fertilizers and seeds.
7. Assist in identification of beneficiaries under financial assistance provided to the farmers who are affected by cyclone/flood.
8. Assist in identification of beneficiaries for providing minor irrigation facilities for coconut growers scheme.
9. Assist in identification of beneficiaries for Farmers Training Centres.
10. Assist in identification of beneficiaries for the Horticulture Training Centres.
11. Assist in identification of beneficiaries for the training schemes for women farmers in agriculture technology (TANWA).
12. Identification of beneficiaries under scheme for distribution agricultural implements.
13. Implementation of scheme for setting up of compost pits.
14. Assist in identification of beneficiaries under scheme for Intensive Cotton Development.
15. Assist in identification of beneficiaries for Oil Seeds Production Programme.
16. Assist in identification of beneficiaries for National Pulses

Development.

17. Assist in identification of beneficiaries for the Drought Prone Area Programme.
18. Assist in identification of beneficiaries for Integrated Dry Land Development Scheme.
19. Assist in identification of beneficiaries for the National Watershed Development under Rain-fed Areas Programme.
20. Assist in identification of beneficiaries for the Command Area Development Programme.
21. The Village Panchayats can advise and assist in the selection of beneficiaries for the distribution of agricultural inputs like quality seeds, fertilizer, bio fertilizers, pesticides and fungicides etc. at appropriate time to increase the agricultural production.
22. Village Panchayats can advice in setting up of godown facilities, cold storage facilities etc. through regulated markets to store and increase the profitability in agricultural produce and particularly in perishable items like fruits and vegetables.
23. The Village Panchayats can assist in publicity to increase farmers participation in the crop yield competitions, by creating congenial and positive competitive spirit among the farmers.
24. The Village Panchayats can assist the Agricultural Departmental staff in identification of beneficiaries under Integrated Programme on Cereals Development, programme for the augmentation and promotion of paddy, minor millets, pulses, oil seeds, cotton etc., plant protection schemes, seed certification programme, integrated pest management programmes, land and water use schemes, crop insurance schemes to small and marginal farmers etc. Village Panchayats can also prepare list of the beneficiaries assisted under various schemes, subsidy disbursed with other details and inform the concerned officials of the Agricultural Department every year.
25. Village Panchayats may plan an important role in attaining self sufficiency with protein and fat (oil) in the food by increasing the production of soya, beans by encouraging their cultivation either as single crop or as inter-crop or as the catch crop in the double crop lands.
26. The Village Panchayats can assist in schemes of the Horticulture Department, by giving free seedlings, seedling under subsidised rates to the farmers for planting in the fields or in thopes. Village Panchayats can also grow such crops in the poramboke lands vested with the panchayats so that the horticultural crop production can

increase by availing the opportunities offered in departmental schemes, Village Panchayats can assist planting of fruit trees in the waste lands under their control.

27. The Village Panchayats can identify suitable lands for the construction of seed storage godowns for scientific storage of the Agriculture Department.
28. Most of the farmers incur loss due to distress sale of their produce immediately after harvest when the price is low either due to lack of storage facilities or due to pressing need for money. To avoid this, Village Panchayats may contact the concerned marketing officers and recommend to get 50% of amount on the value of the grains stored in the rural godowns as advance to the farmers.

2. Land Improvement Implementation of Land Reforms, Land Consolidation and Soil Conservation

1. Assist in the implementation of distribution and development of surplus land and implementation of land ceiling measure.
2. Assist in updating the land records.
3. The Village Panchayats may identify surplus lands and recommend to Government for allocating it to landless poor.
4. In case of poramboke lands encroached by private people, when the identified lands are not usable for common purposes panchayats can recommend for its re-allocation to landless poor.

3.A. Minor Irrigation

1. Village Panchayats can assist the Panchayat Union to identify the tanks with ayacut area of less than 100 acres, and for the collection of information on water spread area, water holding capacity and period of storage to plan and execute necessary works.
2. Taking appropriate action for desilting of tanks with an ayacut of less than 100 acres during summer season for increasing the water storage capacity of the tanks.
3. The Village Panchayats may avail such benefits for reconstruction of supply channels of tanks with an ayacut of less than 100 acres and sinking of deep borewells.
4. Assist in the identification of beneficiaries under Western Ghat Development Programme.

3B. Water Management

1. The respective Village Panchayats can initiate action to collect details regarding the water table of their area from the Geologist and take suitable action.
2. The Village Panchayats may take steps to search for the possibilities of sinking borewells for improving irrigation facilities in cultivable lands.
3. The message of keeping adequate spacing between two open wells as per the opinion of the Geologist may be spread among the public.

3C. Watershed Development

1. The Village Panchayats can assist in the compilation of details on land records, information on cultivable lands, pasture, wastelands, water harvesting structures, tanks bunds and other panchayat lands and community asset, detect encroachments and evict such encroachment.
2. Taking actions to implement all schemes under Watershed Development Programme should be the domain of Village Panchayats. In order to increase the production and proper usage of public land and other assets, Village Panchayats may supervise and take necessary actions. Co-ordinating with various Departments for conservation of natural resources and protecting the ecology and environment.
3. The Village Panchayats can prepare plan and implement the Watershed Development Programme in their areas. They can also identity the type of trees and plants which are suitable to the soil types.
4. Village Panchayats can assist in the identification of beneficiaries under the Watershed Development Programme.

4. Animal Husbandry, Dairying and Poultry

1. Identification of beneficiaries for Artificial Insemination through Sub-Centres.
2. Identification of beneficiaries for frozen semen facilities under IRDP.
3. Identification of beneficiaries and implementation of conducting livestock and poultry show at village levels.
4. Implementation and maintenance of slaughter houses.

5. Assist in the identification of beneficiaries (small and marginal farmers and agricultural labourers) under sheep rearing scheme.
6. Identification of the beneficiaries under piggery schemes.
7. Identification of the beneficiaries under distribution of birds and animals.
8. Assist for setting up rabbit and backyard poultry units.
9. Assist for fodder land development scheme.
10. Assist in getting financial assistance to Milk Producers' Co-operative Societies.
11. Identification of beneficiaries for supply of quality milch animals.
12. Identification of beneficiaries under Hill Area Development Programme.
13. Identification of beneficiaries under Western Ghat Development Programme.
14. The Village Panchayats can intimate the Assistant Director (Animal Husbandry) or Extension Officer (Animal Husbandry) available at the Panchayat Unions regarding outbreak of epidemics and disease to cattle.
15. Supervise and record observations regarding the functioning of the slaughter houses with the technical advice of Assistant Director of Animal Husbandry.
16. Maintenance of slaughter houses in village panchayat area.
17. Undertaking fodder development activities in common lands to improve fodder availability.
18. For the purpose of raising fodder, common lands may be purchased by the Village Panchayats jointly with the Milk Producers Co-operative Societies.
19. Creation and maintenance of fodder banks in local areas to supply fodder during summer and scarcity seasons.
20. Taking action for supply of seeds and saplings of fodder trees to the villagers.
21 Necessary facilities can be created for Milk Producers Co-operative Societies, milk creation centres and poultry centres.
22. Assisting in the identification of beneficiaries under various schemes like development of native breeds, Fodder and Seed Development Schemes, Special Component Plan, Integrated Tribal Development Programme and vaccination of livestock and birds.

5. Fisheries

1. Identification of beneficiaries and implementation of the programme

on development of inland fish culture through Fish Farmer's Development Agency.

2. Identification of beneficiaries for inland water fishing and marketing.
3. Identification of beneficiaries for establishment of fresh water prawn factory.
4. Identification of beneficiaries in establishing inland prawn culture farms.
5. Identification of the beneficiaries and implementation of establishment of brackish water fish farmers agencies.
6. Assist in acquisition of lands for developing fishing harbours.
7. Identification of the beneficiaries for training of fishermen in latest fishing technology and issue of stipends to fishermen.
8. Identification of the beneficiaries for the scheme of providing assistance to fishermen for the purchase of clean containers and tricycles.
9. Identification of beneficiaries for the chemical to fishermen's Catamarans.
10. Assist in execution of prevention of sea erosion projects.
11. Identification of beneficiaries for Fishermen Group Insurance Scheme.
12. Identification of beneficiaries for Fishermen Savings and Relief Scheme.
13. Assist the Department in assessing the loss and damages to houses caused by flood and cyclone and to give publicity regarding fishermen insurance scheme and to encourage the enrolment of fishermen under the scheme.

6. Social Forestry and Farm Forestry

1. For promoting social and form forestry, to maintain the ecology, dissemination of information about protection, identifying community degraded wastelands and planting trees on community lands, the Village Panchayats can coordinate with the Forest Department.
2. Village Panchayats lands can be leased out to groups/individuals interested in the establishment of social forestry on the concept of sharing.
3. For promoting fuel, fodder and timber producing plants for local use, private farmers can be encouraged to take up nurseries and planting and they can be assisted to distributing horticultural seedlings/saplings free of cost to public sector undertakings/

government departments etc. Bamboo estates, raising of plantations in non-forest areas, construction of buildings/tribal welfare schools, formation of roads, establishment of people's nurseries, implementation of social forestry schemes in Rural Development Department and farm forestry scheme in Agriculture Department can be done with the assistance of forest department and also to identify the benefeciaries etc.

4. While implementing afforestation schemes on Externally Aided Projects/Centrally sponsored schemes and state schemes, Village Panchayats committees shall be formed as supervisory body on the pattern in Tamil Nadu Afforestation Project.

7. Minor Forest Produce

1. The Village Panchayats can approach the Forest Department to get permit for the village artisans to collect minor forest produce from the forests, except from protected forests, Wild Life Sanctuaries, National Parks.
2. The beneficiaries of Minor Forest Produce can be identified through Forest Department, which has got the expertise and to explore the feasibilities for implementation by the Forest Department.
3. Village Panchayats can identify and select suitable persons for planting of minor forest produce plants including medicinal plants.

8. Small Scale Industries Including Food Processing Industries

1. Assist identification of beneficiaries for Entrepreneurs Development Programme.
2. Identification of benefeciaries for setting up industries in backward areas.
3. Identification of beneficiaries for sanctioning of loans under schemes implemented through Director of Industries and Commerce.
4. Village Panchayats may assist to give publicity through media so that the scheme announced by the Central and State Government reach the beneficiaries who are interested to start industries in rural areas.

9. Khadi, Village and Cottage Indsutries

1. Assist in identification of village level potential activities and formulation of projects.

2. Identification of beneficiaries for skill development and transfer of technology.
3. Advise the artisans about training centres suitable for their trades and crafts and marketing of their finished goods.
4. Identify the beneficiaries, inform about the training centres and impart training by formulating the projects.
5. Village Panchayats should assist the establishment of marketing centres and for making necessary arrangements for starting industries using locally available raw materials and also fixing the prices of the goods produced by them.
6. Village Panchayats may implement new schemes for the development of khadi industries in consultation of Tamil Nadu Khadi Board.
7. Village Panchayats may plan, monitor and supervise the modernisation of Khadi and handloom weaving in consultation with the officials of Khadi and Handlooms Department.
8. Village Panchayats may assist for providing beehives boxes to the Adi-Dravida and Tribals living in the village to supplement their income and to supervise the implementation of the scheme.
9. Village Panchayats may formulate the schemes for the Khadi Silk weavers for providing Jacquard boxed in consultation with the department concerned and supervise the scheme.
10. Village Panchayats may seek the assistance of the officials of Khadi and Handloom Department to formulate the schemes for producing Khadi based industries to improve living condition of the people below the poverty line.
11. Village Panchayats can formulate the schemes for the people engaged in Palmyra tappers by providing necessary equipments and supervise the schemes.
12. Village Panchayats can implement and supervise the schemes for providing free books, notebooks and stationeries to the children of Palmyra tappers.

10. Rural Housing

1. Identification of beneficiaries for allotment of house sites for SC/ST, BC and MBCs.
2. Identification of beneficiaries under Tamil Nadu Rural Housing Schemes.
3. Identification of beneficiaries for improving the habitations in rural areas.

4. Identification of beneficiaries and implementation of the schemes under Indira Awaas Yojana.
5. Implementation of housing schemes for SC and ST.
6. Assess the needs for the house to the shelterless in the rural areas for the allotment of house sites and to provide assistance under rural housing schemes.
7. Identification of house sites and lands for construction of houses and maintain such data.
8. Selection of house less persons.
9. Assist to the co-operative societies for construction of houses.

11. Drinking Water

1. Maintenance of hand pumps, power pumps open wells, tanks and overhead tanks.
2. Assist in the identification of drinking water supply schemes and locations.
3. Supervision of the distribution of safe drinking water supply and sample testing of the quality of drinking water supplied.
4. Formulate and execute simple water supply schemes themselves with their own funds and also out of the funds allocated by the government and ensure assured water supply in the villages.
5. Supervision of the implementation of rural water supply schemes for the uncovered rural habitations under self-sufficiency programme.
6. Supervision of the implementation of comprehensive piped water supply scheme in excessively fluoride affected areas.
7. Supervision of the implementation of schemes in the supply of safe drinking water to habitations affected with salinity and brackishness under Minimum Needs Programme.
8. Supervision of the functioning of desalination plants under Accelerated Rural Water Supply Programme.
9. Supervision of special water supply scheme implemented under Accelerated Water Supply Programme in Rural Areas.
10. Formation of joint village committee for the maintenance of comprehensive water supply scheme covering less than 5 village panchayats.

12. Fuel and Fodder

1. To take necessary action to raise fuel and fodder plants to meet the

fuel and fodder needs of the village panchayats according to the advice of the Animal Husbandry, Forest Department in the lands belonging to Village Panchayats and Panchayat Unions.

2. Assist the department for the identification of wastelands and degraded lands for taking up fuel wood lots and fodder plantation under integrated wasteland development programme.
3. Encourage public in using the non-conventional energy sources like smokelessness chulahs and solar cookers and identification of similar fuel saving devices and to promote awareness among the public for the same.
4. Along with the Animal Husbandry and the Forest Department firewood and fodder plantations may be undertaken and supervised.
5. Execution of Tamil Nadu Agriculture Development Project (TNADP) Scheme by World Bank, Fodder Development Scheme, implemented under the control of Joint Director (Animal Husbandry), and schemes to issue fodder plants or saplings for fodder development can be supervised and assisted.
6. Assist in the implementation of National Bio-gas Development Programme and Chulah Programme and supervise its implementation.

13. Roads, Culverts, Bridges, Waterways and Other Means of Communication

1. Formation and maintenance of Village Panchayats roads.
2. To levy toll to collect taxes to meet execution and maintenance cost, wherever necessary.
3. Raise and maintain avenue trees/plantation on road sides.
4. Removal of encroachment in the road sides and impose penalty.
5. Supervision of the panchayats road works undertaken with the financial assistance of the concerned department.
6. Services of technical consultants can be utilized for the planning, execution and supervision of works taken up for the improvement of Village Panchayats roads.
7. Supervision of Village Panchayats roads and link road works undertaken under Jawahar Velai Vaaipu Thittam and other development programmes, like M.P. Local Area Development and MLA Constituency Development Schemes and works undertaken with externally aided programmes.

14. Rural Electrification Including Distribution of Electricity

1. Maintenance of street lights and purchase of the lights and other fittings etc.
2. The Village Panchayats will furnish the Electricity Board the list of habitations under 'One light one hut scheme' and under 'Million Wells Scheme'. TNEB will furnish the details of service connections along with the list of benefeciaries to the Village Panchayats.
3. Village Panchayats and Panchayat Unions may be entrusted with the responsibility of identifying the theft of electricity. Tamil Nadu Electricity Board will award 10% of the total amount collected due to the theft of energy to concerned panchayats.
4. While the Tamil Nadu Electricity Board proposing for setting up transformers and poles, it should consult the Village Panchayats for finalising the place.

15. Non-Conventional Energy Sources

1. Identification of beneficiaries for bio-gas plants and windmills.
2. Assist in imparting to benefeciaries at appropriate centres.
3. Assist in supervising the plants at village level.
4. Creating awareness among the people by dissemination of information on non-conventional energy sources and conservation of energy.
5. The Village Panchayats may be empowered to identify the persons to be assisted, the places where those sources of energy such as solar, windmill and bio gas plants be erected and co-ordinate with Block Development Officers, District Rural Development Agency and Branch Manager of Tamil Nadu Energy Development Agency.
6. Tamil Nadu Energy Development Agency and Electricity Board will guide Village Panchayats to educate the rural people on the importance of electricity and its savings.
7. The Village Panchayats may be given the responsibility of imparting training to the benefeciaries selected under non-conventional energy sources like bio-gas and windmill.
8. The Village Panchayats may assist in the proper identification of beneficiaries under these schemes and also in the rural employment generation schemes.

16. Poverty Alleviation Programmes

1. Identification of beneficiaries under Swarna Jayanthi Swarozgar Yojana and other individual beneficiary oriented schemes.
2. Implementation of Jawahar Gram Samriti Yojana (JGSY) and other employment generation programmes entrusted to the Village Panchayats.
3. In case of individual beneficiaries oriented Poverty Alleviation Programmes like "Swarna Jayanthi Swarozgar Yojana" beneficiaries will be selected by village panchayat and arrange for assistance after approval of Gram Sabha.
4. Inform the Panchayat Union, District Collector and the concerned district level officers about the misuse of assets, grant and loan by the beneficiaries.
5. Village Panchayats can utilize the entire allocation under "Jawahar Gram Samridhi Yojana" for the development of infrastructure in the Village Panchayats.
6. Village Panchayats can assist Panchayat Union for the distribution of identity cards under Employment Assurance Scheme and put up information boards about all the works taken up under Employment Assurance Scheme.
7. Assisting the Panchayat Union in preparation of plans for land development schemes.
8. Assisting for the finalisation of schemes/works under Decentralised District Plan at district level.
9. Assist in the selection of beneficiaries under Drought Prone Areas Programme.
10. Identification of eligible beneficiaries under Smarga Awass Yojana.
11. Village Panchayats can ensure proper utilization of funds of Tenth Finance Commission by the local bodies and also to ensure that the scheme works permitted within the Village Panchayats are completed.
12. Identification of beneficiaries under Central Rural Sanitation Programme and Provision of Drinking Water Schemes implemented with DANIDA assistance in Cuddalore and Villupuram districts.
13. Arrange live demonstration under smokeless chulahs scheme and undertake identification to beneficiaries under National Project on improved Chulahs.

17. Educational Including Primary and Secondary Schools

1. Assist and monitor the works regarding maintenance and repairs of school building, latrines, provision of drinking water facilities and sending reports to Assistant Education Officers.
2. Assist the local schools for opening of libraries.
3. To assist children for seeking admission in the primary schools.
4. Village Panchayats may recommend for opening of new primary schools and up gradation of primary schools as middle schools.
5. To assist in the implementation of various schemes in the schools.
6. Set up Education Committee in Village Panchayats and review of the standard school education.
7. Construction of buildings to create infrastructure facilities, repairing the buildings and providing equipments needed for the schools will be the responsibility of Village Panchayats.
8. Provision of learning equipments, tape records and uniforms may be organised from the funds of Village Panchayats.

18. Technical Training and Vocational Education

1. Identification of training needs in specific trades suitable for respective villages.
2. Dissemination of information on training and technical institutions.
3. Assist in identifying the people in the rural areas available for technical training and vocational training.
4. Publicity meeting can be conducted to educate the eligible students on the importance of vocational training so as to secure their admissions for the same.
5. Identifying the locations for establishments for vocational schools and vocational training centres and create favourable atmosphere for its better functioning.
6. Take steps to fulfill the expectations of people by assisting in the establishment of Government and private vocational training centres.
7. Recommend and to take necessary steps for the inclusions of vocational education in the High schools in the panchayats.
8. Identify suitable locations for the starting of new vocational schools for women.

19. Adult and Non-formal Education

1. Supervise the implementation of adult education and Non-formal Education, enrolment of students and arranging facilities therefor.
2. Selection of beneficiary and maintenance of centres in respect of non-formal education, establishment of reading rooms for promotion of non-formal education. Libraries will continue under the Government control.

20. Libraries

1. Opening of new reading rooms and libraries.
2. Construction of buildings for reading rooms and libraries.
3. Village Panchayats will have power to establish Reading Rooms in village areas.

21. Cultural Activities

1. The Village Panchayats can organise locally popuiar games and sports, village festivals and promote performance of local arts. Assistance other than financial assistance may be mobilised from the Department of Art and Culture for organising such events.
2. The Village Panchayats can create awareness amongst public through convergence of folk arts, cultural troops, music, dance and drama etc. with the assistance (other than financial assistance) of Department of Arts and Culture.
3. Village Panchayats will take necessary steps to promote small family norms, national integration, religious harmony, abolition of untouchability, etc.
4. Village Panchayats will identify artists in distress and help them to avail financial assistance provided by the Government.
5. Village Panchayats will make financial contribution to sports Development Authority, establish sports complexes, identify talented players and provide necessary training to them.

22. Markets and Fairs

1. Planning, identification of beneficiaries and supervision of Public Markets.
2. Planning, identification of beneficiaries, co-ordination and supervision

of Private Markets.

3. Assist in co-ordinating the services of Regulated Markets.
4. Co-ordinate and assist Primary Co-operative Marketing Societies.
5. Panchayats are empowered to identity places to open both public markets and private markets.
6. Village Panchayats maintain the buildings in public markets belonging to village panchayat.
7. Village Panchayats can issue license to shops, markets and fairs and festivals and to levy fees.
8. Panchayats will be vested with powers to regulate and control the shops, markets and to cancel license and impose penalties for breach or rules, regulations and conditions.
9. Taking appropriate sanitary measures during the fairs and festivals and other community gatherings in the village panchayat area is one of the mandatory duties of the village panchayats.

23. Health and Sanitation, Including Hospitals, Primary Health Centres and Dispensaries

1. Assist in development of District and Taluk Headquarter Hospitals.
2. Assist in identification of beneficiaries and supervision for the eradication of Tuberculosis, Malaria, Dreaded diseases, AIDs, Leprosy.
3. Assist in the establishment of dispensaries in tribal areas.
4. Assist in identification of beneficiaries for benefiting under Mobile Medical Units services in remote localities.
5. Assist in identification of beneficiaries and involve public in prevention and control of diseases.
6. Involvement of NGOs in conducting Eye and Family Welfare Camps. Identification of beneficiaries.
7. Implementation of construction, supervision and maintenance of Primary Health Centres and Maternity Centres.
8. Creating awareness among public about the importance of health environment and control of diseases.
9. Assist in providing financial assistance and identification of beneficiaries to conduct training for Multi-Purpose Health Workers in Primary Health Centres.
10. Assist in implementation of immunization against Diptheria and Polio for school children.
11. Implementation and supervision of Maternity and Child Health

Centres.

12. Implementation of School Health Scheme.
13. Implementation of Birth and Death registration.
14. Implementation and supervision of sanitation activities.
15. Recommend and assist concerned officials in extending the service area of the Primary Health Centres and Health Sub-Centres.
16. Assist in training of the nurses, doctors and other employees of voluntary organisation through District Training Teams for the benefit of the villagers.
17. Identify qualified and competent persons among the practitioners of Indian system of medicine and encourage the use of indigenous medicine.
18. Render necessary assistance to health workers in compiling statistics relating to pregnant women and women in reproductive age so as to provide health service to the target groups.
19. Collect data on causes of various diseases that affect children and inform the concerned officials to take up remedial measures.
20. Collect information on Infant Mortality Rate and mortality rate among the children under one year and report to the concerned officers for further action.
21. Ensure availability of essential life saving drugs in the Primary Health Centres and Health Sub-Centres on continuous basis.
22. Encourage visits by Village Health Nurses and multi purpose health workers to households and create awareness among the public for proper utilization of health services provided by the Health and Family Welfare Department.
23. Ensure regular health appraisal of Primary and Elementary school children, maintain their health cards and arrange treatment for the ailments, keep health record of adolescent girls identify their nutritional deficiencies and other ailments, organise treatment and to promote health education and nutrition among adolescent girls. Ensure health, nutrition and population education in schools, and co-ordinate the services of concerned departments in this regard.
24. Ensure and encourage periodical visits of the health team to schools to watch the health status of the students.
25. Form village health committee, comprising Panchayat President as Chairman, Village Health Nurses, traditional birth attendants and multi-purpose health workers as members to provide health and medical services to the villagers.
26. Identify endemic and communicable diseases and also complicated

diseases and assist workers of Health Department in providing necessary medical services and arranging referral services.

27. Conduct village level health and medical camps for the benefit of the people.
28. Village Panchayats may render assistance for implementation of the Food Adulteration Act, 1954.
29. Ensure chlorination of over head tanks and open wells and clean them periodically. Ensure cleaning of the private water tanks and community latrines and protect the drinking water sources from pollution/contamination.
30. Construct and maintain drains to dispose of wastes and drainage water in order to prevent stagnation.
31. Organise disposal of solid wastes from disused wells, tanks and ponds to prevent hazards to health and hygiene and also to protect environment.

24. Family Welfare

1. Assist in identification of beneficiaries and establishment and maintenance of Family Welfare Centres.
2. Manage and maintain involvement of local bodies and NGOs in Family Welfare Schemes.
3. Implementation of training programmes for Family Welfare Workers.
4. Implementation of schemes for educating public about Family Welfare Schemes.
5. Assist the multi-purpose health workers in the preparation and maintenance of records relating to provision of health care for pregnant women which is one of the components of family welfare programme.
6. Assist providing proper medical facilities to the pregnant women with the help of the Health Sub-Centres in the villages.
7. Assisting of paramedical staff in ante -natal and post-natal care, safe delivery, survival of new born babies.
8. Mobilise the support of the NGOs, and community organisations in extending medical facilities to the pregnant women, and ensure better health of women and children in their areas by improving the basic facilities.
9. Organise awareness campaign among women to emphasize the importance of breast feeding, and its advantages providing in immunity against diseases to the children with the help of the health staff.

10. Assist in controlling the deficiency of Vitamin-A, iron and iodine, and arrange for anti-rabies vaccination, and ensure better implementation of the schemes, co-ordinate with MCH staff, village officials and Family Welfare Department by holding periodic revival meetings and ensure integrated efforts.
11. Assist in the conduct of special awareness campaign on sexually transmitted disease (STD) AIDs and killers diseases at village level.
12. Promote Mahalir Mandrams People's Groups etc. and organise awareness campaigns for the benefit of pregnant women, and other women in the reproductive age about ante-natal and post natal care, small family norms, breast feeding.

25. Women and Child Development

1. Supervise the Meal Centres functioning in the village.
2. Supervise the Integrated Child Development Scheme/Tamil Nadu Integrated Nutritious Programme (TINP).
3. Implement and supervise the formation pre-school and creches, implementation of Nutrition Schemes in Schools and Integrated Child Development Programme Centres.
4. Assist in starting Balwadis and Schools.
5. Assist in construction of Child Welfare Centres under Swedish assisted Integrated Child Development Programme Centres.
6. Assist, supervision and evaluation of Nutrition Meal Scheme.
7. Assist in prevention of female infanticide and development of children of destitute women.
8. Assist and supervise the Working Women Centres and production units.
9. Assist and supervise various Women Welfare Schemes such as vocational training, poor widow's children and daughter's marriage assistance and orphanages.
10. Assist in implementing the women related economic development activities.
11. Supervise and review of creches for Children of Working and Diseased Women.
12. Assist for implementation of all Women Welfare Schemes.
13. Assist the pregnant women, below the poverty line to get financial assistance.
14. Assist in getting financial assistance for women below poverty line marriage.

15. Assist in getting financial assistance to Female Children Welfare Scheme.
16. Assist in distributing of sewing machines to destitute and deserted women.
17. Assist in distribution of advance to poor widow's daughter's marriage.
18. Assist in implementation of women development under IFAD schemes.
19. Identify the women and children suffering from anaemic, micro-nutrient deficiency (Vitamin-A, iron and iodine deficiency) goitre and inform it to the Social Welfare Department Officials.
20. Assist the concerned department officials in eligible women who come forward for training and to take up self employment ventures.
21. Arrange to co-ordinate the women groups with the Social Welfare Department officials in implementation of Social Welfare Schemes and supervise the same.
22. Creating awareness about the schemes implemented by Government and disseminate information about clean health habits to be adopted, healthy food habits, breast feeding for improvement of standard of living of women and children living in rural areas.
23. Village Panchayats may extend and co-ordinate the following assistance to the Social Welfare Department officials.
24. Inspect the centres assisted by the government, identity the shortcomings and rectify the defects if any.
25. Enlist the local support in the village for supplying of vegetables and other articles required for the Nutritious Meal Centres.
26. The elected women representatives of Village Panchayats can help the Social Welfare Department staff in monitoring of growth of children, pre-natal and post-natal care, care of at risk children, child care activities.
27. Assist the Project Officials for involving the Non-governmental organisations.
28. To assist in taking census and collect statistics related to women and children for evaluation of schemes.
29. To assist in selection of sites for construction of child welfare centres and nutritious meal centres. To assist in identifying the children who require special care and medical attention by means of enumeration of beneficiaries.
30. To assist the Social Welfare Department officials in identifying the child labourers and extend the rehabilitation measures for their upliftment by utlilizing the various schemes of government.

31. Assist in formation of self-help groups among women and inculcate the habit of small savings among them.

26. Social Welfare, Including Welfare of Handicapped and Mentally Retarded

1. Assist and supervise the blind and handicapped rehabilitation centres.
2. Assist and supervision of schools and hostels of handicapped.
3. Assist in issue of scholarship to students of handicapped schools.
4. Assist in implementation of Integrated Polio Eradication Scheme.
5. Assist NGO's for rehabilitation of handicapped and mentally disabled children.
6. Assist in establishment of schools for deaf and dumb for handicapped.
7. Assist the blind who are registered in employment exchange for getting employment.
8. Village panchayats should collect details on number of rural disabled and send it to Panchayat Unions.
9. To create awareness among public regarding causes of disability.
10. To take required efforts for prevention of disability. To find out ways and means to avoid dangerous accidents.
11. To enlist the assistance of non-governmental organisations to protect welfare of disabled and also render help in implementing programmes related to disabled.
12. To take necessary efforts at village level for conducting literacy programmes for disabled children who are above 14 years of age through non-formal education.
13. Utilizing the human resources available with rural based non-governmental organisations to educate the illiterate rural disabled children.
14. To render necessary assistance and support to government officials and non-governmental organisation in their efforts to set up special schools/institutions for hearing, impaired, handicapped, mentally retarded and spastic children.
15. To assist the department officials to identify beneficiaries for supply of aids/appliances such as hearing aid, artificial limbs, folding sticks, tricycles, wheelchairs etc.
16. To assist the officers concerned for implementation of schemes such as old age pension deserted women etc.
17. In order to get rid of this evil and also to create awareness on social evils like alcoholism, women who could undertake this task can be

identified by panchayats and recommended to social welfare department officials.

18. To encourage physically handicapped and mental retarded handicapped, Village Panchayats can conduct special sport meet, cultural programmes and distribute prizes. To this noble task assistance of general public and non-governmental organisation can be enlisted.
19. Village Panchayats may conduct special campaigns with the assistance of non-governmental organisations to propagate the evils of drug abuse to public especially to students.

27. Welfare of the Weaker Sections, and in Particular, of the Scheduled Castes and the Scheduled Tribes

1. Assist in implementation of schemes being implemented by others for the welfare of SC/ST.
2. Implementation of the schemes to provide pathways to burial grounds and burning ghats.
3. Identification of beneficiaries schemes for construction of houses, provision of house sites under various schemes and house improvement.
4. Identification of beneficiaries for electrifying the Scheduled Castes and Scheduled Tribes houses.
5. Identification of beneficiaries for rewarding inter-caste marriages implemented by Social Welfare Department.
6. Identification of beneficiaries for assisting the petty traders.
7. Implementation of Construction of Community Halls, Dhobikhanas Scheme.
8. Implementation of enforcement of the Civil Rights Protection Act, 1995.
9. Implementation of schemes for dissemination of information on the evils of untouchability to the public.
10. Identification of bonded labourers for rehabilitation.
11. Review and evaluate the literacy and educational status of the Scheduled Castes and Scheduled Tribes and send reports to the Panchayat Unions.
12. Assist to bring down the drop-out rates in the schools.
13. Assist in the implementation of programmes, welfare measures for the children in the rural areas.
14. Assist and ensure that special coaching classes are conducted for

the children who obtain low marks.

15. Assisting in the implementation of literacy programmes to benefit the tribal children.
16. Assisting the Panchayat Unions for implementation of schemes to create infra-structural facilities in schools, science lab, teaching materials, class rooms, drinking water, construction of latrine and providing sanitation facilities for the schools.
17. Identification of beneficiaries among Adi-Dravidas/SC for technical training and send it to Panchayat Unions.
18. Providing information on the need for new schools, hostel and their constructions.
19. Assist to upgrade the existing schools into High Schools (or) Higher Secondary Schools.
20. To identify house sites for construction of houses for the Adi-Dravidas and inform the Special Tehsildar for the benefit of Adi-Dravidas and STs.
21. Assisting the Panchayat Unions for providing street lights, provision of electricity, formation of road for the benefit of Adi-Dravidas and STs.
22. To assist in the identification of beneficiaries for getting loan and scholarship.
23. Assisting in the selection of beneficiaries for self-employment and individual entrepreneur programme and self-help groups from among the Adi-Dravidas and STs and ensure that the funds allotted are properly utilized.
24. Sending report to the police on atrocities against Adi-Dravidas and STs based on the 1995 Civil Rights Protection Act and Prevention of Atrocities Act, 1989 where their rights are denied in provision of drinking water and burial ground, use of different vessels in tea shops, prevention in worship places, refusal to attend washing clothes or hair dressing, preventing marriage processions and send information to police on such atrocities.
25. To make aware of the Civil Rights Protection Act, 1955 and Prevention of Atrocities Act, 1989 among the public.
26. Mobilisation of social support and awareness for eradicating untouchability.
27. Assuring the conferment of ownership right on lands given to the Adi-Dravidas and Scheduled Tribes under Land Ceiling Act.
28. Ensure that no compulsory labour on carrying dead bodies, beating of tom tom, digging grave yard etc. on the socially deprived class.

29. Assist in taking action in the identification of bonded labourers and their rehabilitation.
30. Review and Monitor the identification of beneficiaries with the help of NGOs for the scheme of scavengers rehabilitation programmes with financial assistance.
31. Helping Panchayat Union in providing rehabilitation and related activities with financial assistance and rescue them from collection of human excreta.
32. Supervision of school and hostels run for Adi-Dravidas/ST and sending information to the concerned officials.
33. Identification of beneficiaries for Chief Minister Award for continuance of their studies in colleges from among Adi-Dravidas/ST candidates. For this purpose panchayat can give wise publicity in the village and help in creating awareness among the Adi-Dravidas.
34. Identification of beneficiaries for undergoing technical training from among Adi-Dravidas/ST students.

28. Public Distribution System

1. Village Panchayats President of the concerned panchayats will be the Members of Inspection Committee to inspect the ration shops.
2. Review and report to the State and Divisional level committee on the problems noticed during the inspection at the ration shops, by the Panchayat President and its members.

29. Maintenance of Community Assets

1. Plan and supervise the activities relating to the identification, registration and recovery of charges from public users of the community assets.
2. Review and supervision of the sale, lease and transfer of public assets.
3. Review and supervision of social assets and ensure protection against encroachment, damages, losses etc.
4. Planning for eliciting support from NGOs in maintenance of public assets.
5. The Village Panchayats are empowered to collect rent, fees, etc. on their commercial and other assets.
6. Detailed instructions are available in the Tamil Nadu Panchayats Act, 1994 and the orders issued there under to lease out community assets.

7. Village Panchayat may protect community assets from misuse, encroachment and loss and take necessary legal actions in this regard. Village Panchayats may exercise this power in respect of their assets stipulated in their jurisdiction.
8. Sections 124 of the Tamil Nadu Panchayats Act, 1994 permits Village Panchayats to receive donation to discharge their duties and responsibilities to improve and maintain community assets.

Planning by the Rural Local Bodies

Planning for Village Panchayats

Sl. No.	Subject	Department	Officers responsible for Planning at Village Panchayat Level
1.	Crop Production and Protection	Agriculture and Horticulture Departments	Agriculture Officer and Horticulture Officer
2.	Soil and Water conservation	Agriculture and Forest	Agriculture Officer, Forest Range Officer
3.	Animal Husbandry	Animal Husbandry	Livestock Inspector
4.	Dairy Development	Dairy Development Department	Milk Procurement Officer
5.	Fisheries	Fisheries Department	Inspector of Fisheries
6.	Social Forestry	Forest Department (Social Forestry)	Forest Range Officer
7.	Co-operation	Co-operation Department	Sub-Registrar of Co-operative Societies
8.	Rural Development	Rural Development Department	Extension Officer (Panchayats)
9.	Land Reforms	Revenue Department	Revenue Inspector
10.	Social Welfare	Social Welfare & Nutrition Department	Extension Officer (NMP)
11.	Minor Irrigation	Public Works Department	Luskar and Assistant Agricultural Officer
12.	Irrigation Development	Agricultural Engineering Department	Assistant Engineer

13.	Youth and Sports Activities	Education Department Nutrition	Makkal Nala Paniyalarkal, Co-ordinator,
14.	Arts and Cultural Programmes	Tamil Development and Culture Department	Makkal Nala Paniyalar Rural Welfare Officer
15.	Medical	Public Helath & Family Welfare Department	Maternity Assistant, Primary Health Centre
16.	Public Health	Public Health & Family Welfare Department	Village Health Nurse & Maternity Assistant
17.	Water Supply & Sanitation	Rural Development Department	Extension Officer (Panchayats)
18.	Housing	Housing and Urban Deve-lopment Department	Co-operative Inspector (Housing)
19.	Adi-Dravidar/ Tribal Welfare/ Backward Class Welfare	Adi-Dravida and Tribal Welfare	Extension Officer (Adi-Dravida Welfare)
20.	Nutritious Meal	Social Welfare Department	Noon Meal Organiser
21.	Other Social Welfare Schemes	Social Welfare Department	Rural Welfare Officer
22.	Energy	Energy Department	Extension Officer (Panchayats)
23.	Non-Conventional Energy	Rural Development Department	Extension Officer (Panchayats)
24.	Rural and Cottage Industries	Small Industries Department	Extension Officer (Panchayats)
25.	Roads and Bridges	Highways Department	Assistant Engineer, Rural Development
26.	Road and Inland Department	Highways Department	Assistant Engineer, Rural Development
27.	Civil Supplies Department	Food and Co-operation	Revenue Inspector

CASE ANALYSIS

A KARISALPATTI GRAM PANCHAYAT

Introduction

V. Irudayam is a young but the most respected leader of Karisalpatti Gram Panchayat. He has been recognised by his spiritual activities. He is thirty six years old. His way of organising the people in the village is very attractive. When he was at twenty two he organised a padayatra programme to lead men and women to Velankanni church during September to attend the festival and thereby he exhibited his qualities of a leader. The way in which he organised the programme and conducted himself had drawn the attention of all. From that day onwards, he had been the team leader for this programme every year. His passiveness, calmness, understanding capacity and positive attitude attracted the people.

But Irudayam has a few sorrowful memories. He lost his parents when he was nine years old. Himself and his sisters were put in the custody of their grandmother of maternal side. He completed his school final and then took the responsibility of cultivating the lands, he bequeathed from his ancestors. He has three acres of wet land and one acre of dry land. He recollected his earlier days that he was very much interested in farming, even after school hours, visited farm site and engaged in all farming activities.

1982 was the turning point in his life through his marriage. He selected his own partner from his own caste — Vanniar Christian. She is his neighbouring farmer, very hard working lady and so he himself expressed his willingness to marry her, said Irudayam.

Entering into Public Life

During 1984 he entered into public life. He organised padayatra for Velankanni temple. The spiritual contact with the church during his boyhood days and the motivation gained after his sister became a nun culminated in organising a spiritual group. This activity has moulded his personality.

The respondent further informed that he had self-realisation after his marriage that he has to lead a model life and the Holy Bible was the guiding factor for this transformation.

In spite of all his good qualities, the church did not approve his marriage due to his age. And so the church did not permit him and his wife to receive the holy water after the spiritual service. But after he attained the age of twenty one, he was considered as the full fledged member of the church and involved fully in all activities of the church. The respondent felt that he properly understood that unity of people would yield many good results, and a good leader could be a model to public. He served as the vice-president in the Karisalpatti Milk Producers Co-operative Society during the year 1990-92. Since 1991, he is serving as the president of Parent Teachers Association of local primary school, run by the church.

He realised that involvement in politics was essential while doing public activities. Hence he joined Cong.(I) in 1989 and become president of the local unit. In 1993, he become the treasurer of the union committee of Cong.(I) and since 1996 he is with Tamil Manila Congress. Mr. Irudayam attributed the followings reasons for his association with Congress party:

Non-violence as a method

National outlook

Bypassing narrow minded regionalism

He attended the party meetings, conferences, demonstrations held in Chennai, Trichy, Thirunelveli and Erode.

Lead the Agitation for Drinking Water

When a joint action committee of all political parties was formed to take necessary steps for getting drinking water for Karisalpatti and it was decided to organise a road rokho. But none of the members came forward to take the leadership. He stepped in during that crisis and led the demonstration in the year 1994. And they succeeded in their attempt and they got a comprehensive water supply scheme in 1995, and from 1995 there is no water scarcity even during the summer.

His Experiments in the Farming

The respondent wishes to be a model farmer and by which he had drawn the attention of the agriculturists. He is seriously involved in that occupation. He understood the problem that water management is very essential for agriculture. He demonstrated that how effectively one can manage water for agriculture. The vagary of monsoon played on the destiny of farmers. And the respondent was also one of the looser. He suffered a heavy loss in grape farming. And then he switched over to vegetable farming. In vegetable farming one variety of creeper uses to give good yield for a period of three to four months after that it has to be replaced.

He adopted new mode of cultivation and introduced new varieties. He gained a lot of income from his vegetable garden. Within an extend of 0.60 cent he got an income about Rs. 60,000 and so he had an opportunity to voice his experiments to the farming community of Tamil Nadu through AIR, Madurai. He attends any training organised for farmers anywhere in the province. For the past three years he discontinued the use of chemical fertilisers and apply the green manure and compost manure in all his three acres. In addition to his farming, he has animal husbandry, rearing two milch animals. The respondents shared his feelings that due to his new assignment in panchayat and giving more time to panchayat works he has to loose his profit from the farming. This profit loss has created an ill feeling in the mind of his spouse and she was always advising to spare time for personal life also.

His Family Life

He has four children, two daughters and two sons. Realising his inability to devote time for the study of his children, he put the three children in boarding school run by Christian institution. Only one of his son is with him.

The Panchayat Electioneering Process

During the panchayat election, the village panchayat of Karisalpatti witnessed a tough competition in the name of politics. The respondent had to face three opponents, one from DMK, another from CPI(M) and one more from independent. Out of three one was the son of a former president of the Gram Panchayat.

The respondent adopted a unique strategy of circulating a bit notice and by which he appealed the voters that he would initiate a lot of new and good development works with the help of the government and the people at Karisalpatti and he sought their support and solidarity. The villagers acknowledged the spirit of his dedication at the young age, elected the respondent as their president. The minority castes namely Vellalar and Adi-Dravidar preferred him rather the other three contestants as the people suspected their caste supremacy.

Out of 2200 voters, 1700 casted their votes in the election of which 100 votes were invalid. The respondent has secured 951 votes with a margin of 431 votes over his nearest rival.

The respondent's approach in canvassing has made an impact in the minds of the people. He avoided wall writings and other types of canvassing. He put notice board to whom they had to vote. He has used the posters but displayed separately, not pasted on the others property. This culture has influenced 25% of the voters, the respondent explained. Overall expense was around Rs.10,000/- only for the electioneering. The respondent informed that he had decided not to spend more as he was not able to spend. Moreover the amount spent in the election could be compensated only through fraudulent means which will be known to the people.

Panchayat Activities

He conducts monthly meetings regularly. He considers the opinion of all members of the hamlets namely old Kannivadi and Karamadai. He had opposition from a member when he proposed a tap for public at old Kannivadi but with the support of others he completed that work.

The problem of water supply is over as the comprehensive water supply scheme has a perennial water source at Kombai, 8 km distance from this panchayat. And so there are 29 public taps, for the benefit of public at Karisalpatti village panchayat. He informed that there are 51 street lights and they are properly attended to whenever problem arises in street lights.

The maintenance of three overhead tanks and two Televisions is also properly done. He felt that there is only one sweeper and he could not complete his task every day. Considering the problems of sewage disposal, the respondent thought over an innovative sanitation system which has been experimented at four streets, benefiting two hundred houses (A separate case study is done on this innovative sanitary system). He faced a stiff opposition from four members and with the support of the majority *i.e.* five members he carried out this experiment through a donation received from an NGO. He explained that the political interference is in frequency at village level. The responsibility of selection of beneficiaries is with the village panchayat and hence he gets pressures from all corners.

During 1996-97 the IRDP beneficiaries were recommended by each member. The council accepted their recommendation and forwarded to the bank and it was not accepted by the bank because of the fact that most of the ineligible candidates have been recommended by the ward members. The council members without knowing the details of the scheme recommended candidates for IRDP programme based on their party affiliation and hence the proposals were rejected by the bank. And at present he corrected this mistake during the current year 1997-98. Out of twelve IRDP beneficiaries, six have been from the scheduled caste and the remaining six from the backward community. To administer social justice, out of six beneficiaries belonging to backward community two beneficiaries were selected from the economically backward Vellalar community.

While sharing his responsibilities with public, the respondent felt very much about the dependency syndrome of public. They expect everything to be done by the government and all expect loan from the government. To the people "loan" means not refundable. This is the mind set of the people in the rural areas.

To avoid pitfalls in the IRDP, the bank officials made the tie-up arrangement with the co-operative milk producers society so as the IRDP beneficiaries would supply milk to the society and the loan amount instalment would be credited in the concerned bank account and hence repayment of loans is ensured.

Village Development in his Opinion

The respondent had a vision that economic development was the main task of panchayat. He opined that women group formation and introduction of Khadi and Village Industries would uplift the village economy. He suggested that preparation of compost manure in more scientific manner may be a best source for supplementary income as well as for sustainable agriculture. He felt that the level of understanding and knowledge of panchayat members, president and people about the problems of development has to be enhanced. He listed out the following functional groups which ought to be formed and necessary training could be provided to them to become successful groups which facilitate the functioning of village panchayats:

1. Education Committee.
2. Sanitation Committee.
3. Committee to explore employment opportunities to the unemployed youth.
4. Committee to look after transport/road maintenance.

5. Committee for women empowerment.
6. Committee to protect and maintain common property resources.

His Relationship with the other two tiers of PRI

In Tamil Nadu it is a truism that the local body leaders of the three tiers are not maintaining their relationship with each other conducive for development. They fight against each other. Of course there are exceptions. But he is maintaining very cordial relationship with the panchayat union councillor who is a woman from his village. He shares the happenings/activities of his panchayat with her and she had attended all the meetings of panchayat based on his invitation. The councillor discusses with the president before attending the union council meeting so as the village will get the available benefits from all sources. With the help of the union councillor, the village has got a grant to construct a building for ration shop and to black top a road for a kilometre in his village.

The District Councillor is a bit away from the village. And so there is no close relationship between the president and the District Councillor. Even though he is faraway from this village, the president had approached and influenced the District Councillor and got six street lights and allocation of resources for the construction of new building for veterinary hospital. As per his understanding even though there is no organic linkages among the three tiers of the panchayati system as per the Act, he established his connection with other tiers by his approach.

His Relationship with the Vice-President

The age is the uniting factor between the vice-president and the respondent. They are at the same age, same caste and they have mutual trust and faith. As the vice-president is engaged in vegetable trade, he is not devoting his time in village panchayat affairs. But he never acts as hindrance for the activities of the panchayat. In Tamil Nadu, it is general that vice-president is a major hurdle to implement programmes and schemes. In almost all fora resolutions have been passed to remove the powers of the vice-president as they act as stumbling blocks for activities in the panchayats.

Traditional *Vs* New Panchayat at Karisalpatti

The traditional panchayat at Karisalpatti is not a common institution in a real sense. It is an institution consisting of the higher castes. The selection of office bearers is not by voting. The influence of higher caste leaders can be observed in the affairs of the traditional panchayat, the respondent explained.

The respondent informed that when he introduced the innovative sanitation, the traditional panchayat leaders vehemently opposed it. They consider the emergence of new leadership of panchayat as a challenge to the traditional panchayat and so they always try to supersede the new panchayat leadership. While public respect the new leader and recognition is accorded to him, the traditional panchayat committee members ensured that they are in the top of the hierarchy and put the village panchayat president below them. The respondent has overcome this mind set by setting aside their treatment as immature and he does not worry on this treatment. His aim, the respondent said, is not to earn but to serve the society in all his possible ways, irrespective of caste and religion.

The other side

He is pressurised by his wife as he has not concentrated his attention in family matters and spends more money from his packet for public as donation/contribution. No salary for his devoted service whereas he is getting less income from his agriculture. These factors may create a second thought over his future commitment in public life, he felt.

Details of the Communities living at Karisalpatti Village

Five hundred Vanniar Christian families are in this village. Of the families 90% of the households have cultivable lands from the range of one to three acres. The total number of irrigation well owned by this community is about one hundred and fifty and in about 75 to 80 wells have been electrified. It is interesting to note that there is no well in which manual/ animal is used to lift water from the wells at Karisalpatti village.

There are two churches, one is old not in use and another a new church. Father of the church Fr.Gaberial is a young and energetic church authority, mobilising youth and women for gospel services as well as development activities. One primary school is being run by the church. Children belonging to the broken families are receiving support from church for their schooling expenses. Youth are encouraged to utilize their talents in a constructive way by staging drama on social issues, organising sports, celebrating religious functions and events with the help of the church. A team consisting of about two hundred Christians to undertake padayatra to Velankanni every year. The current year is the fourteenth year of their pilgrimage. Panchayat president of Karisalpatti is the organiser of this padayatra team since its inception.

Traditional Community Leadership

There is a village committee consisting of six persons belonging to Vanniar Christian and the committee is responsible for almost all common affairs in the village. The committee members position is as follows:

Nattanmai	1
Maniam	1
Chinna Nattanmai	1
Treasurers	3 (persons)

Apart from this arrangement there is a member in each street. There is community leadership of traditional style in other communities (Vellalar and Adi-Dravida community) also. Hence it was told that any problem arises between communities are locally discussed and settled without reporting it to the police.

Village Panchayat (Traditional)

Every Sunday, near the primary school site, from morning 9 O'clock to afternoon 1 O'clock, the problems relating to individuals, groups and communities have been patiently heard, and arguments and counter arguments have been permitted. Judgments and decisions will be pronounced there itself. The maximum fine imposed on the individuals who have committed mistakes is Rs.100/-. Most of the cases are successfully handled through this community council. They have formulae like compromise, apology and correcting the mistakes. As the Vanniar Christian is the dominant caste, the village committee which is fully represented by Vanniar Christian is accepted by the other communities. The fine amount is managed by the village committee. Apart from setting disputes in the traditional panchayats, they will also participate in the development activities of the new panchayats. Some of them are taking the responsibilities of village development. The committee sends memorandum and other communications to the government officials, ministers and MLA with regard to various civic problems.

The village committee does the cleaning work regularly at the approach path to grave yard belonging to each community. It helps for burial and cremation works during the death of any individual in any community. The village committee organised "Road Rocko" recently demanding proper water supply and successfully exerted pressure on the government machinery and got drinking water pipe lines to all the streets.

Promotion of Communal Harmony

To ensure peaceful and harmonious co-existence, the villagers of Karisalpatti encourage the inter-community participation during the celebration of festival in the villages.

During the month of January, the Vanniar Christians celebrate St. Anthoniar festival in which the first respect of garlanding is accorded to Vellalar community. The Adi-Dravida community people visit church and participate in the celebration of festivals in the churches and communities.

During the month of February/March and March/April the Hindus celebrate Goddess Kaliamman and Goddess Bagavathiamman festivals and they undertake padayatra to Palani Temple. Vanniar Christians used to come forward and give them a warm send off to the padayatrikas. Accepting garlands, exchanging of betal leaf, honouring with ponnadai are reciprocal among the communities of Karisalpatti village. This practice had been in existence for more than hundred years, it was told.

Other Communities

Vellalars and Adi-Dravidas are the other communities living at Karisalpatti. Vellalars have two hundred families, Adi-Dravidas have one hundred families. One hundred and sixty Vellalars have land, owning about fifty irrigation well and about ten families of Adi-Dravida own lands with two irrigation well.

Main Occupation

Agriculture is the main occupation in Karisalpatti supplemented by animal husbandry. During Adi pattam *i.e.,* June/July the farmers sow the grains in the dry land along with green gram and bengal gram. Now maize is an addition. During the Ipasi pattam *i.e.*, November/December they grow coriander, sun flower, sorgum and cotton in karisal land.

Wet land Cultivation

The farmers of wet land have started cultivating vegetables and by which they gain much profit as they have a very big market at Oddanchatram. They grow vegetable creepers very scientifically like grapes adopting proper manuring and pest control. Vegetable like beans variety, roots, guards, onions, chillies and paddy. They grow hybrid grass and utilizing it as animal feeds. In a small plot, brinjal and tomato are being cultivated for domestic purpose. Those who have adequate water for irrigation now are growing fruit bearing trees like sappota.

Marketing Strategy

Earlier most of the farmers depended on the middlemen to whom they had to sell their products. The middlemen sent the commodities to the nearby market Oddanchatram and Dindigul and even to Chennai. Now the farmers directly handle the sales of their product as the market is situated very near to their village. Regular van, mini lorry services are utilized by the farmers jointly. Some individual farmers travel in passenger bus to Oddanchatram and avoiding middlemen and earn the profit everyday.

There is yet another trend emergence of local trades who extend advance loan to the farmers to meet their agriculture operational expenses with the condition that they have to supply their products to the local traders at the price prevailed in the market after harvest. These local traders engage lorry services and directly supply the products to Chennai traders regularly. The telephone communication facilities are properly utilized by the local traders.

The Side Effect of Extensive Vegetable Cultivation

It is told that the farmers are using a variety of chemical fertilisers and pesticides to get more yield and to gain more profit and due to this, the soil condition is deteriorated over the years. Hence they prefer natural and compost manure and showing more interest in animal husbandry also.

The Usage of Agricultural Labour

The wage per day for adult men is Rs. 50 whereas the woman is only Rs. 25. There is a demand that women's wage has to be increased to Rs. 30

or Rs. 35. There are about fifty to sixty families migrated to places like Vellakoil, Palladam for agricultural and other manual work where they get more amount of money as wage. The employment opportunity in agricultural sector is not for the whole year. But apart from farming, there are works like desilting and deepening tanks, transporting of enriched soil to farm site and other agricultural works. Moreover the landless labourers supplement their income by milch animal rearing.

Encroachment/Blocking of Inward Channels

The villagers informed that there are four tanks/ponds namely: 1. Pavadai Iyer Tank, 2. Kanakkan Tank, 3. Percolation Pond, and 4. Vadakkankulam Tank. Most of the tanks do not get adequate water due to the formation of road by which the inward channel route is disturbed.

Conclusion

The villagers of Karisalpatti completely depend on agriculture and animal husbandry. There is a harmonious relationship among the three main communities, Vanniar Christian, Vellalar and Adi-Dravidar. It is told that the drop-out in school is reduced due to counselling and guidance of church authorities. With the help of Church, an attempt is being made to strengthen women and their group activities. It is noted that Karisalpatti village is a traditional one but prepared for further change in the aspects of economic development. Hence the youths are demanding non-farming economic activities.

Milk Co-operative Society in Karisalpatti

Introduction

Vanniar Christians are the majority families of Karisalpatti village panchayat. Earlier they were notorious for their anti-social activities *i.e.* illicit distillation of alcohol and robbery, it was told. But their attitude was changed due to the intervention of church authorities. The church looked into their problems and encouraged them to change their life style. Most of them fell into the advice of the church authorities and engaged themselves in rearing of milch animals.

During 1972 they joined together and established a society in which all families who reared milch animals enlisted as members. In course of time they realised the importance of a registered body and so they registered their society on 10th August 1978.

Status of the Society

The Milk Producers Co-operative Society of Karisalpatti had its long journey during the past two decades. In general the sustainability of any milk producers' co-operative society is doubtful due to unnecessary interventions of the state government and politisation of the institutions. Moreover the state government very often dismisses the elected representatives and their board. Instead of facilitating the growth of the society, the state government and its officials akin to the co-operative department always show their negative attitude towards this institution. In spite of all these environments, the milk producers co-operative society of Karisalpatti successfully come over and got awards two times for its best performance.

At present the total membership of the society is as follows:

Karisalpatti		634		
Palaya Kannivadi		50		
Kurumbapatti		50		
Total		734		
Women members	:	SC - 136	BC - 135	Total - 271
Men members	:	SC - 86	BC - 377	Total - 463
Total	:	SC - 222	BC - 512	Total - 734

The society is administered by a board consisting of fifteen directors, twelve men and three women.

The office administration is looked after by one secretary and two assistants. There are eight vendors. Out of them only three are paid by the society and the balance five vendors are paid by the milk producers themselves, contributing Rs. 60 per month per milk producer.

At present there are 125 milk producers who are selling out the milk to the society. On an average there is 480 litres during morning and 410 litres during evening procured by the society. Out of 125 milk producers who have tie-up arrangements with the society, 32 persons have availed loan from the local branch of a nationalised bank. The loan is extended from non-scheme sector and so without subsidy. But the beneficiaries who availed this loan are very much satisfied that they need not give bribe or loose any amount in subsidy. This non-scheme loan arrangement was initiated by church authorities - Rev. Father and community leadership and so the repayment is assured.

The secretary of the society is a local man continuously serving the society since its registration. He explained that so far about five hundred milch animals were given to the village people through bank loan. The delay in settlement of the money to the members of the society and the frequent dismissal of the elected board created a feeling of insecurity among the members and so there are only 125 members selling milk to the society. The society is having membership with the district milk producers co-operative society and selling the procured milk to the district body. The rate of purchase by the village society is Rs. 8 per litre for cow milk and Rs. 9 per litre for buffalo milk and the society gets a margin of 0.70 paise per litre (irrespective of any kind of milk) from the district society. The payment from the district society has been pending for the past six months all over Tamil Nadu and recently the state government helped the district societies in settlement of dues upto the period of 30th June 1998.

The Economic Feasibility of Milk Vending

Most of the members who rear the milch animals own land where they grow hybrid grass in a small plot or along the bunds of irrigation channel. Further their main crop is at present creeper vegetables and so they have sufficient green leaves, cut down while pruning. Apart from these, they have to purchase paddy husk and concentrated feed, amounting Rs. 15 per day. Those who do not own land have to purchase grass bundle worth of Rs. 10 per day. Altogether the total feeding cost is Rs. 25 per milch animal. Almost all animals are cross-breed and the milk yielding is average 8 litres per day.

The cost is Rs.8 per litre and so the total selling cost is Rs. 8 X 8 = Rs. 64. The feeding expenses is only Rs. 25. From a milching cow on an average Rs. 40 can be earned if the member properly look after the animal. It is argued that the time spared for grazing and the manual labour in maintaining the animal is calculated the profit is not sufficient. But the villagers feel that it is a regular income, available every month which are very much useful to the landless families whereas it augment the income of land holders as the farmers are now realising the importance of natural manure, composite manure for their agricultural crops like vegetable creepers, chilly and onion etc. So the milk vending is now adopted by about three hundred families of Karisalpatti village.

It was told that the enriched and concentrated feed supplied by Aavin was not in good quality and so the society discontinued the purchase of feed from Aavin and advised the members about proper feeding and veterinary care which determine the quality of milk. Thus they prepare feed on their own as they know the device.

Milk Test

To ensure the quality of the procured milk, the society purchased a milk tester at the cost of Rs. 30,000. The secretary informed that in spite of this precaution, sometime, the district society used to deduct 10 or 15 litres by complaining that milk was substandard quality. This lose had to be met out by the local society not by the members.

The Profit earned by the Society

During 1990, the society has earned about Rs. 60,000 to Rs. 70,000 per year. But last three years it was in loss. This year there is a change, the society has earned a profit of Rs. 22,000. Now the average per month procurement is about 600 to 700 litres and if this position is maintained, the society may get a profit of Rs. 1 lakhs per year. The reason for unsteady supply of milk by the producers is that the difference in the margin between the procuring cost of co-operative society and the private vendor. The private vendors purchase the milk at the rate of Rs.10.50 per litre.

Veterinary Care

At present the members of the society avail the facilities of veterinary care at the government veterinary hospital which is available at the village itself. The artificial insemination service is the important facility for which Rs. 10 to 12 is fixed. The members have to depend on the government doctor's time and so they requested the local society to make an alternative arrangement for the artificial insemination and members agreed to pay for it. With the help of the district society, the Karisalpatti society sent a young man of the local area for a training in artificial insemination. The training is for a period of one month and the expenditure towards this training and his one month salary is met by the local society and Rs.750 is shared by the district society towards the total cost. After the training, the society is planned to arrange artificial insemination to the milch animals. It will be more useful to the members.

The Overall Expenses of the Society

Towards the salary of the personnel of society, replacement of milk can, purchase of stationery and record books, electricity charges, maintenance of building and board meeting expenses, the society has to spend about Rs. 90,000.

If the procurement is on an average of 600 litres per day margin at 0.70 per litre for 12 months, the society may earn a profit of Rs. 1.5 lakh. After meeting out the administrative expenses of Rs. 90,000 to Rs.1 lakh per year, the profit Rs. 50,000 will be utilized for providing dividend to the members.

The Secret of Sustainability

The dedicated secretary, committed vendors, production of quality milk, sustainable milk production through proper feeding and veterinary care by the members, along with the elected board's proper administration, the milk producers co-operative society of Karisalpatti is marching ahead. The traditional community leadership among the Vanniar Christian and the church have also contributed further to encourage rearing of milch animals. And the last not the least, the attitudinal transformation of villagers who once engaged in anti-social activities felt a moderately comfortable life in agriculture and animal husbandry.

Innovative Sanitation Arrangement in Karisalpatti

The dwelling area in Karisalpatti has been arranged in an orderly way two sides of the main road which connects the Dindigul town in the east and Kannivadi in the west. The streets are situated in the southern and northern sides of the road. The following toposketch can explain the area.

The eastern side of the road is a high level and so the sewage and rainy water has to pass down to the main road, damaging the main black top road and it has been water logged continuously during the rainy season create unhealthy environment always. Proper drainage provisions are the felt needs of the people in Karisalpatti village. The conventional pattern of drainage is done by stone rubbles masonry construction, using cement is a costly one. Moreover the silt cannot be properly removed from the drainage. The tendency of people with regard to utilization of drainage is an unhealthy one. They dump all waste in the drainage and within a short span of time the drainage is filled up, not useful to drain out sewage water or rain water. Moreover the absorbing capacity of the soil is also poor since it is a marshy land.

The Innovation

The president of Karisalpatti who is a young and energetic personality stormed his brain and found an innovative idea to the problem of drainage. He minutely understood the causes which make the conventional system fail and so he tried to prevent those hurdles, by adopting an innovative system in sanitation.

Its significance lies in the pattern – a collection pot in each house which receives all sewage water and disposals from the house through a inlet arrangement. This collection pot has been connected to a PVC outlet pipe line, which take out the sewage water only leaving the other solid disposal at the collection pot itself as the outlet arrangement at the collection pot is filled with a mesh.

As an experiment, the president had a trial on this innovative sanitation system in one street. The sewage waters come out from the houses situated along the two sides of the street is allowed to come to a collection pot fixed at the side of the main road which used to get damage and where the water has been logged always. Then 3" PVC pipe of 60 metre length was laid down below the ground across the road, upto a common tank situated the other side of the main road.

The sewage water collected in the collection pot flow through the mesh to the PVC pipe line and reach the common tank. For the proper utilization of the water, the president had done another innovative exercise at the tank bund. The bund site is levelled up with enriched soil. Saplings of tamarind, silk cotton, bamboo, neem, poovarasu and vagai are planted in successive rows. The left out area is taken up for floriculture. Now the sewage water of four streets, of 200 houses, is irrigating 200 tree saplings and flower plants. The president auctioned the flower plants for Rs. 3000 for a period of 3 months and within a year there will be three season for a particular flower crop. The overall expenses for this experiment is about Rs. 5000 whereas the value of uncured tank is now enhanced along with an annual income from floriculture, through the tree saplings is grown up.

Innovative Sanitation for the whole Village

The president had submitted the report of this innovative sanitation system to the district collector and to the chief minister. He communicated with all officials tirelessly. And at last he received a communication from the district collector instructing the panchayat union Commissioner of Reddiarchathiram in which jurisdiction the Karisalpatti village falls, to visit and prepare a draft proposal with estimate for the innovative sanitation system covering the whole village.

Cost Effective and Efficient System

The president argued that the construction cost of the conventional drainage system is very high and not sustainably maintained whereas the innovative system is very cheap, involving every user in keeping up the sanitation. To avoid spreading of any flies or mosquitoes, the collection pot has a cover/lid easily handled by every user and any blockade of solid waste or soil can also be removed by the user.

The construction cost per metre for conventional drainage is not affordable to the panchayat as it is between Rs.300 to Rs.400 whereas the innovative system evolved by the president of Karisalpatti is Rs.100. Hence the government machinery is now coming forward to consider the proposal submitted by the president.

Conclusion

It is reported by the majority of the people that this model can be replicated to their street also. There is a counter argument from some of the people. The argument is that the sewage water is led into the public tank which is used for cattle. They fear that the cattle will be affected due to the consumption of this waste water from the tank. At present the access is prevented by fencing. Hence this problem does not arise. But their feeling is respected by the president and he assured them that the sewage water of all streets would be connected and flushed out from the village to a separate place and so the tank may be available for cattle.

Peoples' Observation about Karisalpatti Gram Panchayat

The people of the Karisalpatti village felt that change is essential for the development of the villages. They also stated that during the past fifteen years the village has experienced many changes and hence there is considerable development of the village in many aspects.

Starting of a Co-operative Milk Society: Earlier the village people were unaware of the importance and use of co-operative movement. But due to the efforts taken by the well informed individuals, a co-operative milk society was started. This helped a number of families to get loan from the banks at a lower rate of interest and also with subsidy to purchase milch animals. Further the milk society procured the milk from the members of the society at reasonable rates. This induced a large number of individuals to become members and to get milch animals. This activity helped them (i) in creating assets for the family, and (ii) in getting regular income which reduced the economic burden of the family.

Change in Agricultural Products: The farmers of this village were cultivating only millets and grains which gave them only a marginal income. The introduction of enough transport facilities to this village helped the people to visit their nearby towns and to know about the high cost of vegetables. Also they understood the methods of cultivation of vegetables. As a result, the farmers started shifting their cultivation to vegetables which gave them a good profit. They make use of mini-lorries to transport the cultivated vegetables to the towns. It is to be noted that this farmers are united together and used mini-lorries to transport the vegetables at a cheaper transport cost even to distant places like Chennai.

The Role of Local Church: The services of the priest of the local church Fr. M.Gabriel need to be mentioned here. He used to visit all the houses everyday discuss with them about their family background, source of income and other related matters. During such visits he used to suggest ways and means to solve their family problems. Thus the timely guidance of the priest has helped the village people to develop themselves both socially and economically.

The Services of the Sisters: The sisters of the local church organised the local mahalir mandram and the youth club. In such meetings, the sisters provide moral, health and social education to the members. In these meetings the people of all the caste groups irrespective of their religion participated. The repeated and human approach of the sisters have helped the youth to leave their bad habits. For example, Mr.Velmurugan belonging to the Hindu religion was a regular smoker. In spite of the advises and requests by his parents and friends he could not leave that habit. One day the sister went to his house, talked to him about the origin of smoking, its implications in family and social life. Her positive approach by way of explaining him the evils of smoking struck his mind and gradually he left the habit of smoking. Likewise many individuals in the village have given up many bad habits.

Community Control: The village community has a control over the habits of the people. The village community tries to maintain the values and customs of this village. The committee has a control over the individuals by preventing them from doing any illegal or anti-social activities. If any member of the community or village commits even a small mistake, the committee punishes him with a minimum fine of Rs. 5000. This forces the members to be more loyal and sincere.

Eradication of Alcoholism: This village has no arrack sellers. This means nobody is permitted to sell either arrack or liquor in this village. If anybody of this village is seen in drunken mood, the Father of the church lodges a complaint with the police and he is taken to the police station. Further sometimes back two members of this village died due to over drinking. This also has an influence in preventing alcoholism. Church is playing a vital role in eradicating this evil practice of drinking alcohol.

Karisalpatti Gram Sabha Meeting

People of Karisalpatti are virtually under the control of the traditional panchayat, the new panchayati leader has to adjust with the traditional panchayat leaders. As harmony persists with the intervention of the church, without any hesitation the gram panchayat president calls Gram Sabha. He involves all the leaders of the communities. He convened the Gram Sabha meeting on 15th August 1998.

The following points have been raised during the Gram Sabha meeting held at Community Hall of Karisalpatti village.

* The space at funeral site belonging to Adi-Dravida community is not sufficient. Hence additional place has to be earmarked for funeral.
* The streets are not properly maintained and they should be maintained.
* The irrigational canal scheme announced by the government is not properly planned. It will not benefit Karisalpatti village farmers. Hence panchayat must organise village farmers and draft new and revised scheme which has to be submitted to the government.
* Contract works can be taken jointly by those who are in village. And the quality of works carried out through contract have to be

properly monitored.

* The agricultural women labourer is getting Rs. 25 as wage for a day. It has to be enhanced to Rs. 30 or Rs. 35.
* When important events are being telecasted in TV, the TV operator does not keep on the TV. After a particular time he switches off the TV. Events like cricket is demanded by youth. Hence TV operator has to be instructed to keep the TV on during those programmes.
* Facilities at funeral ground have to be improved by maintaining approach road and providing a shed.
* Electricity supply to all dwelling units has to be given.
* Transporting facilities has to be provided adequately.
* Public telephone facilities is not available at the post office. This has to be looked into by the panchayats.
* Sodium vapour lamp at bazar and main road junction in the village has to be installed.
* There is no rice mill for the villagers and hence some one must come forward to start.
* In the high school, the teachers compelled the students to enlist themselves for a tour. Those who failed to join were not promoted. Panchayat must look into this problem.
* At Kannivadi Government Hospital, some of the hospital staff demand money for treatment. This practice has to be stopped.
* One retired teacher of that locality, has come forward voluntarily to take tuition for the students.
* Bribe in public service institutions has to be checked by the panchayat.
* Pathway lead to funeral ground has to be widened.
* The western side tank has to be desilted.
* Sanitation facilities to all streets should be provided.
* Sweeper services has to be streamlined. They should be instructed to perform their duties perfectly.
* The village boundary has to be earmarked and a name board has to be fixed.
* The MLA fund has to be sought and utilized for development activities.
* The poor in backward community must be provided with housing scheme.
* Library facility is to be provided.
* Ration card distribution for widow/widower is not properly done. They are to be streamlined.
* In some streets, a few street lights are not functioning and they are to

be repaired.

* The arrival and services of the health assistant is not known to public.
* Once in a year the students of Gandhigram must be requested to come and camp at Karisalpatti and must organise cultural programmes, conduct survey on our village.
* The E.B. post and line is not properly planned. At some places the line is very low and disturbing.
* At lamp posts some people tie their cattles.
* Educational standard of school students has to be improved.
* Financial assistance for agriculture has to be arranged.
* The youth power and talent must be properly utilized by the panchayat. They are ready to offer their services to panchayat in its village development activities.
* The encroachment at Kannaikkan Kulam has to be removed.
* The other two common tanks is filled with solid waste and domestic waste in addition to encroachment on them. This has to be dealt with.
* One participant, a farmer is ready to contribute to the panchayat Rs. 3000 if the panchayat is coming forward to do necessary initiatives for digging a new tank and augment rain water harvest for irrigation.

The women who attended Gram Sabha meeting is very limited in number. They did not directly speak. They expressed their feelings through other male member and requested toilet facilities and village industries.

Karisalpatti Village Panchayat
Details of Expenditure (Period from 3/97 to 3/98)

			Rs.
1.	Salary	:	26,860
2.	TA	:	8,540
3.	Stationary and records	:	1,734
4.	Streets maintenance	:	14,414
5.	Panchayat building maintenance	:	1,822
6.	Power pump maintenance	:	12,475
7.	O.H.T., G&R and pipe line maintenance	:	11,855
8.	Street lights	:	879
9.	TV/Radio repair	:	5,105
10.	Sanitation	:	476

11.	Tank maintenance	:	3,252
12.	Road/Small bridge maintenance	:	500
13.	Miscellaneous	:	568
14.	Pipe	:	1,875
	Total	:	***89,476***

These details were read at the Gram Sabha meeting.

Details of Receipt during the period of 1997/98

1.	Finance commission allocation in 4 quarters	:	19,000
2.	Earmarked fund	:	12,000
3.	J.V.V.T. fund	:	1,05,000
4.	H. Tax collection	:	6,900
5.	Professional tax collection	:	9,900
6.	Income from common property resources (Floriculture & Tree)	:	6,400
7.	Contribution received from Kasavanampatti towards the cost of electricity for comprehensive water supply scheme benefiting two village panchayats	:	17,435
	Total	:	***1,71,635***

CASE ANALYSIS

B. VERIAPPUR GRAM PANCHAYAT

Veriappur village panchayat is coming under the jurisdiction of Oddanchatram panchayat union. It has the following hamlets : 1. Veriappur, 2. Kalipalayam, 3. Annamalai Puthur, 4. Velliagoundamputhur, 5. Nagappanpatti, 6. Munur, 7. Uchimahalipuram, 8. Navamarathupatti, 9. Gowandappa Gowndan Valasu, 10. Sundaripalayam, 11. Ponkaliamman Puthur. Total population is 4300 and total number of voters is 2815.

Village Community

Majority of the people belong to Gongu Gownder, next come the SC community. Naidu, Asari, Chettiar are the other castes who are in minority.

Occupation

Agriculture is the main occupation and animal husbandry especially sheep rearing is the supplementary occupation. The nearby town Oddanchatram is the important market for agricultural products. Hence the village farmers transport their commodities to Oddanchatram and earn a lot through vegetable cultivation.

Crops

Onion, tobacco, betroot, carrot, cabbage, brinjal, chilly, jowar are the crops. As the scope for regular transportation is more, most of the farmers possess tyre carts. It is told that there is about eighty tyre carts and six tractors are in the village.

Most of the land is owned by Goundars. About 10 to 15 families of SC community are owning land. In addition to this economic disparity, there is the traditional mentality of dominating the SC community by the majority caste Hindus. Hence the community relationship is not so good. It is told that the people from SC community are taking steps to strengthen their unity with the help of Ambedkar movement. The NGOs namely world vision and DMSS are also supporting them and helping in income generation activities for SC community organisations.

The infrastructure facilities of Veriappur

Overhead tank	:	4
GLR	:	1
Public tap	:	25
Hand pump	:	11
Street light	:	105
Health sub-centre	:	1 (run by Ambilikai Hospital)
Noon meal centre	:	3
Primary school	:	3
Tank	:	3 (two tanks are at the extend of 5 acre, one is 2 acre)

There are 18 coconut trees on the banks of one tank at Munur. But no proper yield out of these trees. There are four community wells but not in use.

Village Panchayat

There are nine members in Veriappur village panchayat excluding the president. Out of nine four belong to SC community and the rest are belonging to Goundar community.

		Men	Women
Total member	9	6	3
Total SC member	4	2	2

It is told that the SC women members are not showing any interest during the panchayat meeting. Whereas the BC woman is actively participating in the deliberations.

Panchayat Meeting

Since the sworn in ceremony of new panchayat council held on 25th September, 1997, they have conducted sixteen meetings in which ninety one resolutions have been passed. The panchayat met four times for emergency meeting. Apart from regular discussion on development issues panchayat council has discussed about the coalition government, and sandalwood smuggler's issue. Requisition for upgrading the veterinary centre, separate ration shop, eviction of encroachment at the community cultural programme site are also among the resolutions of the village panchayat.

Common Property Resources Utilization

At Ramachatiram tank, about 180 Nattukaruvel trees have to be cleared as it is about 15 years old. The village panchayat requested the Forest Department to grant permission to cut down the trees. But the Forest Department has not yet issued order. In the mean time the panchayat is not able to provide a watcher to protect and so some anti-social elements have cut down some of the trees. The village panchayat submitted a proposal for augmenting water sources through percolation pond construction. Due to the difference of opinion between the president and the ex-union chairman who belongs to D.M.K. party, the Oddanchatram union did not consider the proposal of Veriappur panchayat.

Village Panchayat Election

The president Sri. Periasamy belongs to BJP. He had a tough competition during the election. There were two candidates contested against him from the DMK and the TMC. The actual competition was with the former president who was candidate of the DMK party. The former president had served as president continuously since 1958. He is a landlord, owning about 50 acres of land. His political background is also very strong. His daughter is married to the son of former Minister Sri.Thangapandian of the DMK. The former president's sons are also in good position. One is serving as Superintendent of Police and the other one is Joint Registrar of Co-operatives in the Government of Tamil Nadu.

In general the people from SC community as well as the lower economic group among Goundars do not support the authoritative activities of the former president. Moreover they felt that a new leadership has to emerge at least at the village panchayat level. Hence they requested the respondent, Sri. Periasamy to contest in the election. When he refused, the SC community members expressed that they would boycott the election. And hence the respondent contested in the election. The respondent earned a name in the community. He used to help SC community to avail the government facilities. He helped them to purchase site for their colony.

About ten years back, he was compelled to lead the youth wing of Gongu Vellala Goundar. But he refused to give importance to caste. He was so helpful to all who approached him. He allows people to fetch water from his well during the summer season. There was only one main issue, raised during the panchayat election *i.e.,* replacement of traditional leadership.

In the tough competition, he won the election with a margin of 47 votes over his opponent. The respondent explained that the people supported him and at the same time they felt insecure as the former president's son is a high level police officer.

The Problem of Non-performance of the School Headmaster

At the primary school of Veriappur there are only two teachers and among them one is the headmaster. He is continuously serving for 13 years at the same school. He is not a resident of Veriappur. He usually comes late, not showing interest in teaching, and not even encouraged the other teacher to work. His service irregularities were voiced out by the people of Veriappur but there was no proper action against him.

The respondent realised the importance of education and so he approached the headmaster and properly explained to him about the need of the village. The headmaster did not mind his questions. And so a resolution was passed in the village panchayat meeting and the same was forwarded to the officials of the education department. The delegation of people met the D.E.O. and explained the problem. An enquiry was conducted by Dy. Inspector of schools and transfer of the service of headmaster was recommended by the enquiry officer.

The former president who openly supported the headmaster tried his level best to stop the proceedings against the headmaster with the help of his political higher ups. But the people of Veriappur stood unitedly and told the authorities that they will resort to launch an agitation if the problem is not settled. At last the headmaster was transferred to a school run by Muslim community in which he has to serve on Sundays also as Sundays are declared as working day whereas Fridays are declared as holidays in this school.

The former president took this incident as a damaging one against his reputation and his political leadership. And so he is always putting hurdles against the activities of the president of village panchayat.

The Issue of Eviction of Encroachment

At Veriappur, near the primary school, there is a common site, under the usage of village community for their community celebration. The community has a stage for staging drama or any other programmes. At the side of the site, there are seven families who encroached over this common property and construct semi-tiled huts. The village panchayat proposed to vacate all encroachments come up at community sites. A staff of E.B., who is not a local man, but belonging to Goundar community and hence the local people accepted him when he built a small hut at the disputed site. Now he extends further, creating disturbance in the passage to primary school. When the village panchayat passed resolution and requested the revenue authorities to help in evicting the encroachment, the former president protected the wiremen. Moreover he influenced the authorities through his party higher-ups MLAs and minister.

When the enquiry is delayed, the president mobilised people of all hamlets of Veriappur village panchayat, staged a demonstration cum fasting in front of the taluk office. The people showed their unity irrespective of caste and hamlets. The Tehsildar assured to take necessary action. But a communication was sent by the Tehsildar mentioning that the accused put a temporary hut as he proposed repair work at his main house and so the encroachment would be cleared within one month.

In the meantime, the president and the village people met the district collector and explained their problem. He also assured to deal with it as early as possible. But after a period of one month another communication is sent by the Tehsildar mentioning that the panchayat is empowered to evict the encroachment and so the panchayat must take necessary steps to evict the accused. This delay and play of revenue authorities created a tension in the village. The ruling party DMK and local higher-ups unnecessarily interfered in this affairs of village panchayat administration and the district authorities felt it as a headache only but not ready to facilitate the village panchayat administration.

The panchayat president decided to contact the village people and a delegation of the village people would meet the district Collector, police officials and request them to help the panchayat in evicting the encroachment of the government servant.

The Issue of Lack of Co-ordination between the Village Panchayat and the Panchayat Union

The panchayat union of Oddanchatram constructed one building at Munur from the allocation of union general fund. This was due to the pressure of ex-president who tried to earn a goodwill from the villages and at the same time to create dispute between Ponkaliamman Puthur and Munur villages as both of them get water from one OHT. Both the hamlets are receiving water from one OHT, having the capacity of 30,000 litres and there is no water scarcity in these two hamlets.

In the meantime an additional borewell and fixing of motor pump from union fund is not at all necessary. It will be an additional burden on the current bill now itself and it is about Rs.12,000 for two month period. The proposal for a sustainable water source management and laying of a new pipe line for a distance of 1 km, by the panchayat was not seriously considered by the union or district panchayat.

The president took much effort to get a positive sign from the two NGOs, namely SWASTIC and WORLD VISION for the development activities by their financial assistance. The Block officials are not giving any serious thought towards the request of Gram Panchayat but allocates fund for many activities which are not necessary. And while sanctioning work panchayats are not consulted in spite of the fact that the works have to be handed over to the village panchayat as only village panchayat has the power to manage and maintain the water supply sources and constructions. Block and District Panchayats are allocating money for village panchayat to carry out certain activities without knowing whether the activities are relevant or not. Simply because of the fact that they have money, they have allocated to various panchayats and by which they are wasting the money.

The president decided to take this issue to the knowledge of higher authorities through newspaper and planned to meet the MLA and requesting him to reconsider the original proposal of village panchayat by which the goodwill shown by the NGOs would be useful for a sustainable water source.

The Personal life of the respondent

He is a farmer owning ten acre of land. Out of 3 irrigation wells, 2 wells are jointly owned by others along with him. He is a good farmer, scientifically enriching his farm through farmyard manure. His wife is looking after 50 sheeps as well as helping in farming. They have five milch animals also.

The respondent informed that he is earning a lot of profit in agriculture as he maintains crop rotation and composite manuring. The main crop is onion, tomato, groundnut. He opined that he wished to lead a simple life but doing yeoman services to the people. He has three daughters and all are studying in the school in his native town.

Income and Expenditure Account of Veriappur Village Panchayat 1997-98

Income		*Expenditure*	
President Advance	13,600.00	Clerk wages	14,850.00
Commissioner	4,607.00	Sweeper	2,880.00
State Finance Commission Receipt	1,05,207.00	OHT operator	4,080.00
		TA	5,200.00
House tax	10,391.40	EB	12,472.00
Library tax	1,086.80	EB material	23,067.00
Professional tax	8,774.00	Water supply	33,436.00
		Repair/Maintenance	8,883.00
		Cremation subsidy	800.00
		Bank loan	472.00
		Establishment	
		EB repairing bulb	1,200.00
		Clearance of advance to print	13,500.00
		Newspaper subscription	500.00
		Stationery	275.00
		Advertisement	750.00
		Health	420.00
		Donations	500.00
	1,43,684.20		***1,29,985.00***

5

EMPOWERING ELECTED WOMEN REPRESENTATIVES

Section I

PROBLEMS AND PROSPECTS

Introduction

One-third reservation of seats for women in Local Bodies through the Constitutional amendments had opened a channel in the power structure for women from different strata of the society both vertically and horizontally, to occupy the legitimate space. The new entrants are large in number and they have definite roles, however insignificant in terms of their capacity they are, to play in the given structure. The inherent impediments and hurdles associated with the women in Indian society in the political and economic structure are common to the elected women leaders also. Yet, they are in position and performing their role and discharging their responsibilities. How do they perform their role? How are they different from the men leaders? What are the problems they are confronting? How do they manage these problems in their institutions? are the real issues and problems one has to address.

As a student of history and politics, I could not mention from my memory worthwhile literature in the area of women and politics and equally on women studies in history. Till the enactment of the 73rd and the 74th Constitutional Amendment Acts, Academics in Political Science were not sure and specific about the role to be played by the women in the process of the development of the society in general and the development of women in particular. Political Scientists hardly find any role for the women in the political process of the society. Indian Council of Social Science Research had undertaken a major review of studies conducted in India on different areas of polity. I am unable to find a chapter on Women and Politics as I could see on Caste and Politics, Students and Politics and SC/ST and Politics. So this is the status of the studies on women in politics in India. 73rd and 74th Amendments to the Constitution of India prompted the academics to think of the role to be played by the women leaders in the political process at the grassroots level.

Empowering women is a loaded concept which connotes different meanings to different individuals. To me empowerment of women refers to the process by which women are acquiring due recognition as men, to participate in the development process of the society through the political institutions as a partner with human dignity. The barriers which had been very active in the process of development of women have to be removed and for which interventions are imperatives at different levels. Reservation of seats in the local bodies is one of the steps in this direction and this is not the only way to ensure the participation of women in the development process. It has to go a long way in the process of development in society.

The reservation of seats for women has been looked at from many perspectives. One basic question normally addressed in this context is the objectives kept in the minds of the framers of the 73rd and 74th amendments to the Constitution of India, while providing 33.3% of reservation of seats to women. Secondly, the women leaders who are in local bodies should have a clear perception about the objectives of the reservation of seats for women in local bodies. There are other notions on the same issue perceived by the people and the functionaries who are working with the women leaders at the grassroots level. One could see the incongruity and ambiguity in perceiving the role properly.

There is a second aspect, the general perception about the role to be performed by the women leaders as the perceptions are being guided by the historical notion of women folk and their responsibilities and capabilities. This provision of seats in the local bodies makes the women as well as the society to move out from the traditional perception track. This process has been initiated already. But in reality, despite several weaknesses, the elected women leaders are in position and discharging the earmarked responsibilities with varying degree of success. This study makes an attempt to locate the problems encountered by the women leaders and to find out the ways and means to facilitate the women leaders to discharge their role and function effectively in their domain.

Environmental Setting

It is to be noted here that even for the defeat of the 64th Amendment Bill a representative from Tamil Nadu was responsible. Moreover while passing the 73rd Constitutional Amendment Bill, it was only two political parties in the whole country which opposed the Bill — and they are from Tamil Nadu. It is an irony that these two political parties never concurred on any issue so far but they had full argument on one issue namely giving power to panchayats. The political parties are both the AIADMK and the DMK. Both parties are known for anti-panchayats and the institutions are burried fathom deep only during their periods. For the success of the process of decentralisation of power, the political leaders who are managing the affairs of the province should have a political will. Moreover, to reflect the spirit of the Constitutional Amendment a well conceptualised regional Act, along with rules and manuals in a simplified form, a positive and co-operative bureaucracy to work with the elected leaders, capacitated local body leaders and the high level cognition of the people about the new dispensation are essential and imperative for the smooth functioning of local bodies and the better performance of the grassroot level institutions. In the context of the above indicated factors being absolutely absent, one can imagine what would be the conditions prevailing for the functioning of the local bodies.

Women leaders cannot be treated as one entity. Women leaders are drawn from different strata of the society and the problems associated with women empowerment vary from one segment to another. In Tamil Nadu, a sizeable number of subalterns are drawn. Intensity of intervention varies from one group to another. What we find in this small write up is the problems and perspectives of the women leaders who have been in the continuous struggle in establishing their position as leaders in the local body institutions. It cannot be generalized but the observations would indicate the trend of women leadership position in the local body institutions.

Classification of Women Leaders

Never in the political history of Tamil Nadu that the institutions of Governance had such massive number of women in position as what we have been seeing in local bodies at present. All the women leaders who are in position have not volunteered themselves to contest in the election. It is a well known fact that they are driven to these position by an array of organisations, individuals and institutions. But after assuming office women leaders have exhibited their distinctions in terms of their perception, behaviour and performance. Their distinct functions are the result of a number of factors. Before going into the details of the substantive issue of their perception, behaviour and performance we have to classify the category of leaders.

Women leaders are propelled by the male members of their family, oriented by the NGOs for this specific task, oriented by the party, motivated by the community, and sponsored by their husbands with the support of the political party.

Of the five categories, 65% of the leaders belong to the last category. Third and fourth category forms the next largest group around 20%. The other two are having the minimum numbers — 15%. The second and the third group are not having more number of leaders yet their activities are drawing the attention of the people as they have support base for their activities. All the other groups are having a wide variety of problems to be tackled to discharge their role and responsibilities. This classification is not exhaustive but it is done on the basis of experience gained in the training conducted for women leaders at various levels in Gandhigram Rural Institute (It is a deemed university recognised by the Government of Tamil Nadu as nodal centre for training Local Body leaders) sponsored by various funding agencies. The details of the training programme are given in Table 5.1.

Table 5.1 : Elected Women Representatives Trained in Gandhigram

S. No.	Trainee Category	Sponsoring Agency	No. of leaders trained
1.	Gram Panchayati Presidents Block Panchayati Presidents District Panchayati Presidents and ward members of Dharmapuri & Dindigul Districts	Population Foundation of India	0750
2.	Gram Panchayati Presidents and Vice-Presidents Villupuram & Cuddalore Districts	DANIDA	0245
3.	Village Panchayati Presidents of Dindigul, Sivaganga, Madurai, Ramnad districts	CAPART	0425
4.	Village Panchayati Presidents of Theni, Thiruvarur, Salem Namakkal, Virudhunagar Dharmapuri	Social Welfare Board	0825
5.	Chairperson of Town Panchayats Municipalities of Sixteen Districts	Government of Tamil Nadu	2150
		Total	4395

Source : Compiled from the Reports on Training.

Methodology

The data are collected from the leaders who have undergone training in Gandhigram Rural Institute sponsored by various funding agencies. Totally, 4395 women leaders in different tiers and different capacities had been drawn from both rural and urban local bodies. Data have been generated not through interview schedule but through Group discussion arranged in the training programme itself. With the objective of making policy advocacy, focus had been given in their discussion on the vital issues affecting their activities, in the groups. Focus group discussions had been arranged out of the training hours while the leaders were in the campus for a specific period as the training programmes were residential in nature.

Entry into Positions

By and large the performance of the leaders are conditioned by a variety of factors, of which their mode of recruitment is a key factor. As per their perception and understanding they are elevated to position through election on the basis of the caste, party affiliation, family, organisational affiliation, community, peer group, money, own reputation and past services rendered to the community. No single factor worked in an isolation. A combination of factors worked in the process of their elevation to the position. The same factors are responsible for their performance also. The leaders have been oriented by the peer group leaders, family members, community leaders and their husbands and they have to go by the advise of the people who had been responsible for their elevation to these positions through election. NGOs and cadre political parties who have sponsored the candidates have given proper orientation to the women leaders. Certain groups of women leaders who have undergone training have got confusion over their role and responsibility as they are under the control of some extraneous forces. Because of the continuous orientation and capacity building exercise, 40 per cent of the women leaders have started moving out from the clutches of others to their own domain without much noise, through a variety of devices. Yet 60 per cent of the leaders are still struggling in their position due to lack of managerial skill.

Problems Faced

Normally to overcome the problems in discharging the role and functions of the leaders in the Local Bodies, the leader's capacity has to be enhanced. By enhancing the capacity, institutions can be managed effectively. Government has not taken any serious step in the first three years to enhance the capacity of the leaders through the training programme. It took near by three years to impress upon the government about the importance of training. Now the government has taken effort to conduct the capacity building exercise with the financial support of UNICEF, but the leaders have come to the final phase of their tenure.

After elections, the women leaders have entered into the offices without any orientation. The moment the leaders peeped into the offices, the officials have given orientation to the leaders on 'do's' and 'dont's' by reading out some of the provisions of the Tamil Nadu Panchayati Act. This kind of orientation has crippled the initiative of the leaders. Nonetheless steps had been taken by Gandhigram Rural Institute and a number of NGOs to conduct capacity building exercise with the financial support of various funding agencies.

Generally it is a complaint made by 92 per cent of the women leaders that the officials are not co-operating with elected leaders by providing necessary information in time to enable them to perform their functions effectively. Further the leaders who are weak in terms of their capacity are being illtreated and humiliated. The Dalit leaders are not even provided with a chair to sit in front of a clerk in the office. Very rarely one would find officials treating the Dalit leaders with dignity. When fear psychosis is created in the minds of Dalit women leaders in the beginning itself, the leaders never think of meeting the higher officials at the district level during the whole period of their tenure. The Dalit women leaders who are oriented in their issues by the Dalit organisations or NGOs or some political parties are literally in struggle with officials. Officials who had performed the role in the same office without any interference in the absence of panchayat leaders now feel somebody has come and they have taken up the mantle and for them the officials are made accountable. This new system has pushed them from the stage of a decision maker to an executive officer carrying out the decisions of the elected body. Hence their reactions towards the leaders are always negative.

The officials tried their level best to establish their control over the leaders by making use of the ignorance of the leaders. It is a pity that the officials are not properly oriented to new situation. Even in the model states for decentralization of power of the state governments have struggled to mend their officials to cope up with the requirements of the local bodies. It is obvious from the experiences of Kerala and West Bengal. In Tamil Nadu our bureaucracy is committed to party in power. More particularly officials at lower level are corrupt in their thinking and action for the past three decades and their disease had afflicted the higher officials also. Against this background the local body women leaders are functioning. In the absence of power to decide, allocate resources and to plan for meeting the requirements of the local populace the officials perpetuate their hegemony over the leaders. Men leaders are oriented themselves to buckle with the officials and women leaders are not able to do so.

The segments which had supported the women candidates in the election, have not extended their support to the same leaders for their functioning. The leaders who have not indicated a signal that they are working for the people who have caste their votes in the election in favour of them can not get the support of the people of the same segments. Even their party leaders at the grassroot level are not extending their helping hands towards their activities in the panchayats. In the same way, the caste leaders and family members exert pressure on the leaders to yield to their pressures. The caste leaders feel that the panchayat leaders are relying on the support base of the caste. Hence they also exert pressure on them. Husbands are an yet another problem to the elected women leaders. A large number of women leaders have been recruited to these position by the influence of their husbands in the party. When a seat is reserved for women, the male aspirant candidate seeks permission from the party to field his wife for the post. Such is the way most of the women leaders have been recruited.

The male members have fielded the women for leadership position with the thinking that the administration could be controlled by them. Even after the election the husbands have tried their level best to control over the administration but in vain as the government have instructed the officers to check this kind of practice. Moreover wherever the husbands are establishing the administrative control over the panchayats, people have started questioning the capacity of the women presidents in managing the affairs of the panchayats. Over a period of time, the women leaders have oriented themselves by way of participating in the training programme conducted by various organisations, to manage their affairs on their own but they are not in a position to communicate this message to their husbands. Even after three years, the male members of the women leaders family have not changed their perception about the competency and capacity of the women leaders. Still they feel that the women leaders are not having the needed capacity to manage their affairs. Hence they make themselves ready for accompanying the women leaders.

Managerial skill is an imperative for the leaders to manage the personnel and the resources well within the established frameworks of administration. Here the women leaders lack that capacity. In all fora, they have indicated the problem but yet decisions are not on the sight. Yet another problem they face in local bodies is the lack of communication skill. Tamil Nadu politics is known for inflammatory speeches. Political parties are having a separate wing of public speakers. The local body leaders have to share the dais with MLAs and MPs and officials in public functions. Of them, the women leaders from local bodies used to cut a sorry figure as they are not able to communicate their ideas in an effective way as done by the MLAs and MPs. Further, they need a communication skill to mobilise the people and to manage them in Gram Sabha meetings and other public meetings. Nobody gives such orientation to them in the art of effective communication.

By providing this opportunity to women to work in the local bodies as leaders, their workload has been increased enormously both in their houses and offices. Women leaders hailing from upper middle class family have been to some extent relieved of their duties at home as necessary arrangements have been made in the home to look after the affairs which had been looked after by the women leaders before they were elected to positions in local bodies. But women hailing from poor families are facing a number of problems. Their workload has been increased, panchayats are not paying anything to the leaders as salary even after handing over a variety of responsibilities to them on par with a full time officer. In some of the places we find poor men and women assumed responsibilities and discharged their role and function. Poor labourers cannot afford to loose their daily wage by attending the panchayat works. It is natural on the part of the woman leader who is a wage earner to handover responsibility to some one else and performing her duties to the family.

Panchayat leaders at the Gram Panchayati level have to maintain thirty one forms and four accounts. Is it possible for an uneducated woman to maintain all the thirty one forms properly as per the rules and procedures. Even the clerks are finding it very difficult to maintain the same. Most of the women leaders are the victims of the accounting procedure adopted in local body administration in Tamil Nadu. This is a major area one has to concentrate as to how the women leaders could be saved from this ordeal. It is a general problem for all the leaders but it is more specific for women leaders. In the age of information, information flow is stuck below the district level. Every office is instructed to have "peoples charter" and they have to be circulated among the people and their leaders. But now all those documents are kept in the respective offices without circulating them to the people. Officials are not willing to share this information with elected leaders.

Normally women would be sensitive towards women issues and that was the expectation of the leaders who justified the one-third reservation of seats for women in local bodies. But in reality, women leaders are brought and oriented in such a fashion not to be sensitive towards women issues. Women leaders who have been trained properly are sensitive towards the women issues. They are periodically sensitised by the NGOs.

It is true that the administrative procedures which have been introduced in our system to administer development in the rural areas are so complicated not understandable to the common man. But it helps the vested interest to develop a corrupt cotterie in the administrative system. The newly elected women leaders have moved into the office with a sense of hope, but they have seen a different picture in the scenario of administration. The women who are novice in administration have to either yield to the corrupt system or to struggle with the system. If she has chosen the later, she is in need of a supportive system to maintain her rectitude.

The interference of politicians at the level of MLAs and MPs in the local body administration is yet another disturbance faced by the women leaders. The MLAs and MPs with their area development fund have interfered in the administration of panchayats. The women leaders pleas are not respected by the MLAs and MPs as they felt that women leaders cannot mobilise vote for them when they contest in the next general election. Moreover the women leaders at the grassroots level are not inclined towards the political parties.

Need of the Hour

Problems can be projected to any level and they could be visualised in a proper perspective. While analysing all those issues one would be tempted to suggest ways and means to overcome all these issues and problems from the perspective and point of view of a researcher. Here it is deliberately avoided as they have options, suggestions from their perspective. The following are the suggestions of the women leaders.

They need continuous training on the role and responsibilities to be discharged by them within the framework of the established political system at the grassroots level. How to administer development and social justice should be known to every one to perform their role effectively. Through orientation workshop and training, their capacity could be enhanced. This exercise should not be a one time affair. It is a continuous process where the women leaders can have an opportunity to meet and interact with other leaders. By doing so they could easily get the models for emulation. Hence training could be given to the leaders periodically but not by the officials. Officials use to threaten the leaders in their training programmes. Hence officials could be avoided in the training programme. They further demanded that interface programme could be arranged by which the leaders of Tamil Nadu can meet and interact with the leaders of Kerala and Karnataka and by which they can learn more about other states and model leaders. Interface will strengthen the knowledge base of the women leaders. Further the officials who are working in local body Institutions should be given orientation and intensive training on the functioning of New Panchayati Raj System. The officials have a strong mind set and belief that the elected women leaders do not know anything about administration and hence they should be brought under the control of the officials. This mind set has to be changed immediately.

Further, leaders cannot perform their roles and duties without adequate information. Now it is a major handicap that leaders are not supplied with needed information for their functioning. Everywhere it is a cry of the leaders that the government orders are not being sent to the leaders. They are being sent to the offices and officers but they have not been given to the leaders. Unless the leaders have a centre for getting information, they felt that it is very difficult to carry out their activities to the level of the expectations of the people. They require the details of the Act, rules, regulations, procedures, government orders, programmes and schemes of the governments to be carried out in the rural and urban areas.

Next to training and information, the women leaders need a supportive organisation which is able to support the women leaders when they are in trouble. Women leaders are working in a given environment which is not so conducive for effective functioning of the women leaders. All the women leaders who are upright and committed have to face trials and tribulations in the society and they have to swim against the current, and hence they felt need for a supportive organisation. This support can be done by the NGOs very effectively. Because honest women leaders have to face harassment from the vested interests. They are being insulted and humiliated. The intensity of humiliation and insult will increase proportionate to the placement of the leader's caste in the social structure. Unparliamentary words are freely used by the men members in the meetings of the council and sabhas to insult and threaten the women leaders. The Panchayat supportive Non-Governmental Organisations have to sensitise the women leaders periodically, as otherwise they will be non-sensitive towards the women issues. There is yet another expectation from the women leaders that the mentally depressed women leaders in a complicated social structure require proper and timely counselling. There are cases admitted in hospitals and took treatment for mental depression. This was explained by the women leaders at the state headquarter meeting in front of the Secretary of Rural Development, Government of Tamil Nadu, organised by Human Rights Foundation, Chennai. This counselling can be done by some committed NGOs continuously.

Honorarium is yet another demand which could be seen rationally in the backdrop of the workload assigned to the local body leaders. It is our experience that the women leaders who are the bread winners of the family are not taking responsibility without honorarium. Hence whenever programmes are organised for poor women by the NGOs, the women leaders are provided with their wage as they earn in their work spot. Hence corresponding to their workload, honorarium could be fixed and paid properly to them in time for the work done by the women leaders. Otherwise, the poor will not participate in the political and development process of the grassroots level institutions. Dalit women leaders have been driven to the lowest ebb because of the pressure given by the traditional Panchayati leaders. The elected women leaders of Dalit community with the backing of either political party or the community, are able to face the challenges. But this category of leaders are very small in number. Majority of the Dalit women leaders do not have the system. They need the support of the NGOs. Dalit women leaders have expressed that their problems and grievances are being redressed quickly by the higher level authorities at the level of Collectors and above and for which they need the supportive system. Absolutely the Dalit women leaders have last their hopes in the lower level officials. They have attributed that on most of the occasions they have been facing too much of interference in administration by the officials due to instigation of a number of influential groups.

Typology of Leaders

Though they have problems and inadequacies, women leaders have emerged and are able to perform the role and functions assigned to them as effectively and efficiently as men. The women leaders, in the process of making themselves as leaders, exhibited a variety. They are six kinds, namely aggressive leaders, capacitated sober leaders, leaders with *status quo* aspiration, leaders with the aspiration of upward mobility, leaders with a mood of withdrawal and leaders with no idea.

A few cadre parties and a few committed NGOs have been continuously orienting the leaders and extending all their supports to the women leaders who have established their links with the party as party members and NGOs as beneficiary. They always exhibit aggressive character and by which they are able to discharge their duties more effectively than the other leaders. Their strength in the group is only 12 per cent.

There is yet another category of leaders, who have been oriented and trained but not committed to any ideology or organisation. But they are committed in their work. They have participated in the programmes organised by the NGO but they donot have continuous linkage with NGO. They are capacitated leaders concentrating much on their responsibilities and they have performed very well as they have enhanced their capacity. They have aspiration to continue in public service but no specific position. Whether they win or not in the next election, they will remain in public sphere. This group constitutes 22 per cent.

There is another category which is slightly different from the first one. The capacitated leaders have concentrated much on enhancing their capacity continuously and performing their duties. While performing their duties, they see the response of people, based on which they have a desire to continue in office. But this category has fixed an ambition to continue in the same position and for which this category of leaders have developed an art of managing the people in the local bodies. All their deficiencies are compensated by their public relations. Their linkage with the people are stronger as they are always with the people. This category of leaders have come to nearly 24 per cent.

The fourth category leaders have a different aspiration. Though they have a number of deficiencies, by keeping themselves very active in discharging their duties they want to demonstrate to their party leaders that they are the opt candidates for Membership in Legislative Assembly. They are always busy in meeting the people and keeping their life busy by familiarizing themselves with the people. They consider the Panchayati institutions as launching pad for their political entry. But this number is very less but they are the models for emulation. Eighteen per cent of the leaders have developed this type of aspiration.

Another category of leaders who are unable to meet the challenges of the role and unable to bear the pressure of the society and the family have expressed their desire to withdraw from public life. These leaders were brought to the public life by force by their husbands. The relationship between the husband and wife has undergone a change in the whole process of administering development through Panchayati Raj Institutions in most of the cases. Many of the husbands realized the fact that their wives have acquired needed capacity and hence they have to withdraw from the support space. But there is another segment of men who have determined not to allow their wives to attend to their duties on their own. Most of the women leaders have expressed that they have been facing problem in the local body institutions because of the interference of their husbands. This factor cannot be explained to their husbands by the women leaders of panchayats on their own. This group constitutes 20 per cent of the whole lot whom we have interacted.

There is yet another category which has no idea. They are in the hands of the male members of the family despite the pronouncement of the Government. The women leaders have not moved out from their houses for public works. They are not meeting the people. Virtually their husbands are operating the machinery. They are not bothered about it. It is a money spinning device which is ably tackled by their husbands by their muscle and money power. Officials are also co-operating with such leaders. They have no idea about the panchayats and they have no aspiration to contest in the next election. If their husbands ask them to contest they will contest, otherwise, they need not bother about it. They are only 4 per cent yet their cases have been repeatedly quoted in public places. It is true that withdrawal symptom is visible among the women leaders in local bodies. They have a volley of problems from the officials, caste groups, own family members and even their own political party leaders.

Yet majority of the leaders have exhibited their determination to occupy the public space. Having come and tasted power the women leaders have come to the stage of enlisting themselves as members of various organisations to fight for their rights and legitimate spaces. In their struggle they have identified the organisations and institutions which are supporting empowerment of women and through them they have determined to continue their struggle. Further they have started forming their own organisations and federating their organisation with other states/organisations. Another interesting development is that a large number of women are being trained in the self-help group (SHG) to move over to this power domain. Hence the women leaders have come to the public sphere and they will continue to keep their hold over the institutions and try to expand the space for them.

Observation and Conclusion

Women have come to positions in the local bodies as provision has been made in the Constitution. The outlook of the society towards the women has started changing. But the hurdles are continuing in the process of empowering women. Steps are being taken by the women on their own to overcome the hurdles. It is a long drawn process. A structure which had been created over centuries to work against the interest of women cannot be altered within a day or two. It could be changed only by creating a movement by the mass and for which this provision of one-third reservation of seats to women would help. To fight against the designs of the structure, an organised movement of the mass is an imperative need on the ground. In order to make the women to achieve results in their positions an array of interventions are necessary.

They need orientation, sensitization, capacity building, information and counselling continuously through organisations. The ongoing experiments and experiences suggest that periodical training, orientation and sensitization make the women leaders to perform the assigned role in a better way than the novice. When the women leaders are responding to the socio-political challenges in this society, they are to be supported by the organisations and institutions which are working for empowerment of women. Wherever such interventions are obvious, achievements of the women leaders are substantial and impressive. Government will respond to the needs of these women leaders only when they are supported by organisations well known for their credentials.

Section II

CASE ANALYSIS OF GRAM PANCHAYATS (WOMEN)

Case 1: Munnilaikottai

Munnilaikottai Gram Panchayat consists of four hamlets, namely Munnilaikottai, Ariyanallur, Ponnaipatti and Easupalayam. This Gram panchayat is reserved for women general. Mrs. Rajammal Thangavelu is from Ariyanallur hamlet. Mrs. Rajammal had an experience of ward membership in the previous period of local bodies. Her husband is the leader of the block in his party – the DMK. Her husband has been very active in the party for the past twenty five years. She made up her mind to contest the election at the eleventh hour. She has four children.

Since her husband has been very active in his party, her involvement in the activities of the village is more. He intervened in public activities and helped many individuals to get the government schemes. Her electoral victory was mostly influenced by husbands reputation and his party affiliation.

Totally five candidates have contested in the election. Her nomination from the party (DMK) was announced in the eleventh hour by the Minister I. Periyasamy. Minister himself announced her name in the public meeting itself. There were other four candidates representing the AIADMK, the TMC and independents who prepared their grounds well ahead of Mrs. Rajammal. She had to struggle a lot to manage to win the election despite the open support of the local minister and her caste groups. She won the election with a difference of only thirty votes. She said that the whole family members including her daughters have gone for door to door canvassing. She admitted the fact that her electoral victory was more of the achievements and activities of her husband. Till she filed her nomination she did not care to know about the panchayati system. She was not aware of the provisions of the 73rd Amendment to the Constitution of India and the Tamil Nadu Local Body Act of 1994.

Without knowing the implications of the new system she became the president of Gram Panchayat. It is a disease affecting the representative system that the elected members whether for parliament or for state legislature or for local bodies, they never had the inclination to learn but they have developed a perception that they know everything and what they have to do is only to redress the grievances of the people by getting the petitions from the people and placing them in the government offices. They forget the main role of the representatives in the authoritative bodies. She honestly admitted that most of the works are attended to by her husband. She used to receive petition if the people give petition in her house and religiously hand over the same to her husband.

Her husband Mr. Thangavelu visited all the hamlets and received petitions on behalf of his wife. He supervises the group house construction activities. Since he has rich experience in this field she felt that his service is needed and essential. Even to select beneficiaries for government schemes like IRDP and DWCRA she depends on his role in satisfying all council members. Office works are attended to only by her husband. Whether the works are in the panchayat union or in the collectorate they are all attended to by her husband. Since officials are known to him, there won't be any problem in getting things done in the government offices. She used to go to public functions whenever minister comes to her area. For all correspondence reply would be given by her husband with the help of the panchayat clerk. Officials use to respond positively to the request of her or her husband. Her husband's domination has been perceived by her as his assistance to her to carry out her activities. Totally all the activities are done by her husband.

Munnilaikottai panchayat is fully under the control of the president's husband Mr. Thangavelu. There is no SC/ST member in the village panchayat council. There are nine members in the Gram panchayat. Of the nine, six are men and three are women. At the time of election members were divided on party lines but after the election the party rivalry has disappeared. Vice-president of the Gram panchayat belongs to Christianity. Her husband and the Vice-president have decided the beneficiaries for the IRDP and other government programmes. So far she has conducted ten meetings and two emergency meetings. Normally two-third of the members use to attend the meeting. Ward members use to discuss with the husband of the president about the problems of the people in their respective wards. Women member's use to participate in all the deliberations of the council.

Women members use to focus their attention on water supply, medical facilities, facilities for school and employment for women. But they are not vociferous. All their queries are answered properly either by the clerk or by her husband.

Following are the issues discussed in the panchayat council meetings:

a) Group house facilities for economically backward families;
b) Poor maintenance of group houses by the beneficiaries;

c) Construction of T.V. Room in all the hamlets;
d) Construction of thrashing floor for the benefit of the farmers;
e) Repairing work in bridges and culverts;
f) Construction of retaining wall in Ariyanallur village;
g) Getting marriage loan from the block office for the deserving families;
h) Problems in selecting IRDP beneficiaries;
i) Repairing electrical motor in the pumping station;
j) Approval for electricity charges;
k) Maintenance of panchayat roads;
l) T.V. Room maintenance and operation of the T.V.;
m) Extension of drinking water supply pipe line to all the hamlets;
n) Construction of overhead tank and deepening of well;
o) Maintenance of GLR in Munnilaikottai village;
p) Getting JVVT grant;
q) Selection of the beneficiaries of the group houses;
r) Maintenance of school building;
s) Proposal to construct a marriage hall;
t) Giving drinking water supply to all the hamlets;
u) Establishing a ration shop in all the hamlets;
v) Construction of drainage to the hamlets; and
w) Selecting the beneficiaries to DWCRA scheme.

The following are the grants received and activities had been carried out in the Gram panchayat :

1.	JVVT scheme for group houses	Rs. 2,76,000
2.	Retuning wall construction	Rs. 59,000
3.	Construction of T.V. Room	Rs. 18,000
4.	Thrashing floor construction	Rs. 26,000
5.	EAS Thittam	Rs. 1,20,000
6.	Odai maintenance	Rs. 2,00,000
7.	Earmarked fund 1/3 water supply, 2/3 construction of small bridges, drainage	Rs. 16,000
	Total	***Rs. 7,15,000***

To select beneficiaries for IRDP programme, a special meeting of the Gram panchayat council has been convened. Beneficiaries have been selected on the basis of their standard of living. One-third of the beneficiaries are selected from SC and two-third beneficiaries are drawn from caste Hindus. Selection was purely based on the consultation with the ward members of all hamlets.

She used to attend all the meetings in the panchayat union whenever it is convened. She has been accompanied by her husband. Every month review meeting she used to participate along with her husband. She had developed a good rapport with the panchayati union Chairperson as the chair person belongs to the same party. She said that she is maintaining a cordial relationship with all officials hence they are co-operating with her. There is yet another reason for getting active co-operation from the officials. Her husband is a powerful party leader in the block and hence everybody is cooperating with her. She gets many programmes from panchayati union with the support of panchayat union Chairperson. She has completed the work of providing street light to all the hamlets.

She is not aware of the role and functions of the district panchayat. She gets many programmes from DRDA office and in this connection she visits collectorate. She does not know what the district panchayat is doing in the villages. Even in the district collectorate the officials are co-operating with her in sanctioning schemes as she observed.

Major Problems in Her Village

a) A great deal of demand is for houses to caste Hindus belonging to economically poor section.
b) Fund available to repair hand pump and water tank motor is not adequate.
c) Drainage is yet another problem in the villages which needs the attention of the government.
d) Jeevanthara grant is not sufficient to meet the needs of the village.

She openly explained that even though women are elected to different positions, they have a feeling that they are not well equipped to handle the problems.

She is not aware of the schemes available in DRDA or in panchayat union. More over the procedure adopted in the union office is cumbersome and the rules manual handed over to her terrorised her in fact. She feels that she needs periodical training to handle the institution. She does not know the real implications of the New Panchayati Raj. She is not getting the Government orders regularly and even to get the G.O. one has to struggle a lot. She felt that women leaders need an exclusive training programme to overcome the inherent problems. Classes should be handled by the women activists. She felt that she is dependent on her husband as she does not know anything about governance. More member of NGOs and academics have to be involved in the training programme. She is not much aware of MLAs and MPs area development programme. Her exposure to media is limited.

She suggested the following for the success of the Gram panchayat :

a) Giving adequate training to the presidents in the panchayat accounts and maintenance of records.
b) Exclusive programme for women could be arranged and leadership training should be given to the women leaders.
c) Rules and regulations should be flexible so as to meet the requirements of the people.
d) Most of the genuine demands of the people could not be met in the government sponsored programmes and they could be met only through exclusive programme for villages.
e) Provision should be made to allocate more amount of money to meet the demands of the people.
f) Government orders and information should reach the leaders in time without any delay and impediment.
g) Panchayati president should be given salary every month as the work-load of the panchayat president is almost a full time employee.

Case 2: Mallanampatti

Socio-Economic Background

1.	Name of the President	:	Mrs. Kamala Rani
2.	Sex	:	Female
3.	Age	:	40 years
4.	Marital Status	:	Married
5.	Caste	:	Kallar - Backward
6.	Religion	:	Hindu
7.	Education	:	S.S.L.C.
8.	Occupation	:	Agriculture
9.	Annual Income	:	Rs.25,000
10.	Type of House	:	Tiled
11.	Electrification done	:	Yes
12.	Type of family	:	Nuclear

13. Total family members	:	5
14. Land holding	:	1 acre wet land
15. Party affiliation	:	DMK
16. Other social involvement	:	Member in local mahalir sangam
17. Address for communication	:	Mrs. Kamala Rani President Mallanampatti Panchayat Mallanampatti Post Batlagundu Block

Special Information

Mrs. Kamala Rani, a physically handicapped woman has been elected as the President of Mallanampatti panchayat with the active work of her husband and DMK volunteers of Mallanampatti panchayat. Her husband is keen in electing her as President with the active support of DMK members. After elected her as a President, her husband took up the responsibility of panchayat activities even to organise the panchayat council meetings.

Political Activity

Actually she said that she was not interested in politics. She didn't belong to any political party at all. Her husband and her community compelled her to contest in the election and hence she contested in the election. Later on she started moving with politicians and joined in the DMK party with the help of her husband. But her husband is full time party cadre of the village.

Details about Electoral Process

Totally four persons contested in the panchayat election including the respondent. The other details of the candidates are given below in Table 5.2

Table 5.2 : Details of Village Panchayat President Election

S. No.	Name	Community	Party	Votes	Expenditure
1.	Mrs. Kamala Rani	Thevar	DMK	1300	Rs.25,000
2.	Mrs. Susila Natarajan	Thevar	AIADMK	650	Rs.15,000
3.	Mrs. Jeeva	SC	Con.I	130	Rs.10,000
4.	Mrs. Nagalakshmi	Chettiar	MDMK	140	Rs.10,000

Source: Computed.

Mrs. Kamala Rani relegated the other three candidates with the help of villagers support, youths and mahalir sangams. The respondents explained that she spent about Rs. 25,000 for this election. During the election, the money is spent on mobilising local youths, meeting their day-to-day expenses vehicle arrangements for mahalir sangams and her party members expenditure on food. She also informed that the other three candidates spent about Rs. 10,000 to Rs. 15,000. They used more amount of money on vehicle arrangements and wall-posters. But Susila Natarajan, a rich woman used her jeep day and night in the campaign. But she was rejected by people because of her richness.

The total population of this panchayat is 12,000. The number of votes available in the village is 2100. After the announcement of election results everyday she used to visit all five hamlets of Mallanampatty panchayat with the help of DMK volunteers. She is a member of a local mahalir sangam. There are 5 hamlets in the villages in this panchayat. They are :

1. Alagapuri
2. Poosaripatti
3. Mallanampatti
4. Lakshmipuram
5. Krishnapuram

People from Alagapuri, Poosaripatti and Mallanampatti village are mostly supporters of DMK. People believed that she is a good candidate for Mallanampatti panchayat. Her husband has earned a good name in above said three villages and so she was able to defeat her three rivals with the support of her husband. Victory is due to her husband.

Details about Hamlet Villages

In Alagapuri, Gounder, SC and Thevar communities are living. But the dominated caste is Gounder. Poosaripatti, is a multi-caste village. But SC is the dominant community. In Mallanampatti village Thevar community is dominant. In Lakshmipuram, SC and Chettiar are living together. In Krishnapuram is a multi-caste village. The panchayat has the following facilities (Table 5.3).

There are two schools in this panchayat. One union school is situated in the Alagapuri. The other one is a management school and it is situated in the Poosaripatti.

Table 5.3 : Facilities available in the Panchayat

S. No.	Particulars	Total	Good in condition	Not good in condition
1.	Street lights	92	60	32
2.	Hand pumps	12	8	4
3.	Open wells	4	4	—
4.	Water tank	5	3	2
5.	Television	5	5	—
6.	Schools	2	2	—

Source: Computed.

Panchayat Meetings

Monthly once panchayat meeting is conducted in the panchayat office situated in the Alagapuri village. Panchayat clerk is available in the panchayat office from 11 a.m. to 3 p.m. President also informed that her husband is everyday visiting the panchayat union office at Batlagundu, to collect information related to panchayat activities.

The president informed that there are nine ward members in her panchayat and among them three are women including one SC. The other six members are men. Among the six, three are from OBC and three from SC. In the panchayat meeting, along with ward members the staff like OHT operator, sweeper and clerk will also attend.

Panchayat meeting starts at 11 a.m. and continue upto 2 p.m. The SC ward members used to speak about their village problems like the maintenance of hand pumps, borewell, water tank, drainage systems and group houses to SC people. The other ward members are not interested in their own village problems. They participated in the panchayat meetings without any objective. Attendance is always full. They claim Rs. 25. SC members are very much conscious to get as many as schemes for their people. The followings are the major issues discussed in the panchayat meetings.

1. Providing water to individual houses and additional taps to streets.
2. Group houses to SC.
3. Retaining wall is suggested for SC colony as it is situated very near to the main colony.
4. School building and other facilities should be improved. *i.e.*, toilet facilities, classroom benches, chair and tables, compound wall, and adequate teachers also formed items for discussion.
5. Construction of small bridge - BC ward members suggested.

6. Repairing water tanks *i.e.*, leakages of water and damaged in supporting pillars.
7. All the members demanded a full-time health centre, because more than five villagers are coming to our panchayat sub-health centre.
8. The SC representatives came to know various schemes through paper and demanded at panchayat meetings.
9. Problems of street lights and T.V. (frequently under repair conditions).
10. IRDP loan arrangement.

In addition president informed that ward members are not interested in the meeting due to the fact that they are not personally getting any benefit from the panchayat scheme.

Maintenance of Records

The president informed that the following records are maintained at our panchayat office:

1. Agenda note;
2. Attendance register;
3. Tax note *i.e.*, water, house, shop;
4. Resolution note, and
5. Beneficiaries list note.

Major Source of Income

The president informed that there are three types of income for the Gram panchayat. They are as follows:

1. Collection of house tax,
2. Collection of water tax, and
3. Stamp duty.

There is no other source of income to the panchayat. Hence the president pointed out that by planting, fruit bearing trees in the common grounds of the village, revenue could be enhanced.

Grants Received

The panchayat received the following amounts for development of Mallanampatti panchayat and its hamlets :

1.	J.V.V.T.	Rs.1,25,000
2.	MLA scheme	Rs.1,70,000
3.	Earmarked	Rs. 30,000
	Total	***Rs.3,25,000***

In J.V.V.T. Scheme the following works have been done at panchayat level.

1. Drainage system has been completed in SC colony.
2. Retaining wall has been completed.
3. Five houses in group house scheme for 5 SC people.
4. Constructed a small bridge to BC area.

In MLA Scheme, new school building has been constructed for IX and X classes, at Mallanampatti village. In the earmarked fund, we are giving Rs. 200 as funeral assistance to the poor people.

Training

President has undergone one day training programme conducted by block development officer. This training is not so effective. Hence she demanded a separate training programme for the elected leaders along with ward members in the following aspects:

1. Maintenance of records;
2. To raise the sources for panchayat;
3. How to treat the drug addicts;
4. How to deal with communal problem; and
5. How to get loans ? *i.e.*, mainly alcoholic persons and caste problems in getting loan from government.

Relations with Union/District/other Officials

The president told that her husband has a close linkage with panchayat union officials. Since he belongs to DMK party, he is able to get works done. Now-a-days his life is fully devoted for the party. At district level there is no contact with district panchayat. Mostly BDOs are guiding panchayat presidents.

Major Problems at Panchayat Level

1. Sinking borewells in the villages.
2. Repairing of water-tank in all the villages of this panchayat.
3. Group houses to all the families of the SC community who don't have shelter.
4. Illicit liquor is a menace in the villages. Three-fourth of the population is consuming the same. Police is also encouraging the same as they will get money illegally. Nobody knows the solution to this in the

absence of a government policy.

5. Educated women are large in number in this panchayat. They are not getting any employment even at the minimum wage. There are women who know typewriting, tailoring, teaching and yet they do not find gainful employment opportunity.

Women Members Functioning

Women members facing lot of problems in the panchayat. The male members do not co-operate with elected women ward members. It is generally a difficult task for women to attend to both household works and social services. The officials have not recognised the women leaders. Therefore adequate training has to be provided especially to the elected women in the leadership aspects. In addition, our higher officials should also be given training.

Village Plan Exercises

Now, we are planning according to the schemes and money allocation for the needs of our village. But we have not plan for the entire villages. The respondent felt that the panchayat members and herself need a more awareness and skill for village level planning.

For a Successful Panchayat

President simply suggested that without adequate resources we could not see a successful panchayat.

Gram Sabha Meeting

Our ward members have informed that the panchayat meetings can also be considered as the Gram Sabha meeting. President suggested that conducting Gram Sabha meeting is difficult due to each village have different opinions and expectations. Besides panchayat finance is not adequate to share the available funds to all those villages. Besides, people participation is very poor due to their personal interests and occupations.

Bank Accounts and Operation

The bank account is jointly operated by both president and vice-president.

We have three types of accounts as follows :

1. General accounts,
2. Tax accounts, and
3. Scheme accounts.

Panchayat Books, G.O. related with Panchayats

The panchayat president said that she has only one book, namely "Tamil Nadu Panchayati Raj Act, 1994" given by panchayat union. Still now she has not seen any government orders related to panchayats.

Case 3 : Kottur

Nilakottai Block

Kottur is one of the 23 village panchayats in Nilakottai union of Dindigul district. This panchayat union is dominated by the SC community. Nilakottai block is located at the southern part of the Dindigul district. The Nilakottai town is famous for gold ornaments, flowers and brass vessels.

Agriculture is the main occupation of the people in this block. Flower, avarai, tomato are the major crops cultivated in the lands of this block. Wells (farm wells) serve as the main source of irrigation besides the river Vaigai and small tanks.

This Nilakottai block is spread over a total geographical area of 237.5 sq.kms with a population of 117377 and of whom 59013 are males and the remaining 58364 females. There are 31042 scheduled caste and 721 Scheduled Tribe people in this block.

Kottur Panchayat

Kottur is one of the village panchayats as well as revenue village in the Nilakottai block. Geographically, this panchayat is spread over an area of 151.00 hectare with sixteen hamlets. The public amenities available in this panchayat include 13 open wells, 19 hand pumps, four OHTs, one middle school, eight primary schools, seven noon meal centres and one health sub-centre.

For transport, this panchayat has been covered with 6.20 km of panchayat road, 5.6 km of union road and 3.2 km of state highways.

There are 64 tube lights and one fair price shop (ration shop). Also there is a Primary Agricultural Co-operative Society. For irrigation purposes, there are four union tanks and one percolation tank. But the major source is the farm wells.

The total population of this panchayat is 6101 of whom 3037 are males and the remaining 3064 females. There are 1635 Scheduled Caste people in this panchayat.

The Kottur panchayat comprises of 16 hamlets the names of which are as follows :

1. Kottur
2. Thathathapatty
3. Nagamanickampatty
4. K. Pudur
5. Michealpalayam
6. Senkottai
7. Jangalpatty
8. Avayampatty
9. Suttikaladipatty
10. Kanni Asaripatty
11. Achipuram
12. Innasipuram
13. Sundaramallipuram
14. Selvanagar
15. Royappanpatty
16. Somapuram

The panchayat office of the Kottur panchayat is located at Michaelpalayam village.

Panchayat President

This Kottur panchayat presidentship has been reserved for women in the last election. Three candidates contested for the presidentship of this panchayat. All the three candidates were Christians. The names of these three candidates are :

Table 5.4 : Details of the Village Panchayat President Election

Sl No.	Name	Party	Symbol
1.	Stella Mary	DMK	Aeroplane
2.	Lourd Mary	AIADMK	Lorry
3.	Lawrance Mary	Congress	Bulb

Source: Computed.

Of the three candidates, Stella Mary got 660 votes, Lourd Mary got 220 votes and Lawrance Mary got 1586 votes. Thus, Mrs. Lawrance Mary got elected as the president of this panchayat. She is a Congress women.

Socio-Economic Background

This president is 43 years old and studied upto SSLC. She is a native of the Michaelpalayam village and born in a farmer family. She got married to a local person. Her husband is also a farmer. Politically, he is the president of the Congress party at the block level.

Her husband has 25 acres of land with three individual and four partnership wells; all the wells are with motor pump sets. She has five children, two boys and three girls. Two of her daughters got married, one is in the house, one son is looking after the farm (after completing IX std.) and the last son is studying BBA at Dindigul.

Motivating Factor

The president Mrs. Lawrance Mary has served as a nominated member in the same village panchayat during the previous period. During the previous panchayat election, her husband contested for the presidentship of this panchayat, but could not win the election. Because of this, and also as he was a rich landlord his wife Mrs. Lawrance Mary was nominated as a member in the panchayat. This experience as a nominated member helps her to the panchayat effectively, as the president of the panchayat at present.

With regard to the factor that motivated her to enter into politics, she reported that it was her husband who induced her to contest for the presidentship. The reason is that he could not contest for the presidentship as it has been reserved for women. Further he had lost the election during the previous time. So, he planned to get the presidentship at least to his wife this time and so he made his wife to contest the election.

As this family is a Congress family, they have the opportunity of having good relationship with the local MLA. This also helped as a plus point to win the election. According to the president Mrs. Lawrance Mary, her husband had the habit of helping the people even without any party/official position. He used to participate in all family functions in the villages. As he was a good social worker, she could win the election easily, as she reports. She also pointed out that she spent Rs.30,000 towards the election while the other candidate namely Lourd Mary spent only less amount.

But the remaining candidate Stella Mary spent more than one lakh rupees, as was reported by their president. Thus, according to her husband, his social service, the party affiliation, his contact/relation with the local MLA, had helped his wife to win the election easily.

Panchayat Members

The Kottur panchayat has been divided into five wards. The members of these wards are as follows :

Table 5.5 : Details of the Election of Village Panchayat Ward Members

Sl No.	Ward No.	Members
1.	I Ward	L. Savadan D. Kamala
2.	II Ward	Julia Mary Thiruthuvam Sahaya Rani
3.	III Ward	John Peter Maria Arockiam
4.	IV Ward	P.K. Muthalif Dhanapackiam
5.	V Ward	K. Nagarani Oorkalan K. Nagamalai

Source: Computed.

Of these 12 member, K. Nagarani has been elected unopposed. It is also to be noted that there is no nominated member.

Shri. L. Savadan, member of the I Ward from Jangalpatty is the vice-president of this panchayat and he belongs to the AIADMK party.

Panchayat Meetings

The president reported that a total of 13 meetings were conducted till date. She says that the meetings have been convened regularly. Almost all the members use to attend the panchayat meetings. The vice-president, Shri.L. Savadan is reported to be rendering full co-operation in the smooth conduct of the meetings without any problem. She says that her earlier experience as a member in the panchayat helps her in convening and conducting the meetings. She stated that her goal or aim is to improve the road facilities to all the hamlets, to provide safe drinking water and lighting facilities to all the hamlets of the panchayat. Accordingly, the meetings are being conducted by keeping her aim as its main agenda. The following is the list of items discussed in the meetings :

1. Providing street light facilities drinking water facilities and road facilities to all the hamlets of the panchayat.
2. Programmes of women development including provision of toilet facilities.
3. Provision of free houses.

In all the meetings, the members demanded more number of free houses to BC families. Similarly, the government programmes are to be shared both by the BC and SC families. But, in this panchayat, since the BC population is more than the SC population, the proportion of beneficiaries seems to be higher among the SC. In other words, since the SC population is less, the proportion and size of SC beneficiaries seems to be higher than the BC families. This makes the people belonging to BC to demand a major portion of the programmes to the BC which is not permitted by the government. This creates problem among the panchayat members in all the meetings. So, the panchayat president opined that the government programmes must be shared among the people in proportionate to the communities. She also feels that the free housing scheme should be extended to the BC families also.

Gram Sabha

The president admitted that she is not fully aware of the composition and importance of the Gram Sabha. So, she had not taken any step to convene the meeting of the Gram Sabha.

Development Programmes

The president admitted that she is not aware of her powers as well as the various development programmes of the government. Whenever she meets the Project Officer at the DRDA, he directs her to meet the BDO for some programmes. The BDO, on her visit, informs her the various programmes that have been allotted to her panchayat. She understands only those programmes that have been sanctioned and implemented to her panchayat. Even in this case, she is not able to identity various programmes, but her husband keeps in record all such activities. What she does is that with the help of the panchayat members in the meetings and with the advice of her husband, she selects the beneficiaries of various programmes. Similarly, the union engineer helps her by preparing the estimate for various activities and works and also helps in executing the work. The following is the list of developmental activities (village-wise) that were carried out by the president.

Achipuram Village

a) T.V. Room — Rs. 27000 (JVVT)
b) Threshing Floor — Rs. 30000 (JVVT)
c) Check Dam — Rs. 30000 (District Fund)

Jangalpatty Village

a) T.V. Room (2) — Rs. 54000 (JVVT)
b) Street lights (4) — Rs. 15000
c) Threshing Floor — Rs. 28000 (JVVT)
d) School Building — Rs. 2.5 lakhs (MP Fund)

Michaelpalayam

a) T.V. Room (2) — Rs. 54000 (JVVT)
b) Passengers Shed — Rs. 30000 (JVVT)
c) Road (Selvanagar to Michaelpalayam) — Rs. 9 lakhs

Nagamanaickenpatty

a) Check Dam — Rs. 30000 (JVVT)
b) T.V. Room — Rs. 27000 (JVVT)
c) Threshing Floor — Rs. 30000 (JVVT)

Kanni Asaripatty

a) Road — Rs. 30000 (JVVT)

Pudur

a) Road — Rs. 8.75 lakhs
b) Drainage — Rs. 48000 (JVVT)
c) Compressor motor — Rs. 40000 (Collection Fund)

Senkottai

a)	Kitchen	Rs. 30000 (JVVT)
b)	Drainage	Rs. 30000 (JVVT)
c)	Small Bridge	Rs. 30000 (Panchayat Fund)

Suttikaladipatty

a)	T.V. Room (2)	Rs. 54000 (JVVT)
b)	Borewell (2)	Rs. 80000
c)	Hand pump	Rs. 27000

Avayampatty

a)	Drainage	Rs. 60000
b)	Group House	Rs. 160000
c)	Electric Motor	Rs. 18000
d)	Street lights	Rs. 160000
e)	Threshing Floor	Rs. 30000

Apart from the above developmental activities, an amount of Rs.176000 has been sanctioned as subsidy to 44 IRDP beneficiaries. But the amount has not been disbursed to the beneficiaries, as the process of selecting the beneficiaries is not yet over.

The president also reported that the panchayat has cleared the previous year's electricity bill of Rs.17000 and also the present years till of Rs.17000.

Source of Income

House tax is the major source of income to this panchayat. Upto the previous year, an amount of Rs. 14000 per year had been collected as house tax. But this year the rate of house tax has been raised and they have put a demand for Rs. 52000. Of this amount Rs. 32000 had been collected till December 1997.

The other sources of income to this panchayat is the professional tax. The panchayat had collected Rs. 6300 during 1996-97 and Rs. 5700 during 1997-98 upto December 1998. Also, the panchayat got Rs. 600 from 2 'C' patta. The president reported that there is no other source of income to this panchayat. She is of the opinion that the fund allotted to this panchayat is not adequate. She is also of the opinion that the major demand of the people in this panchayat is for toilet, drainage, etc. But the government sanction only check dam which is not necessary here.

Relation with other Officials

The panchayat president reports that the vice-president of this panchayat Mr. L. Savadan is co-operative to all her activities and he render full support. She says that though he is an AIADMK man he helps her in conducting the panchayat meetings properly and in implementing developmental activities.

The BDO also supports her by providing enough schemes to this panchayat.

The union council member J. Amalarani, a native of Michaelpalayam village (from where the president also comes) is a relative to the president. So, they have mutual understanding in implementing development programmes. She also helps the president in getting more developmental programmes to this panchayat.

The district council member Sri. K.P. Chandran is reported to be rendering all support to this president. He is a native of Sempatty, a nearby village of the neighbouring panchayat.

The union Chairman, who is also the local MLA, provides all types of co-operation in getting more funds for this panchayat. As her husband is the president of the congress party at the block level, he has the chance of meeting the Chairman more frequently, discuss with her about various programmes and demand more money. Her husband's contact with the MLA helps the president to come closure with the MLA and others. The president had developed a good rapport with the MLA. At the request of the MLA, the president had joined the TMC party. All these factors helped the panchayat to have cordial relationship with all the officials.

Training Programmes Attended

The president reported that she had attended only one training programme to the Panchayati Raj leader provided by the government. She also said that the training programme she attended was not useful enough to understand completely the Panchayati Raj administration.

Case 4: Kothangudi

The respondent Smt. V. Pitchiammal, an agricultural labourer, belongs to SC community is the president of Kothangudi. The respondent's husband is also an agricultural labourer. They had two acres of land but they have sold the lands to meet the medical expenses of their only one son. As such both of them are coolies.

Now due to her full time engagement in Panchayati Raj administration, she is not working in the field. Her son used to earn for their livelihood and now he is no more and hence they have to earn for themselves. Her husband works and earns to meet the family expenditure. Now they have adopted a boy from her relative.

The president is living in the SC colony, in the house allotted through SC Free Housing Scheme. Her mother-in-law is also with them.

She is illiterate. Now she is able to put her signature with the help of adult literacy programme volunteers. Her husband studied upto fifth standard, and he is able to read and write. During the interview her husband had been there for about ten minutes without any interference. The respondent replied to all questions, and expressed opinions freely without anybody's interference. She is a committed, motivated lady cut out for service. She explained that her orientation in CPI(M) and its women's wing moulded her to do social service courageously.

Panchayat Election

The respondent faced a tough competition from the DMK candidate Smt. K. Leelavathy. The respondent informed that her association with CPI(M) party women's wing activities and participation in village affairs enhanced her image among the people which ultimately helped her to get victory in the election with a margin of 952 votes.

She explained that once in a month on the dark moon day, the village meeting is organised regularly in which village problems are discussed and solutions are found out in the village itself, avoiding police/outsider interference. She involved fully in the activities of the women's forum, participated in agitation for solving problems in public distribution system, wage fixation agreement, hike in bus fare and police atrocities on women.

Panchayat Administration

The respondent informed that there are five hamlets including Kothangudi in her panchayat. The following facilities are available in the panchayat:

121 street lights
21 hand pumps
30 taps
3 wells
3 primary schools

3 noon meal centres
2 PDS centres

Hamlets are: 1. Kothangudi, 2. Ayyur, 3. Thozhudur, 4. Thozhudur Madapuram, 5. Kadambamkudi.

The respondent informed that the villagers common demands are drinking water, road maintenance, cleanliness of well and street light maintenance. Problems in PDS are also reported by people.

As the panchayat office is kept open from 9.30 a.m. to 5.00 p.m.. people used to visit and report to the president who is regularly available in the office on matters of service and facilities. Moreover daily newspapers, Dinamalar and Theekathir are available for common readers in the office. Also there is a T.V. in the office and the youth used to visit and enjoy the serials, cricket and other sports during the day time. The respondent further informed that the officials from panchayat union and union chairman used to visit panchayat office and enquire about the schemes carried out in the panchayat.

The people after experiencing a heavy flood during the last winter, requested the panchayat to desilt the tanks and ponds. They demanded proper steps and construction at the tank site. The people informed that the income from the tank through auction can be improved by proper co-operation from the people themselves.

Panchayat Meeting

The respondent said that the meeting is being convened once in a month and all members enthusiastically participated in the meeting. She explained one incident of decision-making process. Twenty beneficiaries have to be selected for Free Group House Scheme with a ratio of 17 from SC and three from BC. Majority of members suggested that all the beneficiaries can be selected from Kothangudi pocket as it is a big colony and also the next year allocation can be assigned to Ayyur pocket. Only one member representing Ayyur colony refused to this suggestion. The vice-president proposed an alternative suggestion that 10 beneficiaries each from both Kothangudi and Ayyur pocket can be selected. But the Kothangudi members demanded all 20 for Kothangudi. Due to this difference of opinion the Ayyur member did not attend three meetings and made a complaint to the Collector, PO. and panchayati union officials. The BDO and ABDO visited the president and enquired about this allegation. Considering the truth and the other members opinion, the

BDO and ABDO counseled the Ayyur member and then the 20 beneficiaries have been selected from Kothangudi pocket with the consent of the disputed member also. She informed that she would ensure that the next year allotment for Ayyur and more over she could request the Collector to allot all additional number to her panchayat so as the demand of Ayyur can be met.

She said that after the flood, the panchayat did the necessary minor maintenance work at all the hamlets. The rules specification with regard to withdrawal right is very strict. Not more than 300 rupees could be drawn for emergency. This is not adequate, she felt. She further informed that with the help of people, fertilizers have been provided at the tank site steps by putting coconut tree logs etc. around a Katcha step arrangement is provided wherever possible.

Official Relationship

The respondent felt that the union officials are co-operative. She used to meet the ABDO and BDO frequently and discussed with them about the union scheme implementation through panchayat. The group house scheme is going to be implemented by the panchayat itself as the union officials agreed to the request of panchayat. The EOP is also very much positive and properly guiding the president, she told. As such there is no problem with officials from her point of view.

Peoples Expectation

The respondent informed that in spite of her full time dedication for the cause of people, people expect more facilities and not understanding the panchayat procedure, panchayat income etc. The village roads are very long from 2½ km to 5 km distance which can not be maintained by village panchayat. And so she informed that she requested the union to take over the long distanced roads from village panchayat.

Quality of Electric Items

She complained that the spare parts/bulbs supplied by the approved store is not in good quality. The bulbs are burning for about one or two months only. The panchayats have no freedom to purchase the electrical items from the local shops even if it is economical.

Resource Mobilisation

There are 21 tanks, 120 coconut trees, and 40 tamarind trees. Usually the auction on these resources are under the control of village committee of each pocket. Now due to difference of opinion among the political parties, the auction was very much competitive and this year the income from these sources are increased from Rs. 8,000 to Rs. 35,000.

Programme Implementation

The respondent informed that the demands of all ward members have been passed as resolutions. Works are generally allotted to all wards.

Steps to desisting tanks, deepening of wells, cleaning of ponds, improving drainage system, maintaining road, providing culverts, constructing TV room, retaining wall, and water supply provision are the major works undertaken in the panchayat at the cost of about Rs.1,25,000.

Union Works

Tar road	1 km
Group Houses	20 Nos.
Road maintenance	2 Nos. have been done

With the help of union councillor panchayat has approached THADCO and tried to do repair work in 20 houses at AD Colony.

The works under MP area development or MLA scheme have not been sanctioned so far to this panchayat, the respondent informed.

Flood Relief Work and Panchayat President

The respondent informed that during the flood relief work, she accompanied the VAO and helped in distribution of all clothes, cash, and rice to the eligible farmers and individuals.

She informed that the village committee of her Kothangudi village (pocket) had collected all the money due for their farmers and individuals and distributed the money equally to all families at the hamlet, irrespective of their caste. Her participation in this work is fully recognised by the revenue official, she felt.

Political Party's help

She belongs to CPI(M), and the party encourages her involvement. The district level party functionaries regularly visit her area and she used to share her feelings and experiences with them.

The local youth both educated and uneducated, fully stand behind her for helping her in panchayat administration. She has the feeling that if she is an educated person, she would have done much better than this.

Now she has adopted a boy through which she is gaining normalcy after the sorrowful event of the death of her only son.

Training

She expressed that she need regular training in village planning especially to provide employment to educated youth.

A Case Study on the Correspondence Received by the Village Respondent of Kothangudi Panchayat

Date	From whom	Subject
20-10-96	Commissioner	Introductory meeting for newly elected presidents
05-12-96	"	OHT operation ex-gratia amount
28-01-97	"	Duties/responsibilities review
28-02-97	"	Drought/drinking water preparatory meet for review
28-02-97	"	Eye camp
17-03-97	"	Payment to be made to the highways department for tree auction share
20-03-97	"	Advise to collect fee from brick making industry Rs. 35 per 10,000 bricks
27-02-97	DDO	Street light
18-04-97	Commissioner	Information on DRDA review meeting on new accounting system
19-06-97	ABDO	31 registers maintenance training
12-09-97	Collector	Intimation regarding water supply materials purchase approved contractors
17-12-97	ABDO	Funeral grant disbursement details
27-11-97	ABDO	TV visiting of mechanic intimation
20-11-97	ABDO	Selection of beneficiaries for supply of tools at free of cost
2-12-97	ABDO	Low lying area identification for housing plan/ house site patta identification of beneficiaries
20-10-97	DRD	Intimation of financial allocation

04-12-97	ABDO	Jeevandhara IAY - money disbursement guidelines
09-12-97	ABDO	Drinking water supply, cleanliness sanitation/ avoiding of diseases
11-12-97	ABDO	Conversion of village road to union road
16-12-97	ABDO	P.R. Act Tamil Book
10-09-97	ABDO	TV electricity connection
10-09-97	ABDO	TRYSEM beneficiary selection
26-05-97	ABDO	94 to 97 account finalisation
30-05-97	DRD	G.O. 170 received
05-06-97	BDO	Verification of joint account system
11-06-97	DRD	G.O. 248 received
22-07-97	ABDO	Tree planting in public places
13-06-97	Commissioner	Women members family interference avoiding instruction
18-07-97	"	Small saving drive
25-07-97	"	Hand pump spare parts expenditure
17-12-97	ABDO	Tax collection
01-08-97	Addl. Director Agriculture	Crop insurance scheme intimation
01-08-97	District Nutrition Scheme Officer	Awareness generation on nutrition
07-08-97	BDO	Intimation about PA (PD) meeting
07-08-97	PA(PD)	UNICEF/Water harvest project selection o buildings
11-08-97	BDO	50th year of Independence celebration
11-08-97	BDO	TWARD scheme G.O. 252
12-08-97	DRD	10th Finance Commission allocation — guidances for fund utilization
12-08-97	ABDO	To measure the street and mark in the registe of VAO
28-08-97	ABDO	Panchayat clerk appointment guidelines
25-09-97	Asst. Engineer Irrigation Area Dev.	Renovation of tanks — list requested
14-10-97	Commissioner	Preparation for meeting the natural calamitie
28-10-97	ABDO	Guidelines to prepare 1998/99 budget
12-11-97	ABDO	Makkal Nala Paniyalar appointment/ job responsibilities

Case 5: Thirukkuvalai

The respondent Smt. R. Pitchammal belongs to Konar community (BC). Her husband Sri. Ramachandran is an active local leader of DMK since 1962 and he is functioning as the president of DMK local branch. He is now the union representative of DMK party unit.

Election

When the village president position was reserved for women (general) the DMK party decided to nominate the wife of Sri. Ramachandran to contest in the election. The respondent informed that their supporters and volunteers of DMK visited each house and informed the voters that as if the president of Thirukkuvalai village panchayat is from DMK, the panchayat may receive supports from the panchayat union as DMK is a ruling party. And so for the past ten years, the then government neglected the village and did not show any interest and commitment to improve its socio-economic condition as it is the birth place of M. Karunanidhi. The respondent gave assurance to the people that the long pending needs of villagers like – infrastructure facilities to the schools and hospital, drinking water provision etc. can be fulfilled if she is returned to panchayat.

The respondent's husband brought the support of the local leaders from the party and they have worked for Pitchammal. With all these support bases DMK candidate won the panchayat election. She has spent Rs.35,000/- for this election.

Panchayat Meeting

There are 11 hamlet villages including Thirukkuvalai for which there are 9 members (4 women and 5 men) in the panchayat council.

Monthly once the panchayat meeting is conducted. The respondent's husband is also available during the meeting, to provide information to the members as those type of works are handled by the husband of the respondent. The respondent further informed that her elder son is also helping her in administering the panchayat activities. He used to visit the hamlets, ensure the provision of drinking water and street light maintenance etc. Sometime to verify the burning of bulb in night, her son only visiting hamlets during night.

The panchayat passed resolution and sought help from the Chief Minister by informing him that the village is continuously neglected by the then governments for the past ten to fifteen years.

The respondent informed that the members are not properly educated. They demanded the things immediately. Gents in the council are not conducting themselves in the council with a sense of responsibility and not ready to understand the administrative procedures. The respondents husband listed out the following works that are sanctioned to Thirukkuvalai panchayat are carried out in Thirukkuvalai panchayat.:

Sl.No.	Work	Estimate (Rs.)
1.	District Eye Hospital	1 crore
2.	Students Hostel	0.36 lakhs
3.	Sub-station of ED	0.30 "
4.	Higher Secondary School infrastructure	0.08 "
5.	Higher Secondary School laboratory	0.06.5 "
6.	Higher Secondary School Compound Wall	0.08.5 "
7.	Higher Secondary School Playground	0.06.5 "
Under DD Plan Scheme		
1.	Union elementary school	1.5 "
2.	Thar road	1.5 "
3.	Scralai spreading	1.5 "
4.	Scralai spreading	0.8 "
5.	Ration shop building	80,000

Panchayat Works

65% grant Rs. 39,000 and
earmarked grant Rs. 20,460 have been received by the village panchayat.
The income of the panchayat is very minimum.

House tax	Rs. 7,120
PF	Rs. 12,400
Stamp duty	Rs. 13,000
Mahasul (Tree/pond)	Rs. 2,833
Puliur tank	Rs. 2,500

The respondent informed that there are activities to increase the income of village panchayat through tree planting. The village poramboke lands are already encroached and fully occupied by the public. And so tree planting is carried out in highways road side. About 50 coconut tree saplings were planted.

The house tax is now enhanced minimum from Rs.3.50 to Rs.5.50. The income is not sufficient to meet the day to day expenditures in providing basic facilities like street light, water supply and public sanitation provision. There are 185 street lights, 22 hand pumps and 25 water taps in the panchayat.

Programme Implementation

The respondent's husband told that out of total 18 IRDP allocation, 4 SC and 14 BC are selected. He claimed that the ruling DMK does not influence in the selection. All party people views are accepted and the eligible beneficiaries belonging to all parties are selected. He further informed that the numbers are not sufficient. At least there must be a time target to reach all the poor families who are below the poverty line, he suggested.

JVVT

Under JVVT four culverts at the total cost of Rs.1,00,000/- have been constructed. The material like cement, pipe and spare parts are supplied by union. There is no say to village panchayats in this scheme.

Presidents' New Role

A vigilance committee is convened in which the president of village panchayat has to be the president of the committee and VAO has to serve as secretary along with 3 to 4 members representing local farmers. The president has further a role to play in other vigilance committee like Nutrition Noon Meals Programme implementation, PDS and Flood Relief Work. The Village Administrative Officer has taken role as an encroachment to her field and so tried to overshadow the president. The respondent further informed that the supply of free dhotis and sarees, rice and kerosene distribution during the flood relief need close monitoring by the president so as to enable the eligible beneficiaries to get their shares.

The respondent's husband further informed that when highways cleared the roadside, the panchayat planned to plant 13 trees but the people tried to encroach the place. But the respondent and members tried and avoided the encroachment. But the local traditional leaders and political party leaders did not support the panchayat.

The people are not evincing interest in public activities. The representatives are also not immediately bringing the problems to the notice of the panchayat. And so the family members of the panchayat president are helping by visiting various hamlets and in one hamlet there is no member as all the three members of that particular ward have been selected from one pocket. They give information about their area problems.

Administrative Problem

The earmarked fund utilization: Out of the total 2/3 has to be spent on road and 1/3 has to be spent on drinking water. The officials are pressing the panchayat to utilize the fund as early as possible whereas the 1/3 of earmarked fund for drinking water is not sufficient and can be withheld for sometime and after an additional allocation or other allocation, a more planned water supply work could be carried out.

Panchayat Clerk

The clerk has studied only 10+2 whereas he has to maintain 31 records/ registers and accounting procedures are more complicated. He is not fully equipped to manage the administration. And so a periodical training is needed for panchayat clerk also. The old clerks, who were once karnams are helping in maintaining the panchayat accounts of 2-3 villages and earn an amount of Rs.1000/- per month additionally. His services are very much needed and so he has been booked by village panchayat in advance.

Union Scheme *Vs* Panchayat

The union scheme works have been carried out without the knowledge of the village panchayat, the respondent informed. She explained that when a school building work is undertaken newly, there are quality control measures like watering the constructions, and when construction was done there is no assistance from the contractors to watering. If the concerned village panchayat is also given a role in monitoring the scheme, there will be an effective monitoring as the building is going to be handed over to the panchayat after completion. Now it is lacking.

Agricultural Engineering Department Work and Panchayat

Under the auspices of the agricultural engineering department, watershed works are undertaken in two tanks. The department officials approached the panchayat and consulted about the work. About Rs.5,00,000 estimated works are carried out in two tanks. The PWD works like channel renovation, earth removing widening etc. are carried out effectively in consultation with the panchayats.

Women Reservation/Empowerment

The husband of the Thirukkuvalai village panchayat felt that the common people have not yet changed their mind set. They have to co-operate, encourage and help the women representative. Based on this new experiment only, the future success is going to be determined.

The Gram Sabha

The respondent felt that as long as alcohol is freely available in the villages, there is no possibility to organise Gram Sabha as per the new PR system. But a common meeting at hamlets can be organised as there will be a social control when the Gram Sabha deliberations are disturbed by any one.

He further informed that due to party politics, some of the local leaders are not giving due respect and recognition to the panchayat and its new role. They want that it must be a subservient to the state/central governments machineries. The concept of autonomy and decentralised power to the village panchayats are not acceptable to the traditional leaders, the respondent informed.

Observation

The village panchayat president Smt. Pitchammal has not grasped the significance of the interview. But she seldom gave her explanation in a limited way. Her husband only plays the role, it seems. It is mostly a proxy.

Case 6: Athoor

Introduction

Smt. M. Jayamary Karuthuraj is the president of Athoor village panchayat. She is hailing from an agricultural family, owning two acres of wet land, seven acres of dry land. Her husband is a traditional leader, involving in the catholic farmers association of Athoor. They own a tractor.

During the period of 1986 election, her husband contested for president position. But he was defeated. He took it as a prestige issue and so when panchayati election was announced this time, he prepared to contest again. Unfortunately the position was reserved for women (General). Her husband compelled the respondent to contest even though she did not have any orientation in the political or public life.

Athoor village panchayat has only two hamlets: Athoor and Old Sempatti. The village is a heterogeneous one, comprising of Thevar, Muslims, SC (Christians), SC (Hindu), Pillai, Nadar and Brahmin.

There are four wards and the total members are twelve. Out of that four are women and eight are men.

Panchayat Election

There were three contestants including the respondent for the panchayat president position.

1. Ms. Kalarani in support of AIADMK
2. Mrs. Chitra
3. Mrs. Jayamary in support of DMK-TMC

The respondent informed that during the previous election her husband contested. Since her husband owned a licensed arrack shop, meals and arrack were supplied to the volunteers and others who accompanied for election campaign. But this time there was no arrack supply. But every day about 25 to 30 persons visited every house during the evening time. Posters, pamphlets, wall writing were other methods of campaigning. Two days before the polling day with tractor, jeep and lorry, a mass campaign was organised to project her candidature.

The respondent further toid that for canvassing for about 1000 votes from Adi-Dravida community voters, she had given cash to each votes with the support of party/traditional leaders of those pockets. She informed that her caste people *i.e.* cCtholic Christians fully supported her and their family took much hardship in the organising work of Catholic Farmers Association. The popularity of DMK-TMC and her family is the major reason for her success. The respondent won in the election by the margin of more than 500 votes and about Rs.1 lakh was spent, she informed.

Her Function

The respondent said that her only son, being a graduate interested in public affairs is helping the family, looking after their farm activities and also helping the respondent in panchayat raj functions. He deals most of the problem and function as a shadow president.

She informed that she is running the panchayat with the advise and help of her son. During the interview at her house, she furnished details pertaining to Athoor panchayat from a diary, notebook and a file, all in a kit. But she does not able to reply other queries like number of registers, correspondences, government orders etc. pertaining to New Panchayati Raj System. She replied that her son only dealt those things. Further the panchayat clerk is a B.Com graduate and he is properly maintaining all registers.

The Haunting Issue

The previous president collected money from public by promising individual water tap connection. But he failed to do so and there was no account for money collected.

Now, after the introduction of New Panchayati Raj System, the problem of individual water tap connection was raised. The problem was discussed in the panchayat meeting and consulted with the local MLA who is fortunately become a minister Sri. I. Periasamy and with his permission Rs. 500/- was collected. Receipt for Rs.300/- was given to the individual contributors. The balance was kept as unaccountable money to meet other miscellaneous expenses.

In the mean time an order was issued by the State government, banning all new individual water tap connection created tussle in the village. The problem became an issue and public demanded the money. Rs. 200/- is returned to them. The minister could not able to help as the G.O. could not be violated. The problem was figured in the local newspapers also.

The respondent further informed that Rs.40,000 to Rs.50,000 is being spent for proper water supply to the public taps of Adi-Dravida Community pockets. Following this the other caste people demanded the same facilities. The panchayat members also demanded that water supply in all wards has to be improved.

Panchayat Meeting

Monthly once, the panchayat meeting is conducted. The ward members are demanding a copy of the resolution passed during the previous meeting. Sometimes emergency meetings are organised. The resolutions are not properly circulated due to shortage of time. But the members make this as an issue and make wrong propaganda.

The vice-president is belonging to TMC and he is a Thevar community man. The members were divided into groups and so the meeting was disturbed. The members demanded a copy of resolution. Subjects like drinking water, drainage, television, public storage, road facilities were discussed. Rs. 60,648/- is the quarterly allocation from the government and Rs. 1,27,120/- is the JVVT quarterly share for the panchayat.

From the union scheme, a number of works are carried out at Athoor panchayat as the union councillor become the union chairperson. The union Chairperson Smt. Margretmary is the close relative of the respondent.

Union road, graveyard road, Mallayapuram road, ration shop and high school building repair are the works carried out by union. Under MP's fund, three tanks renovation and deepening works are carried out. Since the locality is very close to the minister Sri.I.Periasamy's place, the officials are co-operative to this panchayat.

Her Links

The respondent informed that she used to visit union office, and collector's office frequently. She attends the association meeting of the village presidents association.

IRDP

The allocation is 38 beneficiaries for her panchayat. Twenty beneficiaries are drawn from SC and 18 from BC. Each panchayat member has recommended two beneficiaries. The union Chairman and his brother have also influenced in the selection. There is pressure from the ruling DMK party. But only the poor families are recommended to the bank.

Common Property Resources

The panchayat poramboke sites are under the illegal occupation by consulting of a cattle shed, houses, tree plantation, stocking of paddy and other agricultural commodities straw by a few families. The encroachments are made by mostly well to do families. It is very difficult to clear the encroachments.

The Political Parties

The political parties are in general not creating any problem. Whereas if any petty issue is reflected in panchayat meeting they make it as a big one and spread wrong informations on the president, she informed. Writing unanimous letters, passing information to press etc. is done by the political parties. People's expectation is always increasing. They want that panchayat must do all works immediately. Moreover they are not ready to co-operate with the panchayat.

The Hamlets

The respondent informed that the society is still male dominated one. The traditional leaders are lobbying themselves against panchayat and pressurizing the president to fulfill their demand immediately. They expect that the panchayat president was supported by them and so she must be lenient to them.

Village Panchayat Income (average)

House tax	-	Rs. 10,000.00
Water tax (450 individual connection)	-	Rs. 75,000.00
Professional tax	-	Rs. 40,000.00
Stamp duty	-	Rs.2,00,000.00
License fee	-	Rs. 2,000.00
	Total	***Rs. 3,27,000.00***

Expenses

Salary	-	Rs. 7,000.00
EB	-	Rs. 10,000.00
Pipe	-	Rs. 2,000.00
Street light	-	Rs. 10,000.00
Road and sanitation	-	Rs. 5,000.00
	Total	***Rs. 34,000.00***

Scheme Fund Received

(1/4) JVVT	-	Rs. 65,000	Rs. 2,45,000 (per year)
8th	-	Rs. 65,000	Rs. 2,45,000 (per year)
Earmarked	-	Rs. 36,000	Rs. 36,000 (per year)
		Total	***Rs. 5,26,000***

Corruption

The president informed that corruption is still prevailed in panchayat administration. The officials are demanding percentage to sanction schemes. But the proportion is comparatively less than previous government.

She felt that the village panchayat members expect money like officials expect money to sanction the works, bills, and other administrative procedures.

Expenditure incurred from 1.4.97 to 31.12.97

Current bill	Rs.	2,647
Current bill	Rs.	49,395
Salary	Rs.	66,345
Sitting allowance	Rs.	2,575
Stationery	Rs.	1,342
Street light materials	Rs.	11,895
TV maintenance	Rs.	1,550
Uniform	Rs.	8,076
Funeral grant	Rs.	1,400
Deepavali advance	Rs.	3,400
Other expenses	Rs.	12,342
Earth spreaded on road	Rs.	16,982
Drainage construction in 3 wards	Rs.	3,44,430
Pipe - new extension	Rs.	33,798
Chair/Furniture	Rs.	5,400
Total	***Rs.***	***5,61,568***

Case 7: Noothilapuram

Mrs.M. Kala, president of the Noothilapuram Gram Panchayat of

Nilakkottai block in Dindigul district (32) is hailing from a poor Dalit family. It is fortunate that she had her schooling upto tenth standard. She got married at the age of eighteen. Her husband (Murugan) is a driver by profession settled in Madurai city for sometime to earn their livelihood. The mismatch between their earning and the cost of living has driven them from Madurai to a nearby rural area very near to her husbands native town Noothilapuram. He got a loan from a Nationalised Bank and purchased vehicle and kept it as a tourist taxi and by which the couple spent their days.

Turning point came in their life only when a powerful NGO-ASSEFFA offered a job to Mrs.M. Kala. She was appointed as a field organiser and worked in the same organisation for eight long years. She had been in the field in organising especially women and youth for this organisation. She was familiar with the people in these areas. She shifted her house to her husbands native town Noothilapuram. She also worked as Makkal Nala Paniyalar (peoples welfare worker). In the eight years period she had developed the capacity to speak and to write, to organise the people for social action.

Having realised the gap in the political parties for Dalit's and especially women she had developed and aspiration to move into a political party. She had close contact with the MLA of her constituency Mrs.Ponnammal who happened to be a member of Tamil Manila Congress belong to her caste. Her desire to become a politician has driven her to electoral contest.

Since Noothilapuram panchayat has been reserved for Dalits (SC), she has determined to contest in the election. Along with her there were seven candidates from the same community. It was almost an election on pan with MLA election near about two lakh rupees. Almost three candidates have spent this much of amount.

Since she contested in the MLA election in a reserved constituency of Nilakkottai, she has the capacity to manage the electioneering. Finally she won the election. In her village panchayat jurisdiction there are other caste groups apart from Schedule Caste (majority). They are Piramalai Kallar, Vellalas, Nayakkar, Carpenter and Moopars. Likewise there are twelve small hamlets, namely Noothilapuram, Kulathupatty, Bangalapatty, Achampatty, Sitapuram, Kovilpatty, Vadkku Viralipatty, Therkku Viralipatty, Oothupatty, Chinnamanayakkankottai, Thummalapatty and Perumalpatty. She has to meet the requirements of all the hamlets and all the caste groups.

After her election she had devolved her attention in finding out the financial resources to meet the long felt needs of the people, namely medical facilities, school facilities, providing drinking water supply, providing toilets, providing facilities to farmers, providing housing facilities to the Dalits. Since she had long experience in NGO, she is well aware of the government programmes and schemes:

She has spent two lakh rupees for constructing a medical sub-centre.

She has spent seventy five thousand (75,000/-) rupees for the construction of over head tank for water supply.

She has spent two and half lakhs rupees for constructing school building.

She has earmarked five thousand rupees for constructing community toilets in Noothilapuram.

She has arranged to provide six thrashing grounds with the cost of one lakh eighty thousand rupees.

She has provided road and water facilities to the Graveyard. She has taken steps to provide thirty group houses for the Dalit families.

She is very regular in conducting panchayat council meetings once in a month and if necessary twice in a month. All members of the panchayat council are co-operative. But the vice-president belongs to Backward Community wants to domination in the council. He is non co-operative and refuses to co-operate with the president. She has brought to the notice of the District Collector about the attitude of the vice-president. The District Collector has warned him and now he is attending to the meetings. She is regularly visiting the hamlets and redressing the grievances of the people. She visits the Departments of the government regularly. All the officials are cooperative. She had attended two training programmes conducted by Gandhigram. She does not have any truck with the other two tiers of the panchayats.

With regard to financial position, she informed that one lakh rupees could be mobilised from local taxes. Apart from this funds are mobilised through various schemes of the government for rural development. She is enjoying the confidence of the people and support of the officials and co-operation of her husband. She is not being accompanied by her husband. The primary reason for her success is as stated by her that she has no ego and assumption. She considers herself as a servant of the people.

Beneficiary selection is a stupendous task in the panchayats. Every individual is expecting a benefit from the panchayats. She selects only the deserving in consultation with ward members. Ward members is responsible for beneficiary selection. Nobody can dispute over the selection as the selected individuals are poorest among the poor.

Gram Sabha meeting has been convened with great difficulty. Keeping all caste groups in a common place and allowing them to discuss the issues are the difficult tasks of the leaders. People use to look at issues only from the perspective of the caste. Traditional panchayat leaders want to have their own control over the panchayats. This is the another dimension of the panchayati system.

Case 8: Muthupattinam

Personal Data of the Respondent

Smt. S. P. Indirani, the President of Muthupattinam Gram Panchayat, studied up to ninth standard, married a farmer and she has three children. She belongs to Scheduled Caste Community. She has two acres of dry land.

Her in-laws lived in a village namely Konappattu, situated in Pudukkottai District. But the brother of her mother-in-law handed over all his property to her mother-in law and asked them to go over to Palaya Athankudi village of Muthupattinam Gram Panchayat in Sakkottai Union of Sivagangai District. Hence she migrated from Konappattu to Palaya Athankudi.

The respondent informed that Muthupattinam Village Panchayat has two other hamlets — Padakini Patti and Palaya Athankudi. There are about 1500 families in the panchayat. All of them belong to poor families, living in small huts.

As most of them are illiterate. Adult education was undertaken during the year 1986-87 in this district and the respondent served as a teacher in her village. In 1987, the literacy mission was introduced and the respondent involved herself enthusiastically in the literacy programme.

She felt very much about the poor conditions of huts and hence she has decided to alter the conditions of the huts. She met village administrative officer and he advised her to represent the matter to the Collector. Hence the respondent went to the Collector and explained the problems. The Collector recommended the petitions to the Co-operative Housing Society with the finance help of the housing society, and as a result fifteen houses were constructed for fifteen families.

Panchayat Election

By witnessing her social services, people of that village advised her to contest in the local body election for the presidentship. There was only one opposition candidate — namely Alagarmeenal of that village. The competition was very severe as the SC families joined together and accused her and informed the voters that she and her family was not belonging to the local area. And so all SC families boycotted her joined together to oppose her in the election. But the people of other communities fully supported her and with a margin of about 250 votes the respondent won in the election. There are six members in her panchayat and of them three are men and the rest are women.

Panchayat Meetings

The respondent informed that she has conducted the panchayat meetings regularly. Agenda was served to the members well in advance. Usually the meeting used to be commenced from 10.30 a.m. and it would go upto 3.00 p.m. Members were encouraged to speak about their problems of their ward. Drinking water provisions, street light and pipe maintenance, and public sanitation were the problems usually projected and discussed during the panchayat meetings.

Panchayat Administration

There are two sweepers, eighty-five street lights, one overhead tank, six hand pumps, seven community wells, five television sets available in her panchayat. First she brought all facilities under the control of panchayat. Works have been allocated for sweepers every day. They are supposed to get signature from the people of the area confirming their attendance and work from the respective hamlets.

Every month income/expenditure details are given to members during the meeting. The following works are carried out in the Panchayat:-

Irrigation channel	-	Rs. 17,500.00
Bus shed	-	Rs. 25,000.00
Street maintenance	-	Rs. 15,000.00
Tank deepening	-	Rs. 29,000.00
Irrigation channel panchayati Board	-	Rs. 14,500.00
Tank repair	-	Rs.1,25,000.00
Pipe line — new	-	Rs. 15,000.00
Panchayat Office	-	Rs.1,50,000.00
Community well maintenance	-	Rs. 10,000.00
T.V. room	-	Rs. 33,000.00
PWD tank — it is proposed to deepen one big tank and prepared an estimate for the work	-	Rs.2,50,000.00

Hurdle

The main hurdle in Village Development schemes is getting the technical sanction from the Union Engineers' Office. She informed that she does not give any amount as commission to any officer. This attitude has brought several problems for her smooth functioning. Without giving money, works cannot be carried out.

The Problem of Maternity Women

There is no hospital. About twenty five kilometer distance a full fledged hospital is available at Karaikkudi or Pallathur. People have been suffering due to non-availability of hospital near the village. Hence three village panchayat presidents and Youth Volunteers met together and attempted to meet the Chief Minister in Chennai. They have submitted only memorandum to them. People's expectations are: drinking water facility, TV set and street lights. But officials are not immediately considering the requests of the presidents even though there are provisions in the schemes. The existing water supply system has been functioning in the past twenty five years. Due to this, very often the pipe is broken and disturbed the supply of water. TV repair has to be done only once with the help of the approved mechanic. But there are only two mechanics approved for all Panchayats. The work is delayed as well as expensive.

The Relationship with Officials

The respondent informed that she has a good relationship with the officials. She insisted that the president must every day open the Panchayat Office, meet the people, enlist their problem and based on the priorities, the president must visit the various offices. Because of her sincere efforts, she was able to get Rs. 20,000/- deposited on the name of a girl whose mother has undergone tubectomy operation after two girl children. Rs. 7000/- was received by a poor widow when her husband expired suddenly with the intervention of the president. Two handicapped individuals, one male and one female were provided with IRDP loan. Ration shop — card distribution and essential commodities distribution are regularised with the help of Panchayat. She helped eighty five families to apply properly for ration card. She approached a private land owner and purchased about one and half acres of land for housing to poor, with the help of THADCO, when the rate of the land is more than the Government approved. She convened two needy families and collected their individual contribution so as it can be compensated with the government contribution for purchase of land.

Vice-President relationship

The respondent informed that the administration of the panchayat is openly conducted and each and every activity is discussed with the vice-president and members of the panchayat. The panchayat works are monitored by the members, and inspected by the vice-president and hence there is no quarrel between the president and vice-president. Further there is no friction among the members.

Gram Sabha Meeting

The respondent explained that last year she had organised Gram Sabha meeting. About two hundred members participated. The meeting was conducted between 2.00 to 4.00 p.m. The income and expenditure of village panchayat was read out in the Gram Sabha meeting. The details like: how much financial allocation for various schemes, who are the individual beneficiaries selected for various programmes, what are activities selected for each hamlet have been explained to the people in the Gram Sabha meeting. And then people were asked to articulate their problems. Farmers requested the panchayat to take up maintenance work in the irrigation channel. People demanded two rationshops, individual drinking water supply, group housing, and free house sites for the poor. How then problems can be solved through village panchayat is explained in the Gram Sabha meeting.

The respondent informed that she never demanded power. She believed that service mind is essential for a president. She further explained that she is regularly visiting each hamlet, meeting the members, accompanying the staff like TV operator, water supply attender, EB line men when they are attending the works. So the people understand the panchayat activities. She does not have any serious handicap as being the women president, but her husband felt very unsecured whose candidate was defeated during the election.

Case 9 : Anaikuppam Village Panchayat President

Introduction

Mrs.Ponni Kailasam was one among the ordinary women, looking after the domestic affairs of her family. since her marriage in the year 1982 with Sri.Kailasam, an young and social by committed person of Anaikuppam. Father of Mrs.Ponni Kailasam was an active congress man but a courageous personality. Courageousness seemed to be her inherent quality also. It was evident as she disliked the authority of the local community leadership of Vandaiyar family in her husband village Anaikuppam. When her husband informally shared the village incidents and the authoritarian attitude of Vandaiyar she used to comment on the courage of menfolk of the village. She once during her sharing with her husband, unintentionally informed that "a time would come that she would become a president and challenge vandaiyar". What once she aspired become a reality. She became the village president of Anaikuppam thanks to the reservation to women in local bodies under New Panchayati Raj System and challenged the traditional authoritarian leadership of vandaiyar.

The Factors which Contributed Her Success in the Panchayat Election

Mrs. Ponni Kailasam as an individual of course did not have any attraction or leadership qualities. Whereas her husband Mr.Kailasam is a very serious and socially committed individual. His involvement in the formation of Grama Narpani Manram and its operation brought a reputation to him. And through this public forum, they petitioned for the upgradation of health sub-centre into Primary Health Centre, joined together undertook cleaning work in village ponds and had done a lot of relief works during the time of heavy flood and cyclone.

In course of time, he picked up his leadership qualities and contested in the village panchayat election in the period 1986-91, but did not succeed as the caste factors played a vital role along with the area factor. The village Anaikuppam has many hamlets. As all the times previously the presidents were from the main village Anaikuppam, and this time the hamlet village people joined together and defeated the candidate contested from the main village.

Inspite of the defeat, Mr.Kailasam sustained the spirit of public service, joined the AIADMK party served as the vice-president of

Jayalalitha Peravai. And continued his service and availed various schemes to the village.

After marriage, Mr.Kailasam used to share his public activities with his wife Mrs.Ponni Kailasam and encouraged her to give her suggestions on these activities. He helped her to become the organiser of women association, initiated by union administration. But there was no serious kind of activities in that association.

When the election to the agricultural society was held, Mr.Kailasam contested in the election and became the president. He was waiting for an the opportunity to contest again in the village panchayat election. Since Anaikuppam was earmarked for women he could not contest in the election. Against this background his wife Mrs.Ponni went in to the fray and succeeded in her attempt.

The Election Scenario

The villagers especially the SC and ST who have so far witnessed the authoritativeness of the traditional leadership. They persuaded Mr.Kailasam not to field her wife in the contest. Against the wishes of the traditional leaders, Mrs.Ponni Kailasam contested in the election and defeated the two candidates sponsored by the traditional community leaders.

It was observed here that a candidate from minority community defeated the candidates of majority community Vellalars and Vandayars with the help of SC community. By the public service done by the family of Mrs.Ponni Kailasam, helped her to win the heart of poor. The campaign was so easy. She just visited each hamlet village met the elders/people, reminded them that she contested for their welfare only. She declared that she is a political.

It was told that a few youngsters cutting a cross caste also joined with her in her canvassing as they also decided to bring an end to the authoritarian leadership. Against this background she won the election. Authoritarian, caste dominated panchayat is now in the hands of a leader hailing from a lower middle class family.

Another interesting incident has to be mentioned here that Mr.Kailasam contested for the union ward as he could not able to contest in village panchayat. Hence he concentrated himself in his election campaigning activities did not give any time for his wife's campaign. Inspite of his efforts, he was defeated.

The respondent Mrs.Ponni Kailasam informed that the public was very much influenced by the film hero Rajnikanth's appeal during election and she and the youngsters joined together and made appeal in the style of Rajini. "Even god could not be able to help if you support the bad candidate". Likewise they reminded that if the poor could not be able to cast their vote to Mrs.Ponni Kailasam, the authoritativeness could not be able to replace even by god.

Mrs.Ponni Kailasam as the Women President

She plainly admitted that she did not know more details of New Panchayati Raj System - the three tier pattern - power decentralization. But from the mass media she had gathered that it was an opportunity to improve the village. Her interest was to help poor, providing houses to them encouraging them to send their children to educational institutions, augmenting more income to village panachayat by preventing the illegal exploitation of a few families of the village commons trees, ponds and minor mines etc.

Even though she developed expectation like this, her husband used to explain that the position of village president was not so powerful. But she used to sustain her faith that inspite of limited power, achievements could be made if panchayat at president works hand and builds alliance.

Mrs.Ponni Kailasam studied upto VIII standard. She opted for continuing her study. But it was a social custom in their community that girls were not permitted to go to school if they attained puberty. But her interests in learning does not stop. She learnt the basis of panchayat administration, and developed leadership qualities. With the guidance and encouragement of her husband and the cooperation of her children. She is able to perform her role and responsibilities. She has three girls and a boy.

Her Relationship with Ward Members

Out of nine ward members three are women and four are belonging to SC. As she is apolitical and having faith in cooperation and partnership. She did not find it difficult to manage the council. She was able to muster the support of all members and smoothly conducted panchayat council meetings.

Being women she consider the request of one women member and appointed her husband as the panchayat assistant. moreover she encouraged the vice-president to get explanation from her for all activities as she wished to be transparent in panchayat administration.

The Constraints in Her Administration

The respondent came to panchayat with a different perception and expectations and realities what she has been facing are different. She listed out the following constraints:

1. The people's demands are many; but the allocation to village panchayat is not as enough to meet even the necessary basic amenities to all. She referred that during the first Gram Sabha meet the public submitted 950 petitions.
2. It was to our surprise that none of the requests submitted to the higher officials were attended to and even reply was not given to all those demands.
3. It was a shock to understand that ponds and tanks of village are not the property of village panchayat even though in Chitta it was mentioned as village Natham - Panchayat property but in the custody of village community.
4. All the common properties on the two sides of approach roads, link roads and main street pathways have been encroached. The attitude of revenue officials towards panchayats is not positive in this regard.
5. The procedures to be adopted in the allocation of schemes especially Group houses under Indira Awas Yojana are not in adhered to with what the district authorities referred to. Political interference in sanctioning this scheme is visible in the district.
6. The illegal exploitation of river sand could not be stopped inspite of district higher officials efforts and support. The state government is not interested in protecting the natural resources.
7. The absence of organic linkage with panchayati union makes it difficult to get schemes and programmes from the Block office.
8. Getting the allocation from the MLA fund.
9. About 300 palm trees in the bank of the two canals are under the possession of an individual, who enjoys the income of these trees which ought to be the property of village panchayat.
10. Each and every ward member demands all facilities to their wards and they did not know the financial constraints.
11. The menace of alcoholism in each street and the sale of illicit arracks are the major problems in the villages.

The respondent felt very much when she encountered these realities and did not know the ways and means to face them successfully.

The Process of Her Capacity Building

An encouragement and guidance from her husband, her feeling towards the poor of the village and positive attitude of some higher officials sustained her interest in panchayats. But a turning point occurred in her leadership when she attended the orientation programme Tamil Nadu Social Welfare Board. She stated that till she attended the training programme she had a feeling of withdrawing from the public space as it has got full of obstacles. But in the training programme her confidence was built by the resource persons of Gandhigram University and moreover she was able to comprehend the scope and limitations in the New Panchayati Raj System through the training programmes. She came to know the significance of community mobilisation and peoples participation in panchayat activities.

She picked up the thread systematically interacted with the public and created awareness in their mind and finally successfully she consolidated their support to her activities. The problem of encroachment was solved the public support. Almost all encroachments were removed with the help of people and even a few offered a portion of their patta land for widening the streets and approach roads and link roads.

The menace of alcoholism was also tackled successfully with the help of villagers especially women folk. The respondent met the superindent of police argued the problem with him and the action was immediately taken. Within a week the of arrack sales in all streets were stopped. She encouraged the ward members to monitor and directly inform the police.

Here it is interesting to note that the official cooperated with the panchayat to fackle the menace which is rare in other places.

She identified a suitable site for the construction of a primary health centre which was under the custody of four families. It is a public property. She organised the villagers, and informed them and finally she met the families and persuaded them through government officials. When it failed to get positive response, she with the help of villagers removed the encroachment and kept it clean for the construction. She met immediately the Joint Director and appealed to him to commence the construction activities so as the expectation of the people would be materialised as they themselves involved in the removal of encroachment. The health authorities quickly acted and the building was completed. The PHC is functioning well at present.

The problem in availing group houses was also handled successfully.

By her pursuation, she got twenty seven houses to her panchayat from group house scheme.

The illegal exploitation of sand was also attended to. But still the problem exists and with the help of village people and higher authorities, the removal of sand was regularised. But the revenue officials did not cooperate in containing the illegal removal as it seemed that they have vested interest in permitting other to get sand illegally, the respondent said.

The respondent informed that the union administration was politicalised by the elected representatives. Only one benefit was availed from the union that too through the support from the union officials.

She cited another experience with the panchayat union. When the site earmarked for the construction of TV room by the union was found inappropriate, the respondent selected other site in consultation with the officials and completed the construction. But the union chairman did not approve the work as it was against the earliest decision and delay the payment inspite of the supply of materials by officials. And after one year period, in the presence of higher officials the respondent effectively argued her point and succeeded and got the money.

Influencing the member of the legislative assembly was also a tough task. She met the MLA with a few community leaders and indirectly showed the strength of the community. Atleast two important works have been sanctioned under the local area development scheme of the MLA. Though the panchayat was not able to succeed in bring the village ponds under panchayat jurisdiction, the respondent was able to influence the community which posses the ponds, to contribute fund for availing Namakku Naame scheme from the state government.

Likewise when it was not possible to pool the income of palm trees, growing in the banks and bunds, the responded took efforts to plant palm and it was told that 60,000 seedling were planted in the four years period which would be a valuable asset to the panchayat in future.

The respondent told that the level of understanding of members is improved significantly. Now they are able to prioritise the needs according the available financial resources. They helped the president in achieving cent percent tax collection, maintenance of public taps and other common properties of village panchayat.

The felt needs of farmers ie., desilting of irrigation canal was fulfilled when Namakku Naame Thittam was launched. Emergency meeting was convened with the farmers and their suggestions were sought on this issue. After due consultation with the farmers the farmers came forward to contribute their share to avail the government scheme. An amount of Rs.80,000/- was contributed by the farmers and by which a work with an estimate Rs.3,24,000/- had been carried out. After this, the problem of flood was solved. These innovative activity of the Anaikuppam panchayat was replicated by other near by panchayats. It was told that by mobilising Rs.3.75 lakh from public, under Namakku Naame Thittam Rs.15 lakh worth of works were carried out.

Rapport with Officials

Her rapport with officials helped her in getting grants from various schemes and assistance. A new school building was refused demanded by the people and it was by the union, for a long but now in consultation and guidance of officials, fund was mobilised from the district decentralized plan and carried out the work.

With the support of parent- teachers association, school improvement works were undertaken. Roof maintenance, construction of compound wall and entrance arch were completed. This was possible by bringing the matter to the parent teachers association's meeting and mobilised the contribution from the public.

Women and Child Welfare Activities

She emphasised the importance of education of girl from the poor families. She was referring to the marriage assistance scheme to the poor girls. She created awareness among the eligible couples among the significance of small family norms and helped in organising polio programme and end alcoholism in the village.

The efforts for mobilising women for self-help groups were also initiated. Now there are 30 SHGs with 600 membership. They are now operating the micro credit cum saving activities. Then have a proposal to organise nursery of fruit bearing trees as there is a scope in JGSY and especially to the Adi Dravida community. And as the palm tress are in plenty, skill training is proposed in palm crafts to women to generate additional income. Drinking water problem faced by women folk was also solved by providing new borewells and over head tanks.

The Emerging Women Leadership Qualities of the Respondent

The respondent is now a good orator courageously argued her points in public stages. She had been the president of the District elected women leaders association. Now she has been nominated unanimously as the secretary of Tamil Nadu Women Leaders Association.

She is periodically invited by the district officials for offering suggestions to various issues pertaining to panchayat. She is regularly selected as candidates for training. In general officials do not except any favour from her.

The Other side

Her husband encourage continuously and she shared her aspirations and innovations inspite of her dual responsibility. She admitted that her husband is being used to monitor the records and accounts. She admitted that she has to further equipped in the areas of accounting and maintenance of records in panchayat.

Her Development Perspective

She outlined developmental perspective of her village as follows.

- Priority to desilt all ponds to store more water in tanks for recharge.
- Creating awareness in ecology and environment
- Poverty alleviation through SHGs
- Encouraging youth welfare activities as there is an immense potentials in rural youths.
- Work for accelerating the process of public pressure in demanding 1/3 reservation in assemblies and parliament as the womenfolk can play very effectively in rendering social justice and ensure gender perception in policy making.

Conclusion

It was learnt that if she could further improve her leadership and she would be a successful candidature for Legislative Assembly. She admitted that she also opted for that position provided her husband extend the same encouragement and support.

She has identified her worth and potentials and she has slut down all his inhabitations. She has developed her confidence in managing the public affairs. More particularly she had developed her confidence in managing the public affairs. More particularly she had developed a flaming aspiration to achieve something that provides needed energy to carry out all her activities. She had an advantage in the family. His husband in always positive and cooperative in all her activities. It is proved through her case that panchayat is a nursery of our democracy.

Case 10 : Athoor Block Panchayat

Smt. Margret Mary is the resident of Athoor village. She has completed the secondary school education. She is forty two years old having three children. Her husband is a farmer. The family has got two and a half acres of dry land with electrified motor well and also one acre of Paddy field. With a moderate economic background she has climbed the ladder of the power centre.

Political Background

She had a basic political orientation in the DMK party from her youth hood. Her husband had a tea-shop at Athoor for a long period and because of his interest in public life, the shop and the atmosphere provided a non-formal forum to develop the DMK party in and around Athoor and he gained the benefits from this exercise. She was also attracted towards the party politics and hence she involved herself in the DMK party women's wing activities after her schooling. Her younger brother was also an active worker of the DMK and served two times as the secretary of local branch of the party.

The respondent's husband is a member of the DMK party. Hence after her marriage, the respondent has developed an interest and involvement in the party affairs. With the encouragement and support extended by her husband, she actively participated in the political activities of the party especially in the women wing.

Religious Background

Being a Christian she had the support of the Pillai community both from the Christians and Hindus. There are about four hundred Christian families in Athoor area. They belong to backward community. The church is playing a key role in shaping the character and social life of the respondent. There is a women forum among the BC Christians in the name of "Mariayayee Sena" in which the Christian women involve and engage themselves in both religious and public activities. The members of the sena used to visit those who are sick and prayed for the early recovery.

They collected the necessary material and money and distributed the same to the poor families. This helped a lot in shaping the respondent's knowledge and interest in public life.

Social Background

The respondent has an enterprise in cloth vending in an informal way at her house. Due to this trade, she had an opportunity to meet so many women and their family members. She sold the clothes for competitive price and ensured quality also and earned a name among the members of the community especially among women. The respondent had a claim in getting a ticket to contest due to the service done by her which had been duly recognised by her party. She had the patronage of the local MLA who happen to be the Minister in Tamil Nadu Government.

During Panchayat Election

The respondent contested the union councillor position, which has been reserved for women. She contested as the DMK party candidate and had a tough competition with the AIADMK candidate and other allied party candidates. The respondent promised to provide basic amenities to all the sections of the ward and assured that the problem of drinking water could be solved if she was elected to power. Moreover it was also informed that she would be the candidate for Chairperson position of Athoor Block Panchayat as the same was reserved for women. The assurance given by her consolidated the vote banks at Athoor against her rival. The Scheduled Caste community supported her against her rival as the rival candidate belonged to Thevar community. Against this background, she won the election with a margin of nine hundred votes.

In the Block Panchayat Council Chairperson election she was selected unopposedly as the councillors of both the DMK and the TMC combine are in majority. But, for the position of Vice- Chairman there was a tough competition from the AIADMK to the TMC candidate as the two independent members decision could not have been assessed. And so it was told that the councillors who promised to support TMC candidate were all made available in a far away place one day or two day earlier to the Vice-Chairman election and they were brought to the office only at the time of election. In the meantime the two independent members also extended their support to the TMC candidate by the encouragement and effective canvassing of the DMK.

Panchayat Union Administration

The respondent has the opinion that the old system of Panchayati Raj was comparatively better than the new system especially with regard to union administration. The present scenario in panchayat union administration is not in tune with the principles of decentralization. The Block Development Officer and Assistant Block Development Officer are two separate entities and both of them are really under the control of higher officials. The ABDO never seriously responded to the call of the Union Council. He is not regularly attending the union council meeting. The power and authority to control over the school, health centres, public distribution system. Agriculture are still with the concerned departments of the State Government. The major items of panchayat union work are road, drinking water supply, providing infrastructural facilities like school, public health centres, building for PDS and shop, and bridge. The other items like development schemes of state and central governments are with ABDO, who is functioning independently. He is neither answerable to the council nor to the village panchayats. It is very difficult to comprehend the administration of Block Panchayats.

Union Council Meeting

The meetings are being regularly conducted and all councillors are actively participating in the deliberations. In general the demand are many from the councillors especially for drinking water supply and metal roads. The councillors used to raise the other problems of their villages and village panchayat administration. The women councillors in the union in the initial stages used to echo their husbands suggestion. Later on they have trained themselves to act and deliberate independently. The respondent opined that when the husband of a women councillor is an active cadre of any political party, it is not possible for that women councillor to act independently as the interest and interference of the husband could not be avoided.

The respondent felt that Athoor union's main problem is providing drinking water supply and the union as well as government administration is seriously looking into the demand of all village panchayats in this regard. By a comprehensive water supply scheme, seven to eight village panchayats have been already covered and under a new scheme three wells have been dug at the Perumbarai of Western ghat —Kodai range, situated at a distance of fifteen kilometres. The fund allocated under 10th Finance Commission is also spent on drinking water supply.

She complained that the officials are not properly attending the requests of the people. ABDO is not meeting the Chairman. The presidents of Gram panchayat have the opinion that they need not be at the mercy of the union council. Against this background the union Chairman has to function, she added. The new and innovative scheme "Anna Marumalarchi Thittam" and "Samathuvapuram" are being implemented in Athoor union. The respondent informed that she involved very seriously in identifying and purchasing land to the extend of fifteen acres for Samathuvapuram scheme. It was informed that if the land identification and purchase was delayed, the opportunity would be transferred to Nilakkottai. Hence she was hectically trying to locate a suitable land for Samathuvapuram.

Linkages with the District Panchayat

The respondent felt that the relationship between the union councillors and district councillors is cordial and regularly they meet each other and discuss about the functioning of the system.

Training Attended

The respondent informed that she attended a three day training programme at SIRD, Maraimalai Nagar, Chennai in which women's empowerment was emphasised. She felt that it was very much useful and suggested that the training must be periodical to enhance the capacity of the leaders. The respondent expressed that during group discussion in the training, a few participants told that the officials have not respected the women leader and sometime they are ill-treated if they are not assertive. The respondent further informed that initially the Collector used to convene monthly meeting for all union Chairpersons which helped a lot to share and discuss their problems among the Chairpersons in front of the collector for viable solutions. But at present no such periodical meetings.

She informed that she was the only women Chairperson attended a meeting held by the Public Health Department recently. She told that the meeting was useful as lot of information have been given on health related issues. She felt that all the panchayat presidents should know these informations as they are directly responsible for drinking water provision and maintenance of drinking water sources.

Panchayati Raj and Women's Empowerment

She informed that only through political orientation, women can be empowered. She further told that once in a month in her party meeting, public problems and government functions are being discussed. This opportunity is more or less a training ground for her.

She accepts that there are family constraints which have to be overcome only by mutual understanding between women and other family members. The officials' attitude has not been changed and still it is male dominated one. Women who are dare and courageous can successfully overcome any encounter. For others the position is always an ornamental one. The government is not strictly managing the officials properly for the advantage of the people. She felt that the DMK government is more people oriented, compared to previous AIADMK government, which colluded with corrupt officials and misused the public money.

Panchayati Raj System and Development of Scheduled Caste Community

The respondent said that the fund allocation was based on the population of the village and the block. And the allocation was further distributed in the ratio of 70% to SC's welfare and 30% to others. She further told that, the share extended to SC community in the schemes like Jeevandhara, Group Housing, TRYSEM are also considerably more than other communities. Home sites allocation, distribution of Saree and Dhoti, IRDP loan are very much helping SC community. She further informed that only the educated in the SC community are evincing keen interest in developing themselves and others in the same community are not really having self motive or self-initiative to develop themselves.

The Practical Problems Faced by Women Leadership

1. Lack of information.
2. Lack of political orientation and training in administrative skill.
3. Officials non-commitment and non-cooperation towards women empowerment.
4. People are not recognising the women services.
5. Social issues like caste, religion are not so easy to deal with as they

are now becoming part of local administration. Male leaders are sometime able to deal with them properly.

6. People do not have co-operative attitude towards panchayat bodies. When drainage/road facilities provided, the encroachers are not ready to move out from their places of occupation to help the local bodies to perform their functions properly.
7. Lack of will on the part of the leaders of political parties like Congress, Janata to empower the women through their activities. Parties like the DMK, the AIADMK, the CPI(M) and the CPI have women's wing which have been providing some opportunities to women in holding positions to orient themselves for public life.

The respondent felt that the decision of providing honorarium to Panchayati Raj leaders is a welcoming feature. The state government announced Rs.1000/- for District Panchayat President, Rs. 300/ District Panchayat Councillors, Rs.500/- Union Chairperson, Rs. 200/- Union Councillors, Rs.300/- to village panchayat president an honorarium per month. She hoped that the next period will witness an improvement in the working of Panchayati Raj System in Tamil Nadu. The leaders in panchayati system at present are really the leaders breaking a new path.

Section III

CAPACITY BUILDING FOR ELECTED WOMEN REPRESENTATIVES

Report of the Training

Table 5.6 : Details regarding the attendance

Sl. No.	District	Total No. of Unions	Total No. of Batches	Total No. of Participants
1.	Madurai	13	3	79
2.	Ramanathapuram	11	2	81
3.	Pudukkottai	13	2	78
	Total	37	7	238

Source : Computed.

Backdrop

73rd Constitutional Amendment Act and the subsequent enactment of the State Local Bodies Act of 1994 provide a large number of responsibilities to the local body leaders. To discharge all those responsibilities in a highly fragmented communities and complicated administrative system the local body leaders need adequate skill and capacity. Of all the prerequisites for smooth functioning of local bodies to deliver goods, capacity building exercise for local body leaders is foremost and imperative. It has been indicated in many fora that the leaders or representatives recruited for different authoritative bodies, namely National Parliament and State Legislature should have adequate skill and capacity to perform their role and function in a fast changing socio-political and economic system and thereby training is an imperative need. But nobody took keen interest on it. As a consequence our parliamentary institutions are fastly deteriorating in their standard of performance. The local body institutions cannot and should not follow the beaten path of the higher level representative institutions as these bodies are closely monitored by the people and the representatives in the local bodies are to see the faces of the people every day and they should be so responsive to their calls. Hence a programme of training for Gram Panchayati Presidents was conceived by Rajiv Gandhi Chair for Panchayati Raj Studies and the proposal was sent to CAPART Hyderabad for financial support. As Rajiv Gandhi Chair for Panchayati Raj Studies was instrumental in evolving a training module based on the excise done at the national level in Hyderabad for Tamil Nadu Planning Commission, CAPART Hyderabad was kind enough to approve the module and sanction the required financial support to take up the training programme for Gram Panchayati leaders for about five districts. To start with, the exercise had been planned for all Gram Panchayati presidents in two districts namely Dindigul and Sivaganga and on the basis of the experience in the two districts, the same exercise has been done for women and Dalits in three districts, namely Madurai, Ramanathapuram and Pudukkottai. In the first leg the evolved training module has been tested and accordingly modifications have been effected in the training. This programme was a beginning of a massive exercise. It is being done in batches. Each group consists of forty to forty five presidents of Gram panchayat. The training content of the programme includes the historical aspects of the Panchayati Raj System, constitutional aspects of the panchayats, main provisions of the federal and state acts, planning experience in India for economic growth and development, micro level planning for comprehensive development of the areas, activity dimensions of the panchayats on twenty nine subjects in 11th schedule, behavioural and performance dimensions of the presidents of the Gram panchayats. The methodology of training is more on dialogue and discussion. Vital issues have been video taped and shown to them. Field trips have been arranged to model panchayats to demonstrate the success of programmes by the active involvement of the people. Pre and post evaluation of the training programme has been done through administering an interview schedule. Information have been collected from the leaders on the practical problems faced by them when they perform their role and function in the panchayats.

How we have proceeded?

First eliciting the opinion and perception of the participants about the new dispensation and its activities.

Secondly, a sharing session is devoted to elicit the problems the participants face when they are at work. Here focus was given on the gender issues.

Thirdly, academic sessions devoted to deal with the role and responsibilities to be discharged by the panchayati presidents on the subjects earmarked to the rural local bodies.

Perception of the Leaders on New Panchayati Raj System

Before the commencement of the training exercise a schedule is being circulated among the trainees to elicit their perception and understanding of the New Panchayati Raj System. Their perceptions are explained here.

The perception that panchayats are to perform the service functions is linkering in the minds of leaders as they are not aware of the provisions and main implications of the New Panchayati Raj System. They had a rough idea about the new system that it would fulfill the basic needs of the people and provide basic amenities to the community. They presumed that more powers would be given to panchayats and equally more amount of money would also be given to panchayats. This has been created among the people by the media. They said that they did not find copies of the 73rd Amendment to the Constitution of India and hence they did not read the provisions of the Act. They did not care to read the provisions of the Tamil Nadu Panchayati Act, 1994, even though it was supplied to the Gram Panchayati leaders as the entire Act is in a language which is not understandable to them despite that it is in Tamil. Even the candidates who have contested in the election have not gone through the Act when it was enacted. Likewise they had a notion that the political parties will not evince keen interest in conducting the election. The moment election was announced, they contested in the fray with the hope to enjoy more powers and resources as MPs and MLAs. They have openly admitted that they have spent money for electioneering between rupees thirty five thousand to two lakhs.

In the interview schedule which was administered to elicit the opinion of the leaders, there are about twelve questions. They are:

a) basic objectives of the New Panchayati Raj System;
b) special features of the new system;
c) functions of the New Panchayati Raj System;
d) responsibilities of the presidents of Gram Panchayati;
e) ways and means to perform their role successfully;
f) methodology of organising the people and to involve them in the development activities of the community;
g) possibilities for rural economic development;
h) peoples participation in panchayati activities;
i) women's development;
j) SC/ST development activities;
k) social justice; and
l) the characteristics of a good leader in the panchayat.

Their responses to the above questions are as follows :

a) panchayat is to elicit their basic needs;
b) panchayat is to fulfill the basic needs;
c) panchayat is to implement the Government schemes for the poor;
d) panchayat is to provide basic facilities in the rural areas;
e) panchayat has three tier panchayati system;
f) panchayat will be a permanent entity;
g) panchayat will have 29 subjects in 11th Schedule;
h) panchayat will have a Gram Sabha;
i) panchayat is to select beneficiaries for government schemes;
j) panchayat is to supervise fair price shop;
k) panchayat is to mobilise resources for panchayats;
l) panchayat is to construct culverts, bridges, houses for the poor;
m) panchayat is to lay roads, and dig wells;
n) panchayat is to maintain sanitation;
o) panchayat is to protect the environment;

p) panchayat is to do aforestation activities;
q) panchayat is to protect the common property resources;
r) panchayat is to take steps to women's development;
s) panchayat is to convene the panchayat meetings periodically; and
t) panchayat is to organise Gram Sabha meeting periodically.

The presidents of Gram Panchayats are having a rough idea about what the panchayats can do and again reiterate the service functions as the functions of the panchayats. They forget about the original functions of the local bodies as per the provisions of the Act. They are not well aware of the basic objective of the 73rd Constitutional Amendment. They have not mentioned about the economic development activities and social justice. Because of the past three years, the Gram Panchayati leaders are oriented only in implementing the schemes and programmes of the governments. Even in discussion they ask more questions about schemes. They are not much worried about the planning and resource mobilization for economic activities.

Problems the Women Leaders have Faced in the Field

Group discussions are being arranged to elicit their problems face in the field while performing their role and functions. Their problems are presented here.

1. Presidents of Gram panchayats are not aware of all the rural development programmes and schemes. They know only a few programmes from the officials. Even for a few schemes they are not able to get the full details from the officials.
2. Needs of the people are going on increasing which need enormous amount of resources. To meet all their requirements there is no comprehensive plan and moreover they have no adequate resources.
3. Employees and teachers working in the purview of panchayats, are not employees of the panchayats and they are all employees of the Government and hence the employees are not accountable to local bodies; as a result schools are not properly managed. Yet the presidents are made accountable to the people for the proper functioning of the schools in the villages.
4. Resources (both in the form of money mobilised from within and drawn from outside.
5. Capacity of the workers working in the rural areas are inadequate to

meet the problems in the rural society. Attending the repair works in the street light or motors fixed in over head tanks is not in time and the technicians caused inordinate delay. Rates for the repairing work is very low and hence nobody turns towards these works. For the purchase of materials for the repairing works or replacement, presidents have no option but to give more money than the market rate and where they will go for this extra payment. Naturally, they will indulge in corrupt practice. Even if they want to be honest the system would not permit them to be honest.

6. Providing shelter is a major problem in the rural areas. Whether it is providing patta or getting housing scheme presidents have to face lot of problems as needs are more and available resources are limited. Moreover while providing these facilities discretion of officials plays an important role rather than the procedures of the programmes and schemes.
7. IRDP beneficiary selection is a major problem due to the interference of the politicians, MLAs and MPs.
8. Getting the village map is very difficult from the revenue officials because large number of irregularities have been committed by the revenue officials in the matter of common properties. Absolutely there is no co-operation from the revenue department and other sectoral departments in this regard.
9. It is very difficult to removė encroachment from the common properties. It requires the support of Revenue Department and Police. As per the government order they have to support the panchayat to remove all encroachments of the common properties. It is unfortunate that officials are co-operating with the panchayats for eviction.
10. Common property resources have not been maintained well to yield income to panchayats since they are not under the control of the local bodies. They are being encroached by influencing individuals.
11. Needs are unmet even after the panchayats came into being.
12. No relationship between the needs and the schemes.
13. Still we have complicated administrative procedures at the lower level.
14. Difficult to provide employment opportunities to the needy.
15. Officials domination over the elected leaders is evident and they dictate terms to the leaders.
16. People's mind-set is that everything has to be done by the government. People are only to receive. They expect each and everything to be

taken care of by the local body leaders.

17. Common property resource management should be given to local bodies. Sand, quary and other natural resources are the properties of the community. But now on a single order they are taken away from the people without getting the consent of the community.
18. Powers of the Union Engineer (UE) are unlimited and UE is the embodiment of corruption. He is more powerful than the Block Development Officer. He is the person responsible for clearing bills, proposals and hence he makes the Gram Panchayat presidents to dance to his tune. Union Engineer demands 15% commission for each and every work.
19. Interference of MPs and MLAs in the affairs of local bodies is more and their words are respected and their interference in the local body affairs disturb the activities of the local bodies. Increasing the amount for MLAs and MPs would attempt to kill the local bodies.
20. In all government functions organised in the rural areas, the concerned constituency MP and MLA are invited but the local body leaders are not respected and invited.
21. Presidents are elected by the people and vice-presidents of Gram panchayats are elected by ward members. But to sign the cheque, it was made that vice-president should also sign. It disturbs the atmosphere and administration. Vice-president's demand money to put his or her signature.
22. Women presidents are not respected by the officials. Sometimes they were ill-treated in the offices. They face lot of problems in the offices of the government.
23. More flexibility should be given in the schemes to local body leaders to meet the basic needs of the people.
24. Public distribution system should be supervised by the panchayats in the local areas.
25. Government orders are not properly circulated among the local body leaders.
26. For each and every transaction officials in the panchayat union demand money openly.
27. There is no linkage between panchayat and the co-operatives.
28. Makkal Nala Paniyalargal are in the panchayats and they have to work under panchayats and they have to get their salary from panchayats. Yet, in practice they are not working in co-ordination with the

president. Hence the procedure of giving salary to them in panchayat union office should be stopped. Now only government have raised and they are brought under the control of the Gram Panchayats.

29. Ration cards are to be distributed through Gram Sabha to elimate bogus cards.
30. For making estimate and settlement of bills, officials take lot of time but to execute the programmes and schemes officials give very short duration to the leaders. This has to be avoided.
31. Birth certificate, death certificate, community certificate should be issued by the panchayats through resolution. Erring leaders have to be punished. Now these certificates are being given by the officials (revenue) after getting Rs. 300 as brife.
32. There is no linkage between the revenue department and the development departments.
33. The role of district panchayat is not known to Gram panchayat presidents.
34. MPs, MLAs, District Panchayat Members, Block Panchayat Members are operating funds to execute certain works in the villages without the knowledge of the people and the Gram Panchayats. All these works are to be integrated. Now these works were not on the basis of need and hence lot of money is being wasted by alloting them for construction work.
35. Panchayats are advised to take up works without claiming any advance. Where do they find money for work? Even after completing the work the presidents have to move from pillar to post to get their money from the offices and for which they have to give bribe to officials at all levels.
36. Allocation of money to MP, MLA, District Panchayat Member, Block Panchayat Member tempted the Village Panchayat Ward Members to pose that they should also be given some amount of money for works.

Input given by the Resource Persons

1. Background of 73rd Constitutional Amendment.
2. Salient features of 73rd Constitutional Amendment.
3. Features of the Panchayati Act of Tamil Nadu, 1994.
4. Powers and responsibilities entrusted to panchayats.

5. Government orders passed in Tamil Nadu akin to panchayats.
6. Schemes and programmes of both governments.
7. Water supply and sanitation.
8. Pre-natal and post-natal care.
9. Children and women development.
10. Multi Level Planning in PRI's.
11. Employment generation and administering social justice.
12. Agriculture and Animal Husbandry.
13. Common Property Resource Management.
14. Maintenance of Accounts.
15. Resource Mobilisation.
16. Participatory Planning.
17. Self-Help Groups and Village Industries.
18. Participatory Governance through Gram Sabha.
19. Environmental issues.
20. Communication skill.
21. Improving Leadership qualities.
22. Transparency and accountability.
23. Peoples charter and its implication.
24. Making this institution as peoples institutions.
25. Containing corruption at the grassroots level.
26. Gender sensitization.
27. Special focus on (SGSY).

People's Expectations as Perceived by the Leaders

1. Approach road to the burial ground belonging to SC community and BC community.
2. Upgradation of metal road into Block Toproad.
3. Additional building for PDS due to more family cards.
4. Veterinary sub-centre.
5. Group Housing Scheme.
6. Hand pumps.
7. Replacing the Iron Post (street lights) with cement post as the EB wire man refuses to climb over the iron post.

8. Approach roads to helmet villages.
9. Removal of encroachments of road and street leading to SC habitation.
10. Increasing the number of lineman (EB) according to the number of street lights.
11. Overhead Tank.
12. TWARD board incomplete works must be completed.
13. More trips of buses to their villages.
14. Plan for improving and maintaining Common Property Resources.
15. To provide sanitation facilities during festival time sanctioned amount is not sufficient.
16. Employment opportunities to young men and women.
17. Repair work at over head tanks.

Leaders Perception after the Training

Before the Valedictory session, again an interview schedule is being distributed to elicit their opinion about the implications of training. Apart from filling up the schedule, they openly express their opinion about the training programme in the valedictory session. Some VIP will be there in each programme to distribute the certificate. The session has an advantage for the trainers to correct themselves in their methodology of the training. Their perceptions about the Panchayati Raj after the training programme have been compiled and presented below.

1. They perceived the long-term implications of the New Panchayati Raj System.
2. The mind-set that local bodies are to execute schemes and programmes of the governments has been changed and the new mind-set that local bodies are to work for economic development and social justice has been created.
3. They learnt to make the Panchayats as peoples panchayats and not the governments panchayats.
4. It is not power but it is only responsibility that makes the panchayats as self governing institution.
5. They realise that without money panchayats can do many programmes in the villages.
6. They realise the original functions of the local bodies.

7. They feel that they are change agents.
8. Key provisions of the 73rd Constitutional Amendment Act and Tamil Nadu Panchayati Raj Act are known to the Gram Panchayats presidents.
9. How to prepare perspective plan for rural development? is known to them.
10. It is recognised as a governing institution.
11. Schemes and programmes of the government are known to them.
12. Role and responsibilities of the presidents are known to them.
13. How to create employment opportunities in the villages by making use of the available skills? is known to them.
14. How to mobilize resources in the rural areas? is known to them
15. How to make the panchayats as movement of the people? is known to them.
16. How to get the government orders from the officials? is known to them.
17. How to get the works done in the government offices? is known to them.
18. How to conduct the panchayat administration in a transparent way? is known to them.
19. How to mobilize people and to involve them in the panchayat activities? are known to them.
20. Issues and solutions are known to them.
21. How to protect the environment? is known to them.
22. How to make the rural areas Green? is known to them.

Points Aggregated from the Group Discussion

a) Madurai District

1. Political interference and politization of issues by party men in the villages. They look at panchayats as political institutions and not as development institutions.
2. The people are not at all satisfied with the necessary facilities provided to them. Their demands are always on the increase in geometrical proportion.
3. Selection of beneficiaries is not an easy job. Every political segment

wants to include the names of its candidates in the beneficiary list. Hence the final selection is done by the officials. People have been oriented to obey the officials and not to the leaders. Still people have hopes in the officials.

4. The community control over the society is more than the Panchayat control where one community is large in number. Still community panchayats are powerful.
5. The ward members demanded that their ward must be given in priority in all the works. Every one wants to please the people by hook or crook.
6. The allocation of fund is not proportionate to total population. Wherever SC and ST population is more, fund allocations are abundant. But the conditions of the caste Hindus hamlets are also on par with the hamlets of the SC and ST. In several villages the variation of the total population is more than 2000. Our administration acts on wrong data base.
7. The Hand Pump are not functioning well. The depth of water table has gone down very deeply.
8. The House tax may be increased. But people resist and further party men are instigating the people to resist it. People are willing but politicians are instigating the people not to give.
9. The PHC supposed to be functioning round the clock are not functioning till night. Hence poor people sought panchayats president's support to take the patients to towns for treatment.
10. There must be a special meeting of all representatives to discuss and decide the various developmental activities of the villages and the possible ways and means to augment resources for the same from within and from the state and central governments. This initiative has to be taken by the inspector of panchayats. Inspector of panchayats should have a facilitating role in the panchayati system rather than inspecting role. At present the Inspector of panchayat has come to take action only against the president of the Gram Panchayats.
11. The officials released the fund not in time but they chase the president to complete the work quickly. Hence, quality is not ensured. It seems that the schemes are to spend money and not to ensure facility to the people.
12. Sufficient awareness must be created among the people on the significance of Gram Sabha. In the absence of awareness, Gram Sabha

is a grievance redressal sabha.

13. Anna Marumalarchi Thittam — the selection process is not transparent. The MLAs are expecting commission to select the panchayat. Hence, only poor panchayat should be selected for AMT as per the norms.
14. The village commons should be entrusted to the panchayat. But now they are with traditional panchayats and some of them are with influential individuals. We can control and check the encroachments by entrusting the power and responsibility to panchayats. Further the commons could be enriched and fruitfully utilized. There is a lot of scope for augment resources from the common properties.
15. The government officials especially the field level officials must be asked to stay in the villages. Workers and officials of rural development are not living in the villages. They are also conducting rural development tourism.
16. The police administration is not helpful in dealing with encroachment problem. Eventhough the government order clearly states that the police have to help the panchayats in this regard, the police are always in the hands of the vested interests.
17. The revenue officials are not seriously functioning to protect common property resources. They even allow the individuals to encroach public way to burial ground.
18. At least once in two months the district authorities must meet presidents.
19. MP/MLA fund allocation has to be abrogated or atleast streamlined otherwise a huge amount of money is going to be wasted. MLA's and MPs are doing some work which are not the felt needs of the people.
20. Even to receive ration card, we have to mobilise people and take public action like dharna. This type of indifferent attitude has to be checked on the part of the officials.
21. The irregularities in PDS should be dealt with seriously by the officials or it can be brought under the control of panchayats. People are bringing complaints only to the presidents. For the effective functioning of PDS, central government believes the panchayats can do it better and the state government believes the officials can do better.
22. The ex-presidents and defeated candidates create problems on most of the occasions in the panchayat administration. Instead of co-

operation, they always develop conflict with panchayat council.

23. The grievance reddressal system is very complicated and expensive. For example, when the caste Hindu encroached the land site earmarked for SC community housing, the problem is not sorted out by the officials. The president took the case to the court and redeem the land after a struggle. It takes money, energy and time.
24. The works undertaken in the villages by other tiers of panchayats are not known to the village panchayats and people are not consulted whether that work is needed or not.
25. Training is very essential for panchayat leaders for their effective functioning. But the Government of Tamil Nadu has not given serious attention to the training aspect. Now atleast Gandhigram Rural Institute is giving such training. It should not be a one time affair. It should be a continuous one.
26. The help and support of family male members is needed due to the villagers non-co-operation and groupism.
27. Uneducated and uninterested women presidents only allow their husbands/male members of their family to interfere in the administration of the panchayat and others only seek support and help from the male members of their family. It should not be treated as proxy. It will be proxy only when the space of the women is operated by men or others.
28. The house tap connections permitted during the official tenure have to be disconnected now. When the presidents take necessary steps towards this decision, the officials are not supporting the presidents for their actions. Most of the occasions the officials are creating problems in the villages.
29. To replace the street lights, the E.B. staff demand more money than what is permitted.
30. The existing procedure for repairing electric motors is illogical one. For the whole district two to three persons are given license whereas a large number of motors have to be repaired immediately. In each block, there must be one or two motor mechanics approved by government.
31. The vacancy of positions in village schools should be filled up immediately.
32. The schools are not clean and the environment is not so conducive

for learning. We have no control over school administration. We have to maintain only school building. It is illogical on the part of the government to give building to panchayats and retaining the staff with them.

33. The government appointed Makkal Nala Paniyalarkal are not useful to panchayats. They obey their pay master in union. They are party men doing party work at the cost of the people. Sometimes they are anti-social elements.
34. The G.O. and other guidelines pertaining to local administration are not properly sent to the panchayats.
35. There must be a special fund to improve the poor panchayats.

b) Ramanathapuram District

36. The relationship between the presidents and the officials are smooth because of the intervention of the Inspector of panchayats. But it is not a permanent feature.
37. Due to power fluctuation, the street light burning is always a problem, and hence people are bringing complaints and they are not attended to by the EB staff responsively.
38. We are able to provide tanks, library, drinking water, school building, PDS building shelter to passengers and street lights in the villages. But people expect further facilities such as house tap connection, drainage, cement pavement in the street and sweeper services which demands more finance.
39. We are able to obtain land for overhead tank and PDS shop. It could not be possible during the officials tenure. Yet our achievements are not recognised.
40. Involving community leadership is a technique for smooth functioning and to avoid conflict between official panchayats and traditional panchayats.
41. With the help of women sangams we are doing shramdhan works. But while the noonmeal scheme implementation was evaluated, the sangam of noon meal workers threatened the president. In this situation people have not come forward to help the presidents.
42. The Block level monitoring committee for noon meal scheme appointed by the government is not properly functioning due to its limited membership in the committee.

43. There are still a few villages where there is no drinking water facility. The TWAD scheme is not yet reached there.
44. We have involved ourselves in school activities and we have encouraged sports and cultural events for children in the schools. We collected public fund for upgrading middle school to high school. Even without adequate powers, we are doing our best to provide quality education to our people.
45. The people living in the extension area are expecting all facilities for them in one stroke which is highly impossible at present.
46. We maintain the communal harmony in the villages but the political parties are working in a different style and they are creating clashes among the caste groups.
47. We formed approach road to the remote villages through Namakku Name Thittam.
48. We spent money for improving the bank of the irrigation tanks and we are not able to maintain the same due to the interference of the officials.
49. There are villages where electricity service is not yet reached.
50. The officials are not giving special attention to the buildings of Balwadi/School which need immediate repair work and we find usual delay in this also.

c) Pudukottai District

51. Unaware of the details of fund allocation under various schemes in the various departments of the government.
52. Lack of knowledge and practice in augmenting more resources to improve the financial position of the panchayat.
53. The other two tiers have no link with Gram Panchayats.
54. The MLA, MP area development allocation is not reaching the non-party presidents for their activities in the rural areas.
55. Non-implementation of the resolutions passed in the Gram Sabha meetings resulted in non-co-operation of people to the panchayats.
56. No records available about Common Property Resources in the villages.
57. Officials have helped the influential individuals to encroach the common properties.

58 The auction of social forestry trees is unduly delayed in spite of repeated requests. The revenue officials are indifferent in this assignment.

59. The fishery right is vested with the private party in a village tank. The domination of caste panchayat over the commons is a very big problem in the villages.

60. No special grant for maintenance of CPR. Over 40 years, poor are residing over the sides of the tankbund. But patta is not issuing to them.

61. Poor families in Backward Community are also demanding group housing facility.
    - The repair work at SC group house was not undertaken as promised by higher officials.
    - The MLA, MP fund allocation mostly for their own party people.
    - Untouchability is still persisting in rural areas. Revenue officials do not seriously to attend to this problem. Police force is not coming to protect the SC.
    - VAO, Police and Revenue Officials are joining their hands to protect the selfish interest of the encroachers.
    - The agriculture engineering department, forest department, are not showing any interest in the panchayats when they are implementing their schemes.
    - The Gram Sabha attendance is in the diminishing trend due to non-fulfilling of their earlier demands and expectations.

Materials Supplied to them

1. A Printed Book of 400 pages
   with details of 73rd Constitutional Amendment Act;
   with details of the Tamil Nadu Rural Local Body Act of 1994;
   with a brief history of Panchayati Raj;
   with a brief outline of Planning Experience in India;
   Micro Level Planning and participative development process;
   All schemes and programmes of the centre and state governments with all details;
   Resource mobilization;
   Common Property Resource Management;
   Importance and implications of community action;
   MPs Area development programme details;

MLAs constituency development programme details and the hurdles to make panchayati as self-governing institutions.
2. All government orders pertinent to local bodies.
3. A well desined jute bag.
4. A scribbling pad.
5. A Pen.
6. Important addresses of institutions to get more informations about panchayati activities.
7. A charter of panchayats.
8. A book on people's participation in panchayat activities – Kerala Experiences.

Conclusion

The capacity building exercise for Gram Panchayat Presidents has to go a long way to achieve its results. It is a good beginning by which their mind-set has been changed. Lot of information have been exchanged. Their potentiality has been drawn out. Sixty per cent of attendance has been ensured. Material suppiied to them are properly used by the participants of the training programme. Women leaders have evinced keen interest in listening the lectures. One aspect is obvious from their interactions – *i.e.*, they need a supporting base as government officials are not favourable to them. They feel that they are not properly oriented either by the officials or by the family members who are guiding them for their action. But in the slow process they have gained confidence. They said that their struggle is silent. In the silent struggle a section of the women leaders have come to a conclusion that they have to withdraw from this space. But there is a section with a good number of leaders have determined to continue in the space created for them and they have identified the supportive organisations and through which they gain support and strength. One important aspect that the utilization of the space created for women by the women has to be seriously looked into by our research endeavour.

Notes and References

1. G. Palanithurai, *Report on Empowerment of Panchayati Raj Institutions on issues related Population, Health and Social Development* (sponsored by Population Foundation of India) Rajiv Gandhi Chair for Panchayati Raj Studies, 1997.
2. G. Palanithurai, *Report of the Training Programme Conducted for Gram Panchayati Presidents – Dindigul & Sivaganga Districts* (sponsored by CAPART), Rajiv Gandhi Chair for Panchayati Raj Studies, 1998.

3. G. Palanithurai, *Report of the Training Programme Conducted for Women Presidents of Gram Panchayats in Five Districts.* (sponsored by Social Welfare Board), Rajiv Gandhi Chair for Panchayati Raj Studies, 1998.
4. G. Palanithurai, *Report of the Training Programme Conducted for Presidents and Vice-presidents on Water Supply and Sanitation in Villupuram and Cuddalore Districts.* (sponsored by DANIDA), Rajiv Gandhi Chair for Panchayati Raj Studies, 1998.
5. V. B. Athreya and K. S. Rajeswari, *Women's Participation in Panchayati Raj — A Case Study from Tamil Nadu* (sponsored by Women Commission) M.S. Swaminathan Research Foundation, Chennai, 1998.

6

CAPACITATING LOCAL BODY LEADERS

Section I

IMPORTANCE AND IMPLICATIONS

"Where are the powers? and where is the resource? are the repeated demands of the elected presidents of village panchayats in Tamil Nadu for the past two years after the election to local bodies. It is a general trend in India that elected representatives of State Legislature and National Parliament do not incline to get any kind of orientation or training to perform their role and function both inside and outside those bodies as representatives. The consequence of this trend is the conflicting and ambiguous role perception and performance of the legislators and thereby the legislative institutions have come down to the lowest ebb in terms of their performance. Representatives of the local bodies have also followed the same track to perform their role and discharge their responsibilities. It is obvious that the ambiguous and conflicting role perception of the leaders of local bodies will bring disastrous consequences in the society as they are executives and executing several programmes in the society unlike the legislators of higher level Legislative institutions.

Having realised the implications of training, well meaning leaders and intellectuals from the very beginning of the exercise of installing local bodies insisted that capacity building exercise for the local body leaders at the lowest level is an imperative need. Meaningful exercise has been done at different level to finalize the training module for this excise. National Institute of Rural Development, Hyderabad brought out a handy volume of a training module for local body leaders. Based on this excise Tamil Nadu Planning Commission also evolved a manual suitable to the given environment and published the same. This being the starting point, Rajiv Gandhi Chair for Panchayati Raj Studies in Gandhigram Rural Institute initiated the programme of conducting capacity building exercise for Gram Panchayati presidents in five southern districts of Tamil Nadu with the financial support of CAPART, a wing of the Ministry of Rural Areas and Employment, Government of India.

This unique excise brought wealth of information about what is going on in the rural areas in the name of Panchayati Raj. Despite the Panchayati

Raj Act of 1994, passing of innumerable Government Orders, allocating huge amount of money apart from the funds of MPs and MLAs, the needs of the people are still unmet and they are growing. The increasing inflow of funds from various schemes and programmes of the Government representatives of the people in Block Panchayats and district panchayats, MLAs and MPs has escalated the tension in the villages as to which section is a major beneficiary. There is no doubt, activities are on in the village through various schemes but the president of Gram Panchayat does not know under whose allocation the activities take place. It is unequivocal that as schemes and programmes are available the elected leaders are advised to take up such schemes and execute the same within the stipulated time to make a report that the target is achieved. The irony is that the local bodies have to assess the needs, prepare a plan mobilize resources to meet the needs and to perform all those responsibilities, the bodies need powers but the reality depicts a different picture that the government has schemes and for the execution of schemes it has resources, since they have money, the local bodies have to take up the schemes and execute the schemes certain powers are given. Thus there is no relationship between the needs of the people and the programmes executed in the villages. The demands continue to grow and unmet, contrarily schemes and programmes are proliferated and executed irrespective of the need and by which huge amount of money is being wasted. Many examples have been quoted. For instance retaining wall is a scheme, local body leaders use to execute the scheme irrespective of the need in the village.

There is yet another issue which has been highlighted by all the president of Gram panchayats of Dindigul and Sivaganga districts is the continuing corruption in development works that are being executed in the rural areas. From estimation to clearing of bills for the works executed, one has to bribe the officials and for which there is an accepted percentage. Those who fall in line with the officials need not worry about all the formalities and those who do not follow the officials in this regard has to face the problem. Thirty one guide books with stipulated norms have been handed over to each panchayati president with three sets of pass books of the banks to execute schemes and programmes of the Governments.

The question is whether the Gram Panchayati president with their poor educational background will be able to follow all these rules as officials. Hence panchayat clerks are more powerful than the presidents. To make estimate and to clear the bills, officials take their own time and the officials give very little time to execute the works. To execute JRY schemes the president cannot get advance and the programme has to be executed and then only claims can be made. Who will give advance for taking up the works? Assuming that a few presidents are able to mobilize money and they have executed. Will it be possible to get the amount in one instalment immediately after the execution of the work? without paying the mamool? Likewise the government has fixed rates for repairing works in the street light but the line man of the Electricity Department is not doing the job and with this amount no one is able to do that works. In the same way Government has fixed rates for material to be purchased for street lights which are sometime costlier than the market rates and the shops are faraway from the villages. The articles purchased from the shops approved by the government are durable as a result tube lights will be bright for a few days and they will be dim for a few days and totally they will be off within a short span of time. People bring lot of complaints against this type of mistakes done by the panchayats. Such practical difficulties they face while performing certain service functions.

Common properties are considered to be the lifeline of the poor and the best sources of income to the panchayats but all those properties are now not with the panchayats. They are all encroached by many influential individuals in the rural areas with the support of the political parties. To remove encroachment the presidents need the village map which is available in the revenue department but they are not supplied to them even after repeated demands made by Gram panchayat presidents. Absolutely there is no co-ordination and co-operation between development department and revenue department.

It is the rule that the Gram Sabha of the village panchayat has to be convened at least twice a year without exceeding six months between the earlier meeting and the next one to consider the budget, approve the annual report and to approve the plan for development. As per the latest order one tenth is the quorum for the Gram Sabha meeting. First question is whether decision could be taken in a open air meeting with thousand and more members in a given environment. Do we have such space to accommodate one thousand in a place in the villages? Will the people assemble in a particular place in a multi caste village? It is to be seen.

There is yet another problem the elected panchayat presidents are facing while discharging their responsibilities is the inference of the leaders of the traditional panchayats. Traditional panchayats have their own arrangement with their own resources supported by the people. Often they clash with each other for resource sharing. In most of the places the dual practice stifles the functioning of the New Panchayati Raj System.

In the election almost all the presidents has spend money from thousand to two lakh rupees. They openly agreed that they contested in the election with the hope that more powers would be given and more amount of resources would be given and from the amount minimum of profit could be gained or perks would be fixed for leaders as MLAs and MPs and through which a small potion of the amount could be managed. But the reality is contrary to the expectation. Moreover the Government of Tamil Nadu has published the CBI address in the news paper and people are keeping this address with them. If anybody makes money out of the transaction, people would give petition to CBI. This is the trend prevails in the villages. They feel that there is no control over the officials and they continue to demand money from them. Where will they go for money? is a question.

As the leaders of the people in the local bodies have not read anything about the amendment, the new local bodies act of Tamil Nadu and all the programmes and schemes of the governments both centre and the state. Hence the officials working in Panchayati Union Office and DRDA have oriented them by giving them the details about the schemes and programmes of the government to be executed in the rural areas. Hence the mind-set has been created among the leaders that the panchayats are to execute the schemes of the government.

The five day training in Gandhigram Rural Institute has given needed inputs such as the role of panchayati institutions in economic development and social justice, imperatives of micro level planning, community actions in tackling the basic needs, common property resources management and linkage between the NGO and the panchayats to the Gram panchayat presidents. In the post evaluation test, it is inferred that the mind-set of the leaders that panchayats are to execute schemes has been changed. Further they had the perception that panchayats are the governments panchayats and after training they came to know and feel that it is peoples panchayats. They have realised that even without financial resources lot of activities could be created in the villages. Thus it is necessary that the capacity of the local body leaders have to be enhanced to make them as change agents.

Section II

A REPORT ON TRAINING ON IMPROVEMENT OF PANCHAYAT ADMINISTRATION

Part A

Introduction

It was proposed to implement a massive programme on total sanitation in Cuddalore district with the support of the central government and the state government. Before launching the programme, it was decided to build the capacity of the elected representatives of the people in the rural local bodies on both administration of the panchayats and the total sanitation programme. Steps have been taken methodically to conduct the exercise. Training modules and manuals have been prepared. The whole exercise have been carried out by the Rajiv Gandhi Chair for Panchayati Raj Studies and logistic support had been provided by the officials of DRDA of Cuddalore under the supervision of the Additional Collector. The following are the narrative of the experience gained out of the capacity building exercise done at Cuddalore for the leaders of the people.

Training to Village Panchayat Presidents
Content of the Training Programme

a) Why decentralisation and devolution of power?
b) Improvement of Panchayat Administration.
c) Total Rural Sanitation Programme.
d) Rajiv Gandhi National Drinking Water Mission.

Why this decentralisation of power

- Deepening of democracy – all sections of people to participate in governance.
- Participation for development.
- More responsibilities to people.
- Reduction of Government structure
- Creating responsible citizens.
- Develop human resources.
- Improve human skill.

- Maximum use of human resources.
- Prepare people for planned activities.
- Economic development.
- Social justice.
- Use the facilities for development.
- Facilitate for transparent administration.
- Movement for development.
- Planning from grassroots.
- Pro-nature.
- Pro-women.
- Pro-poor.

Duties and Responsibilities of Village Panchayats

The Constitution has specified duties and responsibilities of the village panchayats to work with a vision of developing the villages. The duties are:

1. Statutory Functions

- Construction, repair and maintenance of all the panchayat roads and culverts.
- put up drainage and sewage
- to provide public and individual latrines
- create and maintain graveyards
- to create (repair and maintain) wells, small ponds and lakes

2. Obligatory Functions

- Planning and maintaining trees on both sides of the roads.
- providing street lights in public places
- organise sandies
- constructing bus shelter
- provide reading rooms, radio/TV rooms, parks, playground and gymnasium.
- work for social education and to create cultural centres

Also the state government has provided development activities in 29 subjects under 11 Schedule. The State Government has issued orders in this regard.

Thus the participants had been oriented to understand clearly all the statutory and obligatory functions role as well as the roles to be performed under 11 Schedule and work for the development of their villages.

Panchayat Administration

The Tamil Nadu Panchayat Act, 1994 provides that village panchayat presidents to function as an Executive Officer of the panchayat and the following are the duties of the president :

1. Carryout the resolutions of the panchayat;
2. Control all the officials and workers of the village panchayat;
3. Prepare and send the annual administrative reports in the prescribed format; and
4. Prepare the income and expenditure statement, get the approval of the council and the approved copy to be sent to the panchayat union.

Thus, presidents as Executive Officers (of the village panchayat), they have to play a dual role and hence to perform their dual role they have to develop enough skill, especially they have to follow the following activities.

1. Day to day activities

- present in the office in time
- tax collection/supervision/deposit it in the bank
- direct visit to the hamlet
- public contact
- supervise the works
- response to letters (communication/relation/contact with other department)

2. Preparation for the meetings/convene the meetings

- council meetings
- Gram Sabha meetings
- special meetings
- meetings for mobilizing the people to take up the schemes like Varummun Kappom, Valvoli Thittam, Animal Health Camp etc.
- successful conduct of these meetings by creating confidence and good rapport with other members.

3. Contact with Government Officer

- understanding the needs for acquiring and improving skill of developing rapport and cordial relations with government officials, creating confidence among the officials working in developmental departments and the need for joint efforts in all developmental activities.

4. **Public Relations**

- Skill in the art of mobilisation of people for participation in development activities.
- Forming seven groups by involving the people.
- Forming advisory committees to solve problems with peoples representation and active participation.
- Motivating and guiding youth groups, helping the womens forum.
- Special arrangements for the development of farmers, artisans etc.

5. **Special Efforts for Social Justice**

- Creating awareness among the people about the need for social cohesion to achieve peace and prosperity.
- Take precautionary steps to prevent social injustice.
- Receive guidance from government higher officials through regular contact.

Thus, the presidents were guided to improve their leadership qualities.

Planning for Village Development

Under this subject, the participants had been oriented to understand the importance of planning and the various approaches in planning.

- Collecting the necessary statistical information on various developmental sectors of their area.
- Assessing the available human and natural resources.
- Planning should be a wholesome process leading to economic development and social justice – integrating human and natural resources through planning for economic development.
- Prioritising the needs.
- Financial resources : panchayats own resources (tax, matching grant etc), state plan allocation, central plan allocation, Finance Commissions awards, income from common property resources and public contribution have been explained to them. The importance of peoples participation in all the above activities was also explained.

Planning with Peoples Participation

One of the features of the New Panchayati Raj System is the Gram Sabha. The Gram Sabha is an instrument for effective functioning of Panchayati Raj Institution that enables the leaders to involve people in every step from identifying the needs of the village society, prioritise them, planning for socio-economic development to evaluating the implementation of the programmes. People with their traditional approach and skills would contribute a lot for planning and to achieve development.

The twin objectives of New Panchayati Raj System are to administer economic development and 'Social Justice'. To achieve these two objectives, peoples participation, their involvement and co-operation in the development activities are essential. Development should be a natural process. Development by dependence is not sustainable. The main reason attributed for the stagnation of development in the rural areas is the dependency syndrome. The dependency syndrome has eaten away the creativity of the people. But in the new system the dependency syndrome has to be eliminated and for which people are to be mobilised to participate in the community activities for economic development and social justice. For this process the present mind-set of the people including leaders and officials has to be changed. These details have been explained to the participants. People should have aspiration to achieve development and they should be in a position to take initiative and the initiative of the people has to be facilitated and supported by the government. Thus a new mind -set has to be created.

In the activities of the New Panchayati Raj Systems peoples participation has been made mandatory. To ensure maximum participation, the following details have been explained to them.

1. Gram Sabha meetings
2. Peoples participation
3. Planning
4. Evaluation of the programmes
5. Budget
6. Social audit
7. Prioritising the needs/works
8. Selection of beneficiaries by Gram Sabha
9. Formation of committees

These committees are, appointment committee, welfare committee, health committee, committee for drinking water and sanitation, public distribution committee, agricultural production committee, implementing committee and educational committee. Social workers and representatives of government departments are the members of these committees. Special programmes like Namakku Namme Thittam, Valvoli Thittam, Varumun Kappom Thittam, Rajiv Gandhi National Drinking Water Mission have been explained to them.

Total Rural Sanitation Programme and Rajiv Gandhi National Drinking Water Mission

The participants were imparted with the following details :

The Panchayati Raj Institutions have been provided with the necessary powers and duties as well as responsibilities to improve the sanitary conditions in their areas. These panchayats have to take necessary steps to implement the programme. They should analyse the prevailing sanitary condition of their villages. More specifically

A – keeping the water sources clean
– purity in drinking water supply
– pre-caution in using drinking water
– necessary arrangements for protected water supply.

B – sanitation of village/street
– arrangement for sullage disposal
– safe measures for solid waste removal
– construction of individual latrines
– construction of public toilets
– manure pit (both public and individual)
– soak pits

C – awareness about sanitation
– cultivating habits
– formation of social habits

D – Prevailing practice of rural sanitation/demonstrations/ uses

E – Health sub-centre
– balwadis
– noon meal centres (TINP Centres)
– School children's health and sanitation

First of all, the presidents should gather necessary information about the existing sanitary condition of the village, analyse them and identify the health/sanitary needs of their respective villages. Then they should know the available schemes and gather full details about such schemes.

Keeping these in mind they must plan for the total rural sanitation programmes for their respective villages.

The latest and appropriate technology has to be adopted in removing the solid and liquid wastes and they should keep in mind the defects in following the present method of removing the wastes.

We should not depend wholly on government to meet the basic health needs. People have to fulfill them on them own. Only the concerned persons are responsible for personal as well as family hygiene and the government can only help to some extent.

The importance of peoples participation in health education and health awareness creation was explained to the participants. Also the joint efforts and activities to be carried out with other departments like education, health, TWAD board, agricultural engineering, agriculture, social welfare, women development were also explained. Since the total rural sanitation programme includes a number of activities, the presidents were guided to improve their talents and skills as well as administrative abilities. Suggestions were offered to the presidents to act carefully in activities like forming committees on drinking water and sanitation, convening committee meetings, distributing responsibilities and in encouraging the committee members in performing their duties. In all these activities, peoples involvement should be ensured properly.

Kerala state is a pioneering example in ensuring peoples involvement in all such activities. The details of how the Panchayati Raj administration with peoples involvement was helpful in each activities like child welfare, health status, personal hygiene and preventive arrangements were explained to the participants. The details regarding the research institutes for quality test were given to them. Details regarding sources of participation, how the land and air pollute the water, the effect of effluents from the mills, household wastes were also discussed in the training programme.

The decreasing ground water level for irrigation, the need for water saving and water harvesting process were also explained to the participants. Similarly, the means of saving the rain water like creating small ponds, digging ring wells in the houses, constructing check dams were explained with government provisions for such activities. The details regarding the activities and programmes of Rajiv Gandhi National Drinking Water Mission were discussed with the participants.

- quality test/protected, safe drinking water
- creating new sources of drinking water
- maintaining the existing water sources

- providing new pipe line connection
- providing water sources to all hamlet
- planning in the panchayat itself
- drinking water administration by panchayat
- peoples contribution – maintain such amount for follow up activities
- The power and responsibilities of the water committee were discussed

Various dimensions like loss of income for the people, loss of production and economic problems, have been explained to the presidents. The main features of the total rural sanitation programme, how many villages are marching towards total sanitation with peoples involvement were also the topics for discussions during the training programmes.

This is a special scheme aimed at creating awareness among the people to make all the 682 village panchayats to be as total sanitation villages.

Roads and buildings are essential for the village but still more essential is the rural sanitation as it provides opportunity to lead a dignified human life in the society. This has been illustrated with the example of how most of the people in the rural areas are leading a sub-human living conditions. This can be achieved not through law or through scheme but with the co-operation of the people and for which a new mindset has to be created.

The meaning of a good toilet, how to protect water, how to protect the nature from pollution and how to construct a good low cost latrine were also discussed with the participants in the training programme. Specimen of variety of toilets were also exhibited with different estimates in the venue of training.

The efforts, special arrangements that have been taken by the district administration to provide health education and awareness creation were also explained. The details about the methodology have also been illustrated. They are :

- wall posters
- phamplets
- wall advertisements
- advertisement boards
- mass advertisements - cinema theatre
- processions//conferences
- training programmes
- cultural programmes

The role of village panchayats in total rural sanitation programme were also explained as :

- forming water and sanitation committees in the panchayats for awareness creation/execution/field level assessment.
- identifying/locating and approaching the financial resources
- individual/social benefit schemes
- making the people to participate in the programmes
- project administration/assessment/reporting.

The panchayat presidents have to understand the implications of the total rural sanitation programme and the Rajiv Gandhi National Drinking Water Mission activities in the rural areas. They will create the following benefits in the villages :

1. Sustainable development/maintenance is assured with the help of drinking water and sanitation committee.
2. Sanitation will be maintained – individual/public latrines will be constructed in the villages.
3. The sanitary status of school/Anganwadi will improve.
4. Cleanliness will be maintained in the streets of the villages.
5. Supply of protected and safe drinking water.
6. Uninterupted supply of drinking water.
7. The community wili become a responsible one by acquiring the needed awareness about the importance of protected drinking water and sanitation.

The two programmes provide opportunities, responsibilities, necessary power and rights to the panchayat presidents to create the above said benefits. The training programme was conducted in such a way to create faith and confidence among the presidents that they can bring a good name to their panchayats and also they can create the sense of responsibilities among the people.

Special Attention

Special attention was given to the following aspects during the training programme :

1. The mismatch between the increasing demands and decreasing resources, has been explained to them.
2. The community has to take interest in the village common property and natural resources which give ample opportunities to the panchayats to augment resources for its activities.
3. 100 per cent collection of taxes – would fetch two times more revenue to the panchayats.
4. Social awareness, women involvement and basic sanitation are the

three basic important components for development.

5. The challenges and opportunities to the panchayats under the new economic situation.
6. The features of the New Panchayati Raj System :
   - three tier structure
   - finance commission
   - election commission
   - reservation of seats – for women and SC & ST
   - Gram Sabha
   - XI schedule – 29 subjects
   - District planning committee
7. Special efforts/activities carried out by the states of Kerala, West Bengal and Madhya Pradesh
   - increase peoples involvement/contribution/commitment;
   - make the officials responsive to the leaders demand;
   - regularise the planning process through District Planning Committee;
   - process of fund allocation and resource management;
   - devolution of powers, resources and functionaries;
   - institutionalising decentralization of powers;
8. The steps taken by the government of Tamil Nadu have been explained. They are :
   - the powers/responsibilities provided to panchayats as per the recommendations of the L.C. Jain Committee and high power committee;
   - the government orders issued till date akin to panchayats;
   - steps to improve the administrative capacity of the leaders;
   - steps to strengthen Gram Sabha activities;
   - state finance commission - formation - research activities and other details.
9. The problems and difficulties in the New Panchayati Raj Systems have also been explained. They are :
   - the three tier system without any organic linkage;
   - the political influence;
   - dependency syndrome;
   - non-cooperation of the bureaucracy;
   - role of caste in panchayat activities; and conflicting perception of the people.

Training Methods

First before starting the exercise the participants awareness has been assessed and based on the awareness, supplementary information were provided. They were supported by the rules, government orders, the success stories were also provided to the participants.

Among the participants those who have succeeded in many of the programme were identified and those leaders were requested to share their experiences with the participants.

Since the department officials were also present in the training programme, their experiences were also used to clarify doubts whenever necessary. The interest and eagerness of the participants were maintained by involving them in small games.

Part B

Participants have been asked to discuss about the issues and the problems confronted by them in their administration apart from the scheme for which the training was organised. A volley of issues have been projected by the leaders.

Participants Views

I. Total Rural Sanitation Programme

- Need yearly allotment of funds for drainage improvement.
- Permission to appoint scavengers based on the population.
- Permission to appoint worker to maintain public latrine.
- Increase of subsidy for household latrine.
- People are to be informed about the diseases, death rates and wastage of money through media.
- Government order should be issued for the co-ordinated activity of the VAO and Village health nurse with the village panchayat in creating awareness about the need for household latrine.
- Put up hand pumps in the graveyards.
- Need adequate finance to maintain the streets.
- Need vehicle to remove solid waste.
- Need police help during quarrels in preventing the persons from digging pits in the water points.
- Need separate place to dump the wastes.
- Need training to construct low cost latrines.

- The officials of the departments of the education, health, sanitation, field publicity and TWAD, have to sit together once in three months in the village analyse the prevailing condition and advice the people accordingly. They should also come forward to talk to the people in the Gram Sabha meetings.
- If the functioning of the PHC, health sub-centre and taluk hospitals are regulated, it will yield good results to the village people.
- It is good to understand that the school children of a few villages have collected money from their parents and contributed for the school latrine.
- Initially people were hesitant and did not come forward to construct house hold latrines. The efforts of the officials by arranging street meetings and individuals meetings, yielded good results and thus 341 house hold latrines were constructed in Chettipalayam village.
- The toilets in the group houses lack facilities and hence only a limited families make use of the toilets.
- Generally the SC colony families do not use the toilets, instead they use the toilets for other purposes.
- Among the BC families only the women use the toilets.
- Every individual must understand that sanitation includes personal habits, safe drinking water, environmental sanitation, use of toilets and disease prevention. For this we need awareness movement.
- People lack awareness about sanitation and even the literate don't feel the importance of toilets. They waste the drainage facilities. They feel that only the government has to work for village sanitation. Sanitation programmes are only target oriented and not with follow up activities. We are providing household latrines. Even after 50 years we have to explain this scheme to the public. In many cases the people sold out the accessories of the toilets. Since there is enough open space, ponds and small tanks and canals with water in the rural area, the people don't feel for it. Instead they feel it discomfort to have toilets in the house.
- It should be made compulsory to share details about the diseases identified during the Varumun Kappom Thittam.
- Provision of subsidy should be given to all sections of people to construct household latrine.
- Target should be fixed to the union/district representatives regarding the construction of latrines. They are provided with funds but not responsibilities. All the difficult works are allotted to the Gram panchayats.

The panchayats should be empowered to take action against those who misused the accessories meant for latrine construction.

- Panchayats should be empowered to take proper action against those who use the public places for open defecation.
- Since the subsidy amount varies in constructing latrines, people expect the schemes providing highest amount of subsidy.
- The women officials should take additional responsibilities to create awareness among the women to take part in the panchayat activities.
- The presidents have now understood the importance of water sources, distribution points, the storage tanks and maintenance of the same.
- The rural women folk do not take interest in the health of their children. An awareness should be created among them in this regard.
- Since the idea of peoples contribution in development activities is new, more publicity is needed in this regard.
- The poor panchayat presidents suffer much due to paucity of funds to advance for the works. So the panchayats should be permitted to use the panchayat funds and replace it within six months.
- The parent-teacher association should be made responsible for constructing school latrine.
- The government officials should visit the village and help in forming the village drinking water committee.
- We should create awareness about the household latrines.
- Drainage facilities should be provided in important places.
- The officials should help the panchayats in collecting the deposit for house tap connection. Government should issue order to disconnect taps who failed to pay the deposit.
- Preference and special subsidy should be given to hand pumps than large scale water schemes.
- The government should insist the members of the self-help groups to construct latrines in their houses.
- The government should issue order to the police and officials to co-operate with the panchayats for disconnecting the illegal water tap connections.
- The quality of water in the borewell should be tested and the results to be informed to the public.
- Additional hand pumps to be put up in many places to facilitate supply of drinking water during power failure.
- Since the water is sucked even below the sea level in Neyveli area, the quality of water as well as the nature of soil gets affected.
- The works carried out by the TWAD board get delayed. The handing

over of the work also is delayed. Even after the government allots funds the work is delayed and as a result people suffer a lot.

- The benefits will be long lasting only if the technical advice of the TWAD board continues to the village panchayats.
- The illeffect of the abandoned well near the hand pump should be shared with the village panchayats and the people.
- Details regarding the rain water harvesting is essential.
- The details of fees for quality test of water should be explained to the leaders.
- At present the people in the village render their co-operation in solving drinking water problems. So, it is opt time to create awareness about this new scheme.

II. Village Panchayat Administration/Meetings

- Circulars and Government Orders regarding administration should be sent to the panchayats directly.
- Field level staff should guide the panchayats in forming people committees for human resources development.
- Since the ward members are not aware of panchayat structure and administration they should also be trained in panchayati administration.
- Vice-presidents do not co-operate with the president for panchayati administration and causing delay in signing the cheque. Even for works carried our properly, they delay in their signature and expect personal benefits from the presidents.

III. Tax and Tax Collection

- Panchayats could not collect the house tax completely. People refuse to pay house tax.
- It should be made mandatory to pay the rent of the fair price shop to the panchayat by the co-operative societies.
- The officials like the VAO do not pay the professional tax.

IV. Street Light

- EB does not co-operate with the panchayat in maintaining the street lights. They demand a higher amount than prescribed by the government for the works attended to by the EB men. So it is better to appoint one staff for each panchayat.

- EB does not co-operate in providing street lights in the newly created colonies.

V. Gram Sabha

- Panchayats have to convene the Gram Sabha meeting four times in a year. The resolution passed in the previous meetings could not be implemented before the next meeting and this creates problem in the Gram Sabha meeting. People get disappointed by this.
- In the meetings, the people raise only questions but do not listen to the explanation offered by the administration
- Among the resolutions, the village panchayats carried out the works with its fund to meet some of the demands for others, the other two tiers have to take steps to carryout works in the panchayats to meet the demands of the people.
- The members of the SHG raise questions in the meetings but do not contribute.
- The defeated candidates disturb the Gram Sabha meetings.
- The presidents should be educated about how to conduct the Gram Sabha meeting properly also proper awareness could be created among the people.
- The participants use to come to the meetings and programmes by expecting loan and subsidy facilities.
- People feel that their responsibilities are over once they inform their demands to the panchayats.
- Politics and caste factors disturb the Gram Sabha meeting.
- Under the free house scheme the beneficiaries selected by the Gram Sabha are neglected and others get with the influence of brokers.
- In the list of below poverty line families, real poor families are omitted but rich families are included by the officials.
- People do not show interest in knowing the venue and time of the Gram Sabha and also do not attend the meetings.
- People are not ready to accept the poor financial position of the panchayat, delay in fund allocation, political influence in the allotment of MLA and MP funds. But they like only the execution of resolutions passed in the Gram Sabha meeting.

VI. Village Common Property Resources

- VAO should provide details of the poromboke lands to the

panchayats.

- Revenue department and police should co-operate in evicting the encroachments because panchayats can augment the panchayat income by planting trees in those lands.
- In the lakes, the brickklin owner dig pits and remove the clay and as a result the condition of the soil is affected. The panchayat should be empowered to regularise these activities.
- Village panchayats should be provided with special powers to maintain the village common property resources.
- Revenue department officials issue pattas even in the road side areas. This makes it critical in widening the road and in constructing drainage facilities.
- Appeal made by the economically well off encroachers in the court against the decision of the panchayats on encroachment lasts for years. The officials and the government should give importance to the panchayats to speed up the eviction process as done in the case of eviction in the places selected for Uzhavar Sandhai.

VII. Education

- Incentive money given to the SC women and children should be given in time.
- Every school should have a fencing or a compound wall and this will facilitate the proper maintenance of school gardens and school latrines.
- In a few places with the support of the parents-teacher association, trees were planted and are properly maintained.
- In the same way government should issue order to maintain all basic facilities in the government aided schools. The government have to accept the report of the village panchayat.
- Steps taken by the panchayats to fill up the vacant post of teacher did not yield any result. But at last due to the pressure of the people, they had to participate in road roko and then only teachers were appointed. Why should the government create such a situation?
- There is a Government Order that in every village, a village education committee should be formed. The government must take action against those officials who did not take any steps to form such committees. Otherwise, the people will loose faith on the government schools.

VIII. Development Schemes – Fund Allocation – Implementation

- Allotted funds should be released in two instalments.
- New ration shops should be created according to the total number of card holders.
- Community halls should be constructed in all the panchayats.
- Panchayats should be consulted in selecting the beneficiaries for the supply of agricultural inputs.
- The rehabilitation scheme for the physically handicapped should be designed to provide complete relief to them.
- Panchayat presidents spend their personal money and render their support in pre arrangements, publicity, food arrangements and other infrastructure facilities for the Varumun Kappom Thittam. But these panchayat presidents are not informed fully about the programme.
- Presidents should be provided with a book containing the details of all welfare programmes.
- Government allots only less funds to the areas with less SC population. But fulfillment of basic needs is common to all the villages irrespective of caste groups.
- Officials should not persuade the presidents to start the works before allotment of funds and without written order.
- There are a few panchayats without receiving any benefits under the MLA, MP and district panchayat member funds. So, in future, these villages must be given preference.
- Due to late release of funds, the water shed programmes are incomplete and this leads to loss of money and human energy.
- Black top roads are quality wise better than the cement roads. So, the panchayat must not be compelled to put up cement road and it should be left to the discretion of the panchayats.
- Poor panchayats should be provided with special funds to meet the basic needs.
- Rules regarding the selection of beneficiaries of the group houses should be uniform throughout Tamil Nadu.
- Noon meal centre, kitchen room, balwadis are functioning in the rented buildings which led to so many problems. They need own building and the government should help in this regard.
- To supervise the public distribution system, women committee should be formed.
- Employment programmes should be prepared village wise and be implemented through panchayats.
- Fund allocation for development takes place at various levels. Unless

panchayats are integrated with the system, the activities of the panchayats may not be scientific.

– Preference has not been given to the villages affected by the drinking water scheme.The water tanks are under repair. Separate fund should be allotted to maintain the water tanks.
– Under the Anna Marumalarchi Thittam, the selected villages are provided with additional funds even after the completion of the schemes to meet the basic needs. This affects the other poor panchayats.
– People are not interested to contribute for the Namakku Naame Thittam. The contribution of people in the form of labour should be accepted.
– Under the group house scheme, the villages must be selected only after field survey.

IX. Employment Assurance Scheme

– The panchayats and the people do not get the details about the works under the scheme. Also, works that provide employment opportunities are not implemented. People are not benefited by this scheme. It is only the owner of the machines gets benefits.

X. Development of Irrigation Tanks

– Since this scheme is under the control of the Agricultural Engineering Department, the chances of panchayats taking part in this is less.

XI. MP, MLA Constituency Development Scheme

– Since political intervention and political bias are involved in this, the panchayats with reasonable demands do not get any benefit under this scheme.
– The delay in getting the Tenth Finance Commission funds should be rectified.
– The panchayat play a responsible role in making the benefits of various development schemes of the Department of Rural Development reach the people in time So, the fund allocation of the union and district panchayats as well as the DRDA should be based on the priority needs of the panchayat as approved by the Gram Sabha. For this, the district administration should convene a union

level meeting of village panchayat presidents once in three months and discuss with them the details.

The allotment for cement concrete road in the streets is very less and not even a single street is put up with cement concrete road fully. So, the people feel that this type of incomplete road is not necessary and we can divert the fund for some other vital works. So panchayats should be permitted to put up cement concrete road at least for a distance of 100 metres.

To make the people contribution effective under the Namakku Naame Thittam, the present level of 25% contribution may be reduced to 10% and then we can slowly increase the people contribution.

The monthly water tax of Rs. 30 should be reduced and the deposit amount of Rs. 1000 should also be reduced. Free house pattas be issued to the poor families living for a long time in a place.

Like the village presidents explaining the activities of the panchayats at the Gram Sabha meeting, the village panchayat presidents should be invited for a meeting and the works of the union and district panchayats should be explained. This will help the presidents understand whether the schemes are implemented at the top level without any bias.

XII. Relations with Union and District Panchayats

Under the Employment Assurance Scheme, both planning and execution should be given to the village panchayats (or) the works suggested by the village panchayats alone should be carried out.

The village panchayats should be given proper information about the works carried out by the other departments in the village.

Whenever public activities like farmers meet are arranged in the panchayat area, the panchayats should be kept informed.

Whenever the presidents meet the officials to get clarifications, the officials do not respond properly. They have to visit many times to the office to complete the accounts.

XIII. Four Years Experience

During the four years experience, they developed the art of patience and public service and got satisfaction in this work. They got opportunity to have interaction with variety of people from political parties to caste groups. They got a chance to understand the government activities. This has created an opportunity to develop aspiration to become a social worker.

Administration is not simple. There are a number of interference in the administration and they are subjected to many government controls and rules. So, they have to think properly and face it. This needs patience and efforts.

Agenda of the presidents for their panchayats :

– To create the basic minimum facilities.
– To meet the basic minimum needs.
– Provision of education to all.
– All people should be concientised on health, and sanitation, and water supply.
– Employment opportunities to earn their daily income to meet their livelihood.
– Support and co-operation with one another and live as an integrated community.

XIV. Opinion of Women Presidents

– The minimum working period of one year should be reduced to six months of the self-help groups to get government funds.
– Proper awareness about health and sanitation should be created first among the women.
– Since there is a large number of political and social problems in the villages, the women presidents need the help of their husbands in panchayat administration. This will hold good in families also. They are helping the women leaders and they are not proxy.
– Initially people doubted the ability of the women leadership. But after they overcome the field problems with the help of the officials, the people have got faith in them.
– They could not meet the MPs and MLAs and get funds for the programmes to be carried out in the villages.
– The mind-set has not been changed in the society to honour the reservation policy.
– They have moved over to the public life from the family life. Fear sychosis has been removed from the minds of the women leaders.
– They have acquired the development thinking. They felt that their social status has gone up.

11th Schedule

Of the subjects given in the 11th schedule for the panchayats, panchayati presidents have indicated the nature of works to be attended to by them. They are given below :

1. In every village agricultural counselling centres should be created.
2. Arrangements have to be made to easy availability of tree saplings for planting.
3. Planning must be carried out at the micro level for maintaining the small lakes, ponds etc with the special funds as well as peoples manual contribution.
4. All the benefits to the farmers should be provided only through the panchayats
5. Panchayats have opportunities in determining the prices of agricultural products.
6. Porombokes under the control of the revenue department should be handed over to the panchayats.
7. Since the cost of fodder is high, the livestock rearers must be informed about the various types of low cost fodder, their technical details of production.
8. The lands with poor fertility should be converted into ponds to cultivate fish.
9. Only today we could understand the 29 subjects. The officials have kept us in darkness till date in this regard.
10. The officials of the agricultural engineering departments do not have rapport with the panchayats. They do not seek our advice in deepening and desilting of our tanks. They don't work in the tanks recommended by the panchayats.
11. The local school teachers are not interested in their work. So teachers should be appointed only from outside.
12. The adult education programme should be properly planned and implemented. They should seek the advice of the panchayats.
13. Need permission to appoint staff to maintain the library and reading rooms in the villages. Need building facilities and books for the library.

Suggestions to Improve the Peoples Participation

- Arrangements to improve the quality of life of the poor and when their needs are satisfied people will be interested to participate.
- All the basic facilities should be provided to the people.

- To create awareness about people's participation mass media, namely the cinema, street play, drama etc. should be properly used.
- Since people do not have the habit of participation in the development activities till now it will take some more time to change their mind-set. Also the Gram Sabha should continue to motivate the people.
- The leaders must meet the people frequently and explain to them in detail about the importance and implication of Gram Sabha.
- In villages, conference should be organised every month and meetings should be arranged on topics akin to problems of the village. Discussion should also be arranged among the people about the various socio-economic programmes of the government.
- If the MLA, MP's also attend the Gram Sabha meetings, more people will participate in the meetings with interest.
- The officials should create awareness about the panchayat administration among the public.
- Arrangements are to be made to encourage the people who participate in the Gram Sabha meeting.

Participant's Views about the Training

1. This training should have been provided four years back.
2. This training should be arranged for at least three days.
3. Since the information were provided within a short time we could not digest them all.
4. Got solution to many rural problems.
5. Understood the depth of many rural problems.
6. Understood the methods of attracting the people for Gram Sabha.
7. The training was simple.
8. Not sufficient time.
9. The opinion of leaders were respected.
10. Need separate training to women.
11. Need separate training to Dalits.
12. Training should be a continuous process and hence it should be arranged periodically.
13. People should also be explained about Panchayati Raj activities.
14. The resource persons were like one among them.
15. The training was like a discussion and not like a lecture programme.

16. Training was given in accordance with the needs of the participants.

Opinion of the Resource Person

1. Most of the presidents were not interested.
2. Generally, the presidents are not prepared to meet the people. They feel it a problem to meet the people.
3. They have spent four years without understanding about the panchayat.
4. The presidents perceive the panchayats as a political institution.
5. Many women presidents are not aware of even their responsibilities in the panchayat.
6. Women presidents were not aware of administration, management, income, expenditure and planning.
7. They reached the training venue late.
8. The special attention provided by the Additional Collector for the training programme is appreciable.
9. The logistic arrangements were good.
10. The importance given by the District Collector for the training programme is appreciable.

7

CAPCITATING OFFICIALS

Training Details

Nature of Training	:	Residential
Duration	:	Five Days
Trainees	:	Project Officers of DRDA and District Level Officials of Development and Sectoral Departments
Districts Covered	:	Karur, Theni, Perambalur, Trichy, Pudukkottai, Tirunelveli, Kanyakumari, Kanjeepuram, Thiruvallur and Dharmapuri.
Campus	:	Gandhigram
Residence	:	KVK Hostel and University Guest House
Training Centre	:	Conference Hall of the Department
No.of Batches	:	Three
Details of Dates	:	17-21 & 24-28 April & 2-6 May, 2000.

Course Core Faculty

1. Dr. G. Palanithurai
   Professor & Head
   Department of Political Science and Development Administration
   Gandhigram Rural Institute, Gandhigram.

2. Dr. B.S. Bhargava
   Senior Fellow
   Institute of Social Sciences
   Bangalore

3. Mr.V.A. Vasudeva Raju, IAS (Rtd)
   Executive Director, IICD,
   Pondicherry

4. Dr. Jose Chathukulam
   Director & Vice-Chairman of
   District Planning Committee
   Centre for Rural Management
   Kottayam, Kerala

5. Dr. N. Narayanasamy
   Professor in Extension Education
   Head, PRA Unit – Specialist in PRA
   Gandhigram Rural Institute, Gandhigram

6. Dr. N.D. Mani
   Reader in Rural Development
   Specialist in Remote Sensing and GIS
   Gandhigram Rural Institute, Gandhigram

7. Dr. N. Lalitha
   Reader in Rural Development
   Specialist in Self Help Groups
   Gandhigram Rural Institute, Gandhigram

8. Dr. V. Ragupathy
   Reader in Political Science
   Specialist in CPR Management
   Gandhigram Rural Institute, Gandhigram

9. Sri. Balakrishnan
   Manager
   District Lead Bank
   Dindigul

Content of the Training

- Training Methodology
- History of Planning in India
- 73rd Constitutional Amendment
- 1994 Tamil Nadu Rural Local Bodies Act
- Approaches towards planning
- Collection of data and compilation of profile
- Basic rules and procedures for planning

- Planning for poverty alleviation
- Matching the needs with programmes in the planning
- Three tiers involvement in the planning exercise
- Integration of sectoral departments with Development Departments in Planning on the subjects in 11th Schedule.
- Integration of Annual credit plan with Development plan.
- Resource Mobilization in Panchayats including CPR Management.
- Peoples participation in the planning exercise through PRA.
- Role of District Planning Cell and District Planning Committee in the preparation of District plan.
- Kerala Experience
- Karnataka Experience
- Visit to various units of Gandhigram Trust to see the employment generation activities.
- Group Discussion.
- Utilizing the services of Remote Sensing and GIS Department

List of Participants
Who have undergone training

Karur District

1.	Sri. R. Balakrishnan	–	Project Officer, DRDA
2.	Sri. M. Muthumanickam	–	Executive Engineer (RD)
3.	Sri. P. Carol	–	District Planning Officer
4.	Sri. A. Natesan	–	APO (EAS)
5.	Sri. A. Amanullah	–	Assistant Executive Engineer TWAD (RWS)
6.	Sri. M. Neelamegham	–	Assistant Divisonal Engineer (HRW)
7.	Sri. R. Nandakumar	–	Assistant Director Statistics

Theni District

1.	Sri. B.R.K. Ramesh	–	Project Officer, DRDA
2.	Sri. T. Sivasankar	–	Executive Engineer (RD)
3.	Sri. P. Anandaraj	–	APO (Regular)
4.	Sri. R. Pandiyaraj	–	Assistant Executive Engineer TWAD (RWS)
5.	Sri. B. Koppaiyan	–	Assistant Divisional Engineer (HRW)

Permabalur District

1. Sri. N. Idimannan – Project Officer, DRDA
2. Sri. M. Vadivelu – Executive Engineer (RD)
3. Sri. K. Ramalingam – APO (Regular)
4. Sri. K. Jayabal – AD Panchayat
5. Sri. K. Chinnadurai – Asst.Exe.Engr. TWAD (RWS)
6. Sri. S.S. Prakasam – Asst.Div.Engr. (HRW)
7. Sri. K. Rengaraj – Asst.Exe.Engr. (Agri.Engg.)
8. Sri.G. Jeganathan – Divisional Statistical Officer
9. K. Sundaram – Asst.Director (Audit)

Trichy District

1. Sri. P. Ponniah – Project Officer, DRDA
2. Sri. M. Ramachandran – Executive Engineer (RD)
3. Sri. V. Ramasamy – District Planning Officer
4. Sri. C.R. Subramanian – APO (Regular)
5. Sri. A. Shanmugasundaram – AD Panchayat
6. Sri. P.Dharmaraj – Asst.Exe.Engr. TWAD (RWS)
7. Sri. K. Durairaj – Asst.Div.Engr. (HRW)
8. Sri. P. Sundar – Asst.Exe.Engr. (Agri.Engg.)
9. Sri.S. Francis Selvaraj – Asst.Dir.Statistics

Tirunelveli District

1. Sri. F.Abdul Razick – Project Officer, DRDA
2. Sri. G. Muralithran Pillai – Executive Engineer (RD)
3. Sri. N. Karuppasamy – APO (Regular)
4. Sri. S. Thanumalayan – AD Panchayat
5. Sri. S. Krishnan – Asst.Exe.Engr. TWAD (RWS)
6. Sri. A. Kolappapillai – Asst.Div.Engr. (HRW)
7. Sri. M. Kaliappan – Asst.Exe.Engr. (Agri.Engg.)
8. Sri.B. Hariharadhas – Asst.Dir.Statistics

Kanniyakumari District

1. Sri. P. Selvarajan – Project Officer, DRDA
2. Sri. S. Kalyanasundararaman – Executive Engineer (RD)
3. Sri. S. Selvaraj – District Planning Officer
4. Sri. N. Kuppusamy – APO (Regular)
5. Sri. A. Mani – AD Panchayat
6. Sri. S. Muthiah – Asst.Exe.Engr. TWAD (RWS)
7. Sri. K. Justin Thambi – Asst.Div.Engr. (HRW)

8.	Sri. C. Vellmani	–	Asst.Exe.Engr. (Agri.Engg.)
9.	Sri.S. Arumuga Nainar	–	Asst.Dir.Statistics

Pudukkottai District

1.	Sri. X.David Thangaraj	–	Executive Engineer (RD)
2.	Sri. V. Arunagiri	–	District Planning Officer
3.	Sri. M.A. Benjamin	–	APO (Regular)
4.	Sri. C. Narasimhan	–	AD Panchayat
5.	Sri. P. Dhakshinamoorthy	–	Asst.Exe.Engr. TWAD (RWS)
6.	Sri. A. Bazheer Ahmed	–	Asst.Div.Engr. (HRW)

Kancheepuram District

1.	Sri. S. Kandasamy	–	Executive Engineer (RD)
2.	Sri. Madasamy	–	District Planning Officer
3.	Sri. N. Sambasivan	–	Asst.Div.Engr. (HRW)
4.	Smt.V. Malathi	–	Asst.Dir.Statistics

Tiruvallur District

1.	Smt. R. Jagadeeswari	–	District Planning Officer
2.	Sri. K. Ravindran	–	APO (Regular)
3.	Sri. Lakshmipathy	–	AD Panchayat
4.	Sri. V. Sivaprakasam	–	Asst.Exe.Engr. (Agri.Engg.)
5.	Sri. J. Elancheyian	–	Asst.Dir.Statistics
6.	Sri. C. Vinayagam	–	ADE (H)

Dharmapuri District

1.	Sri. C. Balu	–	Executive Engineer (RD)
3.	Sri. P. Subbiah	–	District Planning Officer
4.	Sri. A. Narayanan	–	APO (Regular)
5.	Sri. B. Manivannan	–	Asst.Exe.Engr. TWAD (RWS)
7.	Sri. P. Pandian	–	Asst.Exe.Engr. (Agri.Engg.)
9.	Sri.P. S. Janarthanam	–	APO (M)

From State Planning Commission – Chennai

1.	Sri. K. Prakasam	–	Planning Officer
2.	Sri. Mohammed Kalimullah	–	Planning Officer

Details regarding Inaugural and Valedictory Functions for the Three Batches

First Batch :	Inauguration on 17th April, 2000 Chief Guest Sri.**K.V. Palanithurai**, Fulltime Member, State Planning Commission, Chennai.
	Valedictory Session 21st April, 2000 Chief Guest Sri.**M.R. Rajagopalan**, Secretary, Gandhigram Trust, Gandhigram.
Second Batch :	Inauguration on 24th April, 2000 Chief Guest Dr.**N. Markandan**, Vice-Chancellor, Gandhigram Rural Institute, Gandhigram.
	Valedictory Session 28th April, 2000 Chief Guest Dr. **G. Pankajam**, Joint-Secretary and Treasurer, Gandhigram Trust, Gandhigram.
Third Batch :	Inauguration on 2nd May, 2000 Chief Guest Dr.**N. Markandan**, Vice-Chancellor, Gandhigram Rural Institute, Gandhigram.
	Valedictory Session 6th May, 2000 Chief Guest Dr.**N. Markandan**, Vice-chancellor, Gandhigram Rural Institute, Gandhigram.

List of Participants

Who have been selected as Master Trainers

First Batch

1.	B.R.K. Ramesh	- Project Officer	– Theni
2.	N. Idimannan	- Project Officer	– Perambalur
3.	S.S. Prakasam	- Asst.Divisional Eng. (HRW)	– Perambalur
4.	V. Ramasamy	- Dist. Planning Officer	– Trichy
5.	P. Sundar	- Asst.Executive Eng. (Agri)	– Trichy
6.	K. Durairaj	- Asst. Divisional Eng. (HRW)	– Trichy

Second Batch

1.	P. Dhakshinamurthy	- A.E.E. (TWAD)	– Pudukottai
2.	X. David Thangaraj	- E.E. (DRDA)	– Pudukottai
3.	C. Narashimahan	- A.D. Panchayat	– Pudukottai
4.	P. Hariharadoss	- A.D. Statistics	– Tirunelveli
5.	J. Abdul Ruzak	- Project Officer	– Tirunelveli

Third Batch

1.	V. Sivapraskasm	- A.E.E.	– Thiruvallur
2.	K. Prakasam	- Planning Officer	– SPC, Chennai
3.	J. Ilunchizhian	- A.D. Statistics	– Thiruvallur
4.	A. Narayannan	- A.P.O.(Regular)	– Dharmapuri
5.	R. Jagatheswari	- Dist.Planning Officer	– Thiruvallur

1. Training of Trainers on Multi-Level Training – Report

The programme was launched with the traditional prayer of Gandhigram. After the prayer Dr.V.Ragupathy, Reader in Political Science and Development Administration formally welcomed the distinguished guests, resource persons and the participants. Prof. G. Palanithurai the Course Co-ordinator explained the mechanics and logistics of the TOT. He explained the steps taken by Gandhigram Rural Institute in strengthening Panchayati Raj in the past ten years from awareness creation to training of leaders and Functionaries of Panchayati Raj Institution. He succinctly narrated the steps taken by the Government of Tamil Nadu from the enactment of the State Act to the present stage of activating the District Planning Committee. He outlined that the conditions are so conducive for human resource development in Tamil Nadu and our state is comparatively in a better position than many other states of India in terms of physical quality of life index. But he felt that inspite of these conditions and well experienced officials, the rate of growth and development in the villages are not satisfactory. He remarked that there is a need of a sound and strong political will on the part of the leaders at various level in the state and the central level to decentralize power and resources to local bodies along with functionaries. The present conditions can be altered through the bottom up planning to be done with the active participation of the people.

Our democracy within a short span of fifty years after independence achieved spectacular results in many aspects of polity, society and economy. Compared to the performance of many of the countries of the West and North America. But the poor in India did not get their due share in the achievement of the Indian democracy. The decentralization of power will pluck the loop holes in the system and thereby poor can ensure their entitlements through their participation. Services and facilities may be provided by the government but the maintenance and sustenance of the same could only be done by the people themselves. To achieve this goal a new mind-set is needed at this juncture.

At present, there is no clear perception among the partners on the scope and implications of Panchayati Raj Institutions. Government pumped a lot of resources for the socio-economic development of the people. How it can be profitably executed? is a question. It may be possible only by participatory planning. In this context, the role and function of Panchayati Raj Institutions in local area planning is an imperative and the need of the hour is Multi-Level Planning. Imperatives and Conditionalities of the Multi-Level Planning are explained by the Course Director Prof. G. Palanithurai. He underscored the fact that the panchayats should be perceived as peoples organisation rather than government institution.

In his inaugural address Sri.K.V. Palanithurai full time Member, State Planning Commission traced the whole planning exercise and process in the country since Independence. He indicated the contextual need of the multi-level planning. He further outlined that after the formation of District Planning Committee, the State Government took further initiative to strengthen the planning process at the grassroot level as per the constitutional guidelines.

"Government is not the magic tree to deliver whatever we demand" Sri. K.V. Palanithurai observed. He further indicated that it is the duty of the government to provide facilities for the development of the community, and the community has to make use of the facilities to achieve the economic development of the people and for which every citizen has to be oriented. He cited a few examples to illustrate how the centrally and state sponsored programmes could be meaningfully integrated in the multi-level planning and how people could be involved in the planning exercises.

Sri. K.V. Palanithurai indicated the efforts of the government in micro level planning. Anna University and Trichy Bharatidasan University's remote sensing departments have adequate data which could be used. He further shared his concern over the distribution of fund among the district and block councillors. This trend will bring a discredit to the Panchayati Raj Institutions. This will defeat the very principle of planning and sustainable growth. The mind set of the elected leaders has to be changed to suit the new requirement. They need orientation on the concept of sectoral development, integration plan and its with the Development plan of the main department on holistic development. Sri. K.V. Palanithurai further quoted the Chief Ministers budget speech on the planning process at the district level.

Dr. N. Markandan, the Vice-Chancellor of Gandhigram Rural Institute, in his presidential address remarked that the profit of Freedom has not yet reached the poorest of the poor. He found that the slavish mentality and dependency syndrome persist in the minds of our people. The officials could not be blamed for this state of affairs because they obeyed their superiors who have been oriented by the British. He explained further that the government failed to evoke participation of the people for planning since India attained Independence. He insisted that in this context both officials and people have to change their mind-set that everybody is a participant not a giver or taker. The officials must realise that their role is only to facilitate the people to govern themselves. He quoted the special schemes of Tamil Nadu Government "Namakku Naame and Anna Marumalarchi Thittam." in which there is a great amount of scope and space for the people to participate in the development activities.

The Vice-Chancellor emphasised the importance of long-term planning in addition to the annual plan as envisaged by the Planning Commission. Employment generation for the poor should get priority in our plan. Officials and technocrats should find ways and means to enhance the income of poor villagers. Self-sufficiency as per Gandhiji vision may be an utopian concept whereas we have to ensure atleast self-sufficiency in food, shelter and the necessary basic needs and amenities, he said.

We must understand the other side of the development. We have polluted our nature and exploited the natural resources. There is a rethinking on the development model which we have pursued sofar and now we are suggesting an alternative model which will be human and nature oriented. Against this background we need a new and proper approach in Multi-Level Planning with peoples' participation. These steps are only to empower the new rural leadership through which our democracy may sustain and achieve equity and growth.

The Programme Director explained the importance and the need of the TOT. He told that the participants should have a prerequisite to become a master trainer by developing a commitment to learn and to communicate the same to others. A trainer is a learner. Everyone is learning a new thing every day. Prof. G. Palanithurai further remarked that the routine and hectic schedule of officials do not permit them to learn more new things. There is no scope for creativity in their work. But it is essential that official must equip and enhance their capacity to improve the life style of the people. They must learn new skills in development administration. 73rd Amendment to the Constitution and its concepts have to be understood properly by the government officials and then only they can perform their role and function effectively.

The present system of government is expensive and ineffective in its delivery as its size is very big. The planning system sofar handled at the top negated the responsibilities of the citizens. The developmental process is not an outward one; but it is an inward mental process of individuals concerned. And also in the development the individual concerned must take part and must be involved and must have an assertive role. To provide this, there must be a transparent government system and it can be moulded through Panchayati Raj Institutions. To bring the people near to the government and its system, the institutional arrangements like Gram Sabha has to be strengthened in which the politics of development has to be echoed than the politics of political parties.

The existing provision of 11th schedule created a new space for the people as well Panchayati Raj Institutions to perform their participatory role and function. Hence the Multi-Level Planning gets significance. Now the Panchayati Raj Institutions become permanent one and so they should be allowed to play their role in planning.

Prof. G. Palanithurai outlined the characteristics of the decentralization of power, basic features of the 73rd Constitutional Amendment, Tamil Nadu Local Bodies Act, 1994 and indicated the hurdles in this process. He further indicated the role of panchayats in micro-level planning.

The key resource person Sri.Vasudeva Raju in his session traced the evolution of planning in India. He opened his remarks with the good old saying "Good planning is half done". He explained the planning process initiated from the days of Nehru to the present. At every stage he indicated the strengths and weaknesses of the planning.

Mr.Vasudeva Raju shared his experience as an administrator and as a development planner. He criticised the role of ICS officials of the colonial government and asked to evaluate the role of present Indian Administrative Service personnel. The difference is in the contour "exploitation *Vs* development". He explained Gandhiji's experiment on constructive programme and his beneficial thinking on his experiment. In this way we have to review our plan experiment.

He explained relationship between the Department of Finance and Planning Commission and indicated the strenuous efforts of planning bodies in drafting of special component plan for SC&ST, Tribal development plan, Minimum Needs Programme which all ensure growth with social justice and equity. He remarked that they should be the guidelines in planning.

In the other sessions, Sri.Vasudeva Raju focussed on the Multi-Level Planning process and system of spatial distribution and spatial planning. He insisted that a well prepared data base with maps should be available in each village panchayat. This assignment must be given to all key sectoral, development and statistics departments.

He further indicated the indifferent attitude of the staff in the various departments in this regard. The officials do not know and fail to realise to whom this work serves? Integration and coordination of various departments for planning is the need of the hour. He cited the example from Karnataka government's system of district planning and data collection procedures and the personnels involved in the work. He explained the concepts of Multi-Level Planning, participatory planning. In Multi-Level Planning, planning is not only for growth but also for social justice and equity. The whole of his lectures indicated the steps to be taken for multi-level planning from the bottom to the District Planning Committee by following the guidelines prepared by the State Planning Commission.

Dr. Bhargava, a well known academician in the field of development administration started his discussion on the concepts – decentralization, delegation, deconcentration, devolution and privitization. He remarked that the changes accorded have to be noted carefully so that we can change the system and pattern of development plan and administration. Here the weightage is for the cost economy and the effective result. This new set needs institutional framework and finance along with a meticulous and scientific plan with the participation of people.

He further explained in detail the Karnataka experience of decentralization since 1978 under various party rule. He vividly explained the transfer of power from the British to India and the same way from Indian Government to people. We have established the national and state government. But the district level government system is not yet established in order inspite of a sea changes for over a period of time after the Panchayati Raj Institutions have been constitutionally established.

He put forwarded the following suggestions for an effective decentralized planning:

1. Stability in decentralized institution
2. Increased capacity of the local bureaucracy
3. Responsiveness of the system
4. Womens/Dalit participation
5. Clear cut powers/functions/functionaries
6. Unambiguous government orders and guidelines
7. Creating models
8. Strengthening of Gram Sabha
9. Human Resource Development

He conducted his presentation with his rear that if individual is transformed there will be a larger impact on the society.

Prof. G. Palanithurai in yet another session opened his discussion with three basic principles for enhanced activity in planning to achieve desired results, namely collecting data, deriving information from data, making knowledge out of information, enhancing capacity to make use of the knowledge for action.

He remarked that any event is a result of a skill in a particular art and which makes the performance different and distinct from other. He indicated the ways and means to enhance the capacity to become master trainers. He specifically mentioned the methods to release the psychic energy to perform the assigned roles and responsibilities to the maximum expected level. Prof. G. Palanithurai envisaged that the 21st century is the century of knowledge and capacity. In this work, the effective communication plays a vital role.

The best performer must know the length and breadth of the issues and must be able to handle the situation and to keep environment under control. The trainers must be equipped with the capacity of assessing the environment and handling of the environment.

He quoted the example that inspite of modern information technology, there is no proper training module to learn and utilize the same. He insisted that the learner must have a learning spirit and develop interest and understand the systematic transformation and dissemination of information. Foreigners become well verse in the Kuran and the Bagavad Gita and apply for their business promotion. Likewise the trainer must have the capacity to comprehend the things and suit them to our needs.

Prof. G. Palanithurai in his session explained the training methodology, training need assessment, training environment, trainee *Vs* trainer relationship, role of resources in training assessment, monitoring and evaluation technique.

In his next session, Prof. G. Palanithurai emphasised the significance of District Planning. He explained various segments of growth and development. He explained the basic objectives of the planning namely:

a) Orientation for Growth,
b) Orientation for Social Justice,
c) Orientation for Welfare,
d) Orientation for Protecting Environment,
e) Orientation for Integration, and
f) Orientation for Participation.

Here he outlined the necessity of sustainability.

He further explained the role of District Planning Committee in:-

- Consolidation of Plan
- Analysis of Plans
- Redrafting of Plan

- Integration of Plan

These are the basic phases in district developmental plan. He explained in details the process of District Planning System:-

- the principles of integration
- the procedures of removal of disparities
- the adherence of central and state government plan objectives and guidelines
- the ways and means of removal of disparities. Example: growth *Vs* environment and growth *Vs* social justice
- Integration of credit plan with development plan
- the approaches of annual plan and the long-term plan
- the plan implementation stages/phases
- the procedure for monitoring/evaluation
- the scope of re-drafting and improvement in plan draft

He indicated the role and responsibilities of District Planning Committee and District Planning Cell and indicated the structural weaknesses in the District Planning Committee and the Planning Cell.

Dr. N.D. Mani efficiently handled his session on the role of Resource Mapping in Multi-Level Planning. He explained in details regarding the various problems and hurdles in collection of data and its reliability, dependability, and accuracy.

He explained the remote sensing process:

Terrestrial survey
Produce photos and imagines
Aerial survey
Satellite survey - Produce the above with digital data.

He spoke on the application of remote sensing data in the area of town planning, natural resource inventory, and in a few areas. He outlined that still India have to develop further skill in this field and he compared the developed nations like America with us. He explained the role of remote sense – ground control system, down loading and data processing system in our country.

He narrated his project/experiment – Resource Mapping for Dindigul DPAP activities. He further spelt in details the scope of application of remote sensing data in the following field:-

- Crop management / pest control
- Land use / Land development

- Crop inventory
- Waste land mapping
- Water details – Recharging of ground water
- Forest coverage analysis

He emphasised that in District level and Block level planning, we must use remote sensing data. He further disclosed that the state of art is not up to the mark for further down - micro level planning.

Dr.N. Narayanasamy, Prof. in Extension introduced the Participatory Rural Appraisal technique to the participants. He explained the importance of the people's participatory planning and its evolution since 1972. He explained the reasons for the failure or limited success of various scheme introduced by the government. They are:

- Plans and people needs mismatch
- Lack of people participation and involvement
- No follow up

Prof. N. Narayanasamy explained the four type of participation:

- Contractual Participation
- Consulting Participation
- Collaborative Participation
- Collegiate Participation

For an effective participation there is a need for a positive mind-set with a state of awareness. To achieve this we have to provide opportunity, facilities and institutional arrangement to the people for their participation. They have to be involved in all stages of planning. He further explained the technique of Participatory Rural Appraisal, namely Social mapping, Resource mapping and others. Various diagrams are explained for mobility map, institutional map and so on so forth. Transwalk and its significance was explained to the participants. The details regarding seasonal calendar, crop inventory, resource analysis activities have been explained. The principle, technique, skill, application and scope of Participatory Rural Appraisal are explained to the participants in this session.

Mr. Ramachandira Nair from Kerala enlightened the trainees on the Kerala experience on people plan campaign and action. He started his discussion on the events of the plan from the period 1996 to 2000 with an emphasis on the peoples' participation process. Formation of neighbourhood group, role of voluntary agencies, trade unions and political parties in creating public awareness were explained. He outlined that a sensation was created on the minds of mass that it is their right to participate just like it is their right to vote.

Planning and peoples participation were highlighted by the government itself. This generated a speed and action. Special Gram Sabhas were organised in this line in which 27 lakhs of people attended, deliberated and decided.

A well planned design was formulated for State level, district level, block level and local level plan campaign after proper orientation of the people in Training. The resource persons are well versed in various fields in addition with the officials. Twelve sectors have been given importance.

They are namely Agriculture, Animal Husbandry, Fishery, Education, Health, Roads and Transports, Cooperation, SC & ST welfare, Industries and Women and Child Welfare. The people have participated in the gram Sabha discussion seriously on the present condition of the village and future plans. In future plan, the dreams and aspiration of people are also accommodated. The reports of all groups are submitted in the special Gram Sabha. After addition or deletion by the Gram Sabha the report was published. In the IInd stage, collection of data. Primary and secondary and preparation of development report for each Gram Panchayat were done. The report content includes history of the panchayat customs and practices of people, problems, vital statistics, maps and twelve sectoral details in twelve chapters are included. Likewise all 991 village panchayats in Kerala are having a well documented development plan.

Another special Gram Sabha was convened for the approval of the plan. After the approval, Task force for 12 sectors have been formed and in which the convener is the line department officer, joint convener a representative of peoples' forum or body, the chairman is the president of Gram panchayat and 10 to 15 volunteers from the village itself as members.

This Task force will prepare the plan from the development report and submit to the panchayat council with a note on the priority. It was told that inspite of these exercises, there were political mileage in every effort. The Task force become a parallel administration and so the suggestions of Task force are only advisory. Now the government redesigned the role of the Task force.

Mr. Nair explained that each year the peoples participation is improved in quality. Their perception and understanding the concept is improved. The mind-set of officials also under transformation. Mr. Nair admitted that there is no strict control on the corrupt practices inspite of all these initiatives. Mr. Nair succinctly narrated the peoples plan step one to the last as an insider and at the same time he indicated the problems and weaknesses in the whole of the exercise.

Mr. Balakrishnan, Lead Bank District Manager, Dindigul District in his session handled the topic District Annual credit plan and integration of this plan with District Development plan. The role of banks in district annual credit plan for three sectors Agriculture, Industry and Service sectors. He explained that the service area approach was very useful and effective in preparing village credit plan. Block level bankers committee drafted the Block credit plan. Most of the time for these plans data are not properly collected. He informed that the sectoral departments do not facilitate with data for village credit plan. He further told that it is very necessary that peoples' participation must be ensured and he was very positive that people would understand the income, credit, repayment system of many transaction. What is needed is facilities and institutional arrangements for regular interface with the people and transparent in our transactions.

Dr. Lalitha, Reader in Rural Development in her lecture indicated the implications of the poverty alleviation programme in Rural Development. She outlined the various approaches introduced by the government.

- Multi-purpose approach
- Sectoral approach
- Target approach
- Area approach
- Minimum need programme

She made a fair evaluation on the above approaches and the schemes implemented. She cited many examples to illustrate the success of micro enterprises and effective utilization of the schemes and programmes of the government by groups especially the women. She indicated the need of Institutional linkage, namely:

- Training
- Market Facility
- Improved tools at common facility centre
- Awareness on Social and Economic field

Dr. Lalitha cited the features of Self-Help Group (SHG) and the new scheme SGSY. The SHG must be equipped with the institutional linkages and given infrastructure facilities to ensure sustainability.

Dr.V. Ragupathy dwelt at length on the role of Panchayati Raj Institution's in Common Property Management. He indicated the need of establishing local bodies control over resources to make them as autonomous. He brought to light the traditional role of community on the Management of Common Property Resources and its effective utility. He further informed that 200 years back there were no government machineries to take any developmental initiative for the welfare of the villagers. 40,000 tanks/ponds were once maintained by the villagers with the meticulous planning. These are the references for the reasons of successful planning and execution of work by people. He made a question that what are the reasons for the diminishing of people's participation? He outlined that the new step introduced by the British Colonial administration formation of district and appointment of district 'collector' as well as introduction of issuing patta to individual, resulted in the trust gap between people and government.

He shared his study experience on the status of Common Property Resource in Madurai and Sivaganga district. He told that there were a number of panchayats who have earned several lakhs of rupees out of common property resources by-passing government control. Here Dr. V. Ragupathy referred the study of Duke University on "Ecological Culture of Sivaganga District" to explain the role of a stake holders in an enterprise.

He noted that the present 'Namakku Naame Thittam' of Tamil Nadu government was a well conceived plan to generate peoples' participation. But he suggested that to draw the people for common activities is few pre-conditions have to be ensured. He listed out the following pre-conditions:

1. The interest of individual who participate must be looked into
2. The benefit must be to all concerned
3. There must be autonomous status to the Management / Executive Committee which is going to deal.
4. There must be openness in all its transaction.

He commented on the present system of government control over Panchayati Raj Institutions. How a collector can effectively function as the inspector of panchayats? The inspection or monitoring will be more effective if it is done at the local level and by the local people. He compared the system in Kerala state where the social development is in high position and so the community control on the Panchayat Raj Institution was more.

He admitted that in several villages in the name of community control, there were caste, religious or money power domination over the Panchayati Raj Institution in addition to the party politics. In this mind-set, are there successful models? Dr. V. Ragupathy cited an example of the Ralegon model of Anna Hasara, the Sukurmaji models in Chandikar, the Arabaric model of West Bengal. He stated that there are a number villages in Sivaganga or any other districts where the community has a social control like not permitting to cut any tree in the villages, completely prohibited sale of arrack, collect community toll during the trade in agriculture and restricted and regulated water utility during drought seasons.

He shared his concern with the participants to ponder over an idea of appointing a technical official a Forest Officer or a Revenue Officer under District Panchayat to exclusively assist in administering Common Property Resource with peoples participation through Ayakkuttudar Sangam users group or Pani panchayat system.

He envisaged the scope of group activities not only SHG of women sangam but in all civic transaction which can play a vital role in micro-level planning under the new environment.

Educational Tour

The trainees were given exposure to the various income generation activities of the Gandhigram Trust and the university – Soap making, Shampoo making, dying / printing, handicrafts, Sidha units through which employment generation for poor village men and women. They visited Gandhiji constructive Museum and understood the origin and development of various constructive activities. They visited the remote sensing project lab and learned from the computer pictures and data presented in the lab.

Valedictory Session

Prof. G. Palanithurai in the valedictory session, he shared his experience as a trainer and appreciated the mind-set of trainee-officials who were largely attended the classes, without fail in time, plainly interacted with the resource persons and took notes keenly. He admitted that the course materials must be given in advance to the trainers. He further told that training as a continuous process and according to the field environment it has to be improved. The Kerala and Karnataka models are not exact models for all the states and there are failures also in these models. Hence Tamil Nadu must learn lessons from them and draft our own model based on our field situation.

He presented the scenario of our socio-political and administrative system and requested the officials to start our new approach in planning and make the people to realise and make necessary improvement to achieve the desired end.

He appealed to the trainees to shed the inter and intra departmental differences and take part in this exercise in the best interest of the people.

Dr. N. Markandan, in the valedictory session shared Gandhigram Rural Institute project experience in Karatalagan Patti. He explained the various step taken to bring people to organise themselves, to plan socio-economic activities and to do follow up. He realised that a proper alteration should have been done then and there to correct the pitfalls in the plan. Regular and sincere interface programme among all sectors would correct the Multi-Level Planning perfectly to delver the exact results.

He further stressed that environmental protection and upgrdation have to be included in the plan. Health awareness must be part of the plan otherwise the rural poor do not utilize the toilet facilities.

After distributing certificate to the trainees, M.R.Rajagopalan, Secretary of Gandhigram Trust shared his earlier day experience in development administration. He facilitated the state government for the prompt decision of giving this training assignment to the Gandhigram Rural Institute. Sri.M.R. Rajagopalan further explained that the knowledge need not be from the books. He underlined the importance of micro level planning with an objective of providing basic facilities to improve the quality of life. Any development must have two component as a compulsory one namely Health and Education. Gandhigram founders were expert in their field and so their expertise resulted into the present development as a result of health and educational facilities provided to the rural areas. There is a lot of discussion on from where we have to start planning either at the district level or at the village level. We need not think one thing is right the other one is wrong. We can sit and exchange our views. The present need is togetherness in all walks of life. He concluded that a small step towards that integration in the planning process would definitely bring a new trend in our plan process.

Participants Reflections

Participant - I

It was a good opportunity to learn and understand the role of Panchayati Raj Institution's in planning. A lot of information were given by the key resource persons from Tamil Nadu, Pondicherry, Kerala and Karnataka. The rural development department has already implemented various schemes with peoples participation. JRY, EAS, Group House Scheme are implemented with peoples involvement. But people are not evincing keen interest on it. The administrative sanction are given by district panchayat itself.

There is a need for creating a separate and independent development section as the revenue wing. The fund allocation is now increased. About 100 to 125 crores of rupees are spent on the welfare and economic programmes annually. Hence an independent development administration has to be established. Along with development administration, the district planning committee must also be strengthened. All matters related to the development of the district must be decided at the district level. We have to create India-development service like IAS or it may be a separate service cadres in the name of state administrative service for development.

He said that was very much enlightened when the thrust was given on social and environmental aspects in plan. He wanted that clear cut ideas, methodology, course materials for the district level training from the planning commission.

Participant - II

A lot of new information have been given in the training. Considering the various responsibilities of District planning, a good and commanding level official is needed to co-ordinate all the activities effectively. He expressed that the district planning committee must function independently. He shared his happiness that he involved fully and exchanged a lot of information during the sessions.

Participant - III

So far there was no scope for people's participation in the plan preparation. Now we realise the significance of it. He appreciated the resource persons effort to provide the necessary inputs in the trainees mind. He demanded that a further attention is need for training techniques.

Participant - IV

He expressed satisfaction over the way in which the training is being conducted and the content given in the training. Yet he expressed his reservation over the issue of integrating sectoral department with the development department.

He narrated a puranic story from Mahabaratham to illustrate the new mind-set they have after attending the training as servants of the people. He appreciated the teaching method in Tamil handled by Prof.G. Palanithurai.

Participant - V

He disclosed that he had already learned Participatory Rural Appraisal technique. He suggested that a session has to be allotted for analysing group psychology. He wished that the time for the resource persons may be increased as most of them brought a lot of OHP sheets. He wanted to know how the other departments are going to be linked in plan preparation.

He suggested that initiative must be taken to create awareness among the people first about the preparation of development plan. He indicated that Kerala model may not be reapplicable in Tamil Nadu. Let us improve it for our own objective, he added. He recalled that what is learned during the youth still remains hence the concepts such as principle of Participatory Rural Appraisal, Multi-Level Planning should from civic education and they should be taught at high school and higher secondary school levels.

Participant - VI

He was happy that he become a trainer. He told that the government is giving more importance to improve the infrastructure facilities. Now there are a large number of schemes which are location specific and micro level. In this context the peoples' participation in Multi-Level Planning exercise is very much essential. To perform a new task the orientation given in Gandhigram is sufficient.

Weakness Identified in the Yraining

The officials are not informed about this exercise well in advance. Some of them are nearing retirement age. Materials are not supplied to the participants before their arrival. There is no scope for hand on experience. Training content could not be given fully within the five day frame work. No time for discussion. Adequate reading materials could not be supplied due to budget constraints.

Strength Notices

One could notice the presence of well meaning committed officials in the group of trainees. They are sincere in taking notes, raising questions and adding points to the discussion. They are punctual in attending classes and committed in their work. The invited resource persons from outside and Gandhigram Rural Institute have turned up to this programme without fail. The resource persons level of handling the classes have attracted the attention of the participants. The personal attention of the Vice-Chancellor in this programme made the participants more serious in attending their work.

Suggestion

Well prepared reading material have to be handed over to the trainee well in advance so that the trainees are expected to participate in the training with a background knowledge. Before they proceed to participate in the training programme, they must be briefed about the programme and its importance. When the officials are in the training programme they should not be disturbed by their superior officials. All the officials at the district level should be given field level exposure atleast two days in Kerala which will reinforce the programme. The trained staff members have to be given the next assignment immediately otherwise they will loose the grip over the subject. Proper integration of the sectoral departments with development department in the preparation of plan has to be explained clearly by the District Collector well in advance before they participate in the training programme. Though government has passed order fixing responsibility on the part of the official in each sector, the officer concerned has not been informed of his role and responsibility in the District Planning Cell officials have to be sensitised in the new context before they are being drawn to the training as they have to play a dominant and vital role.

3. Evaluation of Training of Trainers
(by the Participants)

		Good	Satisfactory	Poor
1. Training Arrangements				
i)	Class room arrangements	54	10	7
ii)	Lodging arrangements	46	15	10
iii)	Boarding arrangements	54	9	8
iv)	Course content	61	10	—
v)	Course delivery	57	14	—
vi)	Course material	41	15	25
vii)	Educational Tour	20	32	19
2. Sessions Handled				
1st Day	Session I	64	7	—
	Session II	62	9	—
	Session III	67	4	—
	Session IV	68	3	—
2nd Day	Session I	59	12	—
	Session II	57	14	—
	Session III	55	16	—
	Session IV	57	14	—
3rd Day	Session I	59	12	—
	Session II	57	14	—
	Session III	55	16	—
	Session IV	53	18	—
4th Day	Session I	62	9	—
	Session II	64	7	—
	Session III	57	9	5
	Session IV	55	12	4
5th Day	Session I	57	14	—
	Session II	48	16	7
	Session III	51	15	3
	Session IV	48	19	4

3. Suggestion for improvement in the following aspects

I i) Boarding	1.	Hygenic condition must be ensured.
	2.	Quality of food may be improved.
	3.	Dining Hall – sections with table must be provided.
	4.	Non-vegetarian meal may be provided.
	5.	Good drinking water arrangement may be given.
	6.	2 sets of dining arrangement for quick supply.
ii) Lodging	1.	Rooms should be cleaned daily.
	2.	More wash basins are needed.
	3.	More number of bathrooms/toilets are needed.
	4.	Separate rooms instead of dormitory.
	5.	News papers and Television facilities are needed.
	6.	Drinking water arrangement.
	7.	Cubboard arrangement.
	8.	Table /chair facilities.
iii) Classroom arrangment	1.	Generator is needed.
	2.	Table mike for interaction.
	3.	Library facilities.
	4.	Seating arrangements may be improved.
	5.	Seperate Hall not in the Library for Training classes.
	6.	Seating must be rearranged to face the Resource person directly.
iv) Education Tour	1.	It must be according to the training content.
	2.	Village Panchayats must be visited for planning exercise.
	3.	PRA - Practical classes are needed.
	4.	NGO may be visited.
	5.	Every day evening session for Educational tour may be arranged.
	6.	Each topic need education tour/visit

		7.	Participants must be taken to Kerala.
II	i) Session delivery	1.	Lecture session is a long one. It may be shortened.
		2.	More practical classes than theory classes.
		3.	Training Techniques – Practical assessment is needed.
		4.	More time for interaction is needed
		5.	Model planning committee may be formed and practical may be arranged.
	ii) Course content	1.	Notes/details must be given well in advance.
		2.	Group psychology principles must be taught.
		3.	Example must be provided.
	iii) Course materials	1.	Sufficient materials are needed well in advance.
		2.	Session wise course materials are needed.
		3.	Each Resource Person's lecture details details should be given to the participants.
		4.	A well content booklet is needed.

8

ASSOCIATING WOMEN REPRESENTATIVES IN LOCAL BODIES

Step I

NETWORKING NGO's

Introduction

Empowering women is a herculian task in Indian context as social and cultural moorings had established their strong roots in the belief system of the people. As a result, there has always been an uncommon disparity in the upbringing of women and men. All social reconstructions took place only through political activities that too through political systems. Democracy provided enough scope for such reconstructions through polity. Hence every social segment is moving towards power. Yet women hesitate to take part in politics as if the space is for men. In order to break this barrier at a micro level, a new device has been worked out through 73rd Constitutional Amendment Act. This Act provided the women with one-third reservation of seats at all levels in all positions of the panchayati institutions. But this provision has not yielded the expected results as this space is not perceived properly by the women leaders. Because the elected women representatives of this grassroots institutions are facing a variety of problems in their social, political and administrative settings, apart from their personal family life. They have been made ineffective in administration since they have come to these institutions as freshers. Yet laudable achievements are made by women leaders in panchayats. To achieve things in panchayats the women leaders have to face plethora of problems and infact the leaders are overcoming all those difficulties by taking series of efforts. They are in struggle. The leaders have been made insensitive towards their self and women issues. They have been oriented to lose their identity. They are made as instruments to operationalise certain things for others. This process has made them to sink in localism and voicelessness. As a result their space expansion is severely limited. In order to overcome all those hurdles, an attempt is made to associate the women leaders on their own to address all those issues for the general cause of the women in their functioning.

The expectation of this attempt is empowerment of women leaders at the grassroot level by federating themselves with similar Women Representatives Association in Local Government in other states and make them to speak their issues on their own in their platform. An attempt was made on 26th August, 2000 at Gandhigram Rural Institute, Gandhigram by making women activist, gender specialist and feminist to comment on this proposal and discuss how women leaders can be associated in local governance by overcoming the existing difficulties. The outcome of the meet is presented here and it can be called as "proposed agenda for action". They are:

* Awareness creation about their space;
* Periodical sensitisation of the women leaders on women issues;
* Information dissemination;
* Federating the existing Associations;
* Association formation;
* Creating supporting base — Information Centre;
* Organising Interface Programmes;
* Tie-up with NGOs;
* Documenting success stories and other women related issues;
* Conducting women conventions; and
* Policy advocacy.

Why N.G.Os?

N.G.Os have a long cherished history in working at the grassroots for the betterment of the people. In the fifty three years of democratic governance both at the centre and state, opportunity had not been provided for peoples participation. This has resulted in a wide gap between the ruled and rulers. Hence, all the initiatives by the government did not reach the people. As a result an intervention by an outside agency becomes inevitable in the process of facilitation. NGOs have intervened in a massive way to implement some of the government programmes and exhibited success with the participation of the people. So the role of NGOs was realised at the grassroot level for their contact with people.

NGOs play a crucial role in mobilizing the mass for development activities in the rural areas. They have a supporting networking system at the grassroots. So these grassroots NGOs will play a commendable role in empowering women and simultaneously associate women leaders at the grassroots level. Hence NGOs of this kind came forward for a tie-up activity with Gandhigram Rural Institute as they have direct contact with the people at the grassroots level.

Some leading and professional NGOs are doing panchayati activities in their areas for the past four years in awareness creation among the people about the New Panchayati Raj System and conducting capacity building exercise for the grassroots leaders. Hence they are invited to take part in this programme. They are expected to perform certain functions to facilitate the women leaders to federate themselves and to offer training to them.

The Meet

To explore the possibility of the NGOs role in this endeavour, they are asked to look at the issues of the women leaders as they are working in the same field for the past four years. They have been asked to react on the following points:

a) What are the problems faced by the women leaders in performing their role and function?

b) How to help the women leaders to break the barriers in their way to achieve results?

c) To what extent they can work with the women leaders organisation as facilitators?

The participants are :

1. M. Anbalagan
   Programme Coordinator
   VIDIYAL
   Rasingapuram - 625 525
   Theni District

2. S. Nagamani
   Special Officer
   Kamaraj Jaycee Leadership School
   KAJALS
   443, Main Bazar
   Virudhunagar-626 001

3. B.C. Sivagami
   Centre for Rural Health and Social Education
   A/11, Ashok Nagar
   Vellore District - 635 601

4. N. Sivakumar
   Centre for Rural Health and Social Education
   A/11, Ashok Nagar
   Vellore District - 635 601

5. K. Nirmala
   Guide
   10B, Masilamani Nagar
   Kancheepuram Road
   Walajabad
   Kancheepuram

6. J. Imma Culate Mary
   SIGA Community Service Guild
   Ayyalur Village
   Kalambakkam Post
   Thiruvallur District

7. N. Dayalan
   LRSA
   Nehru Nagar
   Vallam Post
   Chengalpattu - 603002

8. N.S. Chidambaram
   Retd A.D.R.D
   Consultant S.I.R.D.
   Maraimalai Nagar - 603 209

9. K. Vallinayagam
   Retd A.D.R.D.
   No.8, Kattabomman Street
   Chitlapakkam
   Chennai

10. Dr. B.S. Bhargava
    Senior Fellow
    ISS South Region
    Near State Bank of Mysore
    No.2, 8th Main Road, 8th Cross
    Malleswarm, Banagalore - 560 003

11. P. Viswanath
    Scientist MSSRF
    Taramani Institutional Area
    3rd Cross, Chennai - 11.

12. R.V.Bhavani
    MSSRF
    Taramani Institutional Area, 3rd Cross
    Chennai - 11.

13. T. Thanulingam
    AWARD
    10/20, Hamedia Nagar
    Valanadu,
    Thoothukudi District - 628252

14. M. Kalaiselvi
    Rural Improvement Project
    Panankulivizai
    Kappukobu (PO)
    Kanyakumari District

15. Bimla Chandresekar
    EKTA, No.6, Duraisamy Nagar
    Ist Cross street,
    Bye pass Road
    Madurai - 6.

16. N. Balachandran
    (Representing RDO Trust)
    25A, Glencross Colony
    Ooty

17. N. Logamani
    Director
    WED Trust
    Chellampatti
    Usilampati,
    Madurai District

18. Dr. N. Markandan
    Former Vice-Chancellor, GRI
    No.3, Sakthi Cross 1st Street,
    Gandhipuram
    Coimbatore

19. Gnana Surabhi Mani
    RCPED
    1A/1, Ponneni Periavar street
    S.S.Colony
    Madurai - 10

20. Dr. B. Guna, E.W.D
    Valparai Road, Angalakurichi
    Pollachi - 642 007

21. M. Thava Singh
    RCPED
    1A/1, Ponneni Periavar street
    S.S.Colony
    Madurai - 10

22. R.K. Murugan
    CODE, Mahdendrapuram
    Radhapuram

23. R.D. Gnanaiah
    CHDP
    Udumalapet

24. K. Parwathi
    MMS
    Chinnamanur

25. M. Ponnuraj
    SIRPI
    Ammapatt
    Theni

26. S. Lispin
    Rural Organisation for Awareness and Development
    Sarathy
    H97, Marthandam
    Kanyakumari District

27. I. Jesuraj
    Secretary
    ARISES
    8/99, South Street
    A Vellodu - 624 307

28. Dr. G. Palanithurai
    Programme Coordinator
    SS Foundation Project
    Department of Political Science
    Gandhigram Rural Institute
    Gandhigram.

29. Dr. V. Ragupathy
    Associate Programme Coordinator
    SS Foundation Project
    Department of Political Science
    Gandhigram Rural Institute
    Gandhigram.

30. Mr. G. Umashankar
    Project Facilitator
    SS Foundation Project
    Department of Political Science
    Gandhigram Rural Institute
    Gandhigram.

31. Ms. G. Uma
    Project Facilitator

SS Foundation Project
Department of Political Science
Gandhigram Rural Institute
Gandhigram.

32. Mr. S. Devaraj
Research Assistant
Department of Political Science
Gandhigram Rural Institute
Gandhigram.

33. Mr. M. Gurusamy
Research Assistant
Department of Political Science
Gandhigram Rural Institute
Gandhigram.

34. Mr. M.A.Thirunavukkarasu
Research Assistant
Department of Political Science
Gandhigram Rural Institute
Gandhigram.

35. Dr. K.S. Nakkeeran
Lecturer
Research Assistant
Department of Political Science
Gandhigram Rural Institute
Gandhigram.

36. Mr. A. Thangathurai
Research Assistant
Department of Political Science
Gandhigram Rural Institute
Gandhigram.

37. Mr. K. Tamilarasan
Research Assistant
Department of Political Science
Gandhigram Rural Institute
Gandhigram.

38. Ms. C. Muthulakshmi
    Chinnamanur (Post)
    Theni District

39. Dr. G. Pankajam
    Associate Secretary
    Gandhigram Trust
    Gandhigram.

40. Sri. M.R. Rajagopalan
    Chairman
    IAC, Gandhigram.

Barring a few all the participants are from NGOs. NGOs are selected on the basis of their past record of work in the field of women empowerment activities.

Mr. G. Umashankar welcomed the participants and in his welcome address, he pointed out the various activities of the Gandhigram Rural Institute for the cause of women since its inception.

Dr. G. Palanithurai, in his introductory remarks gave a detailed picture on "why this decentralization of power" and the work done by Gandhigram Rural Institute in creating awareness on New Panchayati Raj System. He added that awareness creation is not done at the time of election alone. It is a continuous process and hence it has been continued till now. Ever since the Government of Tamil Nadu passed the confirmity legislation, academic exercise had been started in Gandhigram Rural Institute to study the Act and assess its position in the state. It made several recommendations. After the conduct of the election, training programme was started and thereby rural and urban local body leaders have been trained. In the whole process of training, we have learnt the dimensions of the problems of the leaders especially the women. The problems are so acute for Dalit women leaders. These problems have been documented and done policy advocacy and yet there is no sign of qualitative improvement. Their problems are being presented by us and other NGOs. But the issues remain unsolved as we speak for them. Hence we have decided to make them to speak on their own.

When they speak, they would take up issues based on their perception and understanding. But in reality the women leaders have been oriented to think in a different pattern as expected by others. Sometimes the women are insensitive towards their own issues. A careful analysis of the women leaders would suggest ways and means to achieve empowerment of women.

Our experiences with the women leaders and their functioning in the past four years in Tamil Nadu bring a lot of issues to the front for discussion.

Types of Women leaders in Position

1. Women oriented by NGOs
2. Women oriented by political parties
3. Women oriented by families
4. Women oriented by community
5. Women oriented by women organisations

What enabled them to make an entry into the local bodies

- Caste
- Political party affiliation
- Family
- Organisation
- Relatives
- Peer groups
- Money
- Past service
- Own reputation

The status of women leaders
- Aggressive women leaders
- Capacitated and sober women leaders
- Leaders with *status quo* aspiration
- Leaders with the aspiration of upward mobility
- Depressed leaders in the process of withdrawal.

Problems faced by them are due to
- Non co-operation of the officials
- Non co-operation of their own party leaders
- Influence by family members
- Influence by caste leaders
- Influence of MLAs and MPs
- Interference of political party leaders

The Problems are

- Inadequate supply of information
- Inadequate skills and capacity
- Domination of the officials over the elected leaders
- Ill-treatment of the Dalit women leaders by the officials
- Husband's domination in administration
- Increasing workload in the home
- Poor capacity in communication
- Poor skill in mobilising the people
- Poor management of council and crowd, account maintenance
- Planning and preparing of projects
- Unaware of rural development schemes
- Unaware of the basis of the new dispensation
- Unaware of the potentiality of the natural resources
- Unaware of the human resources and their implication
- Conscious of their self
- Non cooperation of the revenue officials
- Complicated administrative procedure
- Presence of corruption at every level
- Influence of MPs and MLAs
- Paucity of funds

So, against this background they are working. Against this background an attempt is made to sensitise them on their own issues and to rise up to the occasion to speak out their issues. They in fact form their association and get collaborated with other organisations and associations in other states. In this exercise we are exploring the possibility of involving the NGOs for federating the women organisations as facilitators. After the presentation of status report by Dr. G. Palanithurai, Dr. N. Markandan (Former Vice-chancellor of Gandhigram Rural Institute) in his presidential address stressed that people must be made aware of what is going on in the world and only then we can achieve development. For the effective functioning of grassroots institutions, proper orientation of leadership is an imperative. Otherwise, they will be oriented to work as a contractor for the government. Even people are not ready to participate in any of the activities relating to their development as they are not sensitised on their issues and the New Panchayati Raj System. Secondly, NGOs who are all involved in this process have to be accredited as they have to be at the back of the women leaders organisations in their struggle. The role of the NGOs and the capacity of the leaders are essential components of this empowerment process of the women. To carryout this task the orientation must be done on non-violent basis. Non-violent techniques have to be taught. This alone can bring peace at the grassroot level and panchayats can achieve desired ends in a sustainable way.

The programme was inaugurated by Dr. G. Pankajam (Executive Secretary of Gandhigram Trust). In her inaugural address she stated that it is a right time now to take stock of the situation after four years of the functioning of the Panchayati Raj Institutions under the leadership of the women folk in the society. For this we have to take into consideration the following aspects :

* In the past four years how far these institutions under the leadership of women have functioned?
* What were the problems faced by the women leaders in their institutions?
* Are the women leaders sensitized and concientised?
* How far the self-help groups are helping the functioning of women leaders in panchayats?
* How far the other associations function with the Panchayati Raj Institutions?
* What were the developments achieved in the past four years by the women leaders?

After the evaluation, steps have to be taken to empower the women leaders in panchayat with appropriate interventions.

Other States Experience

Dr. B.S. Bhargava, Senior Fellow, Institute of Social Sciences, shared the experiences of women leaders in grassroots governance in Karnataka with the participants. The following are the key points:

* Karnataka is a pioneering state for democratic decentralization.
* Women constituted 25 per cent in panchayats when they were given opportunity in 1985.
* There is a well documented literature available for grassroots governance in Karnataka.
* A well established information guide for the panchayat leaders on panchayats are available.
* Proxy leaders are yielding to corruption.

* Women are still on old prison and they move from critical mass to critical action.
* Women leaders have acquired positions more than 42 per cent in the local bodies.
* There are numerous NGOs working at the grassroots for empowerment of women.
* At taluk level there is an association for panchayat leaders.
* Women still are experiencing gender discrimination.
* They worry much about money and muscle power.
* Many women want to withdraw from their office because of non-co-operation of officials and her own colleagues.
* Government is devolving powers through governments orders but not through the Act and this itself is a set back for the effective functioning of the women leaders.
* Radical change has been made in Karnataka by women leaders.

He stressed that in order to make the local body institutions more viable and vibrant the local list has to be added to the Constitution like the state list and central list. After 73rd Constitutional Amendment Act of 1992, the bureaucracy is on the upper hand and the peoples representatives are at the lower level. The alternative can be, the District Panchayat President must be made the real executive and all the ordinances must be made on his name only. He concluded his sharing with one observation that for the empowerment of women leaders, interface programme between Tamil Nadu and Kerala and Tamil Nadu and Karnataka will be very useful and effective. Others experiences will be lessons for the Tamil Nadu women leaders.

In terms of panchayat administration, the problems faced by the women are not different from the men. They face more problems as they are women. The crucial question is how the women leaders are going to mitigate the sufferings of the women living in the rural areas. At every sphere women faces problems starting from the parents to workspot, they have been treated as second rate citizens. Even for the female infanticide, women are the worst victims. They commit such a crime since they were under severe sress in the family and they were terrorised by the family members. Poor women coolie doing the work on par with men getting low pay yet no one is to ask for that women folk. In the same way maid servants were harassed sexually and there was no protection. Due to the influence of alcohol, women are tortured in the family by their husbands. Who speak about their cases? and where they are heard? instances and events can be listed. But all those issues are not finding place in the agenda of the discussion of Gram Sabha. It was only a money business in Gram Sabha. If it is a people's forum all the issues of the people whether they are connected with children or women or Dalit, they are to be discussed and decision has to be taken. These are some of the points highlighted in the inaugural sessions.

The meet was arranged in two sessions. The first session in the forenoon and the second session in the afternoon.

Session I

The first session theme was "Assessment of Women Leaders Performance in Panchayati Raj Institutions and the Problems Faced by the Women Leaders in Panchayats".

Shri.Vallinayagam Retd Additional Director of Rural Development, Government of Tamil Nadu and an advocate chaired the session. In his introductory remarks he highlighted the following issues :

* 73rd and 74th Constitutional Amendment Acts have created a space for women but the maintenance and expansion of the space depends not on the Acts but on the efficient management of the institutions provided to them and concientising themselves properly to keep up the space. It was hoped and believed that with the inclusion of the marginalised section the misery of the women folk would be mitigated. The newly recruited women for the leadership have to prepare themselves to face the challenges in many fronts. They have to respond to the multipronged attack and for which they have qualify themselves by enhancing their capacity. To safeguard themselves, they have to rely on the strength of organisations.
* Officials especially the District Collectors use the Section 205 in the Tamil Nadu Panchayati Act to remove the Gram panchayat leaders. Till date 98 panchayat presidents have been removed from office and out of the 98, 66 are women. This has created a sense that women leaders are incompetent. It is not the fact, women leaders are not aware of their rights, powers and functions. So a small deviation creates a big confusion. Awareness creation is a must on the part of the women leaders and the people. Enlightenment is empowerment, so women leaders must be enlightened. People have notion that effective laws will create wonders in the society. Law cannot create wonders. It is the people who handle the law can bring wonders. Hence "participation" has been considered as a key for social

transformation.

* Women leaders at the grassroots level cannot change the existing syndrome all of a sudden. They have to equip themselves to demonstrate their competence. They have to be concientised properly to address the issues. They should cultivate the habit of working in an organised structure to galvanize the support of the organisation for their struggle in the society. They have to be supported by the women leaders at the higher level and for which reservation for women in the State Legislature and National Parliament was saught.
* Against this background it is thought that awareness creation must be the primary aim of the organisations and institutions towards the women leaders.

There is a comment everywhere about the women representation. The women representation in the country that too in the grass roots institutions is only a proxy and they are the instruments of the male family members. Partially there is truth in it. But the conditions are changing fastly that has to be recognised. It is the responsibility of the government to take initiative to build the capacity of the women leaders and see the powers of the leaders should not be encroached. There are explicit and implicit forces working in the system to project the women are in competent to manage these institutions. And this has been taken as an advantage by the family members in the name of helping the women presidents, they do all those activities. Even the officials are co-operating with them for this proxy leadership as to quicken the process of carrying out their activities without much trouble.

It is demonstrated in many places that the capacitated women leaders are carrying out their activities on their own without the help of the male family members. It is true in the case of the women leaders oriented by the party and NGOs. So what is needed is the capacity building.

There is yet another issue which has to be taken note of seriously. In the name of training the women leaders have been oriented in such a way to forget about the self and made to think in a form which is suited to government and bureaucracy. Success and failures of administrations are in terms of the amount spent in panchayats and not in terms of the issues that they have dealt with. There are a large number of issues being confronted by the people and especially the marginalised and excluded women and Dalits, but they are not taken note of. It is only the schemes and programmes of the governments carried out in the panchayats are considered as parameters of success. The basic issues remain dormant. They are made insensitive towards their own issues. Because they are not included in 11th Schedule and 12th Schedule and for all those issues the governments have not allocated money and evolved schemes and programmes. These issues need only a change of mind-set on the part of the leaders and the people to bring the needed change of mind-set a struggle has to be waged and for which women leaders have to be prepared. It could be done not in isolation but through an organisation and a movement. As of now there is a legitimate political space created for women. It has come to a critical mass. It has to move into a phase of critical action. For critical action, the women leaders have to be prepared.

Gram Sabha is yet another legitimate space created for discussion of issues faced by the people, where people can bring their issues for discussion of the community. But time has not come sofar to bring the issues of the women folk. And women folk has not come to such level to bring all those issues to the public for discussion. As agenda has been prepared by the government officials, items relating to income and expenditure, proposal for schemes and programmes have been included in the agenda. No issues connected with dowry or unequal wage for women in farming operation or female infanticide or foeticide or education to women children or employment to women included in the items of agenda of Gram Sabha discussion.

Even the women leaders are not sensitive towards those issues. Because they have been oriented to treat all those issues as non-issues. This is the saddest part of the whole exercise. Even if they are sensitise towards those issues, they cannot take all those issues because they have to meet the dair consequences from their own families. It requires an analysis and altogether it needs a new approach for those who work with panchayat leaders for empowerment of people and women. The above posited points have been discussed by the participants in the first session.

Session II

The focal theme of Session II is "How can we facilitate women leaders for their effective functioning in their space by keeping ourselves as outsiders". This session was chaired by Sri.Chidambaram, Retd Additional Director of Rural Development, Government of Tamil Nadu. In his introductory remarks he stressed the following aspects:

There is no substitute to training. The women leaders have to be trained. This training might have imparted in the beginning of the term itself. Content must have due bias towards feminism and discriminationism. With a new content, women leaders are to be oriented on issues. It is a general trend that efforts should be taken to make the women to participate. The question is participation for what? It should be on an issue. More participation would reflect only the role of a spectator. Women leaders are not spectators.

Further when women leaders take up the core and basic issues of the women, they need organisational support otherwise they will be terrorised by the vested interest in the society. It has been noticed from the women movement from Andhra Pradesh. Even the government would not support. Hence it is necessary to concientise the women leaders on their issues. Make them to take up issues according to their capacity. When they deal with the issues they would be provided with all moral and legal support by the organisations. The purpose of federating their organisations with the help of the NGOs is to keep their space intact for the women continuously and to expand the space and they should deal with development issues more specifically on issues affecting the women.

Dr. G. Palanithurai, in his concluding remarks stated that, before we plan for a course of action, we must be very clear about the issues. It should be noted that issues vary from region to region. Therefore, when we talk about the state level convention, we have to first work at the regional level and consolidate it at the state level. Orientation has to be given on the part of panchayat presidents and members. After the discussion, they have identified the issues which are to be dealt within the whole process. They are listed here.

Issues to be Considered

The issues to be considered while the process of associating women representatives in local governance are.

I. Social Issues

1. Female foeticide
2. Female infanticide
3. Malnutrition
4. Domestic harassment
5. No consideration for feelings and aspirations
6. Sexual harassment in workplaces
7. Gender discrimination

8. Education beyond primary level for women
9. Denial of technical education
10. Dual responsibility both in home and working place
11. Sexual exploitations
12. Increasing workload
13. Denial of basic amenities in working place
14. Lack of health facilities
15. Food habits
16. Lack of medical care
17. Domestic situations
    Drinking Water
    Fuel wood
    Public Distribution System
    Child care results in tension
18. Forced sex against their will
19. Liquor consumption
20. Viewing women as a child bearing machine
21. Denial of property – non-implementation of law
22. Made women victims of different kinds of violence
23. No security in unorganised sector
24. Widow remarriage is still dream

II. Economic Issues

1. Wage differences
2. Over workload less wage
3. Employed in hazardous industries
4. Total dependence
5. A notion is there that the work done by women are easy

III. Political Issues

1. Voting rights are denied
2. Name sake participation alone is allowed in political activities.
3. Not easy to form an organisation or association
4. Very difficult to approach the political leaders
5. Character assassination
6. When women enter into politics, they are not considered as leaders, they are treated as proxies.
7. Judiciary is still conservative. Judgments are mostly based on the

judges.

8. Women's rights are still in papers only.

Dr.V. Ragupathy, in his consolidated report observed the following:

* Out of certain difficulties women leaders are functioning effectively in certain areas.
* Problems have to be identified region-wise and the women leaders are to be concientised on those issues.
* When those issues are taken for action at the micro level, the experience of the leaders are to be documented.
* The whole transformation process has been visualised and observed carefully.
* Capacity building exercise, for the women leaders and their members has to be done with a new perspective. Gender, discrimination and feminism should be the components in the perspective.
* Interface programme with Kerala and Karnataka has to be conducted.
* Document the successful leaders and make it available for as role model for others.
* The programmes should be proactive and constructive.

By federating the women leaders organisations, the documented issues have to be utilized for policy advocacy and they have to articulate their problems in their fora. All state level conventions are meant for politicising the issues for larger consumption.

Sri. M. R. Rajagopalan (Chairman, Administrative Committee) gave the valedictory address. In his address he stressed that motivation is a must for adding efficiency in individuals. Training programmes must be planned in such a way that it should change the individuals mind-set. Training programme must have the content of planning. While taking the planning exercise, special component plan for women and Dalit development should find a place. The major concern of the activities in the panchayat are to be economy oriented. Economy orientation does not mean growth derived from Globalization. We have to be very selective in choosing the option. What type of economy we want? How it should be achieved? All these issues are to be cleared. Our activities should be oriented towards the poor, nature and women. In this regard NGOs must play a key role to make the panchayats to function effectively and achieve the desired results.

Ms. G. Uma proposed vote of thanks.

What to do

1. Network the Women Leaders Association
   Let them be first sensitised on women issues
   Women are working solitarily at the grassroots level. They all must be brought under one umbrella.
2. Information dissemination
3. Establishing a monitoring cell to monitor the activities
4. Documentation of cases of conflict and achievement
5. Projection of role models through documentation
6. A sense of security must be made to the women leaders
7. Legal assistance to be provided
8. Policy advocacy has to be done
9. Urging the government to have gender analysis in its policy and programmes.

How to do

1. Tamil Nadu has 28 districts and they are divided into five zones. namely

   Zone I
   Erode
   Namakkal
   Coimbatore
   Nilgiri
   Salem
   Dharmapuri

   Zone II
   Kanyakumari
   Tirunelveli
   Tuticorin
   Virudhunagar
   Madurai
   Ramanathapuram
   Sivaganga

Zone III
Dindigul
Theni
Karur
Thiruchirappalli
Perambalur

Zone IV
Tanjore
Tiruvarur
Nagapattinam
Pudukkottai

Zone V
Kancheepuram
Cuddalore
Vellore
Thiruvannamalai
Thiruvarur
Villupuram

1. In each and every district one or two NGOs will function as network agencies or partners and for every zone there will a co-ordinating agency which will work with Gandhigram Rural Institute.
2. These NGOs will identify the women leaders and associate them.
3. Zonal level meetings will be conducted and finally a state level convention will be conducted.
4. From the above said activities women leaders will be sensitised on the issues identified.
5. Necessary support would be extended from different spheres to the women leaders.
6. Documentation on every step will be done.
7. Role models will be identified and made available for others.
8. Interface and exchange programmes will be organised for them.
9. Finally the Tamil Nadu Federation will be associated with the federation of the other three southern states.

NGOS for tie-up activities

Zone I

1.	Erode	Womens Organisation in Rural Development (WORD) 449, Thiruchengode Road Pallipalayam - 638 006
2.	Namakkal	WORD 35, Middle Street Post Bag : 1 Pandamangalam Namakkal
3.	Coimbatore	Rural Development Organisation
4.	Nilgiris	Gramya Bhavan Aruvanakadu The Nilgiris
5.	Salem	Peoples Movement for Development Prof. Aruthur Nilayam (Opp) Ward : 8 Nangavelli Main Road Taramangalam - 636 502
6.	Dharmapuri	ARCOD 4/637, Krishnagiri Road Royakottai - 635 116

Zone II

7.	Kanyakumari	ROAD SAARATHY 1-197/A, Kulasekaram Road Marthandam - 629 165
8.	Tirunelveli	CODE Mahendrapuram Radhapuram - 627 111

9. Tuticorin	AWARD 10/20, Hameethia Nagar Vallanadu - 628 252
10. Virudhunagar	KAJALS Idhayam 442, Main Bazaar Virudhunagar - 626 001
11. Madurai	RCPED 1-A/1 Ponmeni Periyavar street, SS Colony Madurai - 625 010
	EKTA Plot No.6, Lakshmi Nivas First Cross Street, Duraisamy Nagar Bye pass Road Madurai - 625 010
12. Ramanathapuram RCPED	1-A/1, Ponmeni Periyavar Street, S. S. Colony, Madurai-625010.
13. Sivaganga	GRAAMA IYAKKAM Pudukattampur - 630210 Tirupathur Sivaganga District

Zone III

14. Dindigul	CHERU Vellbommanpatty Vadamadurai - 624 802
	PEACE Trust New Police Colony Trichy Road Dindigul - 624 005

15. Theni	SIRPI 1-A, Raja Street Near Lakshmi Theater Periyakulam Road Theni - 625 531
	VIDIYAL Karippanpatti Rasingapuram Valliyoor - 627 117
16. Karur	AREDS Ranganathapuram Krishnarayapuram Karur - 639 108
	ARPE 42/3 Vanchinathan Nagar Thanthondrimalai Karur - 639 005
17. Tiruchirapalli	DOW 18, Arulnayagam street Near Sakthivinayagar Koil Crawford Tiruchirappalli
18. Permabalur	IFPAW N. H. Road, Thuraimansalam (Post) Perambalur (Distt.)-621220

Zone IV

19. Tiruvarur	Bharathi Women Development Centre 28, Kannaki Building Thiruvarur Road Thiruthuraipoondi

20. Tanjore	Mulit Purpose Society
21. Nagapattinam	SEVALAYA Mr. M. Murugapaerumal Thirukuvalai (PO)
	SNEHA Ilancheran Nagar 55, Muthumariamman Koil Street, Velipalayam - 611 001
22. Pudukkottai	STEPS Steps Women's Centre Near Union Office Pudukkottai - 1.

Zone V

23. Kancheepuram	GUIDE JCK Nagar Chengalpet - 603 001
	LRSA P.O.Box No. 20 Chengalpet - 603 001
24. Thiruvallur	SIGA E.Block, F.21 PST Quarters Anna Nagar 11th Main Road Bharati Avenue Chennai - 600 040
25. Villupuram	Peoples Development Centre Marakkanam - 604 303 Tindivanam Taluk
26. Vellore	CRHSE A-11 Ashok Nagar Tirupattur - 635 601

27. Thiruvannamalai M. K. Gandhi Rural Development Seva Centre
Eanthal (Post)
Vandhavasi (TK)
Thiruvannamalai-604502

Coordinating Agency for Five Zones

Zone I

1. Rural Development Organisation – Aruvankadu Nilgiris

Zone II

1. RCPED
2. EKTA – Madurai

Zone III

1. Rajiv Gandhi Chair for Panchayati Raj Studies
   Gandhigram Rural Institute

Zone IV

1. STEPS – Pudukkottai

Zone V

1. LRSA – Chengalpattu

Step - II

STATE LEVEL CONSULTATION ON FEMINIST PERSPECTIVES

Report

Elected women representatives to the grassroots level institutions have been facing numerous problems in their social, political and administrative settings apart from their families since their entry into the local bodies. This has led to ineffective administration of the bodies by the women leaders. They don't have a common platform to express their grievances and get them redressed. Experiences of capacity building exercise programme conducted in the various parts of the state have propelled us to prepare an action programme for empowerment of women leaders at the grassroots level by federating themselves with similar women representatives association in local government in different parts of the country and make them to speak their issues on their own.

To perform this activity a state level consultation was conducted on 26th August, 2000 at Gandhigram Rural Institute, Gandhigram by the active involvement of the women activists, gender specialists and feminists. This programme was part of the major action project "Associating Women Representatives in Local Government" sponsored by Ford Foundation through Singamma Sreenivasan Foundation, executed by the Rajiv Gandhi Chair for Panchayati Raj Studies, Department of Political Science and Development Administration, Gandhigram Rural Institute, Gandhigram.

Why this Programme?

The outcome of the capacity building programme is that women leaders are in demand of an alternative arrangement for the continuous flow of the information and consultancy to stabilize their activities for development. The existing grassroots leaders organisations are not providing space for grievance redressal of women leaders. Moreover the requirements of the women leaders are not adequately fulfilled by these organisations. Therefore it has resulted in demanding a fullfledged professional organisation to assist the women local body leaders. Against this background, a facilitating centre for grassroots women leaders is being thought of at the Gandhigram Rural Institute. Before proceed further it is necessary to have a glance on the problems of the women leaders.

Problems faced by the women leaders in the Panchayats
(Problems are generated from the Training Programmes)

1. Village community does not whole heartedly accept the women as leaders. It is the reality one has to accept.
2. Personal constraints —dual responsibility family as well as panchayat — lack of time to manage both effectively and efficiently.
3. Social inability — lack of knowledge on the local politics and illiteracy.
4. Lack of opportunity to meet others and share their experiences and common forum to improve their capacity and personality.
5. Male members of the family don't believe the capacity of their women.
6. Alcoholism, gender discrimination are the real hurdles for the women leaders in panchayats.
7. Women leaders find it difficult to contact and convince government officials.
8. Women presidents are illtreated in the government offices.
9. Most of the women presidents are not showing any interest initially in the training programme. They said that they have nothing to do with the panchayat administration since it was only their husbands who are looking after the entire activities.
10. They need information on the self employment and entrepreneurship opportunities for women.
11. They need information to build women's organisations and co-operation.
12. They need regular information dissemination through a news letter/ magazine.
13. The segments which had supported the women candidates in the election, have not extended their support to the same leaders for their functioning after the elections.
14. The leaders who have not indicated signal that they are working for the people who have casted their votes in the election in favour of them cannot seek the support of the same segments of the people.
15. Even her party leaders at the grassroots level are not extending their helping hand towards her activities in the panchayats.
16. In the same way the caste leaders and family members exert pressure on the women leaders to yield to their pressures.

17. The caste leaders feel that the panchayat leaders are relying on the support base of the caste. Hence they exert pressure on them.
18. Husbands are the yet another problem to the elected women leaders. A large number of women leaders have been recruited to these positions by the influence of their husbands in the party.
19. When a seat is reserved for women, the male aspirant candidates seek permission from the party to field his wife for the post. Such is the way most of the women leaders have been recruited.
20. Women leaders are not able to communicate their ideas in an effective way.
21. Poor women leaders cannot afford to loose their one day wage by attending panchayat works. So it is natural on the part of the women leader, who is a wage earner to hand over her responsibility to some one and perform her family duties.
22. Normally women will be sensitised towards women issues but in reality women leaders are brought and oriented in a fashion to be non-sensitive towards women issues.

The Consultation

To get these problems rectified and to make the women leaders empowered and effective in functioning with the Gender and feminist perspective the state level consultation was organised on 26th August, 2000, by inviting women activist, feminist scholars, academicians, lawyers, and representatives from women organisation working for grassroots women leaders development. The participants are :

1. Ms. Mythili Sivaraman
   Working President - AIDWA
   13, Mosque Street, Chepauk,
   Chennai - 600 005.

2. Ms. Gabriele Dietrich
   Director Centre for Social Analysis
   37, Janaki Narayan Salai
   S.S. Colony, Madurai

3. Ms. Bimla Chandrasekar
   EKIA, Plot No : 6, Lakshmi Nivas
   First Cross Street, Duraisamy Nagar
   Bye Pass Road, Madurai - 620 010

4. Dr. G. Pankajam
   Joint Secretary & Treasurer
   Gandhigram Trust, Gandhigram

5. Ms. Ramani Mathew
   B-6, M.V.M. Nagar
   Bechi College Post,
   Dindigul

6. Dr. N. Lalitha
   Reader in Extension
   Department of ACE & E
   Gandhigram Rural Institute
   Gandhigram.

7. Dr. M. Kuruvammal
   Head incharge
   Department of Tamil
   Gandhigram Rural Institute
   Gandhigram.

8. Dr. K.P. Vasantha Devi
   Reader in Home Science
   Gandhigram Rural Institute
   Gandhigram.

9. Ms. Rajini
   Centre for Dalit Solidatory
   Flat No : 5 LC Colony
   K.K. Nagar, Madurai.

10. Ms. Shenbagavalli
    Advocate
    C 187 A Thirunagar, Madurai

11. Dr. G. Palanithurai
    Programme Coordinator
    Singamma Sreenivasan Foundation Project
    Department of Political Science
    and Development Administration
    Gandhigram Rural Institute
    Gandhigram.

12. Dr. V. Ragupathy
Associate Coordinator
Singamma Sreenivasan Foundation Project
Department of Political Science
and Development Administration
Gandhigram Rural Institute
Gandhigram.

13. Dr. K.S. Nakkeeran
Lecturer
Department of Political Science
and Development Administration
Gandhigram Rural Institute
Gandhigram.

14. Mr. S. Devaraj
Research Assistant
Department of Political Science
and Development Administration
Gandhigram Rural Institute
Gandhigram.

15. Mr. M. Gurusamy
Research Assistant
Department of Political Science
and Development Administration
Gandhigram Rural Institute
Gandhigram.

16. Mr. M.A. Thirunavukkarasu
Research Assistant
Department of Political Science
and Development Administration
Gandhigram Rural Institute
Gandhigram.

17. Mr. A. Thangathurai
Research Assistant
Department of Political Science
and Development Administration
Gandhigram Rural Institute
Gandhigram.

18. Ms. N. Sumathy
    Agri.Extn. Specialist
    PRA (ADP) Project,
    Faculty of Agri & A.H, Gandhigram

19. Ms. G. Uma
    Project Facilitator
    Singamma Sreenivasan Foundation Project
    Department of Political Science
    and Development Administration
    Gandhigram Rural Institute
    Gandhigram.

20. Mr. G. Umashankar
    Project Facilitator
    Singamma Sreenivasan Foundation Project
    Department of Political Science
    and Development Administration
    Gandhigram Rural Institute
    Gandhigram.

Dr.V. Ragupathy welcomed the gathering. In his welcome address he highlighted the pioneering attempts made by the Gandhigram Rural Institute in the context of empowerment of grassroots leaders since the inception of New Panchayati Raj Institution in the state.

Dr.G. Palanithurai initiated the consultation by giving a brief account of the proposed programme. They are :

Objectives of the Programme

1. To sensitise the women leaders periodically on gender and social development issues;
2. To activate, strengthen and network the organisations of leaders of women panchayat leaders;
3. To provide necessary information for their organisational activities;
4. To interact with the leaders of the organisation and aggregate their demands for policy advocacy;
5. To build the capacity of the leaders of the organisation to manage their organisations and to address the issues of the Women panchayati leaders;

6. To process their problems and to take them to appropriate bodies for reddressal; and
7. To extend legal guidance to women leaders when they face problem while perform their role and function legitimately.

Major Activities Proposed

1. Networking the women leaders organisation
2. On request, organising interface programme for the office bearers of the organisations in other States – *eg.* Kerala and Karnataka
3. Supporting the women leaders organisation while organising conferences to discuss their problems annually
4. Organising periodical meetings to sensitise the women leaders on gender and social development issues
5. Performing the role of policy advocacy – aggregating the problems of the women leaders and transmitting the same for policy and decision making at the appropriate level
6. Organising counselling for the leaders who are under mental depression
7. Organising capacity building exercise for office bearers of the Association to manage their organisation
8. To provide necessary information to the office bearers for their conduct of their role and responsibilities as leaders of panchayats
9. To bring all those issues of the women leaders to the media for wide publicity
10. To provide legal assistance to women leaders through their organisations whenever they demand. (Women Lawyers Association of Tamil Nadu has agreed to provide such assistance).

Expected Results

1. Building a Women Panchayati Leaders movement in Tamil Nadu to address their issues on their own
2. Making their organisations stronger and sustainable in the years to come to function on their own even after our withdrawal
3. Establishing an information dissemination Centre for Women Panchayati Leaders in Gandhigram Rural Institute
4. Women Leaders will be made sensitive towards gender and social development issues.

Dr. G. Pankajam : The women members of the grassroots institutions must be involved in a fullfledged way in all the activities of the panchayats and they must be activated with necessary information. Then only we can expect efficiency and effectiveness in their functioning. Gram Sabha meetings may be used to mobilize large number of women members and by which they can gain the organisational support.

Ms. Mythili Sivaraman : Women are made victims in most of the occasions as we have seen that there are lot of loop holes in the existing panchayats system. But certain women leaders function effectively due to organisational backings. Even with the support of the organisation they are not able to function. The best example is Mrs. Leelavathy. This shows that women leaders have an array of problems, hurdles and barriers. Women can function effectively only with the support of institutions or organisations. In the absence of such support women will be in the hands of the male member of the family. So, it is a must to organise grassroots women leaders. Secondly women leaders face an yet another crisis in the panchayat due to the caste consciousness of the people. A women leader from the SC community finds it very difficult to function as the president.

She interestingly quoted a typical case from Villupuram district. A women Gram Panchayat President hailing from SC community has been relentlessly fighting against the atrocities of the party leaders. He is able to respond to the challenges only because of the backing of the organisations. The need of the hour is some supportive organisation to the women leaders to assist them continuously.

Dr. G. Palanithurai : The experiences of training programmes have brought the following :

1. Women leaders are not ready to share their ideas and even if they are ready they are not allowed to do so.
2. They are not in a position to understand the existing problems from a proper perspective.
3. They are not ready to speak out the issues because they feel that they will become victims without organisational support. Rarely they speak issues and if they speak, they have orientation and perspective.
4. Women leaders who have come to power through an organisational background of anykind are successful, because for every action they are being supported by the organisation.
5. Women's problems will be highlighted and redressed only by

the women leaders.

The women leaders can organise themselves at the state level and it can be linked with other state level organisations of the south. The outcome will be the reddressal of the problems faced by the women leaders through their organisations. For example, the difficulties in management of accounts can be sorted out by gaining experience from other states. The experience of Kerala is much useful in this respect as the panchayats are in the hands of the people in Kerala where as the panchayats are in the hands of officials in Tamil Nadu. Further the issues of the women leaders can be addressed in a larger association and by which their issues will be highlighted. In the absence of their own associations and organisations women leaders oriented to think and perceive issues from the perspective of Government and other organisations. They are always in the hands of others or they are made to be in the hands of others. Women leaders must look at themselves as leaders. They may be agricultural labourers or a coolie. They should perceive their role properly. At present the women leaders are to be oriented in the issues which are affecting the life of the poor and the women. As long as the issues of the poor and the women are highlighted by others, the problems should not gain momentum. Hence the problems should be highlighted only by the affected lot.

Hence we can make women leaders to function effectively by orgainising themselves. That organisation must be a full fledged feminist organisation where the women leaders can perceive and prepare a plan of action according to their own perception. There is a notion among the politicians and officials that in the name of training programmes the women leaders are oriented and instigated to fight against the state government. But is not the fact. It is just a capacity building exercise only. It is vital to note that government is telling how a women leader should think? What women leader should think? This has to be removed and for this purpose and to make women leaders a full fledged grassroots development worker an orgnaisational structure is an imperative. Gandhigram Rural Institute is working on various dimensions for the enhancement of grassroots governance especially with women leaders in nine districts of Tamil Nadu. Gandhigram is having a long and cherished history on the part of empowerment of women. We have our own strategy and programmes to work with them. This has made us to see the issues in a feminist perspective and we can look at the problems faced by the women leaders in a feminist perspective. Todays discussions will perfect our approach in this regard.

Mr. Thirunavukkarasu : A journal or a periodical carrying articles from women's perspective must be made available for women leaders.

Mr.Thangathurai : Women leaders must be oriented in the issues of women and issues of development.

Dr. G. Pankajam : The burden of Indian women leaders has to be reduced because women leaders are under severe stress and it makes them not to be aware of their issues. They are not able to realise and express their difficulties. Secondly, husbands of women leaders are ruling the women leaders and the women leaders made proxy of their husband. Hence the suppression of women starts from the home or family itself. This is mainly due to the fact that the male members of her family are having sound political background and not having proper orientation. Thus women are not recognised and are not allowed to be conscious of their problems. In addition women are forced to take care of the children and other domestic works even after they become leaders and showldering public responsibility.

The alternative for this can be

1. Creating awareness among the women leaders about the role, rights, duties, powers and functions of the women leaders;
2. Creating opportunity for effective functioning through organisational means;
3. The concept of "all are equal" and information dissemination to all must be put into practice effectively.

The ACP principle *i.e.*, affective, cognitive and psycho motor principle can be adopted. The women leaders are not aware of the functioning of primary institutions in their locality. Women leaders must be sensitised on women specific issues and about the primary institutions. They must be made to function totally independent of others. We have experiences in sensitising women leaders and changes in the same process. Women must be made enough to conduct the Gram Sabha meetings on their own. In practice husband's of women leaders are running the panchayat administration. We can quote as many examples as possible. Moreover political backing or any organisational backing is a must for effective conduct of Gram Sabha. Today we see women self-help groups are functioning effectively in sensitising women's issues. So we can start with women self-help groups. To make things effective, information dissemination is a must. An organizational support in the context of making women leaders to work is important. The organisation which is to be established must be accepted by all. The organisation must be based on the principles of cognitive action, zero rivalry, and mutual trust among the members of the organisation.

Dr. G. Palanithurai : The husband's role has to be viewed seriously. We have seen, there are husbands who assist their wives in the panchayat activities by standing behind them. They are facilitating and enabling women leaders to perform their functions effectively. As long as the husbands of the Women Local Body Leaders are not taking the legitimate space of the women in the panchayats, men should not be viewed as proxy. The experiences of Madhya Pradesh in training both the women leaders and their husbands is a milestone in differentiating the role of women leaders in panchayats with the help of their husbands. This may be followed in the case of Tamil Nadu also. But in practice, we have not trained the women leaders in the early days of their office. This practice has to be changed. The sense of individual management by women leaders is possible and this belief must be developed among the husbands of the women leaders.

Dr. G. Pankajam : The role of husband must be made invisible.

Mr. Thirunavukkarasu : Women are made victims of the rivalry of men on the grounds of caste religion and politics.

Ms. Mythili Sivaraman : Words like "Gender Sensitisation" "Feminism" have raised a sort of fear among the middleclass men. The resistance by the male has to be broken down in the area of providing women to play the role of leadership. This has to be done by giving a new definition, scope and shape to the leadership by the women. The notion created by male leadership is totally far away from the path of performance and administration. Women leadership must be looked into a new perspective *i.e.,* a new leadership model has to be developed. This should be done by having a proper proportion of male and female components in the leader *i.e.*, a male leader can have feminine characters and vice versa. So this new dimension has to be incorporated when leadership is discussed. The alternative for exciting women leadership can be heard from the experiences of West Bengal, where a women minister who hailed from a womens association is functioning very effectively by giving a new definition to women leadership. Attitudinal change is a must for women leadership in the rural areas. Because caste and class differences are still existing among them whether she may be a upper caste or lower caste women. Rubber stamp recapturing movement of North Indian Women is a best example to be followed by our women. We find many husbands are enthusiastically helping their female counterparts. This enthusiasm should not cross the limits. This should be supportive and not suppressive.

To make women leaders performance more effective the working hours of women are reduced by four hours in Maharashtra in all women panchayats. This may be followed in Tamil Nadu also. The specific areas in which women leaders are to be sensitised are :

1. Public Distribution System
2. Primary Education
3. Primary Health Care
4. Environmental Sanitation
5. Family Planning

Women must have the access to all facilities at the primary health centre especially family planning methods. Women should not be forced to adopt family planning methods. The attitude of the women leaders about the casteism and feudalism must be changed.

The land reforms in Kerala and West Bengal has opened a new chapter in the life of panchayats. This may be adopted by all other Indian states. Family burdens must be reduced by sensitising the men and fear psychosis among the men has to be removed. Women has to be seen as a part of the male gender sensitisation process. Humanness must be in practice in every action. A close liason has to be established between the womens organisations in the village and the panchayats. Interface programme has to be organised for women leaders. To make the women leaders aware of their roles, responsibilities, modules can be developed and they are to be trained. Finally, newsletter focussing on womens issues and women development has to be brought out in a simple way. The women leader must change her life style apart from personal reservations and commitments. Another attitudal change has to be brought out among all and women leaders on their rights and duties.

Dr. M. Kuruvammal : Women leaders have to over come the problems associated with their duties and responsibilities. They are :

1. Inferiority complex
2. Identity crisis
3. Social and cultural bondages
4. Economic dependence
5. Fear of character assassination

6. Harassment of various kinds

Women has to think that problems are nothing when they become leaders. Secondly, exclusive leadership training programmes for women must be organised. Women's issues has to be visualised separately. Self-confidence, courage and communicative skills have to be developed among women. Women should not expect appreciation. They must be mentally prepared for action.

Dr. G. Palanithurai : In most of the occasions women fail to realise that they are leaders.

Dr. Gabriele Dietrich : To make women leaders as leaders we have to answer the following questions.

1. What is development?
2. For whom this development?
3. Why this development has to take place?
4. How this development is going to take place?

In the age of globalisation, we have to define this concept 'development' in a new framework. We have to incorporate women component in development. Because women are closely associated with economic production and distribution. The various problems associated with these two economic activities are much affecting the women especially in child care, health, education and domestic activities.

Todays technological development has created wider gap between the women and the reality. This will ultimately affect women in many spheres. This scenario has to be changed and women must be made as the nucleus for development. For example traditional system of farming or production is closely associated with the women. This can be put into practice today as an alternative. All the advancements must be pro-nature, pro-poor, and pro-women. A new outlook has to be made when development is talked about. Women must be made aware of the following aspects :

1. What is development?
2. Basic economic problems
3. Gender issues
4. Adding efficiency
5. Problems associated with basic facilities
6. Other issues

To achieve this, the relationship between man and women has to be changed.

Dr. G. Palanithurai : The concept of development should be redefined because there is an abiquity in the concept that development can be achieved through people's participation or by technological transformation. People's participation is a must for any change. But leaders feel that technology can transform the society.

Ms. Bimla Chandrasekar : Situational analysis is a must for any activity. For example 50 years of independent life has made us to destroy the natural resources, leading to starve for drinking water and water for irrigation and so on. Again globalisation process has created a wide gap between the micro and macro linkages.

To make women leaders effective, we have to create awareness on certain basic elements *i.e.*, a change in the public distribution system must be brought out. Secondly, the identity crisis of women leaders leads to non-functioning. This has to be changed. Importance is given for fulfillment of basic needs alone. This has to be extended to all other spheres. Existing disparity has to be removed and sense of oneness has to be made. Women must be brought out from the invisible position to the visibie position. For all these things we have to exercise or perform physical and mental mobility of women. As we have lot of loopholes in the existing panchayat system women are made victims.

The process of associating women leaders in local governance has to consider various aspects. Similarly women leaders have to be sensitised on various issues. The primary considerations should be given to the following aspects:

1. Review of the public distribution system (need based).
2. Integration of different organisation/associations. For example a creche and a old age home in a village can be integrated.
3. Awareness about migration, feminisation, poverty.
4. An exclusive leadership training for women leaders leading to perceptional change on the concept of leadership.
5. A sense of realisation that rights always go with responsibilities and duties.
6. An attitude that makes them to function as, this is my village and I have to work for its betterment as I work for my family.
7. Making the male counterpart to understand that feminism is not for asserting one's own rights by denying others rights. It is for protecting the rights of the women.
8. Documenting successful leadership and making it available for others as role models.

9. Media has to picture these components without affecting the performance of women leaders.
10. A clear cut idea about the rotational system of reservation has to be made.
11. A clear cut understanding must be established among various segments especially during the Gram Sabha meetings to have better interaction.

Dr. G. Palanithurai : Development indicators at the macro level can be easily framed. Whereas at the micro level it is very difficult to fix the indicators. Women leaders must be aware of existing environment and they should plan their course of action accordingly. To identify the problems persisting in the rural societies, the N.G.Os must collaborate with other institutions. In particular, women specific issues can be identified by this course of action. Research works will be effective when academic institutions and N.G.Os join together.

Dr. G. Pankajam : A panchayat can do its level best what a state and central government cannot do it and only when it is provided with the necessary provisions.

A company called Thapar Dupont Ltd was originally to be launched in Goa. But due to stiff resistance by the Gram Panchayat and its people on the basis of severe environmental hazzards, it shifted its site to Gummidipoondi. Like this a women leader must be a committed and support seeking leader in her functioning. Beyond this, women leader must create awareness among other women in the areas of resource mobilization and utilization.

Women leader should play the role of an educator *i.e.*, she has to educate her women about democracy, and importance of people's participation.

Ms. Bimala Chandresekar : The mental block existing among the women has to be removed and they should have a feeling that they have a confidence that they are able to do or function independently with panchayat administration. But they have a fear that how this message can be communicated to their husbands or family members *i.e.*, who will tell the male members that women are capable of performing independently and they need assistance only from outside the framework.

Dr. G. Palanithurai : Any discussion or demand must be made on the basis of data support. Women leaders must be provided with necessary information to pressurize the government regarding the issues raised by them. Only data can speak and get results. Data will give confidence and courage to women leaders. In this regard certain N.G.Os and academic institutions are very effective and they conduct research and create a data base which can be used.

Dr. M. Kuruvammal : Women leaders must be aware of the M.N.Cs as these Multi National Companies (M.N.Cs) are knocking our doors. The full implications of the M.N.Cs are to be sensitised among the women.

Ms. Ramani Mathew : Today panchayats are functioning like business centres or service centres. They give statistical information about income and expenditure on various activities. Their orientation is like contractors and it must be changed.

Women usually neglect and avoid to take part in panchayat activities as criminalisation and demoralisation of women is being done at the grassroots level in a massive way. We have to appreciate and extend a supportive hand to the women who come out of these hurdles and function in the panchayats.

Certain other women leaders try their level best to overcome the hurdles. But they lack supporting base. The establishment of forum to support and assist the women leaders gains considerable momentum. It is a difficult task to create a support base for women. But continuous effort in this regard must be made.

This supporting base must be created at various levels. In addition this base must make the women leaders to think, act and react.

A second support structure at the family level must be made. These support structures must make women leaders committed with the common agenda for action. Nature of common agenda must be made in such a manner that, we can do this on our own, we can do this with the joint effort of others. Modules on self empowerment, conflict resolution, capacity building and leadership qualities has to be developed in a way that it will fulfill the needs of the common rural women. A consistant and continuous need based training must be planned for women leaders. These training programmes must create a deep sense of convictions and course of actions among the women leaders. In addition to this, they must be made to know about the utilization of power, finance and personnel. Kerala model campaign can be adopted.

Ms. Rajini : Women leaders are made victimsout of caste differences. The alternative is migration from rural areas to urban areas as stated by Ambedkar. Because modernisation is faster in the urban areas. To make Dalit women leaders to overcome the difficulties, small panchayats must be clubbed together and made as town panchayats/satellite towns.

Dalit women panchayat presidents are ineffective in panchayat administration and they are removed from office due to said caste differences. This has to be changed totally. Because of this fact, the functioning of women leaders are limited.

For the effective functioning of the Gram Sabha women presidents have to be given protection. To make the empowerment process very effective, there must be proportional representation, multi seat constituency in the context of women and Dalit.

Ms. Shenbagavalli : We have to give special attention to Dalit women leaders also. In practice we find rivalry and revenge even after this Dalit women leaders acquire office. They experience non-cooperation, disturbance of different kinds in their office. This situation must be changed by providing certain measures which safeguards Dalit Women Leaders.

Dr. G. Palanithurai : Associating Dalit Women Leaders is a must in the present context. We find, people are working together in various places without any hierarchy. But when they come out from the organisation the social hierarchies will emerge. This makes much differences among women as majority of them are labourers. This situation has to be changed. Economic emancipation of women is a must. It is very difficult to achieve development on a massive scale. To empower women leaders, they must be educated or as an alternative, educated women has to come to politics. Secondly, an organisational support must be made for women leaders. Husbands of women leaders has to be oriented in such a way that the women are having all the abilities and potentials to function as leaders. There is a need for creating a space for women leaders to express their views.

Dr. M. Kuruvammal : Women who are treated as untouchables assert their rights and becoming powerful. This is taking place slowly. This process has to be speeded up. A quorum must be insisted for women and Dalit's presence in Gram Sabha. This will ultimately enhance the empowerment process of women.

Ms. Rajini : We experience untouchability still persisting in villages. This makes women not to come out of the social and cultural bondages.

Dr. G. Pankajam : Education and employment should become accessible for Dalit women. Making access alone is not important but also providing opportunities to make use of the facilities is much more important. N.G.Os can play a pivotal role in this regard.

Dr. G. Palanithurai : Specialized government schemes for Dalits are not reaching the targets. Information related to the schemes are not disseminated. We have people's charter every where but in practice they are in black and white. But they are not being circulated.

Ms. Rajini : Women must be oriented in health and sanitation.

Dr. G. Palanithurai : It is important that how are we going to provide opportunity for Dalit and women to make use of facilities. We can take the Dalit and women to the next phase of development by extending the opportunities, to make use the various kinds of common property resources.

Ms. Rajini : Steps have to be taken to protect the reservation policy.

Ms. Mythili Sivaraman : Is there any idea to bring a bulletin exclusively for women leaders in this project?

Dr. G. Palanithurai : We can make the women empowered and make them to be a part in the process of development only when we educate them, create awareness, providing opportunities and support. We have to work for these aspects.

Proposed Agenda for Action

* Awareness creation
* Sensitisation
* Information dissemination
* Association formation
* Creating supporting base — Information centre
* Organising interface programmes
* Tie-up with N.G.Os
* Documenting success stories other women related issues.
* Conducting women convention meetings

* Policy advocacy.

The Highlights

- *Women are shy, ignored and not ready to share their ideas and this mind-set has to be changed. To change this, information dissemination is an imperative. Information dissemination will empower the women.*
- *The prevailing fear among the men out of Gender sensitisation and feminism can be removed only by sensitising both men and women and make them to realise that every individual should have the charter of a man and women.*
- *The prevailing leadership in our polity should not be the role models for the new women leaders. They are to be oriented and sensitised in a different way and they should be the role models for others. Hence we have to recognise the tough task a head.*
- *To make the women leaders to function effectively in the panchayats, their burden has to reduced to a larger extent. Secondly, the role of women leaders husbands will be supportive. If they stand behind them, without occupying their space, i.e., women leaders can be drawn easily from the invisible position to visible position.*
- *Women leaders performance can be analysed from the perspective of the organisational/associational backings. As a leader with sound organisational or associational backing the performance is more positive. It makes the women leaders to overcome several hurdles. Hence organisational support is a must for empowerment of women at the grassroots.*
- *Women leaders must have a tight hold over Public Distribution System, Primary Education, Primary Health Care, Environmental Sanitation and Family Planning, as the major issues affecting the women in the rural areas. Access to these basic facilities will make the women leaders to sensitise various problems faced by women.*
- *Awareness through dissemination of information about the clear objective of reservation of seats for women and its implication, the role expectations of the women leaders will make them to realise the importance of their role in the development process of women and children in the society.*
- *Overcoming the personal hurdles like inferiority complex, and identity crisis become inevitable for a women leader to realise herself as leader. This realisation will enhance the women*

empowerment process at the grassroots level. They should realise their worth.

- *Access to education and employment will make the women to overcome the social and cultural bondages which they have inherited from tradition.*
- *NGOs, academic institutions and activists can bring specific issues more effectively to the women leaders and can assist them to resolve the issues. Periodical sensitisation can be done by these institutions. Collaborative work is possible between a women leader and said institutions.*
- *Women leaders function does not ends with the panchayats alone. She has to integrate different organisations in her locality and add efficiency in administration, settlement of disputes and sharing of resources to maintain equity. We need more number of role models. Hence, documentation of such role models is essential. The dissemination of such role models will be immense use for women empowerment. Women leaders must be provided with opportunities to learn about the successful leaders.*
- *Periodical training is an imperative for the women leaders. They need information for their functioning and for which a newsletter or a magazine is very essential.*
- *Women leaders must be oriented and made to know, what is development? for whom this development is meant why this development has to take place? and how this development is going to take place?*
- *Situational analysis is a must by the women leaders to get long with lasting results. In addition, all the information about the various schemes have to be disseminated to women leaders. Right to information will empower the women leaders and enhance her performance as the leader of a panchayat.*

What Next?

Women leaders of local bodies have to be sensitised on the women issues. They should have orientation to look at issues perspectively otherwise they will be lost and their identity will be lost. Further they should know clearly what is development in the context of Globalization and for whom the new economy is being pursued? and the linkage between the resources and institutions. Sofar in all training programme representatives are oriented towards ensuring participation of the people in the process of governance. At present they are to be sensitised on what for participation? They should go beyond participation.

The issues which are affecting the people even to ensure their entitlements are to be taken up for sensitization. When the women representatives are oriented towards issues, they will acquire their grip over the problems and methods to be adopted to fight against all kinds of exploitation. Further sensitization is needed not only for the women leaders but also for their husbands or the male members of their families. Issue based activities has to be designed and where from higher level linkages have to be established. Unless the women leaders are not linked with the issues, the women association will became a get together clubs not as an organisation of the marginalised who are struggling for decent life in the society. It is equally important that the women leaders organisations should find a critical mass by expanding its activities horizontally all over the state and for which partnership building is essential and imperatives. With whom partnership could be developed is a basic question. There are NGOs who have deep commitment on women empowerment, grassroots democracy and empowering marginalised and they will be accommodated with the women leaders organisation. The linkages are activity based. Till concretising the organisation of the women leaders in the society for women empowerment, it is necessary to rope in organisations which are coming forward to help this kind of activities. Periodical interventions, sensitization, capacity building and extending support to their activities and struggles are imperatives. The women leaders organisations can take up location specific issues and more in their own mode with their issues. Issues need not be the same all over the state. Associations will mutually help each other to realise their objectives.

9

OBSERVATION AND CONCLUSION

The analysis of cases of Panchayati Leaders of Gram Panchayats, Block Panchayat and district Panchayat and especially the Women Leaders brought valuable information to us. It is a well known fact that the success of panchayat institutions is always influenced by a constellation of factors from the content of the central act to the intent of the leaders who assume responsibilities in panchayats. Though it is declared constitutionally that panchayati institutions are to be made as Self-governing Institutions, in real terms they are not so and these institutions are being made to run only by the efforts of the state and central governments. It is obvious from the facts given by the leaders that the flow of money to local areas is very high. It is a major question how money is being utilized and spent for development activities in the rural areas. Knowingly and unknowingly our leaders are oriented to speak in terms of quantum of money to be spent not in terms of volume of works to be done. From the member of Parliament to Gram Panchayat President, allocation refers only the earmarked money for positions. The quantum of money does not bring any transformation in the society, unless appropriate traits are developed among the people to develop themselves. Institutions are to be made as facilitators not as factors of development.

In Tamil Nadu, the Act what had been passed in the year 1994 has its own major drawbacks and weaknesses and it does not reflect the spirit of the 73rd Constitutional Amendment Act. Further to operationalise the new Act, a conductive environment has to be created by way of creating awareness among the people and among the bureaucracy about the importance of the new institution. After creating awareness among the bureaucracy and people the political leaders who are in the helm of affairs at the State Government should have needed political will to overcome the difficulties which the leadership faces while operationalising the new dispensation.

The elected leaders of local bodies should be trained in the art of governance with much emphasis on ensuring the participation of people in the development process of the community from planning to evaluation of the development works. It is an imperative that the mind-set of the leaders have to be changed to the new environmental setting. A well thought out training programme has to be formulated to prepare the leaders to meet the new challenges of governance at the local level and their capacity has to be enhanced. Equally the mind-set of the officials who are involved in the development process of the community at the local level has to be changed and their capacity has to be increased to meet the increased aspirations and expectations of the people and their leaders. People are not participants of development and they are to be concientised with the sole objective of making them as development participant. It requires much skill. The above said are the prerequisites for the smooth and effective functioning of the local bodies.

But in reality, Tamil Nadu local bodies are projecting a dismal picture of performance contrary to expectation. The observations are based on the studies conducted at the grassroot level. The case studies which have projected in this work bring wealth of information about the functioning of local bodies. For effective functioning of any institution, the roles assigned to these institutions are to be perceived properly by the individuals who are placed in the institutions. The individuals who have rules and responsibiiities have to perceive the role without any ambiguity and conflict and then only they will discharge their roles and function properly and effectively. The question here is whether the leaders have perceived their roles properly. Role clarity has to be brought in the minds of the eaders and that could be done only in the training by the trainers who train the Leaders in the act of governance at the local level. In this context one has to be consider the role perception of trainers who are the officials of the government working in the development departments at the grassroot level. The officials have no such clear cut perception about their own role in the new situation and equally the leaders do not have needed perception. Both the leaders and functionaries have moved into the beaten track of development which is contradictory to the expectation.

What is the perception of the new leaders? is a major question now. They believe that like MLAs and MPs, they should have funds and they should also distribute the money to different works to meet the aspirations of the people. They always equate themselves with the MLAs and MPs. It is a truism that the representatives of the people in India have role ambiguity. The local body leaders have earmarked role and responsibility as per the provisions of the Act. The leaders have to perceive their role properly and perform their faction effectively and for which the leaders are to be oriented and trained. Training is not a one time affair and it is a continuous process. All the needed skills cannot be imparted into the leaders all of a sudden in a day or two. It will take time. But steps have to be taken to change the mind-set of the leaders of local bodies. In Tamil Nadu serious efforts have not been taken to train the local body leaders. In the name of training, the officials have conducted one day orientation course for them and in which they have taught administrative and accounting procedures.

Devolution of power refers to the decentralization of political, financial and administrative powers. Here political power has been decentralized. But financial and administrative powers have not been decentralized. Thus the leaders have to act as the agents of the central and state governments to implement their programmes. Since powers have not been devolved on administrative and financial domains, the panchayat leaders have no discretion and the leaders cannot decide on the basis of the needs of the people. They have to execute the programmes and schemes simply because the government has schemes and programmes. Thus there is no dearth of resources and equally problems are also many. There is no match between the peoples needs and governments schemes. Government goes on implementing its schemes irrespective of the need of the people. Money has been spent but peoples needs have not been met. Even after the establishment of the Panchayati Raj System, the tendency of proliferating centralised schemes continues.

In all the fora from the leaders of the federal government to the officials who work at the bottom speak about the need of empowering the panchayats but in the reality it does not take place in an expected line. At every stage the local body institutions find hurdles. Hurdles are in many forms. MPs, MLAs and officials in fact, have to help panchayat institutions to grow and develop. Peoples representatives and officials are in real terms not helping the Panchayati Institutions to perform their duties and they found so much of interference from many quarters.

In panchayati activities the officials are the supporting mechanisms and they are not helping panchayati leaders to discharge their role and responsibilities. This is a general complaint of all the representatives of local bodies. There is yet another reason for this kind of behaviour attributed by the leaders. The reason is that in the absence of elected representatives in the Local Bodies officials have carried out all the activities on their own. But now they have to carry out works as per the discussions of the elected leaders.

Women have specific problems in the local bodies. The problems in the rural local bodies are peculiar as the social settings are prone to conflict and conditions are different form that of the urban local bodies. The prevailing gender discrimination has disturbed the normal mind-set of the leaders at the grass root level. Councils of the panchayats are also non-cooperative. The domination of male members of the family has not allowed the women leaders to act independently in the functioning of panchayats.

The officials in the Block and District have not respected the women leaders who belong to lower echelons of the society. Most of the occasions they have been ill-treated. This was brought to the notice of the government. The Government has issued strict warnings to the officials. Yet the practice continues. But there is a considerable change in the perception and performance of the leaders as a result of their interaction with NGO's and other women organisations. At present women leaders of rural local bodies have formed their own associations to tackle their problems. Women leaders, who have well trained in the art of managing the crowd, have performed well in the panchayats.

The MPs and MLAs are also in the activities of the local bodies as they have two crore rupees and thirty lakh rupees every year respectively for area development programmes. The representatives normally won't consult the local panchayats and ascertain the needs of the people and instead they contact local party men to fix the priorities and allocate money for works in the rural areas and bywhich huge amount of money has been wasted. Commissions and corruptions are abundant in distributing the works from local area development programme to the contractors through officials.

In the local body people should have more representations and they have to participate in the development activities of the panchayats. But in reality, for the past fifty years people had been oriented to relinquish their responsibilities and look forward to get more facilities and services from the government machinery. This tendency has grown to the maximum level. Now people's expectations are increased as governments have developed practices of introducing populist programmes over the year. Hence it is a general belief among the people that local bodies would distribute doles to the people as MLAs and MPs.

It is unequivocal from the performance of the panchayats that enormous amount of money has been spent in different programmes and schemes of the central and state governments apart from the area development programmes of the MLAs and MPs and yet the basic needs of the people are not met. Further to ensure the participation of the people in the development activities of the panchayats steps are being taken and yet it is not materialised as the steps are only ornamental in nature and not real and result oriented. Peoples participation in the panchayati activities is dismal and not significant. It is inbuilt in the system that panchayat has to administer social justice but in reality panchayats are facing crisis due to the social conflict as the panchayats are not vested with needed financial and administrative powers. The prevailing conditions in local bodies need drastic changes in many aspects of the new system.

The Tamil Nadu Panchayati Raj Act has to be changed drastically to enable the local bodies to get adequate administrative and financial powers to declare the local bodies as self-governing institutions. The officials who are all working in the local bodies upto district panchayats have to be made as officials of the local bodies and they are accountable to the local bodies. Local bodies are to be equipped to mobilize and generate resources on their own. The local body leaders have to be trained in the art of managing development instead of practicing as contractors to execute the schemes of the governments. Likewise the officials are to be oriented to work in consonance with the objectives and principles of panchayats. People should be given a sense that panchayats are not panchayat of officials but of the people. They should be given orientation in preparing plans at the local level to bring development in the rural areas.

THE

TAMIL NADU

PANCHAYATS

ACT,

1994

CONTENTS

THE TAMIL NADU PANCHAYAT ACT, 1994

The following Act of the Tamil Nadu Legislative Assembly received the assent of the Governor on the 22nd April 1994 and is hereby published for general information:

ACT NO. 21 OF 1994[1]

[Corrected upto 30.06.2002]

An Act to repeal and re-enact the Tamil Nadu Panchayats Act, 1958

WHEREAS it is expedient to repeal and re-enact the Tamil Nadu Panchayats Act, 1958, for establishing a three tier panchayat raj system in the State to the elected bodies at the village, intermediate and district level in keeping with the Constitution (Seventy-third Amendment) Act, 1992, relating to panchayats for greater participation of the people so as to make them institutions of self-government and for more effective implementation of rural development programmes;

Be it enacted by the Legislative Assembly of the State of Tamil Nadu in the Forty-fifth Year of the Republic of India as follows:

CHAPTER – I

PRELIMINARY

1. Short title, extent and commencement

(1) This Act may be called the Tamil Nadu Panchayats Act, 1994

(2) It extends to the whole of the State of Tamil Nadu except.-

(i) the City of Chennai;

(ii) the City of Madurai constituted under the Madurai City Municipal Corporation Act, 1971(Tamil Nadu Act 15 of 1971)

(iii) the City of Coimbatore constituted under the Coimbatore City Municipal Corporation Act, 1981; (Tamil Nadu Act 25 of 1981)

(iv) the municipalities, town panchayats and industrial townships constituted under the Tamil Nadu District Municipalities Act, 1920; and (Tamil Nadu Act V of 1920)

(v) the cantonments constituted under the Cantonments Act 1924 (Central Act II of 1924)

(3) It shall come into force on such date as the Government may, by notification, appoint.

2. Definitions. – In this Act, unless the context otherwise requires.-

[2][(1) Deleted)]

[3][(1A) 'building' includes a house, out-house, tent, stable, latrine, shed, hut, wall (other than a boundary wall not exceeding 2.5 metres in

---

[1] This act has been brought into force with effect from 22.04.1994 in GO.MS. No.84 R.D. (C1 dated 22.04.1994)

[2] Inserted by Act No.30/1995 but deleted by Act 15/1996

[3] Re-numbered by Act 30/1995

height) and any other such structure, whether of masonry, bricks, wood, mud, metal or any other material whatsoever;]

(2) 'casual vacancy' means a vacancy occurring otherwise than by efflux of time and 'casual election' means an election held to fill a casual vacancy:

(3) 'Chairman' means the chairman of a panchayat union council or a district panchayat, as the case may be:

[1][(4) omitted]

(5) 'Collector' means the collector of a revenue district;

(6) 'Commissioner' means the commissioner of a panchayat union;

(7) 'Company' means a company as defined in the Companies Act, 1956 (Central Act 1 of 1956) and includes a foreign company within the meaning of section 591 of that Act;

(8) 'District' means a revenue district;

(9) 'District Panchayat' means the district panchayat constituted under sub-section (1) of section 24;

(10) 'Drain' means a rain or storm water drain and water tables, chutes and the side drain exclusively meant to drain away the rain water falling on the surface of any street, bridge or causeway, but does not include a drain or sewer within the meaning of the Chennai Metropolitan Water Supply and Sewerage Act, 1978. (Tamil Nadu Act 28 of 1978)

[2] [(11) 'executive authority' means a person notified as such by the Government under section 83"]

(12) 'Government' means the State Government

(13) 'Grama Sabha' means a body consisting of persons registered in the electoral rolls relating to a penchant village comprised within the area of village panchayat concerned.

(14) 'house' means a building fit for human occupation, whether as a residence or otherwise, having a separate principal entrance from the common way, and includes any shop, workshop or warehouse or any building used for garaging or parking buses or as bus-stand.

(15) 'hut' means any building which is constructed principally of wood, mud, leaves, grass or thatch and includes any temporary structure of whatever size or any small building of whatever material made, which the panchayat may declare to be a hut for the purposes of this Act;

(16) 'Inspector' means any officer not below the rank of a Collector appointed by the Government to exercise or perform any of the powers or duties of the Inspector under this Act;

(17) 'latrine' includes privy, water-closet and urinal;

(18) 'member' means a member of the village panchayat, he panchayat union council or the district panchayat, as the case may be;

---

[1] *Omitted the word "Chief Executive Officer" by Act 28/1999*

[2] Substituted by Act 21/1996

(19) 'ordinary vacancy' means a vacancy occurring by efflux of time and ordinary election ' means an election held to fill an ordinary vacancy;

(20) 'owner' includes -

(a) the person for the time being receiving or entitled to receive whether on his own account or on behalf of another person as agent, trustee, guardian, manager or receiver or for any religious or charitable purpose. the rents or profits of the property in connection with which the word is used; and

(b) the person for the time being in charge of the animal or vehicle in connection with which the word is used;

(21). 'panchayat' means a village panchayat a panchayat union council or a district panchayat constituted under this Act;

(22). 'panchayat development block' means the area declared by the Government from time to time to be a panchayat development block for the purpose of this Act;

(23). 'panchayat union' means any local area which is declared to be a panchayat union under this Act;

(24). 'panchayat union council' means the body constituted for the administration of a panchayat union under this Act;

(25). 'panchayat village means any local area over which a village panchayat has jurisdiction;

(26).'president' means the president of a village panchayat;

(27). 'private road' means any street, road, square, court, alley, passage, cart-track, foot-path or riding-path which is not a ' public road' but does not include a path-way made by the owner of premises on his own land to secure, access to, or the convenient use of , such premises;

(28). 'public road' means any street, road, square, court, alley, passage, cart-track, foot-path or riding-path, over which the public have a right of way, whether a thoroughfare or not, and includes-

(a) the roadway over any public bridge or causeway;

(b) the footway attached to any such road, public bridge or causeway; and

(c) the drains attached to any such road, public bridge or causeway, and the land, whether covered or not by any pavement, veranda, or other structure, which lies on either side of the roadway upto the boundaries of the adjacent property, whether that property is private property or property belonging to the State or Central Government;

(29). a person is deemed to have his residence or to 'reside' in any house if he sometimes uses any portion thereof as a sleeping apartment, and a person is not deemed to cease to reside in any such house merely because he is absent from it or has elsewhere another dwelling in which he resides, if he is at liberty to return to such house at any time and has not abandoned his intention of returning;

(30). 'revenue district' means any local area which for the purposes of revenue administration is under the charge of a Collector, after excluding there from all areas included in -

(a) the City of Chennai;

(b) the City of Madurai constituted under the Madurai City Municipal Corporation Act, 1971; (Tamil Nadu Act 15 of 1971)

(c) the City of Coimbatore constituted under the Coimbatore City Municipal Corporation Act, 1981; (Tamil Nadu Act 25 of 1981)

(d) the municipalities, town panchayats and industrial townships constituted under the Tamil Nadu District Municipalities Act, 1920; and (Tamil Nadu Act V of 1920)

(e) the cantonments constituted under the Cantonments Act, 1924, (Central Act II of 1924)

(31). 'Scheduled Castes' shall have the same meaning as in the Constitution;

(32). 'Scheduled Tribes' shall have the same meaning as in the Constitution;

[1] [(32-a) 'Secretary' means the Secretary of a District Panchayat];

[2] [(33). Tamil Nadu State Election Commission'] means the Tamil Nadu State Election Commission referred to in section 239;

[3] [(34).'Tamil Nadu State Election Commissioner'] means the Tamil Nadu State Election Commissioner referred to in Section 239

(35). 'unreserved forest' means a forest not notified under section 4 of the Tamil Nadu Forest Act, 1882 (**Tamil Nadu Act V of 1882**) and includes unreserved land at the disposal of the Government;

(36). 'village' means any local area which is declared to be a panchayat village under-sub-section

(1) of section 4, and 'revenue village' means any local area which is recognised as a village in the revenue accounts of Government after excluding therefrom the areas, if any, included in-

(a) the City of Chennai;

(b) the City of Madurai constituted under the Madurai City Municipal Corporation Act. 1971; (Tamil Nadu Act 15 of 1971)

(c) the City of Coimbatore constituted under the Coimbatore City Municipal Corpora-tion Act, 1981; (Tamil Nadu Act 25 of 1981)

(d) the municipalities, town panchayats and industrial townships constituted under the Tamil Nadu District Municipalities Act, 1920; (Tamil Nadu Act V of 1920) and

(e) the cantonments constituted under the Cantonments Act, 1924; (Central Act of II/1924)

(37). 'village panchayat' means a panchayat constituted as a village panchayat under sub-section (1) of section 6;

(38). "water-course" includes any river, stream or channel, whether natural or artificial;

(39). 'year' means the financial year:

---

1 Inserted by Act 28/1998. [The word 'secretary' is substituted for the words "Chief Executive Officer" wherever they occurred in this Act.]

2&3 *Substituted by Act 28/1998. [The words "Tamil Nadu" have been added wherever the expression "State Election Commissionpr State Election Commissioner" occurs in this Act].*

CHAPTER – II

GRAMA SABHA

3. Gram Sabha. – (1) There shall be a Grama Sabha for every village panchayat consisting of persons registered in the electoral roll relating to the panchayat village, comprised within the area of the said village panchayat.

[1] [(2) Subject to the general orders of the Government, the Grama Sabha shall meet at least twice in a year but six months shall not intervene between any two meetings.

(2-A) Every, meeting of the Grama Sabha shall be convened by the president of the Village Panchayat. If the president fails to convene the meeting of the Grama Sabha, the Inspector shall convene the meeting"]

(3) (a) The Grama Sabha shall –

(i) approve the village plan;

(ii) approve the village budget for the year;[2] [..]

[3] ["(ii-a) approve the audit report on the village panchayat accounts of the previous year; and";]

(iii) review the progress of the implementation of all schemes entrusted to the Village Panchayat

(b) The Government may by notification, entrust to the Gram Sabha such other functions as may be specified

(4) The village panchayat shall give due consideration to the recommendations and suggestions of the Grama Sabha.

(5) The quorum for a meeting [..[4]] and the procedure for convening and conducting such meetings of the Grama Sabha shall be such as may be prescribed

(6) Every meeting of the Grama Sabha shall be presided over by the president and in his absence, by the vice-president and in the absence of both the president and vice-president, by a member chosen by the members present at the meeting.

CHAPTER III

FORMATION AND CONSTITUTION OF VILLAGE PANCHAYATS, PANCHAYAT UNION COUNCILS AND DISTRICT PANCHAYATS

VILLAGE PANCHAYATS

4. Formation of Panchayat Village. – (1) The Inspector

(a) shall, by notification, classify and declare every local area comprising a revenue village or villages or any portion of a revenue village or contiguous portions of two or more revenue

---

[1] Substituted by Act. 28/1998

[2] *Inserted by Act. 28/1998*

[3] *Omitted by Act. 28/1998*

[4] *Omitted by Act. 28/1998*

villages with a population estimated at not less than five hundred as a panchayat village for the purposes of this Act; and

(b) shall, by notification, specify the name of such panchayat village

(2) (a) The Inspector may, by notification, exclude from a panchayat village any area comprised therein, provided that the population of the panchayat village after such exclusion, is not less than five hundred.

(b) In regard to any area excluded under clause (a), the Inspector shall by notification under sub-section (1) declare it to be a panchayat village if it has a population of not less than five hundred or if its population is less than five hundred, include it in any contiguous panchayat village under clause (c) (i).

(c) The Inspector may, by notification , –

(i) include in a panchayat village any local area contiguous thereto; or

(ii) cancel or modify a notification issued under sub-section (I) ; or

(iii) alter the name of any panchayat village specified under sub-section (I).

(d) Before issuing a notification under clause (a) or under clause (b) read with sub -section (I) or under clause (c), the Inspector shall give the village panchayat or village panchayats which will be affected by the issue of such notification, a reasonable opportunity of showing cause against the proposal and shall consider the explanations and objections, if any, of such village panchayat or village panchayats.

(3) Any rate-payer or inhabitant of such areas or any village panchayat concerned, may, if he or it objects to any notification under sub-section (1) or sub-section (2), appeal to the government within such period as may be prescribed.

(4) The Inspector may pass such orders as he may deem fit –

(a) as to the disposal of any part of the property vested in a village panchayat which has ceased to exist, and the discharge of its liabilities;

(b) as to the disposal of any part of the property vested in a village panchayat which has ceased to exercise jurisdiction over any local area, and the discharge of the liabilities of the village panchayat relating to such property or arising from such local area.

(5) An order made under sub-section (4) may contain such supplemental, incidental and consequential provisions as the Inspector may deem necessary and in particular may direct—

(i) that any tax, fee or other sum due to the village panchayat or where a village panchayat has ceased to exercise jurisdiction over any local area, such tax, fee or other sum due to the village panchayat as relates to that area shall be payable to such authorities as may be specified in the order;

(ii) that appeals. petitions, or other applications with reference to any such tax, fee or sum which are pending on the date on which the village panchayat ceased to exist or, as the case may be, on the date on which the village panchayat cease to exercise jurisdiction over the local area, shall be disposed of by such authorities as may be specified in the order.

[1] [**"4-A Special provisions relating to town panchayat constituted as village panchayats.** – (1) Notwithstanding anything contained in this Act, –

(a) the Chairman and members of a town panchayat holding office as such immediately before the date of constitution of such town panchayat as village panchayat under this Act consequent on the cancellation or modification of the notification declaring it as town panchayat under section 3-B of the Tamil Nadu District Municipalities Act, 1920 (Tamil Nadu Act V of 1920) , shall be deemed to be the elected president and members of such village panchayat under this Act and such president and members shall continue to hold office upto such date as the Government may, by notification, fix in this behalf or in case no such date is fixed, up to the date on which their term of office would expire under the Tamil Nadu District Municipalities Act, 1920 (Tamil Nadu Act V of 1920) if they had been elected as Chairman or members of the town panchayat and such president and members shall exercise all powers and perform all duties conferred on the president and members by or under the provisions of this Act.

(b) Provided that such village panchayat shall have no representation in the panchayat union council or the district panchayat, as the case may be, till such president and members of the village panchayat continue to hold office as such president and members under this sub-section.

(c) all the employees, other than the provincialised employees, of the town panchayat immediately before its constitution as village panchayat shall be the employees of such village panchayat under this Act. The provincialised employees shall continue to serve under the village panchayat and they shall be transferred by the Director of Town panchayats within three months from the date on which such village panchayat is constituted under this Act.

(2) Subject to the provisions of sub-section (1), the provisions of this Act and the rules made thereunder shall apply to the village panchayat referred to in sub-section (1)"]

---

[1] *Inserted by Act 29/1998*

5. Extension of provisions of Tamil Nadu district Municipalities Act, 1920 or of any rules made thereunder. – (1) The Inspector may, whether at the request of the village panchayat or otherwise, by notification, declare that any of the provisions of the Tamil Nadu District Municipalities Act,1920 or of any rules made thereunder, shall be extended to, and be in force in, the panchayat village or any specified are therein. (Tamil Nadu Act V of 1920).

(2) The provisions so notified shall be construed with such alterations (not affecting the substance) as may be necessary or proper for the purpose of adapting them to the panchayat village or specified area therein.

(3) Without prejudice to the generality of the foregoing provision, all references in the provisions so notified to a municipal council or the chairman or the executive authority thereof shall be construed as references to the village panchayat or the president or the executive authority of the village panchayat and all references to any officer or servant of a municipal council as references to the corresponding officer or servant of the village panchayat, and all references to the municipal limits as references to the limits of the panchayat village or specified area therein, as the case may be.

6. Constitution of village panchayats and their incorporation. – (1) A village panchayat shall be constituted for each panchayat village consisting of such number of elected members, with effect from such date as may be specified in the notification issued in that behalf by the Inspector.

(2) Subject to the provisions of this Act, the administration of the panchayat village shall vest in the village panchayat but the village panchayat shall not be entitled to exercise functions expressly assigned by or under this Act or any other law to its president or to any panchayat union council or the district panchayat or other authority.

(3) Every village panchayat shall be body corporate by the name of the panchayat village specified in the notification issued under section 4, shall have perpetual succession and a common seal, and subject to any restriction or qualification imposed by or under this Act or any other law, shall be vested with the capacity of suing or being sued in its corporate name, of acquiring, holding and transferring property, movable or immovable, of entering into contracts, and of doing all things necessary, proper or expedient for the purposes for which it is constituted.

[1]["(4) The Government may, by notification, classify village panchayats into various grades for the purpose of effective administration of the said village panchayats in accordance with such norms as may be prescribed:"]

---

[1] *Added by Act. 29/1998*

7. Alteration of classification of panchayat villages. – (1) The Government may alter any classification notified under sub-section (1) of section 4, if in their opinion the panchayat village satisfies or ceases to satisfy the conditions referred to in that sub-section.

(2) Any decision made by the Government under this section shall not be questioned in a court of law.

8. Strength of a village panchayat. – (1) Notwithstanding anything contained in section 12 or any other provisions of this Act, the total number of members of a village panchayat (exclusive of its president) shall be notified by the Inspector in accordance with such scale as may be prescribed with reference to population of the panchayat village concerned, as ascertained at the last preceding census of which the relevant figures have been published.

(2) The Inspector may, from time to time, by notification alter the total number of members of a village panchayat notified under sub-section (1).

(3) The number notified under sub-section (1) or the number as altered by notification under sub-section (2) shall not be less than five or more than fifteen.

9. Duration of village panchayat. – (1) Every village panchayat unless sooner dissolved, shall continue for five years from the date appointed for its first meting after each ordinary election and no longer. (Duration of Village Panchayats).

(2) Where a village panchayat is dissolved before the expiration of the said period of five years, election to constitute such village panchayat shall be completed in accordance with the provisions of section 214 as soon as may be, and in any case before the expiration of a period of six months from the date of such dissolution:

Provided that where a village panchayat is dissolved, within six months before the expiration of the said period of five years, it shall not be necessary to hold any election to such village panchayat.

[1] [“**9-A. Appointment of special officer in certain circumstances.** – (1) Notwithstanding anything contained in this Act, or in any other law for the time being in force, in respect of village panchayats specified in Schedule – VI, which cannot be constituted on the 25th day of October 2001 even after resorting to election process, the Government may, be notification, appoint special officers to exercise the powers and discharge the functions of the village panchayats, until the day on which the first meeting of the village panchayats are held after elections to the said village panchayats.

(2) The special officer appointed under sub-section (1) shall hold office only for [2][one year] from the date of his appointment or for such

---

[1] *Inserted by Act. 3/2002*
[2] *Substituted by At. 8/2002*

shorter period as the Government may, by notification, specify in this behalf"].

10. Election of members of village panchayat. – The members of the village panchayat shall be elected in such manner as may be prescribed:

[1][Provided that no person shall be eligible to be elected as a member of more than one ward in the same village panchayat or as a member of more than one village panchayat].

[2]["Provided further that a person who stands for election as a member of a village panchayat shall not be eligible to stand for election as president of a village pancayat,a member of a panchayat union council or a member of a district panchayat"].

[3]["Provided also that no member of a village panchayat shall be eligible to stand for election as president of a village panchayat, a member of a panchayat union council or a member of a district panchayat"].

11. Reservation of Seats. – (1) Seats shall be reserved for the persons belonging to the Scheduled Castes and the Scheduled Tribes in every Village Panchayats and the number of seats so reserved shall bear as nearly as may be, the same proportion to the total number of seats to be filled by direct election in that Village Panchayat as the population of the Scheduled Castes in that Village Panchayat area or of the Scheduled Tribes in that Village Panchayat area bears to the total population of that area.

Provided that for the first election for the Village Panchayat to be held immediately after the commencement of this Act, the provisional population figures of the Panchayat Village as published in relation to 1991 census shall be deemed to be the population of the Panchayat Village.

(2) Seats shall be reserved for women belonging to the Scheduled Castes and the Scheduled Tribes from among the seats reserved for the persons belonging to the Scheduled Castes and the Scheduled Tribes which shall not be less than one third of the total number of seats reserved for the persons belonging to Scheduled Castes and the Scheduled Tribes

[4][(2-A)]

[5][(2-B)]

[(3) Seats shall be reserved for women in the Village Panchayat and the number of seats reserved for women shall be, as nearly as may be, one third (including the number of seats reserved for women

---

1 *Substituted by Act 21/1996*

2 *Added by Act. 30/1995*

3 *Inserted by Act. 30/1995, but omitted by Act. 15/1996*

4 *Inserted by Act. 30/1995, but omitted by Act. 15/1996*

5 *Added by Act. 30/1995*

belonging to the Scheduled Castes and the Scheduled Tribes) of the total number of seats in the Village Panchayat:][1]

Provided that such seats reserved for women shall be allotted by rotation to different wards in such a manner as the Inspector may, by notification, direct.

(4) The reservation of seats under sub-sections(1) and (2) shall cease to have effect on the expiration of the period specified in Article 334 of the Constitution.

12. Division of Panchayat Village into wards. – For the purpose of election of members to a village Panchayat, the Inspector may, after consulting the Village Panchayat, by notification, divide the Panchayat Village into wards and determine the number of members to be returned by each ward in accordance with such scale as may be prescribed.

13. Term of office of members. – (1) The term of office of the members of every Village panchayat, who are elected at ordinary elections, shall, save as otherwise expressly provided, be five years from the date appointed for the first meeting of such Village Panchayat after ordinary election.

(2) Ordinary vacancies in the office of an elected member of the Village Panchayat shall be filled at ordinary elections which shall be fixed by the Tamil Nadu State Election Commissioner to take place on such day or days within six months before the occurrence of the ordinary vacancies, as he thinks fit.

(3) The member of a Village Panchayat elected in a casual vacancy shall enter upon office forthwith, but shall hold office only so long as the member in whose place he is elected would have been entitled -to hold office if the vacancy had not occurred.

14. Electoral roll for village panchayats. – (1) Subject to the provisions of sub-section (2) the electoral roll of the Panchayat Union Council for the time being in force in a Panchayat Village shall be deemed to be the electoral roll for such Village Panchayat.

(2) No amendment, transposition or deletion of any entry in the electoral roll of the Panchayat Union Council made after the last date of making nominations for an election in any Village Panchayat ward and before the notification of the result of such election, shall form part of the electoral roll for such election for the purpose of this section.

(3) The executive authority of the Village Panchayat shall maintain in the prescribed manner, an electoral roll for each ward of the Panchayat Village.

---

[1] *Amended by Acts. 30/1995 and 15/1996 (the expression 'Backward classes of citizens' was inserted by Act. 30/1995, but omitted by Act. 15/1996).*

PANCHAYAT UNION COUNCIL

15. Formation of Panchayat Union Council. – (1) The Government may, from time to time, publish a notification of their intention, –

(a) to declare any local area forming a development block for the purposes of the National Extension Service Scheme or Community Development, to be a panchayat development block; and

(b) to constitute for every such panchayat development block a panchayat union.

(2) Any inhabitant of a local area in respect of which any such notification has been published may submit his objection in writing to anything contained in the notification to the Government within six weeks from the publication of the notification and the Government shall take all such objections into consideration.

(3) After the expiry of six weeks from the publication of the notification and after considering the objections, if any, which have been submitted, the Government may, by notifications –

(a) declare the local area to be a panchayat development block.

(b) declare the said panchayat development block to be a panchayat union; and

(c) specify the name of the panchayat union

(4) The Government may, by notification--

(i) exclude from a panchayat development block any area or village comprised therein, or

(ii) include in a panchayat development block any area contiguous to it, or

(iii) cancel or modify a notification issued under sub-section (3), or

(iv) alter the name of a panchayat union.

(5) Before issuing a notification under sub-section (4), the Government shall consult the district panchayat concerned and give the panchayat union council or panchayat union councils and the village panchayat or village panchayats which will be affected by the issue of such notification, a reasonable opportunity for showing cause against the proposal and shall consider their explanations and objections, if any.

(6) The Government may pass such orders as they may deem fit:

(a) for the disposal of the assets of, or institutions belonging to, the Panchayat union council which has ceased to exist, and for the discharge of the liabilities, if any, of such Panchayat Union Council relating to such assets or institutions, or

(b) for the disposal of any part of the assets of, or institutions belonging to a Panchayat Union Council which has ceased to exercise jurisdiction over any Panchayat development block and for the discharge of the liabilities, if any, of the Panchayat Union council relating to such assets or institutions.

(7) An order made under sub-section (6) may contain such supplemental, incidental and consequential provisions as the Government may deem necessary, and in particular may direct-

(i) that any tax, fee or other sum due to the Panchayat Union Council or where a Panchayat Union council has ceased to exercise jurisdiction over any Panchayat development block, such tax, fee or other sum due to the Panchayat Union council as relates to that block shall be payable to such authorities as may be specified in the order;

(ii) that appeals, petitions or other applications with reference to any such tax, fee or sum which are pending on the date on which the Panchayat Union Council ceased to exist, or as the case may be, on the date on which the Panchayat Union council ceased to exercise jurisdiction over the Panchayat development block, shall be disposed of by such authorities as may be specified in the order.

16. Constitution of Panchayat Union Councils and their incorporation. – (1) A Panchayat Union Council shall be constituted for each Panchayat Union with effect from such date as may be specified in the notification issued in that behalf by the Government.

(2) Subject to the provisions of this Act, the administration of the Panchayat Union shall vest in the Panchayat Union Council but the Panchayat Union Council shall not be entitled to exercise functions expressly assigned by or under this Act or any other law to its chairman or the Commissioner or to the Village Panchayat or district Panchayat or any other authority.

Provided that if and so long as there is no Village Panchayat in any part of a Panchayat Union, the Panchayat Union Council shall exercise all the powers including the power of taxation, discharge the duties, perform the functions and be credited with the receipts and debited with the charges of the Village Panchayat, and the Chairman and the Commissioner of the Panchayat Union Council shall exercise the powers, discharge the duties and perform the functions of the president and the executive authority, respectively in such part of the Panchayat development block.

(3) Every panchayat union council shall be a body corporate by the name of the panchayat union specified in the notification issued under section 15, shall have perpetual succession and a common seal, and subject to any restriction or qualification imposed by or under this Act or any other law, shall be vested with the capacity of suing or being sued in its corporate name, of acquiring, holding and transferring property, movable or immovable, of entering into contracts, and of doing all things necessary, proper or expedient for the purposes for which it is constituted.

[1][**"17. Strength of a Panchayat Union Council.** – A panchayat union council constituted for any panchayat union, shall consist of the elected members as notified under section 19"]

---

[1] *Substituted by Act. 21/1996.*

18. Duration of Panchayat Union Council. – (1) Every panchayat union council unless sooner dissolved shall continue for five years from the date appointed for its first meeting after each ordinary election and no longer.

(2) Where a panchayat union council is dissolved before the expiration of the said period of five yeas, election to reconstitute such panchayat union council shall be completed in accordance with the provisions of section 215 as soon as may be, and in any case, before the expiration of a period of six months from the date of such dissolution.

Provided that where a panchayat union council is dissolved within six months before the expiration of the said period of five years it shall not be necessary to hold any election to such panchayat union council.

[1][*"19. Election of members of Panchayat Union Council.* -- *Every panchayat union council shall consist of persons elected from the wards in the panchayat union, as may be notified from time to time by the Government at the rate of one member, as nearly as may be, for every five thousand population of the panchayat union area as ascertained in the last preceding census of which the relevant figures have been published. Such a ward of the panchayat union area may either comprise a full ward or one or more wards of the village panchayats:*

Provided that no person shall be eligible to be elected as a member of more than one ward in the same panchayat union or as a member of more than one panchayat union council under this Act:

Provided further that a person who stands for election as a member of a panchayat union council shall not be eligible to stand for election as a member of a village panchayat, president of a village panchayat or a member of a district panchayat:

Provided also that no member of a panchayat union council shall be eligible to stand for election as a member of a village panchayat, president of a village panchayat, or a member of a district panchayat:"]

20. Reservation of Seats. – (1) Seats shall be reserved for the persons belonging to the Scheduled Castes and the Scheduled Tribes in every panchayat union council and the number of seats so reserved shall bear as nearly as may be, the same proportion to the total number of seats to be filled by direct election in that panchayat union council as the population of the Scheduled Castes in that panchayat union area or of the Scheduled Tribes in that panchayat union areas bears to the total population of that area:

Provided that for the first election for the panchayat union council to be held immediately after the commencement of this Act, the provisional population figures of the panchayat union as published in

---

[1] *Two additional provisos were added by Act.30/1995 to the original section with had only one proviso. But the whole section has been substituted by Act. 21/1996.*

relation to 1991 census shall be deemed to be the population of that panchayat union.

(2) Seats shall be reserved for women belonging to the Scheduled Castes and the Scheduled Tribes from among the seats reserved for the persons belonging to the Scheduled Castes and the Scheduled Tribes which shall not be less than one-third of the total number of seats reserved for the persons belonging to the Scheduled Castes and the Scheduled Tribes.

[1][(2-A) Omitted]

[2][(2-B) Omitted]

[3][(3) Seats shall be reserved for women in the panchayat union council and the number of seats reserved for women shall not be less than one-third including the number of seats reserved for women belonging to the Scheduled Castes and Scheduled Tribes of the total number of seats in the Panchayat Union Council].

Provided that such seats reserved for women shall be allotted by rotation to different wards in such manner as the Inspector may, by notification, direct.

(4) The reservation of seats under sub-sections (1) and (2) shall cease to have effect on the expiration of the period specified in Article 334 of the Constitution.

(2) Only one member shall be elected from each ward.

21. Division of panchayat union into wards. – (1) For the purpose of election of members to the panchayat union council, the Inspector shall, after consulting the panchayat union council, by notification, divide the panchayat union area into wards and determine the number of members to be elected in accordance with such scale as may be prescribed.

22. Term of office of members. – (1) Except s otherwise provided in this Act, members of the panchayat union council elected at an ordinary election, shall hold office for a term of five years.

(2) The term of office of the members elected at an ordinary election shall commence on the date appointed for the first meeting of the panchayat union council after ordinary election.

(3) The member of a panchayat union council elected in a casual vacancy, shall enter upon office forthwith but shall hold office only so long as the member in whose place he is elected would have been entitled to hold office if the vacancy had not occurred.

23. Electoral roll for Panchayat Union Council. – (1) Subject to the provision of sub-section (2) , the electoral roll of the district panchayat for the time being in force for such part of the panchayat union shall be deemed to be the electoral roll for such panchayat union council.

1, 2 *Substituted by Act 30/1995 but omitted by Act. 15/1996*

3 *The expression 'Backward classes of citizens' was inserted by Act 30/1995, but was omitted by Act. 15/1996.*

(2) No amendment, transposition or deletion of any entry in the electoral roll of the district panchayat made after last date for making nominations for an election in any panchayat union council ward and before the notification of the result of such election , shall form part of the electoral roll for such election, for the purpose of this section.

(3) The Commissioner of panchayat union council shall maintain in the prescribed manner, electoral roll for each ward in the panchayat union.

DISTRICT PANCHAYATS

24. Formation and incorporation of district panchayat. – (1) The Government may, by notification, constitute for each district with effect from such date as may be prescribed in the said notification, a district panchayat having jurisdiction over the entire district excluding such portions of the district as are included in a municipality or town panchayat or industrial township or under the authority of a municipal corporation or a cantonment.

(2) Every district panchayat shall be a body corporate by the name of the district, shall have perpetual succession and a common seal and subject to such restrictions as are imposed by or under this or any other enactment, shall be vested with the capacity of suing or being sued in its corporate name, of acquiring, holding and transferring property, movable or immovable, whether without or within the limits of the area over which it has authority, of entering into contracts and of doing all things, necessary, proper or expedient for the purpose for which it is constituted.

[1][“**25. Constitution of district panchayat.** – (1) the district panchayat shall consist of-

(a) all the elected member as determined under section 27;

(b) the members of the House of People and the members of the State Legislative Assembly representing a part or whole of the district whose constituencies lie within the district:

(c) the member of the Council of States who is registered as elector within the district.

(2) Members of the house of people, the State Legislative Assembly and the Council of the States, referred to in clause (b) and (c) of sub section (1) , shall be entitled to take part in the proceedings [2][and vote at the meeting of the district panchayat].

26. Election of Members. – The number of elected members of a district panchayat shall consist of persons elected from the wards in the district panchayat, as may be notified from time to time by the Government based on the population of the district as ascertained at the last preceding census:

---

[1] *Whole section substituted by Act. 21/1996*

[2] *Substituted by Act. 37/1997*

[1] ["Provided that no person shall be eligible to be elected as a member of more than one ward in the same district panchayat or as a member of more than one district panchayat"].

[2]["Provided further that a person who stands for election as a member of a district panchayat shall not be eligible to stand for election as a member of a village panchayat, president of a village panchayat or a member of panchayat union council"].

[3]["Provided also that no member of district panchayat shall be eligible to stand for election as a member of a village panchayat, president of a village panchayat or a member of a panchayat union council"].

27. Determination of elected members after census. – Upon the publication of the figures for each census, the number of elected members of a district panchayat shall be determined in accordance

Provided further that for the first election to the district panchayat to be held immediately after the commencement of this Act, the provisional population figures of the district panchayat as published in relation to 1991 census, shall be deemed to be the population of the district panchayat as ascertained in that census.

Provided that the determination of the members as aforesaid, shall not affect the then composition of the district panchayat until the expiry of the term of office of the elected members then in office:

28. Delimination of territorial wards. – The Government shall, by notification-

(a) divide the area, within the jurisdiction of every district panchayat, for the purpose of election to such district panchayat into as many single member territorial wards as the number of members required to be elected under Section 26;

(b) determine the extent of each territorial ward which shall be a panchayat village or panchayat union or part of a panchayat village or panchayat union; and

[4][(c) determine the territorial ward or wards in which seats are reserved for the Scheduled Castes, Scheduled Tribes and women],

29. Term of office members. – (1) Except as otherwise provided in this Act, members of a district panchayat elected at an ordinary election, shall hold office for a term of five years.

(2) The term of office of the members elected at an ordinary election shall commence on the date appointed for the first meeting of the district panchayat after ordinary election.

---

[1] *Existing proviso substituted in Act. 21/1996*

[2] *New Provisos added by Act. 30/1995*

[3] *New Provisos added by Act, 30/1995.*

[4] *The expression 'Backward classes of citizens' was inserted by Act 30/1995, but was omitted by Act. 15/1996.*

(3) The member of a district panchayat elected in a casual vacancy, shall enter upon the office forthwith but shall hold office only so long as the member in whose place he is elected would have been entitled to hold office, if the vacancy had not occurred.

30. Electoral roll for district panchayat. – (1) The electoral roll of a district panchayat shall be the same as the electoral roll of the Tamil Nadu Legislative Assembly prepared and revised in accordance with the provision of the law for the time being in force in the district and as revised, modified, updated and published in accordance with the provisions of sub-section (2).

(2) Subject to the superintendence, direction and control of he Tamil Nadu State Election Commission , the electoral roll shall be revised , modified, up-dated and published by such officer as may be designated by the Tamil Nadu State Election Commission in this behalf in the prescribed manner.

(3) No amendment, transposition or deletion of any entry in the electoral roll of the Tamil Nadu Legislative Assembly made after the last date for making nomination for election in any district panchayat territorial ward and before the notification of the result of such election, shall form part of the electoral roll for such election, for the purpose of this section.

31. Duration of district panchayat. – (1) Every district panchayat constituted under this Act unless sooner dissolved, shall continue for five years from the date appointed for its first meeting after each ordinary election and no longer.

(2) Where a district panchayat is dissolved before the expiration of the said period of five years, election to reconstitute such district panchayat shall be completed as soon as may be and in any case, before the expiration of a period of six months from the date of such dissolution.

Provided that where a district panchayat is dissolved within six months before the expiration of the said period of five years, it shall not be necessary to hold any election to such district panchayat.

32. Reservation Seats. – (1) Seats shall be reserved for the persons belonging to the Scheduled Castes and the Scheduled Tribes in every district panchayat and the number of seats so reserved shall bear as nearly as may be, the same proportion to the total number of seats to be filled by direct election in that district panchayat as the population of the Scheduled Castes in that district panchayat area or of the Scheduled Tribes in that district panchayat area bears to the total population of that area:

Provided that for the first election for the district panchayat to be held immediately after the commencement of this Act, the provisional population figures of the district panchayat area as published in relation to 1991 census, shall be deemed to be the population of that district panchayat area.

(2) Seats shall be reserved for women belonging to the Scheduled Castes and the Scheduled Tribes from among the seats reserved for the persons belonging to the Scheduled Castes and the Scheduled Tribes which shall not be less than one-third of the total number of seats reserved for the persons belonging to the Scheduled Castes and the Scheduled Tribes.

[1][(2-A) Omitted]

[2][(2-B) Omitted]

[3][(3) Seats shall be reserved for women in the district panchayat and number of seats reserved for women shall not be less than one-third (including the number of seats reserved for women belonging to the Scheduled Castes and the Scheduled Tribes) of the total number of seats in the district panchayat].

Provided that such seats reserved for women shall be allotted by rotation to different territorial wards in such manner as the Government may, by notification, direct.

(4) The reservation of seats under sub-sections (1) and (2) shall cease to have effect on the expiration of the period specified in Article 334 of the Constitution.

(5) Reservation of seats under this section, section 11 and section 20, shall be made by the Government or by any officer authorised by the Government in this behalf.

(6) While determining the number of seats in village panchayats, Panchayat union councils and district panchayats under this section, section 11, and section 20 for the purpose of reservation, any fraction thereof shall be disregarded.

QUALIFICATION, DISQUALIFICATION, ETC., OF MEMBERS

33. Qualification of Candidates. – No person shall be qualified for election as a member or president [4][***] of a panchayat unless-

(i) his name appears on the electoral roll of the concerned panchayat; and

(ii) he has completed his twenty-first year of age

34. Disqualification of officers and servants of Government and local bodies etc. – (1) No Village Administrative Officer, or village servant and no other officer or servant of the State or Central Government or of a village panchayat, panchayat union council, district panchayat, municipal council or the municipal corporation of Madras, or of Madurai or of Coimbatore or of any other municipal corporation that may be constituted under any law for the time being in force or of any industrial township or of cantonment or of any body corporate,

---

[1,2] *Substituted by Act 30/1995 but, omitted by Act. 15/1996*

[3] *Substituted by Act. 30/1995 but omitted by Act. 15/1996*

[4] *The words "or chairman" omitted by Act. 21/1996*

owned or controlled by the State or Central Government, shall be qualified for election as a member or for holding office as a member.

(2) If any question arises either before or after an election whether any person is or is not disqualified under this section, the question shall be referred to the Government whose decision shall be final.

(3) Before taking any decision on any such question, the Government shall obtain the opinion of the Tamil Nadu State Election Commission and shall act according to such opinion.

35. Disqualificqation of persons convicted of election offences. – Every person convicted of an offence punishable under sections 58 to 71 of this Act or under Chapter IX-A of the Indian Penal Code, or is so disqualified by or under any law for the time being in force for the purposes of election to the Legislative Assembly of the State or is disqualified by or under any law for the time being in force, shall be disqualified from voting or from being elected in any election to which this Act applies or from holding the office of president or member of a village panchayat or of the office of chairman or member of a panchayat union council or a district panchayat, for a period of five years from the date of his conviction.

36. Disqualification of voters. – No person who is of unsound mind and declared so by a competent court and no person who is disqualified under section 35 shall be qualified to vote so long as the disqualification subsists.

37. Disqualification of candidates. – (1) A person who has been sentenced by a criminal court to imprisonment for any office involving normal delinquency (such sentence not having been reversed) shall be disqualified for election as a member [1][while the sentence is in force] and for [2][six years] from the date of the expiration thereof.

(2) A person convicted of an offence punishable under the Protection of Civil Rights Act, 1955, shall be disqualified for election as a member for a period of [3][six years] from the date of such conviction.

(3) A person shall be disqualified for election as a member if, at the last date for filing of nomination or at the date of election he is-

(a) of unsound mind, or a deaf-mute;

(b) an applicant to be adjudicated as an insolvent or an undischarged insolvent:

(c) interested in a subsisting contract made with or any work being done for, any panchayat except as a share holder (other than a director) in a company;

---

[1] *Substituted for words "while undergoing the sentence" by Act. 1/2001*

[2] *Substituted for words "five years" by Act. 1/2001.*

[3] *Substituted for words "five years" by Act, 1/2001.*

(d) employed as paid legal practitioner on behalf of the panchayat or as legal practitioner against the panchayat:

[1]["(dd) found that he does not belong to Scheduled Caste or Scheduled Tribe for contesting any seat reserved for Scheduled Caste or Scheduled Tribe in a Panchayat"].

(e) already a member of a panchayat, whose term of office will not expire before his fresh election can take effect or has already been elected as a member of a panchayat whose term of office has not yet commenced: or

(f) in arrears of any kind due by him (otherwise than in a fiduciary capacity) to a panchayat upto and inclusive of the previous year.

[2]["(4) If the Tamil Nadu Tamil Nadu State Election Commission is satisfied that a person-

(a) has failed to lodge an account of election expenses within the time and in the manner required by or under this Act, and

(b) has no good reason or justification for the failure, the Tamil Nadu Tamil Nadu State Election Commission shall, by order published in the Tamil Nadu Government Gazette, declare him to be disqualified for being chosen as, and for being, a member or president, as the case may be, and any such person shall be disqualified for a period of three years from the date of the order"].

38. Disqualification of members. – Subject to the provision of section 41, a member shall cease to hold office as such, if he –

(a) is sentenced by a criminal court to such punishment and for such offence as is described in sub-section (1) of section 37;

(b) is convicted of an offence punishable under the Protection of Civil Rights Act 1955; (Central Act XXII of 1955)

(c) becomes of unsound mind or of deaf-mute;

(d) applies to be adjudicated, or is adjudicated, as an insolvent;

(e) acquires any interest in any subsisting contract made with or work being done for any panchayat except as a shareholder (other than a director) in a company or except as permitted by rules made under this Act;

(f) is employed as paid legal practitioner on behalf of any panchayat or accepts employment as legal practitioner against any panchayat;

[3]["(ff) is found that he does not belong to Scheduled Caste or Scheduled Tribe, but has been elected from the seat reserved for Scheduled Caste or Scheduled Tribe"].

(g) is appointed as an officer or servant under this Act;

(h) ceases to reside in the village, the panchayat union or the district, as the case may be

---

[1] *Inserted in by Act. 2/1999*

[2] *Added by Act. 54/1998*

[3] *Inserted by Act. 2/1999*

(i) fails to pay arrears of any kind due by him (otherwise than in a fiduciary capacity) to any panchayat within three months after such arrears became due; or

(j) absents himself from the meetings of the panchayat for a period of three consecutive months reckoned from the date of the commencement of his term of office, or of the last meeting which he attended, or of his restoration to office as member under sub-section (1) of section 39, as the case may be, or if within the said period, less than three meetings have been held, absents himself from the three consecutive meetings held after the said date:

Provided that no meeting from which a member absented himself shall be counted against him under this clause if –

(i) due notice of that meeting was not given to him; or

(ii) the meeting was held after giving shorter notice than that prescribed for an ordinary meeting; or

(iii) the meeting was held on a requisition of members.

[1][**38-A. Disqualification for president, vice-president, chairman, vice-chairman and member** – Notwithstanding anything contained in this Act, no person shall be qualified for being elected as, and for being, a president, vice-president or member of a village panchayat or a chairman, vice-chairman or member of a panchayat union council or of a district panchayat if he is a member of the Legislatie Assembly of the State or a member of either House of Parliament"].

39. Restoration of members to office. – (1) Where a person ceases to be a member under section 35 or clause (a) or clause (b) of section 38, such person shall be restored to office for such portion of the period for which such person was elected, as may remain unexpired at the date of such restoration, if and when the conviction or sentence is annulled on appeal or revision; and any person elected to fill the vacancy in the interim, shall on such restoration, vacate office.

(2) Where a person ceases to be a member under clause (j) of section 38 the executive authority or the commissioner or the Secretary as the case may be, shall , at once intimate the fact in writing to such person and report the same to the panchayat concerned at its next meeting. If such person applies for restoration suo moto to the panchayat concerned on or before the date of its next meeting or within fifteen days of the receipt by him of such intimation, such panchayat may at the meeting next after the receipt of such application restore him to his office of member.

Provided that a member shall not be restored more than twice during his term of office.

40. Oath or affirmation to be made by members. – (1) Notwithstanding anything contained in the Oaths Act, 1969, (Central

---

[1] *Inserted by Act. 28/2002*

Act X of 1969), every person who is elected to be a member or who becomes a member shall, before taking his seat, make at a meeting of the panchayat an oath or affirmation in the following form , namely:-

"I, A.B, having been elected a member- having become a member of this village panchayat/panchayat union council-district panchayat do swear in the name of God/solemnly affirm that I will bear true faith and allegiance to the Constitution of India as by law established, that I will uphold the sovereignty and integrity of India and that I will faithfully discharge the duty upon which I am about to enter".

(2) Any person who, having been elected to be a member or who, having become a member, fails to make within three months of the date on which his term of office commences or at one of the first three meetings held after the said date whichever is later, the oath or affirmation laid down in sub-section (1) , shall cease to hold his office and his seat shall be deemed to have become vacant.

(3) Any person who has been elected to be a member or who has become a member shall not take his seat at a meeting of the panchayat or do any act as such member unless he has made the oath or affirmation as laid down in sub-section (1),

(4) Notwithstanding anything contained in sub-section (3) , the president or the chairman of a panchayat or the member of a committee constituted under this Act, who has not made the oath or affirmation as a member, shall be entitled to act as such president, chairman or member provided he makes the oath or affirmation and takes his seat at the first meeting of the panchayat which he attends within two months after he is elected or appointed as, or becomes entitled to exercise the functions of, the president, chairman or member, as the case may be.

Explanation – For the purposes of this section-

(i) 'president' includes a vice-president exercising the functions of the president under sub-section (1) or sub-section (2) of section 47 and the temporary president appointed under sub-section (3) of that section; and

(ii) 'chairman' includes vice-chairman exercising the functions of the chairman under sub-section (1) or sub-section (5) of section 54 or a revenue divisional officer who is ex-officio chairman under sub-section (2) of that section.

41. Authority to decide questions of disqualification of members. –

(1) Whenever it is alleged that any person who has been elected as a member of a panchayat or who becomes a member of a panchayat is not qualified or has become disqualified under sections 33,35,37,38 and 40, the executive authority or the commissioner or the Secretary as the case may be, shall, by notice in writing inform such member of the allegation and place the matter at the next meeting of the panchayat concerned. If before the date of the expiry of two months from the date of receipt of such notice, such member does not apply to the prescribed judicial authority under sub-section (2), he shall become not qualified or disqualified from such date of expiry of the said two months.

(2) The executive authority or the commissioner or the Secretary, as the case may be , if so directed by the panchayat or by the Tamil Nadu Tamil Nadu State Election Commissioner, shall, or any such member or any other member may apply to the prescribed judicial authority whose decision on such allegation shall be final.

(3) Where an application has been made under sub-section (2), the member shall, pending decision on such application be entitled to act as if he is qualified or was not disqualified.

(4) Nothing contained in this section shall be deemed to affect the provisions of section 39.

PRESIDENT AND VICE-PRESIDENT OF VILLAGE PANCHAYAT

42. President and vice-president of village panchayat. – There shall be a president and a vice-president for every village panchayat.

43. Election of president. – (1) (a) The president shall be elected by the persons whose names appear in the electoral roll for the village panchayat from among themselves in accordance with such procedure as may be prescribed.

(b) If at an ordinary or casual election, no president is elected, a fresh election shall be held;

[1]["Provided that a person who stands for election as president shall not be eligible to stand for election as a member of village panchayat, a member of panchayat union council or a member of district panchayat;

Provided further no president shall be eligible to stand for election as a member of village panchayat, a member of panchayat union council or a member of district panchayat"];

(2) The election of the president may be held ordinarily at the same times and in the same places as the ordinary elections of the members of the village panchayat.

(3) The term of office of the president who is elected at an ordinary election shall, save as otherwise expressly provided in, be five years beginning at noon on the day on which the ordinary vacancy occurs.

(4) Any casual vacancy in the office of the president shall be filled by a fresh election and a person elected as president in any such vacancy shall enter upon office forthwith and hold office only so long as the person in whose place he is elected would have been entitled to hold office, if the vacancy had not occurred.

(5) Unless the Tamil Nadu Tamil Nadu State Election Commissioner otherwise directs, no casual vacancy in the office of the president shall be filled within six months before the date on which the ordinary election of the president under sub-section (1) is due.

---

[1] *Substituted by Act. 30/1995 for 3 existing provisos*

(6) The provisions of sections 34 o 41 (both inclusive), shall, as far as may be, apply in relation to the office of the president as they apply in relation to the office of an elected member of the panchayat.

(7) The president shall be an ex-officio member of the village panchayat and shall have all the rights and privileges of an elected member of the village panchayat.

44. Election of Vice-president. – (1) The vice-president shall be elected by the village panchayat from among its elected members in accordance with such procedure as may be prescribed.

(2) If at an election held under sub-section (1), no vice-president is elected, a fresh election shall be held for electing a vice-president.

45. Cessation of office as president and vice-president. – The president or vice-president shall cease to hold office as such-

(a) in the case of the president, on his becoming disqualified for holding the office or on his removal from office or on the expiry of his term of office or on his otherwise easing to be a president;

(b) in the case of the vice-president, [1][“on his becoming disqualified for holding the office or on his removal from office or”] on the expiry of his term of office as a member or on his otherwise ceasing to be a member.

46. Functions of the president. – (1) The president shall-

[2] [“(a) convene the meetings of the village panchayat and of the Grama Sabha”]

(b) have full access to the records of the village panchayat;

(c) discharge all the duties specifically imposed and exercise all the powers conferred on the president by this Act.

(2) No official correspondence between the village panchayat and the Government shall be conducted except through the president. The president shall be bound to transmit communications addressed through him by the executive authority to the Government or by the Government to the executive authority.

47. Devolution of [3][**] president’s functions and filling up of vacancies in the office of presidents. – (1) When the office of president is vacant, the vice-president shall exercise the functions of the president until a new president is declared elected and assumes office.

(2) If the president has been continuously absent from jurisdiction for more than thirty days or is incapacitated, his functions during such absence or incapacity shall, except in such circumstances as may be prescribed, devolve on the vice-president.

---

[1] Inserted by Act. 29/1999

[2] Inserted by Act. 29/1999

[3] *The words “and delegation” omitted by Act. 29/1999*

(3) When the office of president is vacant or the president has been continuously absent from jurisdiction for more than thirty days or is incapacitated and there is either a vacancy in the office of vice-president or the vice-president has been continuously absent from jurisdiction for more than thirty days or is incapacitated, the functions of the president shall devolve on a member of the village panchayat appointed by the Inspector in this behalf, and if no member of the village panchayat is available for such appointment, on such person as may be appointed by the Inspector in this behalf.

The member of the village panchayat or the person so appointed (who shall be called as the temporary president) shall perform the functions of the president subject to such restrictions and conditions as may be prescribed, until a new president or vice-president is declared elected and assumes office, or either the president or the vice-president returns to jurisdiction or recovers from his incapacity, as the case may be.

(4) Any vacancy in the office of president shall be reported to the Tamil Nadu State Election Commissioner by such person and within such time as may be prescribed and the Tamil Nadu State Election Commissioner shall arrange for the election of the president.

(5) The president shall have power to control and revise the exercise or discharge of any functions devolving on the vice-president under sub-section(2).

48. Delegation of functions of president. – Subject to such restrictions and control as may be prescribed, the president may by an order in writing delegate any of his functions as such to the vice-president and in the absence of the vice-president to any other member, provided that the exercise or discharge of any functions so delegated shall be subject to such further restrictions and conditions as may be laid down by the president and shall also be subject to his control and revision:

Provided that he shall not delegate any functions which the village panchayat expressly prohibits him to delegate.

CHAIRMAN AND VICE-CHAIRMAN

49. Chairman and vice-chairman of panchayat union council. – There shall be a chairman and a vice-chairman for every panchayat union council.

50. Election of chairman of panchayat union council. – (1) The chairman shall be elected by the panchayat union council from among its elected members in accordance with such procedure as may be prescribed.

(2) If at an election held under sub-section (1) , no chairman is elected, a fresh election shall be held for electing a chairman.

51. Election of vice chairman of panchayat union council. – (1) The vice-chairman shall be elected by the panchayat union council from among its elected members in accordance with such procedure as may be prescribed.

(2) If at an election held under sub-section (1) , no vice-chai an is elected, a fresh election shall be held for electing a vice-chairma

52. Functions of the chairman. – (1) The chairman shall –

(a) convene the meetings of the panchayat union council. and

(b) discharge all the duties specifically imposed and exercise all the powers conferred on the chairman by this Act and the rules made thereunder.

(2) The chairman shall have full access to all the records of the panchayat union council and no official correspondence between the council and the Government shall be conducted except through the chairman. The chairman shall be bound to transmit communications addressed through him by the commissioner to the Government or by the Government to the commissioner.

53. Cessation of office of chairman and vice-chairman of a panchayat union council. – The chairman and vice-chairman shall cease to hold office as such: –

(a) in the case of the chairman of a panchayat union council on his becoming disqualified for holding the office or on his removal from office or on the expiry of his term of office or on his otherwise ceasing to be chairman or member of the panchayat union council;

(b) in the case of the vice-chairman [1]["on his becoming disqualified for holding the office or on his removal from office or"] on the expiry of his term of office as a member of the panchayat union council or on his otherwise ceasing to be a member of the panchayat union council.

54. Devolution and delegation of chairman's functions and filling up of vacancies in the office of chairman. – (1) When the office of chairman is vacant, the vice-chairman shall exercise the functions of the chairman until a new chairman assumes office.

(2) When the office of chairman is vacant and there is either a vacancy in the office of vice-chairman, or the vice-chairman, or the vice-chairman has been continuously absent from jurisdiction for more than thirty days or is incapacitated and until a new chairman or vice-chairman is elected and assumes office, or the vice-chairman returns to jurisdiction or recovers from his incapacity, as the case may be, the revenue divisional officer shall, notwithstanding anything contained in this Act, or in the rules or notifications issued thereunder, be ex-officio member and chairman of the panchayat union council.

(3) An out-going chairman or vice-chairman is eligible for re-election.

---

[1] *Inserted by Act. 29/1999*

(4) The chairman may, by an order in writing, delegate any of his functions to the vice-chairman:

Provided that he shall not delegate any functions which the panchayat union council expressly forbids him to delegate.

(5) If the chairman has been continuously absent from jurisdiction for more than thirty days or is incapacitated, his functions during such absence or incapacity shall, except in such circumstances as may be prescribed, devolve on the vice-chairman.

(6) If the vice-chairman also has been continuously absent from jurisdiction for more than thirty days or is incapacitated or if the office of vice-chairman is vacant, the chairman may, by an order in writing, delegate any of his functions to any member of the panchayat union council who shall be called "chairman delegate" during the period of delegation:

Provided that –

(i) when an order of delegation made under this sub-section is in force, no further order of delegation of any function shall be made in favour of any member other than the member in whose favour the order in force was made;

(ii) no delegation under this sub-section shall be made for any period exceeding in the aggregate ninety days in any year without the special sanction of the panchayat union council; and

(iii) every order made under this sub-section shall be communicated to the panchayat union council at its next meeting.

(7) The exercise or discharge of any functions delegated under this section shall be subject to such restrictions, limitations and conditions as may be laid down by the chairman.

55. Chairman and vice-chairman of district panchayat. – There shall be a chairman and a vice-chairman for every district panchayat.

56. Election of chairman and vice-chairman of district panchayat. – (1) The elect members of the district panchayat shall as soon as may be elected two members from among themselves, to be respectively the chairman and vice-chairman.

(2) The provisions of [1]["sub-section (2) of section 50, sub-section (2) of section 51 and sections, 52, 53 and 54"] shall as far as may be, apply in relation to the office of the chairman and vice-chairman of district panchayat, as they apply in relation to the office of the chairman and vice-chairman of panchayat union council and any reference to panchayat union council or commissioner in the said sections shall be deemed to be a reference to the district panchayat or Secretary as the case may be, in so far as it applies to the office of chairman and vice chairman of district panchayat.

---

[1] *Substituted by Act. 29/1992*

57. Reservation of seats in the office of president, chairman etc. – (1) Office of the presidents of village panchayats, chairmen of panchayat union councils and chairmen of district panchayats, shall be reserved for the persons belonging to the Scheduled Castes and the Scheduled Tribes and the number of seats so reserved shall bear as nearly as may be, the same proportion to the total number of offices in the State as the population of the Scheduled Castes in the State or the Scheduled Tribes in the State bear to the total population of the State:

[1][**]

[2]["(1-A). Offices of the presidents of village panchayats, chairmen of panchayat union councils and chairmen of district panchayats shall be reserved for women belonging to the Scheduled Cases and the Scheduled Tribes from among the offices reserved for the persons belonging to the Scheduled Castes and the Scheduled Tribes which shall not be less than one third of the total number of offices reserved for the persons belonging to the Scheduled Castes and the Scheduled Tribes"].

[3][(1-B) (omitted)]

[4][(1-C) (omitted)]

[5]["(1-D). Offices of the presidents of village panchayats, chairmen of panchayat union councils and chairmen of district panchayats in the State shall be reserved for women which shall not be less than one third (including the number of offices reserved for women belonging to the Scheduled Castes, the Scheduled Tribes of the total number of such offices in the State"]

[6]["Provided that the offices reserved under this section, shall be allotted to different panchayats at each level in such manner, as may be prescribed"].

(2) Reservation of the offices of the presidents of village panchayats, chairmen of panchayat union councils and chairmen of district panchayats, shall be made by the Government or by any officer authorised by the Government in this behalf.

(3) The reservation of the offices of presidents of the village panchayats, chairmen of the panchayat union councils and chairmen of the district panchayats made under sub-section (1) in respect of the persons belonging to the Scheduled Castes and the Scheduled Tribes shall cease to have effect on the expiration of the period specified in Article 334 of the Constitution.

(4) While determining the number of offices of presidents of village panchayats, chairmen of panchayat union councils and chairmen of district panchayats, under sub-section (1) for the purpose

---

[1] *Proviso omitted by Act. 30/1995*

[2&3] *Inserted by Act. 30/1995*

[4&5] *Inserted by Act. 30/1995 but omitted by Act. 15/1996*

[6] *Inserted by Act. 15/1996*

of reservation, any fraction thereof shall be disregarded. [1][any fraction which is less than half shall be disregarded and half and more than half shall be regarded as one]

CHAPTER IV

OFFENCES RELATING TO ELECTIONS

58. Infringement of secrecy of election. – Every officer, clerk, agent or other person performing any duty in connection with the recording or counting of votes at an election who, except for some purpose authorised by law, communicates to any person any information showing directly or indirectly for which candidate any voter has voted, and every person who by any improper means, procures any such information, shall be punished with imprisonment which may extend to six months or with fine, or with both.

59. Minimum penalty for personation. – Notwithstanding anything contained in section 171-F of the Indian Penal Code (Central Act. XLV/1860), any person who in connection with an election under this Act commits an offence of personation punishable under that section shall be punishable with imprisonment for a term which shall not be less than six months and not more then two years and with fine.

60. Promting enmity between classed in connection with election. – Any person who in connection with an election under this Act promotes or attempts to promote on grounds of religion, race, caste, community or language, feelings of enmity or hatred between different classes of the citizens of India shall be punishable with imprisonment for a term which may extend to three years or with fine, or with both.

61. Prohibition of public meetings on the day preceeding the election day and on the election day. – (1) No person shall convene, hold or attend any public meeting in any local area comprised in a panchayat within forty-eight hours before the date of termination of the poll or on the date or dates on which a poll is taken for an election in that panchayat.

(2) Any person who contravenes the provisions of sub-section (1) shall be punishable with fine which may extend to two hundred and fifty rupees.

62. Disturbances at election meeting. – (1) Any person who at a public meeting to which this section applies acts or incites others to act, in a disorderly manner for the purpose of preventing the transaction of the business for which the meeting was called shall be punishable with fine which may extend to two hundred and fifty rupees.

---

[1] *Substituted by Act. 29/1999*

(2) This section applies to any public meeting of a political character held in any local area comprised in a panchayat between the earliest date for making nomination of candidates for an election and the date in which such election is held.

(3) If any police officer reasonably suspects any person of committing an offence under sub-section (1), he may, if requested so to do by the chairman of the meeting, require that person to declare to him immediately his name and address and, if that person refuses or fails so to declare his name and address, or if the police officer reasonably suspects him of giving a false name or address, the policy officer may arrest him without warrant.

63. Restrictions on printing of pamphlets posters etc. – (1) No person shall print or publish or cause to be printed or published, any election pamphlet or poster which does not bear on its face the names and address of the printer and the publisher thereof.

(2) No person shall print or cause to be printed any election pamphlet or poster.

(a) unless a declaration as to the identity of the publisher thereof signed by him and attested by two persons to whom he is personally known, is delivered by him to the printer in duplicate; and

(b) unless, within a reasonable time, after the printing of the document, one copy of the declaration is sent by the printer together with one copy of the document to the execute authority or commissioner or the Secretary, as the case may be.

(3) For the purposes of this section –

(a) any process for multiplying copies of a document, other than copying it by hand, shall be deemed to be printing and the expression 'printer' shall be construed accordingly; and

(b) "election pamphlet or poster" means any printed pamphlet, hand-bill or other document distributed for the purpose of promoting or prejudicing the election of a candidate or group of candidates or any placard or poster having reference to an election, but does not include any hand-bill, placard or poster merely announcing the date, time, place and other particulars of an election meeting or routing instructions to election agents or workers.

(4) Any person who contravenes any of the provisions of sub-section (1) or sub-section (2) shall be punishable with imprisonment for a term which may extend to six months, or with fine which may extend to two thousand rupees, or with both.

64. Officers, etc., at elections not to act for candidates or to influence voting. – (1) No person who is a returning officer, or an assistant returning officer or a presiding or polling officer at an election, or an officer or clerk appointed by the returning officer or the presiding officer to perform any duty in connection with an election shall in the conduct or the management of the election do any act (other than the giving of vote) for the furtherance of the prospects of the election of a candidate.

(2) No such person as aforesaid, and no member of the police force, shall endeavour-

(a) to persuade any person to give his vote at an election, or

(b) to dissuade any person from giving his vote at an election, or

(c) to influence the voting of any person at an election in any manner.

(3) Any person who contravenes the provisions of sub-section (1) or sub-section (2) shall be punishable with imprisonment for a term which may extend to six months or with fine, or with both.

65. Prohibition of canvassing in or near polling stations. – (1) No person shall, on the date or dates on which a poll is taken at any polling station, commit any of the following acts within the polling station or in any public or private place within a distance of one hundred metres of the polling station, namely-

(a) canvassing for votes; or

(b) soliciting the vote of any elector; or

(c) persuading any elector not to vote for any particular candidate; or

(d) persuading any elector not to vote at the election ; or

(e) exhibiting any notice or sign (other than an official notice) relating to the election.

(2) Any person who contravenes the provisions of sub-section)1) shall be punishable with fine which may extend to two hundred and fifty rupees.

(3) An offence punishable under this section shall be cognizable.

66. Penalty for disorderly conduct in or near polling stations. – (1) No person shall, on the date or dates on which a poll is taken at any polling station-

(a) use or operate within or at the entrance of the polling station, or in any public or private place in the neighbourhood thereof, any apparatus for amplifying or reproducing the human voice, such as a megaphone or a loudspeaker, or

(b) shout, or otherwise act in a disorderly manner within or at the entrance of the polling station or in any public or private place in the neighbourhood thereof , so as to cause annoyance to any person visiting the polling station for the poll, or so as to interfere with the work of the officers and other persons on duty at the polling station.

(2) Any person who contravenes, or wilfully aids or abets the contravention of the provisions of sub-section (1) shall be punishable with imprisonment for a term which may extend to three months or with fine, or with both.

(3) If the polling officer of a polling station has reason to believe that any person is committing or has committed an offence punishable

under this section, he may direct any police officer to arrest such person, and thereupon the police officer shall arrest him.

(4) Any police officer may take such steps and like such force, as may be reasonably necessary for preventing any contravention of the provisions of sub-section (1) and may seize any apparatus used for such contravention.

Explanation – In this section, the expression "polling officer" means the polling officer of a polling station or if there is a presiding officer at the polling station, such presiding officer.

67. Penalty for mis-conduct at the polling station. – (1) Any person who during the hours fixed for the poll at any polling station misconducts himself or fails to obey the lawful directions of the polling officer may b removed from the polling station by the polling officer or by any police officer on duty or by any person authorised in this behalf by such polling officer.

(2) The powers conferred by sub-section (1) shall not be exercised so as to prevent any elector who is otherwise entitled to vote at a polling station from having opportunity of voting at that polling station.

(3) If any person who has been so removed from a polling station re-enters the polling station without the permission of the polling officer, he shall be punishable with imprisonment for a term which may extend to three months or with fine, or with both.

(4) An offence punishable under sub-section (3) shall be cognizable.

Explanation – In this section, the expression "polling officer" has the same meaning as in section 66.

68. Penalty for illegal hiring or procuring of conveyance of elections. – (1) No candidate or his agent or any other person with the consent of a candidate or his agent shall hire or procure whether on payment or otherwise any vehicle or vessel for the conveyance of any elector (other than the candidate himself, the members of his family or his agent) to or from any polling station:

Provided that nothing in this sub-section shall apply to—

(a) the hiring of a vehicle or vessel by an elector or several electors at their joint cost for the purpose of conveying him or them to or from the polling station, if the vehicle or vessel so hired is a vehicle or vessel not propelled by mechanical power; and

(b) the use of any public transport vehicle or vessel or any railway carriage by any elector at his own cost for the purpose of going to or coming from the polling station.

Explanation – In this sub-section, the expression "vehicle" means any vehicle used or capable of being used for the purpose of road transport whether propelled by mechanical power or otherwise and whether used for drawing other vehicles or otherwise.

(2) Any person who contravenes the provisions of sub-section (1) at or in connection with an election shall be punishable with fine which may extend to two hundred and fifty rupees.

69. Breaches of official duty in connection with election. – (1) If any person to whom this section applies is without reasonable cause guilty of any act or omission in breach of his official duty, he shall be punishable with fine which may extend to five hundred rupees.

(2) No suit or other legal proceedings shall lie against any such person for damages in respect of any such act or omission as aforesaid.

(3) The persons to whom this section applies are the returning officers, assistant returning officers, presiding officers, polling officers and any other person appointed to perform any duty in connection with the receipt of nomination or withdrawal of candidatures, or the recording or counting of votes at an election; and the expression "official duty" shall for the purpose of this section be construed accordingly, but shall not include duties imposed otherwise than by or under this Act.

70. Removal of ballot papers from polling stations to be an offence.– (1) Any person who at any election fraudulently takes or attempts to take a ballot paper out of the polling station, or wilfully aids or abets the doing of any such act, shall be punishable with imprisonment for a term which may extend to one year or with fine which may extend to five hundred rupees, or with both.

(2) If the presiding officer of a polling station has reason to believe that any person is committing or has committed an offence punishable under sub-section (1) , such officer may before such person leaves the polling station arrest or direct a police officer to arrest such person and may search such person or cause him to be searched by a police officer.

Provided that when it is necessary to cause a woman to be searched, the search shall be made by another women with strict regard to decency.

(3) Any ballot paper found upon the person arrested on search shall be made over for safe custody to a police officer by the presiding officer or when the search is made by a police officer, shall be kept by such officer in safe custody.

71. Other offences and penalties therefore. – (1) No person at an election shall-

(a) fraudulently deface or fraudulently destroy any nomination paper; or

(b) fraudulently deface, destroy or remove any list, notice or other document affixed by or under the authority of a returning officer; or

(c) fraudulently deface or fraudulently destroy any ballot paper or the official mark on any ballot paper; or

(d) without due authority supply any ballot paper to any person or receive any ballot paper from any person or be in possession of any ballot paper; or

(e) fraudulently put into any ballot box anything other than the ballot paper which he is authorised by law to put in; or

(f) without due authority destroy, take, open or otherwise interfere with any ballot bo.. or ballot paper then in use for the purpose of the election; or

(g) fraudulently or without due authority, as the case may be, attempt to do any of the foregoing acts or wilfully aid or abet the doing of any such acts.

(2) Any person who contravenes the provisions of sub-section (1) shall –

(a) if he is a returning officer or an assistant returning officer or a presiding officer at a polling station or any other officer or clerk employed on official duty in connection with the election, be punishable with imprisonment for a term which may extend to two years or with fine, or with both:

(b) if he is any other person be punishable with imprisonment for a term which may extend to six months or with fine, or with both.

(3) For the purpose of this section, a person shall be deemed o be on official duty if his duty is to take part in the conduct of an election or part of an election including the counting of votes or to be responsible after an election for the used ballot papers and other documents in connection with such election , but the expression " official duty" shall not include any duty imposed otherwise than by or under this Act.

(4) An offence punishable under clause (b) of sub-section (2) shall be cognizable.

72. Cognizance of certain election offences. – No court shall take cognizance of any offence punishable under section 64 or under section 69 or under clause (a) of sub-section (2) of section 71 except on complaint in writing made by order of, or under authority from the Government.

REQUISITIONING OF PROPERTY FOR ELECTION PURPOSES

73. Requestioning of premises, vehicles etc, for election purpose.—

(1) If it appears to the Government , that in connection with an election under this Act—

(a) any premises other than residential building actually occupied are needed or likely to be needed for the purpose of being used as a polling station or for the storage of ballot boxes after a poll has been taken or

(b) any vehicle, vessel or animal is needed or is likely to be needed for the purpose of transport of ballot boxes to or from any polling station, or transport of members of the police force for maintaining order during the conduct of such election or transport of any officer or other person for performance of any duty in connection with such election, the Government may, by order in writing, requisition such premises, or such vehicle, vessel or animal, as the case may be and may make such further orders as may appear to them to be necessary or expedient in connection with the requisitioning.

Provided that no vehicle, vessel or animal which is being lawfully used by a candidate or his agent for any purpose connected with the election of such candidate shall be requisitioned under this sub-section until the completion of the poll at such election.

(2) The requisition shall be effected by an order in writing addressed to the person deemed by the Government to be the owner or person in possession of the property, and such order shall be served on the person to whom it is addressed.

(3) Whenever any property is requisitioned under sub-section (1) , the period of such requisition shall not extend beyond the period for which such property is required for any of the purposes mentioned in that sub-section.

(4) In this section-

(a) 'premises' means any land, building or part of a building and includes a hut, shed or other structure or any part thereof;

(b) 'vehicle' means any vehicle used or capable of being used for the purpose of road transport, whether propelled by mechanical power or otherwise.

74. Payment of amount. – (1) Whenever in pursuance of section 73, the Government requisition any premises, the persons interested, shall be paid by the Government, an amount which shall be determined by the Government by taking into consideration the following, namely;-

(i) the rent payable in respect of the premises or if no rent is so payable the rent payable for similar premises in the locality;

Provided that the rent payable in respect of the premises to which the provisions of the Tamil Nadu Buildings (Lease and Rent Control) Act, 1960 (Tamil Nadu Act 18 of 1960) apply shall be the fair rent payable for the premises under the Act.

(ii) If in consequence of the requisition of the premises, the person interested is compelled to change his residence or place of business, the reasonable expenses if any, incidental to such change:

Provided that where any person interested, being aggrieved by the amount so determined makes an application to the Government within one month from the date of service of the order determining the amount, for referring the matter to an arbitrator, the amount to be paid shall be such as the arbitrator appointed by the Government may determine:

Provided further that where there is any dispute as to the title to receive the amount or as to the apportionment of the amount it shall be referred by the Government to an arbitrator appointed in this behalf by the Government for determination and shall be determined in accordance with the decision of such arbitrator.

Explanation – In this sub-section, the expression " person interested" means the person who was in actual possession of the premises requisitioned under section 73 immediately before the requisition, or where no person was in such actual possession, the owner of such premises.

(2) Whenever in pursuance of section 73, the Government requisition any vehicle, vessel or animal, there shall be paid by the Government to the owner thereof an amount which shall be determined by the Government on the basis of the fares or rates prevailing in the locality for the hire of such vehicle, vessel or animal.

Provided that where the owner of such vehicle, vessel or animal being aggrieved by the amount so determined makes an application to the Government within one month from the date of service of the order determining the amount for referring the matter to an arbitrator, the amount to be paid shall be such sum as the arbitrator appointed in this behalf by the Government may determine:

Provided further that where immediately before the requisitioning, the vehicle or vessel was by virtue of a hire purchase agreement in the possession of a person other than the owner, the total amount determined under this sub-section payable in respect of the requisition shall be apportioned between that person and the owner in such manner as they may agree upon, and in default of agreement, in such manner as an arbitrator appointed by the Government in this behalf may decide.

75. Power to obtain information. – The Government may, with a view to requisitioning any property under section 73 or determining the amount payable under section 74, by order, require any person to furnish to such authority as may be specified in the order such information in his possession relating to such property as may be so specified.

76. Power of entry into and inspection of premises etc. – (1) Any person authorised in this behalf by the Government may enter into any premises and inspect such premises and any vehicle, vessel or animal therein for the purpose of determining whether and if so in what manner, an order under section 73 should be made in relation to such premises, vehicle, vessel or animal or with a view to securing compliance with any order made under that section.

(2) In this section, the expression "premises" and "vehicle" shall have the same meaning as in section 73.

77. Eviction from requisitioned premises. – (1) Any person remaining in possession of any requisitioned premises in contravention of any order made under section 73 may be summarily evicted from the premises by any officer empowered by the Government in this behalf.

(2) Any officer so empowered may, after giving to any woman not appearing in public, reasonable warning and facility to withdraw, remove or open any lock or bolt or break open any door of any building or do any other act necessary for effecting such eviction.

78. Release of premises from requisition. – (1) When any premises requisitioned under section 73 are to be released from requisition, the possession thereof shall be delivered to the person from whom possession was taken at the time when the premises were requisitioned, or if there were no such person to the person deemed by the Government to be the owner of such premises and such delivery of possession shall be a full discharge of the Government from all liabilities in respect of such delivery, but shall not prejudice any rights in respect of the premises which any other person may be entitled by due process of law to enforce against the person to whom possession the premises is so delivered.

79. Delegation of function of the Government with regard to requisitioning. – The Government may, by notification, direct that any power conferred or any duty imposed on the Government by any of the provisions of sections 73 to 78 shall, under such conditions, if any, as may be specified in the direction, be exercised or discharged by such officer or class of officers as may be so specified.

80. Penalty for contravention of any order of requestioning. – If any person contravenes any order made under section 73 or section 75, he shall be punishable with imprisonment for a term which may extend to one year or with fine, or with both.

MEMBERS

81. Rights of individual member. – (1) Any member may call the attention of the executive authority or the commissioner or the Secretary, as the case may be, to any neglect in the execution of panchayat work, to any waste of panchayat property or to the wants of any locality, and may suggest any improvement which may appear desirable.

(2) Every member shall have the right to move resolutions and to interpolate the president or chairman on matters connected with the administration of the panchayat, subject to such rules as may be prescribed.

(3) Every member shall have access during office hours to the records of the panchayat after giving due notice to the executive authority or commissioner or the Secretary, provided that the executive authority or commissioner or the Secretary may, for reasons recorded in writing, forbid such access.

82. No president, vice-president, chairman, vice-chairman or member to receive remuneration. – No president, vice-president chairman, vice-chairman or member shall receive, or be paid from the funds at the disposal of or under the control of the panchayat, [1]["any salary or other remuneration except travelling allowance, fixed monthly travelling allowance, daily allowance and sitting fees as may be fixed by the Government from time to time"] for services rendered by him whether in his capacity as such or in any other capacity.

CHAPTER-V
POWERS AND DUTIES OF THE EXECUTIVE AUTHORITY

83. Executive authority of village panchayat. – [2]["The Government may by notification, appoint any person, who shall, subject to such rules as may be prescribed, exercise the powers and perform the functions of the executive authority of a village panchayat:"]

84. Functions of executive authority. – The executive authority shall—

(a) carry into effect the resolutions of the village panchayat:

Provided that where the [3]["executive authority"] considers that a resolution has not been legally passed or is in excess of the powers conferred by this Act or that, if carried out, it is likely to endanger human life or health or the public safety, the executive authority shall refer the matter to the Government for orders and their decision shall be final;

(b) control all the officers and servants of the village panchayat

(c) discharge all the duties specifically imposed and exercise all the powers conferred on the executive authority and subject to all restrictions and conditions imposed. by or under this Act, exercise the executive power for the purpose of carrying out the provisions of this Act and be directly responsible for the due fulfillment of the purposes thereof.

THE COMMISSIONER

85. Commissioner. – (1) A commissioner shall be appointed by the Government in the case of each panchayat union council. Such commissioner shall ordinarily be the Development Officer appointed in pursuance of the National Extension Service Scheme to Community Development for the panchayat development block.

(2) No recovery shall be made from the panchayat union council towards the salary and allowances paid to any commissioner or towards his leave allowances. pension and provident fund.

(3) The Government shall have power to regulate the method of recruitment, conditions of service, pay and allowances and discipline and conduct of the commissioner appointed under sub-section (1)

(4) The commissioner shall-

---

[1] *Substituted by Act. 28/1998*
[2] *Substituted by Act. 21/1996*
[3] *Substituted by Act. 2/1999*

(a) have the right to attend the meetings of the panchayat union council or of any committee thereof and take part in the discussions thereat, but without the right to move any resolution or to vote;

(b) attend any meeting of the panchayat union council or of any committee thereof if required to do so by the chairman;

(c) carry into effect the resolutions of the panchayat union council;

(d) furnish to the panchayat union council such periodical reports regarding the progress made in carrying out the resolutions of that body and in the collection of taxes as the council may direct;

(e) control all the officers and servants of the panchayat union council;

(f) perform all the duties specifically imposed and exercise all the powers conferred on the commissioner by this Act and subject, whenever it is hereinafter expressly so provided, to the sanction of the panchayat union council and subject also to all other restrictions, limitations and conditions hereinafter imposed, exercise the executive power for the purpose of carrying out the provisions of this Act and be directly responsible for the fulfillment of the purposes of this Act.

(5) Notwithstanding anything contained in sub-section (2) of section 16 and subject to all other provisions of this Act and the rules made thereunder the panchayat union council shall have power to issue such specific directions as it may think fit regarding the performance by the commissioner of any of the functions assigned to him under this Act.

Provided that where such directions relate to any National Extension Service Scheme of Community Development or any other scheme specially entrusted by the Government to the panchayat union council, the directions issued by the council shall be in conformity with the terms and conditions of such entrustment.

(6) Subject to any directions given or restrictions imposed by the Government or the panchayat union council, the commissioner may, by an order in writing, delegate any of his functions to any officer or servant of the panchayat union council or to any servant of the Government. The exercise or discharge of any functions so delegate shall be subject to such restrictions, limitations and conditions as may be laid down by the commissioner and shall also be subject to his control and revision.

86. Emergency power of executive authority and Commissioner. – The executive authority or the commissioner may in cases of emergency direct the execution of any work or the doing of any act which requires the sanction of the village panchayat or the panchayat union council, as the case may be, and the immediate execution or doing of which is, in his opinion, necessary for the health or safety of the public and may direct that the expenses of executing such work or doing such act shall be paid from the Village panchayat Fund or the Panchayat Union Fund, as the case may be:

Provided that –

(a) he shall not act under this section in contravention of any order of the village panchayat or the panchayat union council prohibiting the execution of any particular work or the doing of any particular act, and

(b) he shall report the action taken under this section and the reasons therefor to the village panchayat or the panchayat union council at its next meeting

THE SECRETARY

87. Secretary. – (1) The Government shall appoint an officer not below the rank of [1]["Divisional Development Officer in the Tamil Nadu Panchayat Development Service"] as Secretary of the district panchayat.

(2) The Government shall have power to regulate the method of recruitment and conditions of service, pay and allowances and discipline and conduct of the Secretary appointed under sub-section(1).

88. Functions, powers and duties of Secretary. – (1) The Secretary shall –

(a) exercise all the powers specially imposed or conferred upon him by or under this Act or under any other law for the time being in force:

(b) supervise and control the execution of all works of the district panchayat, and have the right to attend meetings of the district panchayat or any committee thereof and take part in the discussions thereat, but without the right to move any resolution or to vote;

(c) attend any meeting of the district panchayat or any committee thereof if required to do so by the chairman;

(d) carryout the resolutions of the district panchayat;

(e) furnish to the district panchayat such periodical reports regarding the progress made in carrying out the resolutions of that body and in the collection of taxes as the council may direct;

(f) control the officers and servants of the district panchayat;

(g) exercise such other powers and discharge such other functions as may be prescribed.

(2) Notwithstanding anything contained in sub-section(1) , the district panchayat shall have power to issue such specific direction as it may think fit regarding the performance by the Secretary of any of the functions assigned to him under this Act.

(3) Subject to any directions given or restrictions imposed by the Government or the district panchayat, the Secretary may, by an order in writing, delegate any of his functions to any officer or servant of the district panchayat or to any servant of the Government. The exercise or discharge of any function so delegated shall be subject to such restrictions, limitations and conditions as may be laid down by the Secretary and shall also be subject to his control and revision.

---

[1] *Substituted by Act. 29/1998*

(4) The Secretary shall within fifteen days from the date of the meeting of the district panchayat or of any of its committee, submit to the Government every resolution of the district panchayat or any of its committee which in his opinion is inconsistent with provisions of this Act or other law and it shall not implement such resolution otherwise than as decided by the Government.

CHAPTER – VI

PROCEDURE

89. Presidency at meetings of panchayat. – (1) Every meeting of a panchayat shall be presided over by the president or the chairman, as the case may be, and in the absence of the president, chairman, vice-president , vice-chairman, by a member chosen by the members present at the meeting to preside for the occasion.

(2) The president or the chairman, as the case may be, shall preserve order and decide all points of order arising at or in connection with meetings. There shall be no discussion on any point of order and the decision of the president or chairman, as the case may be, on any point of order shall be final.

(3) A vice-president, a vice-chairman or member presiding for the occasion shall, for that meeting and during the period he presides over it, have all the powers of the president or chairman, as the case may be.

90. Meetings of panchayat. – Every panchayat shall meet at such times and places and shall, subject to the provisions of section 89, observe such rules of procedure in regard to transaction of business at its meetings (including the quorum at meetings) as may be prescribed:

Provided that no more than sixty days shall elapse between any two meetings of the panchayat.

91. Members when to abstain from taking part in discussion. – (1) No member shall vote on, or take part in the discussion of, any question coming up for consideration at a meeting of the panchayat or any committee if the question is one in which, apart from its general application to the public he has any direct or indirect pecuniary interest by himself or his partner.

(2) The president or chairman, as the case may be, may prohibit any member from voting or taking part in the discussion of any matter in which he believes such member to take such interest, or he may require such member to absent himself during the discussion.

(3) Such member may challenge the decision of the president or chairman, who shall thereupon put the question to the meeting. The decision of the meeting shall be final.

(4) If the president or chairman is believed by any member present at the meeting to have any such pecuniary interest in any matter under discussion, he may, if a motion to that effect is carried, be required to absent himself from the meeting during such discussion.

(5) The member concerned shall not be entitled to vote on the question referred to in sub-section (3) and the president or chairman concerned shall not be entitled to vote on the motion referred to in sub-section (4)

Explanation – The terms "president" and "chairman" in this section include a vice-president, vice-chairman or member presiding for the occasion.

92. Minutes of Proceeding. – A copy of the minutes of the proceedings of every meeting of a panchayat as well as of all minutes of dissent in respect of such proceedings received from any member present at the meeting, within forty eight hours of the close thereof, shall be submitted by the president or chairman, as the case may be, within three days of the date to the meeting to the Inspector:

Provided that the Inspector may direct that such minutes shall be submitted either generally or in any specified classes of cases to any officer empowered by him in this behalf.

93. Power of panchayat to call for records. – A panchayat may require the executive authority or the commissioner or the Secretary as the case may be, to produce any document which is in his custody and he shall, subject to such rules as may be prescribed comply with every such requisition.

94. Proceedings of panchayat and committees. – (1) The proceedings of every panchayat, and of all committees thereof shall be governed by such rules as may be prescribed and by regulations, not inconsistent with such rules or the provisions of this Act, made by the panchayat with the approval of the Inspector.

(2) The Inspector may remit for reconsideration and re-submission any regulation or part thereof to the panchayat

Provided that it shall be competent for the Inspector to add to, omit or alter any regulation which contravenes the provisions of this Act or the rules made there under.

95. Appointment of joint committee. – (1) A panchayat may, and if so required by the Inspector, shall, join with one, or more than one, other local authority in constituting a joint committee for any purpose for which they are jointly responsible.

(2) The constitution, powers and procedure of a joint committee and the method of settling differences of opinion arising in connection with the committee between the local authorities concerned shall be in accordance with such rules as may be prescribed.

96. Committees. – (1) (a) There shall be an Appointments Committee for every panchayat union, which shall be composed of the chairman of the panchayat union council, the commissioner and one member elected annually by the panchayat union council. The chairman of the panchayat union council shall be the chairman of the committee. Subject to the provisions of section 102 and to such rules as may be made by the Government in this behalf, appointments to all posts under the panchayat union council, the pay of which is debitable to the funds of the panchayat union council shall be made with the prior approval of the committee.

(b) (i) There shall be an Agricultural Production Committee for every panchayat union, which shall be composed of the chairman of the panchayat union council who shall be the chairman of that committee, the commissioner and three persons nominated by the panchayat union council.

(ii) No person shall be nominated under sub-clause (i), if

(A) he is not a member of the panchayat union council; or

(B) in the opinion of the panchayat union council, he does not possess adequate knowledge of and experience in, agriculture.

(c) There shall be an Education Committee and a General Purposes Committee in every panchayat union. The panchayat union council may, and if so required by the Government, shall appoint such other committees as may be necessary for the efficient performance of its duties and functions under this Act. Each of the committee constituted under this clause shall consist of such number of members as may be specified by the council and shall include the chairman ex-officio. The members of each committee constituted under this clause, other than the chairman, shall be elected by the panchayat union council from among its elected members.

(2) Subject to such rules, as may be made by the Government in this behalf, the panchayat union council shall have power, by regulations made from time to time, to determine the powers and duties of every committee constituted under sub-section(1).

97. Standing committees. – (1) (a) For the purpose of assisting the district panchayat in exercising such of its powers, discharging such of its duties and performing such of its functions specified under this Act, a district panchayat may constitute standing committees for dealing with –

(i) food and agriculture; (ii) industries and labour; (iii) public works; (iv) education; (v) health and welfare including prohibition;

(b) a district panchayat may constitute additional standing committees for such purposes as it thinks fit.

(2) Each standing committee shall consist of such number of persons not exceeding five including the chairman as specified by the district panchayat and elected by the district panchayat from among its elected members.

(3) The chairman of the district panchayat shall be the ex-officio member in all the standing committees constituted by the district panchayat

(4) Each standing committee shall elect its own chairman from among its members who are elected members of the district panchayat

(5) No member of the district panchayat shall be eligible to serve on more than two standing committees.

(6) The Secretary shall nominate one of the officers under his control as ex-officio secretary for each of the standing committees. The Secretary shall be entitled to attend the meetings of all the standing committees.

ADMINISTRATION REPORTS

98. Administration reports of village panchayat. – (1) Every village panchayat shall submit to the panchayat union council a report on its administration for each year as soon as may be after the close of such year and not later than the prescribed date, in such form, with such details and through such authority as may be prescribed.

(2) The report shall be prepared by the executive authority and the village panchayat shall consider it and forward the same to the panchayat union council with its resolution thereon.

99. Administration report of Panchayat Unioin Councils and district panchayats. – (1) Every panchayat union council shall submit to the district panchayat a consolidated report on its administration and on the administration of all village panchayats in the panchayat union for each year as soon as may be after the close of such year and not later than the prescribed date, in such form, with such details and through such authority as may be prescribed.

(2) The report shall be prepared by the commissioner and the panchayat union council shall consider it and forward the same to the district panchayat with its resolution thereon.

(3) The district panchayat shall prepare a general report on the administration of panchayat union councils and village panchayats in the district and submit the same to the Government before such date as may be prescribed. The district panchayat shall also send a copy of the report to the Inspector.

(4) The report and resolution thereon shall be published in such manner as the Government may direct.

100. Acts of village panchayat, Panchayat Union Council and district panchayat, etc. not to be invalidated by infirmity vacancy etc. – No act of a village panchayat or of a panchayat union council or of a district panchayat or of a committee thereof or of any person acting as president, vice-president, chairman, vice-chairman or member of such village panchayat or panchayat union council or district panchayat or committee, shall be deemed to be invalid by reason only of a defect in the establishment of such panchayat or committee, as the case may be, or on the ground that the president, vice-president, chairman, vice-chairman or member of such village panchayat or panchayat union council or district panchayat or chairman or member of a committee was not entitled to hold or continue in such office by reason of any disqualification or by reason of any irregularity or illegality in his election or by reason of such act having been done during the period of any vacancy in the office of president, vice-president, chairman, vice-chairman or member of such village panchayat, panchayat union council or district panchayat or committee.

CHAPTER VII

ESTABLISHMENT, POWERS AND FUNCTIONS OF PANCHAYATS

101. Establishment of panchayat. – (1) The sanction of the panchayat shall be obtained for all proposals for fixing or altering the number, designations and grades of its officers and servants and the salaries, fees and allowances payable to them.

(2) Such proposals shall be taken into consideration by the panchayat, only at the instance of the executive authority or the commissioner or the Secretary, as the case may be, and the panchayat may sanction the proposal with or without modifications.

Provided that no proposal adversely affecting any officer or servant of a panchayat who has been in the permanent service of such panchayat for more than five years and is drawing a salary of not less than five hundred rupees per mensem shall be considered except at a special meeting convened for the purpose and no such proposal shall be given effect to unless assented to by atleast one-half of the members then in the panchayat.

(3) Notwithstanding anything contained in sub-sections (1) and (2), the Government in the case of panchayat union councils and district panchayats and the Inspector in the case of village panchayats shall have power to fix or alter the number, designations and grades of, and the salaries, fees and allowances payable to the officers and servants of any village panchayat or panchayat union council or the district panchayat or any class of such officers and servants and it shall not be open to the village panchayat or panchayat union council or the district panchayat to vary the number, designations, grades, salaries, fees or allowances as so fixed or altered except with the previous sanction of the Government in the case of panchayat union councils and district panchayats and of the Inspector in the case of village panchayats.

[1][“Provided that the Inspector shall observe any guidelines issued by the Government in this regard”].

102. Conditions of service of officers and servants of panchayats. –

(1) The Government shall have power to make rules regarding the authorities who may appoint the officers and servants of panchayats, other than the commissioners and the secretaries and the classification, method of recruitment, pay and allowances, discipline and conduct and conditions of service of such officers and servants.

Such rule may provide for the constitution of any class of officers or servants of village panchayats, panchayat union councils and the

---

[1] *Added by Act. 28/1998*

district panchayats, as the case may be, other than the commissioners and the Secretaries, into a separate service for the whole or any part of the State.

(2) Subject to the provisions of this Act and any rules which the Government may make in this behalf, the panchayat union council or the district panchayat, as the case may be, may frame regulations in respect of the officers and servants on the staff of the panchayat union council or the district panchayat—

(a) fixing the amount and nature of the security to be furnished

(b) prescribing educational and other qualifications;

(c) regulating the grant of leave, leave allowances acting allowances and travelling allowances;

(d) regulating the grant of pensions and gratuities;

(e) establishing and maintaining provident funds and making contributions thereto compulsory;

(f) regulating conduct; and

(g) generally prescribing conditions of service:

Provided—

(i) that the grant of any leave, leave allowances, pension or gratuity provided for in such regulations shall in no case, without the special sanction of the Government exceed what would be admissible in the case of Government servants of similar standing and status;

(ii) that the conditions under which such allowances are granted or any leave, superannuation or retirement is sanctioned shall not without similar sanction, be more favourable than those for the time being prescribed for such Government servants.

(3) A role may be made under sub-section (1) in so far as it relates to officers and servants of village panchayats and panchayat union councils, so as to have retrospective effect on and from a date not earlier than the date of commencement of this Act.

103. Appointment of common officers. – Two or more village panchayats or two or more panchayat union councils may, subject to such rules as may be prescribed, and shall if so required by any authority empowered in this behalf by rules, appoint the same officer or servant to exercise or discharge any powers or duties of a similar nature for both or all of them.

104. Transfer of officers and servants of village panchayats and Panchayat Union Councils. – (1) Any officer or servant of a village panchayat may be transferred to the service of any panchayat union council or any other village panchayat by the Inspector:

Provided that no officer or servant shall be so transferred except after consulting the commissioner or the executive authority concerned:

Provided further that in making a transfer under this sub-section, the Inspector may issue such general or special directions as may in his opinion be necessary for the purpose of giving due effect to such transfer.

(2) Notwithstanding anything contained in this Act or the Tamil Nadu District Municipalities Act.1920, any officer or servant of a panchayat union council (including the commissioner) may be transferred by the Government to the services of any other panchayat union council or any municipality constituted under the Tamil Nadu District Municipalities Act. 1920: (TN.Act.V of 1920).

Provided that no officer or servant (other than the commissioner) shall be so transferred except after consulting the panchayat union councils or municipal councils concerned:

Provided further that the Government while making a transfer under this sub-section may issue such general or special directions as may in their opinion be necessary for the purpose of giving due effect to such transfer.

105. Power of Government to tranfer of officers and servants of district panchayat. – (1) Notwithstanding anything contained in this Act or in the Tamil Nadu District Municipalities Act, 1920, (Tamil Nadu Act V of 1920), the Government shall have power. –

(a) to transfer any officer or servant of the district panchayat (including the Secretary) to the service of any other district panchayat or to any municipality constituted under the Tamil Nadu District Municipalities Act, 1920

(b) to issue general or special direction as they may think necessary for the purpose of giving due effect to any transfer made under clause (a)

106. Power to punish officers and servants. – Subject to such control as may be prescribed, the executive authority, the commissioner or the Secretary may censure, fine, withhold increments or promotion from, or reduce to a lower rank in the seniority list, or to a lower post or time-scale or to a lower stage in a time-scale, suspend, remove or dismiss any officer or servant in the service of village panchayat or panchayat union or the district panchayat, as the case may be, for any breach of departmental rules or discipline, or for carelessness, unfitness, neglect of duty or other misconduct.

107. Applicability of certain directions to public health establishment. – Subject to the provisions of section 109, the provisions of sections 101 to 106 shall also apply to the public health establishments of panchayats, notwithstanding anything contained in the Tamil Nadu Public Health Act, 1939.

108. Teachers including headmaster and basic servants in the panchayat union schools to be Government servants. – (1) Notwithstanding anything contained in this Act or in any other law for the time being in force, on and from the 1st June 1981, all teachers (including headmasters) and basic servants in the panchayat union schools in the State of Tamil Nadu shall become whole-time Government servants.

(2) Notwithstanding anything contained in sub-section(1) of section 96 or in any other provisions of this Act and subject to the provisions of Article 311 of the Constitution, the Government may make rules regulating the conditions of service of the teachers (including headmasters) and basic servants in the panchayat union schools.

109. Health Assistants, Auxillary Nurses, Mid-wives and Maternity Assistants in Public Health Establishments of Panchayat Union Councils to be Government servants. – (1) Notwithstanding anything contained in this Act or in any other law for the time being in force, on and from the 1st October 1982, all health assistants, auxiliary nurses, mid-wives and maternity assistants in the public health establishments of panchayat union councils, in the State shall become whole-time Government servants.

(2) Notwithstanding anything contained in sub-section(1) of section 96 or in any other provisions of this Act and subject to the provisions of Article 311 of the Constitution, the Government may make rules regulating the conditions, of service of the health assistants, the auxiliary nurses, mid-wives and maternity assistants in the public health establishments of panchayat union councils.

CHAPTER VIII

FUNCTIONS, POWERS AND PROPERTY OF VILLAGE PANCHAYATS, PANCHAYAT UNION COUNCILS AND DISTRICT PANCHAYATS

110. Duty of village panchayat to provide for certain matters. – Subject to provisions of this Act and the rules made thereunder, it shall be the duty of village panchayat, within the limits of its funds, to make reasonable provision for carrying out the requirements of the panchayat village in respect of the following matters, namely:

(a) the construction, repair and maintenance of all village roads, that is to say, all public roads in the village (other than those classified as National Highways, State Highways, major district roads and panchayat union roads) and of all bridges, culverts, road-dams and causeways on such roads:

[1]"[(aa) The extension of village sites and the regulation of building;"]

(b) the lighting of public roads and public places in built-up areas;

(c) the construction of drains and the disposal of drainage water and sullage not including sewage;

(d) the cleaning of streets, the removal of rubbish heaps, jungle growth and pricklypear, the filling in of disused wells, insanitary

---

[1] *Inserted by Act. 37/1997*

ponds, pools, ditches pits or hollows and other improvement of the sanitary condition of the village:

(e) the provision of public latrines and arrangements to cleanse latrines whether public or private;

(f) the opening and maintenance of burial and burning grounds:

(g) the sinking and repairing of wells, the excavation, repair and maintenance of ponds or tanks and the construction and maintenance of water-works [1][“for the supply of water for drinking, washing”] and bathing purposes; and

(h) such other duties as the Government may, by notification, impose

111. Power of village panchayat to provide for certain other matters. – Subject to the provisions of this Act and the rules made thereunder a village panchayat may also make such provisions as it thinks fit for carrying out the requirements of the village in respect of the following matters, namely:-

(a) the planting and preservation of trees on the sides of all public roads in the village subject to mutually agreed terms and conditions between the village panchayat and the authority which maintains the road in case the road is not maintained by the village panchayat itself

(b) the lighting of public roads and public places in areas other than built-up areas;

(c) the opening and maintenance of public markets other than markets which are classified as panchayat union markets;

(d) the control of fairs and festivals other than those classified as panchayat union fairs and festivals;

(e) the opening and maintenance of public landing places, halting places and cart-stands and of public cattle-sheds;

(f) the opening and maintenance of public slaughter-houses;

(g) the opening and maintenance of reading rooms;

(h) the establishment and maintenance of wireless receiving sets [2][“television sets”] playgrounds, parks, sports clubs and centres of physical culture;

(i) the opening and maintenance of literacy centres and centres for imparting social education; and

(j) the construction of works of public utility and the provisions of other facilities for the safety, health, convenience, culture or recreation of the inhabitants of the village;

[3][**] – omitted

112. Duty of Panchayat Union Council to provide for certain matters. – Subject to the provisions of this Act and the rules made thereunder, it shall be the duty of a panchayat union council, within the

---

[1] *Substituted by Act. 28/1998*

[2] *Inserted by Act. 29/1999*

[3] *Existing proviso was omitted by Act. 29/1999*

limits of its funds, to make reasonable provision for carrying out the requirements of the panchayat union in respect of the following matters, namely;-

(a) the construction, repair and maintenance of all public roads in the panchayat union which are classified as panchayat union roads and of all bridges, culverts, road dams and cause ways on such roads;

[1] "(aa` the construction of water works for the supply of water for drinking , washing and bathing purpose",

[2] ["(aaa) the construction and maintenance of comprehensive water supply schemes for the supply of protected drinking water covering one or more village panchayats as may be notified by the Government"]

(b) the establishment and maintenance of dispensaries and the payments of subsidies to rural medical practitioners:

(c) the establishment and maintenance of maternity and child welfare centres, including the maintenance of a that service and offering advice and assistance to mothers in family planning;

(d) The construction and maintenance of poor houses, orphanages, shops, stalls, plinths, the training and employment of vaccinators, the removal of congestion of population and the provision of house-sites;

(e) the opening and maintenance and expansion or improvement of elementary schools, including the payment or grants to private managements in respect of elementary schools;

(f) preventive and remedial measures connected with any epidemic or with malaria;

(g) the control of fairs and festivals classified by the panchayat union council as those reserved for control by it;

(h) veterinary relief;

(i) [3][***]

(j) opening and maintenance of public markets which are classified as Panchayat Union Market

(k) the maintenance of statistics relating to births and deaths;

(l) the establishment and maintenance of choultries;

(m) improvements of agriculture, agricultural stock and the holding of agricultural shows;

(n) the promotion and encouragement of cottage industries: and

(o) such other duties as the Government may, by notification, impose.

113. Entrustment of execution of National Extension Service Scheme of Community Development to Panchayat Union Councils. – The Government shall as soon as may be after the constitution of a panchayat union council for a panchayat development block under this Act entrust to the panchayat union council subject to such conditions and restrictions as may be specified by the Government, the execution in the panchayat development block of the National Extension Service

---

[1] *Inserted by Act. 28/1998*
[2] *Inserted by Act. 29/1998*
[3] *Omitted by Act. 37/1997*

scheme of Community Development, including in particular, all measures relating to the development of agriculture, animal husbandry and village industries organised on an individual or co-operative basis.

114. Entrustment of certain schemes to panchayat union councils. –

(1) Save as otherwise provided in section 113, the Government may, subject to such conditions and restrictions as may be specified, entrust all or any of the schemes, programmes and activities for economic development, whether such schemes, programmes and activities are to be executed as implemented either by the Government or by any statutory body or other agency to the panchayat union council for its execution or implementation.

(2) The panchayat union council may, if so notified by the Government, review the schemes, programmes and other activities executed by the Government or by any statutory body or other agency within the panchayat union.

115. Power of panchayat union council to provide for certain other matters. – Subject to the provisions of this Act and the rules made thereunder, a panchayat union council may, within the limits of its funds, make such provisions as it thinks fit for carrying out the requirements of the panchayat union in respect of measure of public utility other than those specified in section 112, calculated to promote the safety, health, comfort or convenience of the inhabitants of the panchayat union:

[1][Proviso] – omitted

116. Common burian and burning grounds, etc. – Subject to the provisions of this Act and the rules made thereunder, two or more village panchayats:

(i) may construct and maintain water-works for supply of water for washing [2][for supply of water for drinking, washing] and bathing purposes from a common source and may also provide a common burial and burning ground, and

(ii) may entrust to the panchayat union council with its consent and on such terms as may be agreed upon , the management of any institution or the execution or maintenance of any work.

117. Lighting of public roads and public places. – Notwithstanding anything contained in clause (b) of section 111, the Government may, by general or special order, direct any village panchayat or panchayat union council [3][“or district panchayat”] to provide for the lighting of public roads and public places within its jurisdiction and it shall be the

---

[1] *Omitted by Act. 29/1999*
[2] *Substituted by Act. 29/1999*
[3] *Substitued by Act. 29/1999*

duty of the village panchayat or panchayat union council [1]["or district panchayat"] to provide for such light:

Provided that where such a direction is given, the Government shall make such provision for the cost of lighting as they may consider reasonable and the decision of the Government shall be final.

118. Maintenance of common dispensaries, child welfare centers. – Subject to the provisions of this Act and the rules made thereunder, two or more panchayat union councils may establish and maintain common dispensaries, child welfare centres, and institutions of such other kind as may be prescribed.

119. Transfer of immovable property, management of institutions, execution or maintenance of works, etc, to a village panchayat. – (1) The panchayat union council may, subject to such control as may be prescribed, by notification declare that any immovable property vested in itself shall vest in any village panchayat in the same panchayat union and such property shall, from the date specified in the said notification, vest accordingly.

(2) Subject to such rules as may be prescribed, [2]["the Government, Director of Rural Development or any other Head of Department or the Collector,"] the district panchayat, the panchayat union council or the Secretary, the commissioner, or any person or body of persons, may transfer to the village panchayat, with its consent and subject to such conditions as may be agreed upon, the management of any institution, or the execution or maintenance of any work, or the exercise of any power or the discharge of any duty, whether within or without the village and whether provided for in this Act or not.

120. Transfer to village panchayat of unreserved forests. – (1) (a) All unreserved forests in the village at the commencement of this Act shall vest in the village panchayat and be administered by it for the benefit of such village.

(b) In respect of every forest so vested, the village panchayat shall , if so required by the Collector, pay to the Government such rent as the Collector may, from time to time, subject to the control of the Commissioner of Land Administration, fix in this behalf.

(2) (a) If the Revenue Divisional Officer is of opinion that a village panchayat is not administering properly a forest vested in it under sub-section (1), he may be order, withdraw such forest from the control of the village panchayat for such period as may be specified in the order,not exceeding the period if any, prescribed in this behalf . He may in respect of such forest direct that it be vested in the panchayat union council and be administered by it.

---

1 *Substitued by Act. 29/1999*

2. *Substituted by Act, 29/1999.*

(b) The Revenue Divisional Officer may, from time to time, by order, extend the period specified in any order issued under clause (a) subject to the period prescribed in this behalf.

(c) Before issuing an order under clause (a) or (b) a reasonable opportunity shall be given to the village panchayat to show cause against such issue.

(d) When an order is issued under clause (a) or (b) , the village panchayat concerned may, within three months of the service of the order, appeal against it to the Collector and the Collector may confirm, modify or reverse the order.

(3) The Commissioner of Land Administration may, at any time, either suo moto or on application, call for and examine the record of any order issued by the Revenue Divisional Officer or the Collector under sub-section (2) for the purpose of satisfying himself as to the legality or propriety of such order, and may pass such order in reference thereto as he thinks fit.

121. Power of Government to resume possession of unreserved forest vested in village panchayat and payment of compensaion etc. – (1) If in the opinion of the Government any unreserved forest vested in a village panchayat under section 120 is required for any public purpose, they may, by notification, resume the possession and administration of such unreserved forest and upon such resumption by the Government, all rights and interest created in or over such unreserved forest before such resumption shall as against the Government cease and determine.

(2) Whenever the possession and administration of such unreserved forest is resumed by the Government under sub-section (1) , there shall be paid to the village panchayat concerned compensation for any improvement made by such village panchayat in such unreserved forest, as determined in the manner hereinafter provided by the Collector within whose jurisdiction such unreserved forest is situated.

Explanation – For the purposes of this sub-section, 'improvement' means any work or product of a work which adds to the value of the unreserved forest or is suitable to it and consistent with the purpose for which it was vested in the village panchayat and shall include the following works or the products of such works—

(a) the erection of buildings or any other structure, the construction of tanks, wells, channels, dams and other works for the storage or supply of water for agricultural or domestic purposes:

(b) the preparation of land for irrigation;

(c) the reclamation, clearance, enclosure or permanent improvement of land for agricultural purposes:

(d) the renewal or reconstruction of any of the foregoing works or alterations therein or addition thereto:

(e) the planting or protection and maintenance of fruit trees, timber-trees and other useful trees and plants.

(3) The compensation payable in respect of the improvement referred to in clauses (a) to (d) of the Explanation to sub-section (2) shall be the actual value of such improvements as on the date of resumption of the unreserved forest by the Government which shall include actual cot of the labour, supervision thereof, and of the materials, together with other expenditure,if any, which would be required to make such improvements, less a reasonable deduction on account of the deterioration, if any, which may have taken place from age or other cause. The compensation payable inrespect of improvement referred to in clause (c) of the Explanation to sub section (2) shall be such sum which the trees or plants might reasonably be expected to realise if sold by public auction to be cut and carried away at the time of resumption of the unreserved forest by the Government:

Provided that in computing the actual value of such improvements the value of the unreserved forest to which such improvements have been made shall not be taken into account:

Provided further that if any grant for the purpose of making such improvements has been paid by the Government to the village panchayat concerned then, the amount of such grant paid shall be deducted from the amount of compensation payable in respect of such improvements;

Provided also that in the case of trees and plans in the unreserved forest which are of spontaneous growth, the compensation payable in respect of such trees and plants shall be the proper cost of protection and maintenance of such trees and plants.

(4) The amount of compensation referred to in sub-section(2) shall be given to every village panchayat, at its option-

(a) in cash in such annual instalments with interest at such rates as may be prescribed or

(b) in saleable or otherwise transferable promissory notes or other securities or stock certificates of the Government, or

(c) partly in cash or partly in such securities specified in clause (b), as may be required by the village panchayats.

(5) The option of the village panchayat referred to in sub-section (4) shall be exercised by such village panchayat before the expiry of a period of three months from the date of resumption of the possession and administration of he unreserved forest by the Government and the option so exercised shall be final and shall not be altered or rescinded after it has been exercised. Any village panchayat which omits or fails to exercise the option referred to in sub-section (4) within the time specified above shall be deemed to have opted for payment in securities and stock certificates referred to inclause (b) of sub-section (4). The amount of compensation payable in instalments shall be paid, and the securities and stock certificates referred to in clause (b) of sub-section (4) shall be issued, within sixty days from the date of receipt by the Government of the option referred to above or where no such option has been exercised from the date before which such option ought to have been exercised.

(6) Any village panchayat aggrieved by an order relating to compensation under this section may appeal to the Commissioner of Land Administration within such period and in such manner as may be prescribed. The order of the Commissioner of Land Administration on such appeal and where no appeal is preferred, the order which has not been appealed against, shall be final and shall not be called in question in any court of law.

122. Power of Commissioner of Land Administration to transfer or resume control of endowments and imams. – (1) (a) Subject to the control of the Government, the Commissioner of Land Administration may, by notification, make over to a panchayat union council, with its consent, the management and superintendence of any charitable endowment in respect of which powers and duties attached to the Commissioner of Land Administration under the provisions of the Tamil Nadu Endowments and Estates Regulation, 1817; (Tamil Nadu Regulation VII of 1817) and thereupon all powers and duties attached to the Commissioner of Land Administration in respect thereof shall attach to the panchayat union council as if it had been specially named in the said Regulation, and the panchayat union council shall manage and superintend such endowment.

(b) The Commissioner of Land Administration may, of his own motion and shall on a direction from the Government , by notification resume the management and superintendence of any endowment made over to a panchayat union council under clause (a) and duties attached to the panchayat union council in respect of the endowment shall cease and determine.

(2) The Government may assign to a panchayat union council with its consent, a charitable inam, resumed by the Government or any other authority, providcd that the net income from such inam can be applied exclusively to any purpose to which the funds of such panchayat union council may be applied; and may revoke any assignment so made.

(3) The management and superintendence of any charitable endowment which immediately before the constitution of a panchayat union council for any panchayat development block under this Act was vested in a district board under the Tamil Nadu District Boards Act, 1920 (Tamil Nadu Act XIV of 1920) shall, on such constitution, vest in the panchayat union council exercising jurisdiction over the place where the endowment is situated.

123. Government's power to add to function of Panchayat Union Councils. – Subject to such rules as may be prescribed, [1]["the Government, the Director of Rural Development or any other Head of Department or the Collector"] or any person or body of persons may transfer to the panchayat union council with its consent and on such terms as may be agreed upon, the management of any institution or the

[1] *Substituted by Act. 29/1999*

execution or maintenance of any work, or the exercise of any power or the discharge of any duty whether within or without the panchayat union and whether provided for in this Act or not.

124. Limitation of power to accept donations and trusts. – A panchayat may accept donations for, or trusts relating exclusively to, the furtherance of any purpose to which its funds may be applied.

125. Vesting of public roads in village panchayat. – (1) All public roads in any village (other than roads which are classified by the Government as National Highways or State highways or a s major district roads or as panchayat union roads) shall vest in the village panchayat together with all pavements, stones, and other materials thereof, all works, materials and other things provided therefor, all drains, drainage works, tunnel and culverts whether made at the cost of the village panchayat or otherwise, in, alongside or under such roads, and all works, materials and things appertaining thereto.

(2) The Government may, by notification, exclude from the operation of this Act any such public road, drain, drainage work, tunnel or culvert and may also modify or cancel such notification.

126. Vesting of public roads in Panchayat Union Councils. – (1) All public roads in any panchayat union which are classified as panchayat union roads shall vest in the panchayat union council together with all pavements, stones and other materials, thereof, all works, materials and other things provided therefore, all drains, drainage works, tunnels and culverts, whether made at the cost of the panchayat union council or otherwise, in, alongside or under such roads, and all works, materials, and things appertaining thereto.

(2) The Government may, by notification, exclude from the operation of this Act any panchayat union road, drain, drainage work, tunnel or culvert and may also modify or cancel such notification.

127. Duty of village panchayat in respect of public roads excluded from the operation of the Act. – Where any public road has been excluded from the operation of this Act under sub-section (2) of section 125 or sub-section (2) of section 126 and placed under the control of the Highways Department of Government (hereinafter referred to as the Highways Department), the village panchayat may and if so required by the Government shall make provision—

(a) for the watering and maintenance of the drainage of such road;

(b) for the provision, maintenance and repair of the drains in, alongside or under such road;

(c) for the provision, maintenance and repair of foot-ways attached to such road;

Provided that where in carrying out of the above provisions it is necessary for the village panchayat to open and break up the soil or pavement of any such road, the village panchayat shall obtain the previous consent of such officer of the Highways Department as the Government may, by general or special order, specify;

Provided further that in cases of emergency the village panchayat may, without such consent, open and break up the soil or pavement of any such street, but shall, as far as practicable restore such soil or pavement to the condition in which it was immediately before it was opened and broken up; and a report of the action so taken and the reasons therefor shall be sent forthwith to the officer specified under the foregoing proviso:

Provided also that where the execution of any work is required by the Government, the Government shall make provision for the cost thereof.

128. Precautions in case of dangerous structures. – (1) If any structure adjoining a public road vested in a panchayat union council or a village panchayat appears to the commissioner or the executive authority, as the case may be, to be in a ruinous state and dangerous to the passers by, the commissioner or executive authority may, by notice require the owner of the said tree to secure, lop or cut down the said tree to as to present any danger here from.

(2) If immediate action is necessary, the commissioner or executive authority shall himself, before giving such notice or before the period of such notice expires, fence off, take down, secure or repair such structure or fence off a part of any road or take such temporary measures as he may think fit to prevent danger, and the cost of doing so shall be recoverable from the owner or occupier in the manner hereinafter provided.

129. Precautions in case of dangerous trees. – (1) If any tree or any branch of a tree standing on land adjoining a pubic road vested in a panchayat union council or village panchayat appears to the commissioner or executive authority to be likely to fall and thereby endanger any person using, or any structure on such road, the commissioner or executive authority may, by notice, require the owner of the said tree to secure, lop or cut down the said tree so as to prevent any danger therefrom.

(2) If immediate action is necessary, the commissioner or executive authority shall himself, before giving such notice or before the period of such notice expires, secure, lop or cut down the said tree or fence off a part of the public road or take such other temporary measures as he thinks fit to prevent danger and the cost of so doing shall be recoverable from the owner of the tree in the manner hereinafter provided.

130. Fencing of building or lands and pruning of hedges and tress against. – Where a public road is vested in a panchayat union council or village panchayat, the commissioner or executive authority may, by public notice, require the owner or occupier of any building or land near such road to-

(a) fence the same to the satisfaction of the commissioner or executive authority;

(b) trim or prune any hedges bordering on such road so that they may not exceed such height from the level of the adjoining roadway as the commissioner or executive authority may determine; or

(c) cut and trim any hedges or trees overhanging such road and obstructing it or the view of traffic or causing it damage; or

(d) lower an enclosing wall or fence which, by reasons of its height and situation, obstructs the view of traffic so as to cause danger.

131. Prohibition obstructions in or over public roads, etc. – (1) No person shall, except as permitted by rules made under this Act and except in accordance with the conditions imposed by any licence made requisite by such rules-

(a) build any wall or erect any fence or other obstruction or projection or make any encroachment whatsoever, whether permanent or temporary, [1][“in or over any public road or any property vested in or belonging to or regulated or owned by, a village panchayat or panchayat union council”];

(b) make any hole or deposit any matter [2][“in or upon any public road or any property vested in or belonging to or regulated or owned by, a village panchayat or panchayat union council”];

(c) work a quarry in or remove stone, earth or other material from any place within twenty metres of a public road or of other immovable property vesting in or belonging to a village panchayat or a panchayat union council, provided that nothing in this clause shall be deemed to apply to any work which, in the opinion of the Inspector, is done in connection with a bona fide agricultural operation;

(d) erect any building over any drain or any part thereof;

(e) plant any tree on any public road of other property vesting in or belonging to a village panchayat or a panchayat union council; or

(f) fell, remove, destroy, lop or strip bark, leaves, or fruits from or otherwise damage, any tree which is growing on any such public road or other property or on any poramboke land, the use of which is regulated by a village panchayat under section 134 or section 135 and the right to which has not been established by such person as vesting in or belonging to him.

(2) It shall be the duty of the Village Administrative Officer of every revenue village to report on encroachments on properties vested in village panchayats or panchayat union councils to the executive authority or the commissioner concerned and to the officer of the Revenue Department, and [3][“it shall be the duty of the executive authority or the commissioner concerned either suo moto or on

---

[1&2] *Substituted by Act. 29/1999*

[3] *Substituted by Act. 29/1999*

obtaining a report from the Village Administrative Officer in this regard"] to institute proceedings under this Act and secure the removal of the encroachments within such time as may be specified by the Government by general or special order. If the removal of the encroachments has not been secured within the period specified in such order, the officers of the Revenue Department shall institute proceedings under the Tamil Nadu Land Encroachment Act, 1905 (Tamil Nadu Act III of 1905) and secure such removal.

[1]["**131-A. Prohibition of erection of certain hoardings.**— Notwithstanding anything contained in this Act or in any other law for the time being in force.—

(a)(i) or of after the date of the commencement of the Tamil Nadu Panchayats (Third Amendment) Act, 2000 (hereafter in this section referred to as the amendment Act), no person shall erect any hoarding (other than traffic sign and road sign) visible to the traffic on the road and which is harzardous and disturbance to safe traffic movement so as to adversely affect free and safe or traffic;

(ii) where any hoarding is ereced in contravention of sub-clause (i), it shall be confiscated and removed by the executive authority without any notice;

(b)(i) where any hoarding (other than traffic sign and road sign) visible to the traffic on the road is hazardous and disturbance to safe traffic movement so as to adversely affect free and safe flow of traffic and which is in existence immediately before the date of the commencement of the amendment Act, the executive authority shall, by notice in writing, require the owner or any peson in possession of such hoarding, to remove such hoarding within such time as may nbe specified in the notice.

Provided that suc time shall not exceed fifteen days from the date of issue of such notice;

(ii) where the hoarding referred to in sub-clause (i) is not removed within the time specified in the notice, the executive authority shall, without further notice, remove such hoardin and recover the expenditure for such removal as an arrear of land revenue.

Explanation.—For the purpose of this section, "hoarding" means any screen of boards at any place whether public or private used or intended to be used for exhibiting advertisement including the framework or other support, erected, wholly or in part upon or over any land, building wall or structure visible to public wholly or partly"][2].

132. Vesting of communal property or income in village panchayat. – Any property or income including any fishery right which by custom belongs to, or has been administered for the common benefit of the inhabitants of the village or of the holders in common of village land

---

[1] *Inserted by Act. 27/2000*

[2] *Inserted by Act. 27/2000*

generally or of the holders of lands of a particular description or of the holders of lands under particular source of irrigation shall, if so declared by the Government, vest in the village panchayat and be administered by it for the benefit of the inhabitants or holders aforesaid.

133. Maintenance of irrigation works, execution of kudimaramat, etc. – (1) Subject to such conditions and control as may be prescribed, the Government may transfer to any village panchayat or to any panchayat union council the protection and maintenance of any irrigation work, the management of turns of irrigation, or the regulation of distribution of water from any irrigation work to the fields depending on it.

(2) The village panchayat or the panchayat union council shall have power, subject to such restrictions and control as may be prescribed, to execute kudimaramat in respect of any irrigation source in the village and to levy such fee and on such basis for the purposes thereof as may be prescribed;

Provided that nothing contained in this section shall be deemed to relieve the village community or any of its members of its or his liability under the Tamil Nadu Compulsory Labour Act, 1858, (Central Act I of 1858) in respect of any irrigation source in the village in case the village panchayat makes default in executing the kudimaramat in respect of that irrigation source.

(3) Where the maintenance of any irrigation work, is transferred under this section, the fishery rights of Government in such work shall be transferred to and be vested in the village panchayat or the panchayat union council, as the case may be, subject to such terms and conditions including terms and conditions regarding the utilisation of the income, as may be specified by the Government.

134. Village panchayat to regulate the use of certain porambokes in ryotwari tracts. – Village panchayat to regulate the use of certain porambokes in ryotwari tracts. –

(1) The provisions of this section shall apply only in ryotwari tracts.

(2) The following porambokes, namely, grazing grounds, threshing floors, burning and burial-grounds, cattle-stands, cart-stands and topes shall vest in the village panchayat, and the village panchayat shall have power, subject to such restrictions and control as may be prescribed to regulate the use of such porombokes, provided the porambokes are at the disposal of the Government.

(3) The Collector, after consulting the village panchayat, may, by notification, exclude from the operation of this Act, any poramboke referred to in sub-section (2), and may also modify or cancel such notification.

(4) The village panchayat shall also have power, subject to such restrictions and control as may be prescribed, to regulate the use of any other poramboke which is at the disposal of the Government, if the

village panchayat is authorised in that behalf by an order of the Government.

(5) The village panchayat may, subject to such restrictions and control as may be prescribed, plant trees on any poramboke, the use of which is regulated by it under sub-section (2) or sub-section (4).

135. Village panchayat to regulate the use of certain communal lands in estates governed by the Tamil Nadu Estates Land Act, 1908. – (1) In estates governed by the Tamil Nadu Estates Land Act,1908, (Tamil Nadu Act I of 1908) not withstanding anything contained in that Act, the village panchayat shall have power subject to such restrictions and control as may be prescribed-

(a) to regulate the use of lands which are set apart for any of the purposes referred to in item (b) of clause (16) of section 3 of the said Act, namely, threshing floors, cattle-stand, village-sites and other lands situated in the village which are set apart for the common use of the inhabitants of such village;

(b) to exercise the powers vested in the Collector by section 20-A of the said Act, namely to direct that any land referred to in clause (a) which is no longer required for its original purpose shall be used for any other specified communal purpose, provided that the sanction of the Collector is obtained therefor; and

(c) to plant trees on any land the use of which is regulated by the village panchayat under clause (a) ;

Provided that nothing contained in clause (b) shall be deemed to affect in any way the operation of the proviso to sub-section (1) of the said section 20-A.

(2) After an estate ceases to be governed by the Tamil Nadu Estates Land Act, 1908, (Tamil Nadu Act I of 1908) the provisions of sub-section (1) shall apply to the lands referred to in that sub section, to such extent and with such modifications, as may be prescribed.

136. Collected rubbish etc., to belong to village panchayat. – All rubbish, filth and other matter collected by a village panchayat under this Act shall belong to it.

137. Immovable property required by village panchayats union councils may be acquired under the Land Acquistion Act, 1894. – Any immovable property which any village panchayat or panchayat union council is authorised by this Act or any rules made thereunder to acquired may be acquired under the provisions of the Land Acquisition Act, 1894, (Central Act I of 1894) and on payment of the compensation awarded under the said Act, in respect of such property and of any other charges incurred in acquiring it, the said property shall vest in the village panchayat or panchayat union council, as the case may be.

138. Contributions from persons having control over places of pilgrimage, etc. – Where a mosque, temple, mutt or any places of religious worship or instruction or any place which is used for holding fair or festivals or for other like purposes is situated within the limits of a village or in the neighbourhood thereof and attracts either throughout the year or on particular occasions a large number of persons, any special arrangement necessary for public health, safety or convenience, whether permanent or temporary, shall be made by the village panchayat; but the Government may after consulting the trustee or other person having control over such place require him to make such recurring or non-recurring contribution to the funds of the village panchayat as they may determine.

139. Power to order closure of places of public entertainment. – In the event of the prevalence of any dangerous disease within a panchayat development block or a village, the commissioner may by notice require the owner or occupier of any building, booth or tent used for purposes of public entertainment to close the same for such period as they may fix.

140. Minor suffering from dangerous disease not to attend schools. – No person being the parent or having the care or charge of a minor who is or has been suffering from dangerous disease or has been exposed to infection therefrom shall, after a notice from the commissioner or any person duly appointed by such commissioner in this behalf that the minor is not to be sent to school or college permit such minor to attend school or college without having procured from the commissioner or such person or a registered medical practitioner a certificate that in his opinion such minor may attend without risk of communicating such disease to others

Explanation – In this section and in section 139 "dangerous disease" means an infectious disease within the meaning of section 52 of the Tamil Nadu Public Health Act, 1939, (Tamil Nadu Act III of 1939) which is notified as a dangerous disease by the Government.

141. Compulsory vaccination. – The panchayat union council shall enforce vaccination throughout the panchayat union and it may enforce revaccination throughout the panchayat union or in any part thereof, in respect of such persons, to such extent, and in such manner, as may be prescribed.

142. Obligation to give information of small pox or cholera. – Where an inmate of any dwelling place is suffering from smallpox or cholera the head of the family to which the inmate belongs and in default the occupier or person in charge of such place, shall give intimation of the fact to the commissioner or the Village Administrative Officer with the least possible delay.

143. Precautions in case of dangerous tanks, wells, holes, etc. – (1) If any tank, pond, well, hole, stream, dam, bank or other place appears to him to be, for want of sufficient repair, protection or enclosure, dangerous to the public health or safety, the commissioner or executive authority may with the approval of the panchayat union council or village panchayat, as the case may be, by notice required the owner to fill in, remove, repair, protect or enclose the same so as to prevent any danger therefrom.

(2) If immediate action is necessary, he shall, before giving such notice or before the period of notice expires, himself take such temporary measures as he thinks fit to prevent danger, and the cost of doing so shall be recoverable from the owner in the manner hereinafter provided.

144. Removal of fifth or noxious vegetation from lands and buildings. – (1) The commissioner or executive authority may by notice require the owner or occupier of any building or land which appears to him to be in a filthy or unwholesome state or overgrown with any thick or noxious vegetation, trees or undergrowth injurious to health or dangerous to the public or offensive to the neighbourhood, or otherwise a source of nuisance, to clear, cleanse or otherwise put the building or land in proper state or to clear away and remove such vegetation, trees or under growth or to take such other action as may be deemed by the commissioner or executive authority necessary to remove such nuisance within such period and in such manner as may be specified in the notice.

(2) If it appears to the commissioner or executive authority necessary for sanitary purposes so to do, he may by notice require the owner or occupier of any building or land to cleanse or lime-wash the same in the manner and within a period to be specified in the notice.

145. Power of Commissioner or executive authority to use or sell materials of dangerous structure taken down, etc. – (1) When the commissioner or executive authority takes down any structure or part thereof or cuts down any tree or hedge or shrub or part thereof in virtue of his powers under this chapter, the commissioner or executive authority may sell the materials or things taken down, cut down or remove and apply the proceeds in, or towards payment of the expenses incurred.

(2) If after a reasonable enquiry it appears to the commissioner or executive authority that there is no owner or occupier to whom notice can be given under any section in this chapter, he may himself take such order with the property mentioned in such section as may appear to him to be necessary and may recover the expenses incurred by the sale of such property (not being immovable property) or of any portion thereof.

146. Limitation of compensation. – No person shall be entitled, save as otherwise expressly provided, to compensation for any damages sustained by reason of any action taken by the authorities of a panchayat union council or a village panchayat in pursuance of their powers under this chapter.

147. Public Markets. – (1) The panchayat union council may, after obtaining the previous written permission of the Inspector, provide places for use as public markets and, with the sanction of the Inspector, close any such market or part thereof.

(2) Subject to such rules may be prescribed, the village panchayat or panchayat union council may after obtaining the previous written permission of the Inspector, levy any one or more of the following fees in any public market at such rates, not exceeding the maximum rates, if any, prescribed in that behalf as the panchayat union council or village panchayat may think fit:-

(a) fees for the use of, or for the right to expose goods for sale in such market;

(b) fees for the use of shops, stalls, pens or stands in such market;.

(c) fees on vehicles including motor vehicles as defined in the Motor Vehicles Act, 1988 (Central Act 59 of 1988) or pack animals bringing, or on persons taking into such market any goods for sale;

(d) fees on animals brought for sale into or sold in such market;

(e) licence fees on brokers, commission agents, weighmen and measures practising their calling in such market.

148. Licensing of private markets. – (1) No person shall open a new private market or continue to keep open a private market unless he has obtained a licence from the village panchayat or panchayat union council, as the case may be, to do so. Such licence shall be renewed every year.

(2) (a) The village panchayat or panchayat union council, as the case may be, shall grant the licence applied for subject to such conditions as it may think fit as to supervision and inspection, sanitation, weights and measures to be used, rents and fees to be charged and such other matters as may be prescribed.

(b) The village panchayat or panchayat union council as the case may be, may, modify the conditions of licence to take effect from a specified date.

(c) The village panchayat or panchayat union council, as the case may be, may at any time, suspend or cancel any licence granted under clause(a) for breach of the conditions thereof.

(d) Any person aggrieved by an order of the village panchayat or panchayat union council under clauses (a), (b) or (c) may appeal against such order to the Inspector who may, if he thinks fit, suspend the execution of the order pending the disposal of the appeal.

(3)(a) Any person claiming to levy in a private market lawfully established prior to the coming into force of the Madras Local Boards Act, 1884 (Madras Act V of 1884) fees of the nature specified in sub-section (2) of section 147, shall apply to the Inspector for a certificate recognizing his right in that behalf; and the Inspector shall pass order on such application after giving due notice to the village panchayat or panchayat union council, as the case may be, and considering any representations made by it.

(b) Any person aggrieved by an order of the Inspector refusing to grant a certificate under clause (a) may, within six months from the date of communication of such order, institute a suit to establish the right claimed by him, and subject to the result of such suit, the Inspector's order shall be final.

(4) When a licence granted under sub-section (2) does not permit the levy of any fee, it shall be granted free of charges; but when such permission is given, a fee not exceeding fifteen per cent of the gross income of the owner from the market in the preceding year shall be charged by the village panchayat or panchayat union council, as the case may be, for such licence.

(5) The village panchayat or panchayat union council as the case may be, or any officer duly authorised by it may, close a private market which is unlicensed or the licence for which has been suspended or cancelled, or which is held or kept open contrary to the provisions of this Act.

149. Decision of disputes as to whether places are markets. – If any question arises as to whether any place is a market or not, the village panchayat or panchayat union council, as the case may be, shall make a reference thereon to the Government and their decision shall be final.

150. Prohibition of sale in unlicensed private markets. – No person shall sell or expose for sale any animal or article-

(a) in any public or licensed private market without the permission of the executive authority or commissioner or licensee, as the case may be, or of any person authorised by him, or

(b) in any unlicensed private market.

151. Prohibition against sale in public roads. – The executive authority or commissioner may, with the sanction of the village panchayat or panchayat union council as the case may be, prohibit by public notice or licence or regulate the sale or exposure for sale of any animal or article in or upon any public road or place or part thereof

152. Classification of markets. – The Government shall have power to classify public and private markets situated in a panchayat development block as panchayat union markets and village panchayat market, and provide for the control of any such market, and for the opportionment of the income derived therefrom between the panchayat union council and the village panchayat or the payment of a contribution in respect thereof to the village panchayat or the panchayat union, as the case may be. It shall be open to the Government to revise from time to time the apportionment of income ordered or the contribution directed to be paid under this section if such revision is recommended by the district panchayat.

153. Acquistion of right of persons to hold private market. – (1) A panchayat union council may acquire the rights of any person to hold a private market in any place in a panchayat development block and to levy fee therein. The acquisition shall be made under the Land Acquisition Act, 1894 (Central Act I of 1894) and such rights shall be deemed to be land for the purposes of that Act

(2) On payment by the panchayat union council of the compensation awarded under the said Act in respect of such property and any other charges incurred in acquiring it, the rights of such person to hold a private market and to levy fees therein shali vest in the panchayat union council.

154. Public landing places and cart-stands, etc. – Subject to such rules as may be prescribed, the village panchayat may-

(a) provide public landing places, halting places and cart-stands (which last expression includes stands for animals and vehicles of any description including motor vehicles) and levy fees for their use; and

(b) Where any such place or stand has been provided, prohibit the use for the same purpose by any person, within such distance thereof of any public place or the sides of any public road as the village panchayat may, subject to the control of the Inspector, specify.

155. Private cart-stand. – (1) No person shall open a new private cart-stand or continue to keep open a private cart-stand unless he obtains from the village panchayat a licence to do so. Such licence shall be renewed every year.

(2) The village panchayat shall, as regards private cart-stands already lawfully established, and may at its discretion as regards new private cart-stands grant the licence applied for, subject to such conditions as the village panchayat may think fit as to supervisions and inspection, conservancy and such other matters as may be prescribed; or the village panchayat may refuse to grant such licence for any new cart-stand.

(3) The village panchayat may modify the conditions of the licence to take effect from a specified date

(4) The village panchayat may at any time suspend or cancel any licence granted under sub-section (2) for breach of the conditions thereof.

(5) The village panchayat may levy on every grant or renewal of a licence under this section, a fee not exceeding two hundred rupees.

156. Public slaughter-houses. – A village panchayat may provide places for use as public slaughter-houses and charge rents and fees for their use.

157. Prohibition or regulation of the use of places for slaughtening animals and the licensing of slaughterers. – The Government shall have power to make rules for – (a) prohibiting or regulating the slaughter, cutting up or skinning of animals specified in the rules on all occasions not excepted therein, at places other than public slaughter-houses;

(b) licensing persons to slaughter animals specified in the rules for purposes of sale to the public; and

158. Numbering or naming of building, etc. – (1) In any area to which this Act applies, such authority as may be prescribed in this behalf, may cause a number to be affixed to he side or outer door of any building or to some place at the entrance of the premises.

(2) With the approval of the Government , the village panchayat or the panchayat union council shall give name to new village road or panchayat union road, as the case may be, and shall also give name to park, playground, bus-stand, arch or new property belonging to, or vesting in, village panchayat or panchayat union council and may, subject to the approval of the Government, alter the name of any such road, park, playground, bus-stand, arch or property.

(3) No person shall, without lawful authority, destroy, pull down or deface any such number.

(4) When a number has been affixed under sub-section (1) , the owner of the building shall be bound to maintain such number and to replace it if removed or defaced; and if he fails to do so, the authority referred to in sub-section (1) may by notice required him to replace it.

159. Purposes for which places may not be used without a license. – (1) The Government may, by notification, specify the purposes which in their opinion, are likely to be offensive or dangerous to human life or health or property.

[1][“(2) The village panchayat may, with the previous approval of the prescribed authority, notify that no place within the limits of the panchayat village shall be used for any of the purposes specified in the notification issued under sub-section (1) without a licence and except in accordance with the conditions specified in such licence”].

(3) No notification issued under sub-section (1) of Sub-Section (2) shall take effect until sixty days from the date of its publication.

[2][“(4) The village panchayat shall be the authority competent to grant the licence or to refuse to grant it:]

160. Permission for construction of factories and the installation of machinery. – No person shall, without the permission of the panchayat union council in panchayat village and except in accordance with the conditions specified in such permission,-

(a) construct or establish any factory, workshop or workplace in which it is proposed to employee steam power, water power or other mechanical power or electrical power, or

---

[1] *Substituted by Act, 19/1999*

[2] *Substituted by Act, 19/1999.*

(b) install in any premises any machinery or manufacturing plant driven by any power as aforesaid not being machinery or manufacturing plant exempted by the rules.

161. Power of Government to make rules in respect of the grant and renewal of licenses and permissions. – **(1)** The Government may make rules-

(a) prohibiting or regulating the grant or renewal of licences under section 159 and the period for which such licences shall be valid;

(b) as to the time within which applications for such licences or renewals thereof shall be made; and

(c) prohibiting or regulating the grant of permissions under section 160

(2) Rules made under clause (c) of sub-section (1) may empower the panchayat union council in panchayat villages and panchayat unions to set apart specified areas for industrial purposes and provide for the refusal of permissions under section 160 in respect of any factory, workshop, workplace or premises outside such areas and also, subject to the sanction of the prescribed authority for the removal to such areas, of any factory, workshop or work place which has been already established at any place or any machinery which has already been installed in any premises, situated outside such areas:

Provided that no such rule shall authorise the removal of any factory, workshop or workplace or machinery installed in any premises, in the occupation or under the control of the Central or the State Government or of a market committee established under the Tamil Nadu Agricultural Produce Marketing (Regulation) Act, 1987. (Tamil Nadu Act 27 of 1989)

(3) The Government may either generally or in any particular case, make such order or give such directions as they deem fit in respect of any action taken or omitted to be taken under section 159 or section 160.

(4) The income derived from fees on licences under section 159 and on permission under section 160 shall, if received by the panchayat union council, credited to the funds of the village panchayat concerned.

162. Modification of the Tamil Nadu Places of Public Resort Act, 1888 (Tamil Nadu Act II of 1888). – Notwithstanding anything contained in the Tamil Nadu Places of Public Resort Act, 1888, when the Government extend that Act to any village, or part thereof-

(a) the authority to whom application shall be made for a licence under the Act in respect of any place or building to be used exclusively for purposes other than the holding of cinematograph exhibitions, and whom may grant or refuse such licence, shall be the commissioner in the case of panchayat villages;

(b) the appeal from the order of the commissioner granting, refusing, revoking or suspending a licence, shall lie to the panchayat union council;

(c) the income derived from fees on licences under this section shall, if received by the panchayat union council be credited to the funds of the village panchayats concerned.

163. Functions of district panchayat. – (1) The district panchayat shall advise the Government on all matters concerning the activities of village panchayats, panchayat union councils in the district as well as on all matters relating to the development of the economic resources of the district and the services maintained therein for promoting the culture and welfare of the inhabitants of the district.

(2) In particular, it shall be the duty of the district panchayat to perform the following functions, namely:-

(a) advising the Government on all matters relating to the services maintained by and all development schemes undertaken by all village panchayats and panchayat union councils in the district as well as those agencies in the district, which are under the administrative control of the Government;

(b) watching the progress of the measure undertaken by the Government, village panchayats, panchayat union councils and departmental agencies in respect of the services and development schemes aforesaid;

(c) advising the Government on matters concerning the implementation of any provision of law or any order specifically referred to by the Government to the district panchayat such as-

(i) classification of markets as village panchayat markets and panchayat union markets and fixing rates of contribution payable by one authority to the other;

(ii) classification of fairs and festivals as village panchayat fairs, village panchayat festivals and panchayat union fairs and panchayat union festivals;

(iii) classification of public roads (other than roads classified by the Government as National Highways, State Highways and major district roads) as panchayat union roads and panchayat village roads;

(d) advising the Government on all matters relating to development of road transport.

164. General powers of district panchayat. – For the purpose of efficiently performing its functions under this Act, every district panchayat may, within the limits of its jurisdiction-

(a) undertake such measures as it deems necessary;

(b) collect such data as it deems necessary;

(c) publish statistics or other information relating to the various aspects of the regulation or development of the activities of panchayat union councils and village panchayats in the district;

(d) require any panchayat union council or village panchayat to furnish such information as may be required by it in relation of the measures undertaken by that panchayat union council or village panchayat for the regulation or development of its activities and such other matters as may be prescribed.

165. Annual report of district panchayat. – (1) The district panchayat shall prepare in such form and at such time each year as may be prescribed, an annual report giving a true and full account of its activities during the previous year and copies thereof shall be forwarded to the Government.

(2) The Government shall lay on the table of the Legislative Assembly all such reports together with their comments thereon.

166. Returns and reports of district panchayat. – Every district panchayat shall furnish to the Government such returns, reports, statistics and other informations with respect to its activities as the Government may from time to time require.

CHAPTER IX

TAXATION AND FINANCE

167. Local Cess. – (1) There shall be levied in every panchayat development block, a local cess at the rate of one rupee on every rupee of land revenue payable to the Government in respect of any land for every fasli.

Explanation – In this section and in section 168, 'land revenue' means public revenue due on land and includes water cess payable to the Government for water supplied or used for the irrigation of land, royalty, lease amount or other sum payable to the Government in respect of land held direct from the Government on lease or licence, but does not include any other cess or the surcharge payable under section 168, provided that land revenue remitted shall not be deemed to be land revenue payable for the purpose of this section.

(2) The local cess payable under sub-section (1) shall be deemed to be public revenue due on all the lands in respect of which a person is liable to pay local cess and all the said lands, the buildings upon the said lands and their products shall be regarded as security for the local cess.

(3) The provisions of the Tamil Nadu Revenue Recovery Act, 1864, (Tamil Nadu Act II of 1864) shall apply to the payment and recovery of the local cess payable under this Act just as they apply to the payment and recovery of the revenue due upon the lands in respect of which the local cess under this Act is payable.

[1][“(4) The local cess so collected in every panchayat development block shall be credited to the village panchayat fund concerned”].

---

[1] *Sub sections (4) & (5) have been substituted with one sub-section namely sub-section (4) by Act.30/1999*

168. Local cess surcharge. – Every panchayat union council may levy on every person liable to pay land revenue to the Government in respect of any land inthe panchayat union, a local cess surcharge at such rate as may be considered suitable as an addition to the local cess levied in the panchayat development block under section 167 provided that the rate of local cess surcharge so levied shall not be less than five rupees and not more than ten rupees on every rupee of land revenue payable in respect of such land.

169. Rules regarding collection of local cess. – The Government may make rules not inconsistent with this Act for regulating the collection of the local cess, the payment thereof to the village panchayats [1][***] and the deduction of any expenses incurred by the Government in the collection thereof.

170. Land Revenue Assignment. – The Government shall pay to each panchayat union council a sum representing one rupee for each individual of the population of the panchayat development block concerned from out of the total land revenue (including water-cess) collected in the State during that year. The sum thus credited to the panchayat union council shall be referred to as the Land Revenue Assignment of that Block.

171. Taxes leviable by village panchayats. – (1) Every village panchayat shall levy in the panchayat village a house-tax [2][*****].

(2) A duty shall also be levied in every panchayat village on certain transfers of property in accordance with the provisions of section 175.

(3) Subject to such rules as may be prescribed and with the sanction of the Inspector and subject to such restrictions and conditions, if any, as may be imposed by him either at the time of granting sanction or later, the village panchayat may also levy in the village a tax on agricultural land for a specific purpose.

172. House-tax. – (1) The house-tax shall be levied on all houses in every panchayat village on the basis on which such tax was levied in the local area concerned immediately before the commencement of this Act or on the basis of classified plinth area at the rates specified in Schedule I, as the village panchayat may adopt subject to the provisions of sub-section (3).

(2) The house-tax shall, subject to the prior payment of the land revenue, if any, due to the Government in respect of the site of the house, be a first charge upon the house and upon the movable property,

---

1 *The words "panchayat union councils and district panchayats" have been omitted by Act. 30/1999.*

2 *The words "and a vehicle tax" have been omitted by Act. 29/1995*

if any, found within or upon the same and belonging to the person liable to such tax.

(3) The Government shall, by notification, determine in regard to any panchayat village or any class of panchayat villages whether the house-tax shall be levied every half-year or year and in so doing have regard to the following matters, namely:-

(a) the classification of the local areas under section 4;

(b) the annual receipts of the village panchayat;

(c) the population of the panchayat village and the predominant occupation of such population; and

(d) such other matters as may be prescribed

(4) The Government may make rules providing for-

(a) the persons who shall be liable to pay the tax and the giving of notices of transfer of houses;

(b) the grant of vacancy and other remissions;

(c) the circumstances in which, and the conditions subject to which, houses constructed, reconstructed or demolished, or situated in areas included in, or excluded from the panchayat village during any half-year or year, shall be liable or cease to be liable to the whole or any portion of the tax.

(5) If the occupier of a house pays the house-tax on behalf of the owner thereof, such occupier shall be entitled to recover the same from the owner and may deduct the same from the rent then or thereafter due by him to the owner.

[1][“**172-A. Levy and collection of advertisement tax.** – Every person who erects, exhibits fixes or retains upon or over any land, building, wall, hoarding or structure any advertisement, or who displays any advertisement to public view in any manner what-so-ever in any place whether public or private, in the panchayat village shall pay on every advertisement which is so erected, exhibited, fixed retained or displayed to public view, a tax calculated at such rates and in such manner as the village panchayat may, determine in accordance with such rule as may be prescribed:

Provided that the rates shall be subject to the rates that may be prescribed by the Government and different rates may be prescribed for different village panchayats taking into consideration the location, the size of the advertisement board, the period and the types of advertisements:

Provided further that no tax shall be levied under this section on any advertisement or a notice-

(a) of a public meeting; or

[2][“(b) of an election to the Parliament, Legislative Assembly, or a Panchayat; or”]

(c) of a candidature in respect of such an election:

---

[1] *Sections 172-A and 172-B have been inserted by Act. 32/1999*

[2] *Substituted by Act. 1/2001*

Provided also that no such tax shall be levied on advertisement which is not a sky-sign and which –

(a) is exhibited within the windows of any building; or

(b) relates to the trade or business carried on, within the land or building upon or over which such advertisement is exhibited, or to any sale or letting of such land or building or any effects therein or to any sale, entertainment or meeting to be held upon or in the same; or

(c) relates to the name of the land or building upon or over which the advertisement is exhibited, or to the name of the owner or occupier of such land or building; or

(d) relates to the business of any railway administration; or

(e) is exhibited within any railway station or upon any wall or other property of a railway administration except any portion of the surface of such wall or property fronting any street.

Explanation – For the purpose of this action –

(i) the expression "structure" shall include any movable board on wheels used as an advertisement medium;

(ii) the expression "sky-sign" means any advertisement supported on or attached to any post, pole, standard, frame-work or other support wholly or in part upon or over any land, building, wall or structure which, or any part of sky-sign which shall be visible against the sky from some point in any public place and includes all and every part of any such post, pole, standard, frame-work or other support. The expression "sky-sign" shall also include any balloon, parachute or other similar device employed wholly or in part or the purposes of any advertisement upon or over any land, building or structure or upon or over any public place but shall not include -

(a) any flag staff, pole vane or weather-cock, unless adopted or used wholly or in part for the purpose of any advertisement, or

(b) any sign, or any board, frame or other contrivance securely fixed to or on the top of the wall or parapet of any building or on the cornice or blocking of any wall, or to the ridge of a roof:

Provided that such board, frame or other contrivance shall be of one continuous face and not open work, and does not extend in height more than one metre above any part of the wall, or parapet, or ridge to, against or on, which it is fixed or supported. Or

(c) any advertisement relating to the name of the land or building, upon or over which the advertisement is exhibited, or to the name of the owner or occupier of such land or building; or

(d) any advertisement relating exclusively to the business of a railway administration and placed wholly upon or over any railway, railway yard station platform or station approach belonging to a railway administration and so placed that cannot fall in any street or public: or

(e) any notice of land or building to be sold, or let placed upon such land or building:

(iii) the expression "public place" means any place which is open to the use and enjoyment of the public whether it is actually used or enjoyed by the public or not ;

(iv) the expression "advertisement" shall not include any advertisement published in any newspaper].

172-B. Prohibition of advertisements. – No advertisement shall after the levy of tax under section 172-A as determined by the Village Panchayat be erected, exhibited, fixed or retained upon or over any land, building, wall, hoarding or structure within the panchayat village, or shall be displayed in any manner whatsoever in any place except in accordance with the rules made under this Act:

Provided that the Village Panchayat shall regulate the height of the advertisement in the Panchayat Village and shall remove such objectionable advertisement in such manner as may be prescribed:

Provided further that the Government may, by notification, prohibit advertisements in any place within any panchayat village".][1]

[2] **[173.Vehicle-tax.** – [****] (Omitted)]

174. Appeal against assessments. – An appeal shall lie to such authority and within such time, as may be prescribed against any assessment of tax made in pursuance of [3]["Sections 171, 172 and 172-A"]

175. Duty on transfer of property. – (1) The duty on transfer of property shall be levied-

(a) in the form of a surcharge on the duty imposed by the Indian Stamp Act, 1899 (Central Act II of 1899), as in force for the time being in the state of Tamil Nadu, on every instrument of the description specified below, which relates to immovable property situated in the area under the jurisdiction of a village panchayat; and

(b) at such rate, as may be fixed by the Government, not exceeding five per cent on the amount specified below against each instrument:-

(i) Sale of immovable property. – The market value of the property as set forth in the instrument, and in a case where the market value is finally determined by any authority under section 47-A of the Indian Stamp Act, 1899, the market value as so determined by such authority.

(ii) Exchange of immovable property. – The market value of the property of the greater value as set forth in the instrument and in a case where the market value is finally determined by any authority under section 47-A of the Indian Stamp Act, 1899, (Central Act II of 1899) the market value as so determined by such authority.

(iii) Gift of immovable property. – The market value of the property as set forth in the instrument, and in a case where the market

---

[1] *Inserted by Act. 32/1999*

[2] *Omitted by Act. 29/1995*

[3] *Substituted by Act. 29/1995 for the expression "sections 171 and 172"*

value is finally determined by any authority under section 47-A of the Indian Stamp Act, 1899 (Central Act II of 1899) the market value as so determined by such authority.

(iv) Mortgage with possession of immovable property. –The amount secured by the mortgage as set forth in the instrument.

(v) Lease in perpetuity of immovable property. – An amount equal to one sixth of the whole amount or value of the rents which would be paid or delivered in respect of the first fifty years of the lease, as set forth in the instrument.

(2) On the introduction of the duty aforesaid-

(a) section 27 of the said Indian Stamp Act shall be read as if it specifically required the particulars to be set forth separately in respect of property situated outside such on the area under the jurisdiction of the village panchayat and in respect of property situated area;

(b) section 64 of the said Act shall be read as if it referred to the village panchayat as well as the Government.

(3) The amount collected in the panchayat village in the panchayat development block as surcharge on the duty on transfers of property under this section shall e pooled every year for the entire block and distributed among all the village panchayats in the block in proportion to the land revenue of the panchayat village.

(4) The Government may make rules not inconsistent with this Act for regulating the collection of the duty, the payment thereof to the village panchayat and the deduction of any expenses incurred by the Government in the collection thereof.

176. Exemption. – No exemption from the payment of any surcharge or tax specified in section 168 or 171 shall be granted by the village panchayat or the panchayat union council except in accordance with such rules as may be prescribed:

Provided that in any particular case, such exemption may be granted with the previous sanction of the Government.

177. Power to require land revenue staff to collect taxes and fees due to village panchayat. – Subject to such rules as may be prescribed, the executive authority or the commissioner shall have power to require the staff of the Land Revenue Department to prepare at quinquinnial intervals a House-tax Assessment Register in such form as may be prescribed and to collect any tax or fee due to the village panchayat or panchayat union council on payment of such remuneration not exceeding 6 1/4 per cent of the gross sum collected as the Collector may, by general or special order, determine.

178. Write-off of irrecoverable amounts. – Subject to such restrictions and control as may be prescribed, a village panchayat or panchayat union council may write-off any tax, fee or other amount whatsoever due to it, whether under a contract or otherwise, or any sum payable in connection therewith, if in its opinion such tax, fee, amount or sum is irrecoverable.

Provided that where the Collector or any of his subordinates is responsible for the collection of any tax, fee or other amount due to a village panchayat or panchayat union council the power to write-off such tax, fee or amount or any sum payable in connection therewith, on the ground of its being irrecoverable, shall be exercised by the Commissioner of Land Administration or subject to his control, by the Collector or any officer authorised by him.

179. Local Education Grant. – The Government shall pay annually to every panchayat union council a Local Education Grant the amount of which shall be calculated as follows:

The total amount of expenditure approved by the Government for being debited to the Panchayat Union (Education) Fund shall be divided into slabs in the manner specified below:-

So much of the expenditure as may be equal to the land revenue assignment of the block referred to in section 170 shall constitute the first slab.

So much of the expenditure as may be in excess of the first slab subject to a maximum of 250 paise for each individual of the population of the panchayat development block concerned shall constitute the second slab.

To each panchayat union council, the Government shall make a Local Education Grant which shall be a proportion of the second slab not less than fifty per cent and not more than eighty per cent as may be specified by the Government in respect of that block.

[1][**180. Local Cess Surcharge Matching Grant.** – [*** Omitted].

181. Classification of panchayat development blocks. – For the purpose of sanctioning grants to panchayat union councils, the Government may classify panchayat development blocks in such manner as they may deem fit once in every five years and it shall be open to the Government to sanction grants at varying rates for the different classes of panchayat development blocks. It shall also be open to the Government to revise the classification of panchayat development blocks once in every five years.

[2]["**181-A. Deposit of fund of panchayat.** – Any panchayat having surplus fund shall, with the prior approval of the Inspector, deposit such surplus fund in any of the financial institutions specified by the Government:

---

1 *Omitted by Act. 30/1999*

2 *Sections 181-A to 181-D have been inserted by Act. 23/2000*

Provided that no such deposit shall be made when there is need to utilize this fund for administration or development work during the next twelve months.

181-B. Grant or loan for scheme or project. – (1) The Government may take grant or loan to a panchayat for the execution of specific scheme, project, programme or plan relating to any of the matters administered by such panchayat subject to such terms and conditions as may be prescribed.

(2) Such panchayats shall utilize such grant or loan only for the purpose for which such grant or loan is given.

(3) The provisions of the Local Authorities Loans Act, 1914 (Central Act IX of 1914) shall apply in respect of the loan given by the Government under this section.

181-C. Raising of loan by panchayat. – Every panchayats shall be competent to raise loan in full or in part from any financial institution or agency or bank for any of the following purposes, subject to the conditions imposed by the Government in this behalf, namely:-

(a) to carry out any of the works connectd with the improvement and development of infrastructure in panchayat areas;

(b) to carry out relief works at the time of natural calamities;

(c) to undertake any measure in connection with, or ancillary to, the above purposes; and

(d) to carry out any of its other statutory functions.

181-D. Procedure for inter-panchayats lending. – (1) Any panchayat may raise loan from any other panchayat and any panchayat may sanction loan to another panchayat to carry out any of its functions of for the creation of capital assets or income generating assets, with the prior sanction of the Inspector.

(2) The procedure for the receipt, utilization and repayment of the loan under this section and section 181-C shall be subject to such terms and conditions, as may be agreed upon by the financial institution or agency or bank or lending panchayat, as the case may be, and the borrowing panchayat. Every panchayat shall maintain in respect of the loan, such books of accounts, as may be prescribed.

(3) Every panchayat shall utilize the loans only for the purposes for which such loans are borrowed"][1].

[2][**182. Local Roads Grant. – ****]** Omitted

[3][**183. Village House-tax Matching Grant** – [****]Omitted

[4][**184. Deduction from grant in certain cases.** – [****] Omitted.

---

[1] *Inserted by Act. 23/2000*

[2,3,4] *Omitted by Act. 30/1999*

185. Constitution of panchayat union fund and village panchayat fund. – There shall be constituted –

(a) for each panchayat union, a Panchayat Union (General) Fund and a Panchayat Union (Education) Fund:

(b) for each village panchayat, a village panchayat fund.

186. Panchayat union (general) fund. – The receipts which shall be credited to the panchayat Union (General) Fund shall include-

[1][(a). [****]Omitted].

(b) the local cess surcharge collected in the panchayat development block under section 168;

[2][(c) [****] Omitted]

[3][(d) [****]Omitted]

(e) fees on licences issued and permissions given by the panchayat union councils;

(f) fees levied in public markets classified as panchayat union markets after deducting the contribution, if any, paid by the panchayat union council to the village panchayat on the scale fixed by the Government;

(g) the contribution paid to the panchayat union council by village panchayats in respect of markets classified as village panchayat markets;

(h) fees for the temporary occupation of roads or road margins;

(i) fees for the use of choultries;

(j) receipts from dispensaries maintained by the panchayat union council;

(k) income from endowments and trusts under the management of the panchayat union council;

(l) the proportionate share of the proceeds of the entertainments tax received by the panchayat union council under section 13 of the Tamil Nadu Entertainments Tax Act, 1939 (TN.Act X of 1939);

(m) contributions from Government other panchayat union councils, municipalities, other local authorities and persons in aid of every institution or service maintained or financed from panchayat union funds or managed by the panchayat union council;

(n) sale-proceeds of tools and plants, stores and materials and of trees and avenue produce appertaining to panchayat union roads;

(o) income from panchayat union ferries and fisheries;

(p) interest on loans and securities;

(q) interest on arrears of revenue

(r) income from and sale-proceeds of, buildings, lands and other property belonging to the panchayat union council

(s) unclaimed deposits and other forfeitures;

(t) fines and penalties levied under this Act by the panchayat union council or at its instance or on its behalf

---

[1,2,3] *Omitted by Act. 30/1999*

(u) all sums other than those enumerated above or in section 187 which arise out of or are received in aid of, or for expenditure on, any institutions or services maintained or financed from the panchayat union funds or managed by the panchayat union council;

(v) all other moneys received by the panchayat union council.

187. Panchayat Union (Education) Fund. – The receipt which shall be credited to the Panchayat Union (Education) Fund shall include-

[1][(a) [****] Omitted]

(b) the land revenue assignment paid by the Government under section 170;

(c) the Local Education Grant paid by the Government.

(d) such contribution from the Panchayat Union (General) Fund as the Government may decide to be necessary in any year in order to balance the budget of the fund for that year:

(e) all fines and penalties levied within the jurisdiction of the panchayat union council under the provisions of the Tamil Nadu Elementary Education Act, 1920 (TN Act. VIII of 1920);

(f) all income derived from any endowments or other property owned or managed by the panchayat union council for the benefit of elementary education;

(g) all other sums which may be contributed or received by the panchayat union council for the purposes of elementary education.

188. Village Pancahayat Fund. – [2][(1)] The receipts which shall be credited to the village panchayat fund shall include-

[3]["(a) the house-tax and any other tax or any cess or fee, levied under sections 171 and 172"]

[4]["(b) The profession tax levied by village panchayat under Chapter IX-A:"]

(c) the proceeds of the duty on transfers of property levied under section 175.

[5][(d) [****]the local cess under section 167]

[6][(e) [****] (Omitted)]

(f) the taxes and tolls levied in the village under sections 117 and 118 of he Tamil Nadu Public Health Act, 1939; (TN Act. VIII of 1939);

(g) fees levied in public markets classified as village panchayat markets after deducting the contributions, if any, paid by the village

---

[1] *Omitted by Act. 30/1999*

[2] *The whole section 188 has been renumbered as sub-section (1) of that section by Act. 54/1997.*

[3] *The whole section 188 has been renumbered as sub-section (1) of that section by Act. 54/1997.*

[4] *Substituted by Act. 30/1999*

[5] *The expression "the share of" has been omitted by Act. 30/1999*

[6] *Omitted by Act. 30/1999*

panchayat to the panchayat union council on the scale fixed by the Government;

(h) the contribution paid to the village panchayat by panchayat union councils in respect of markets classified as panchayat union markets;

(i) fees for the temporary occupation of village sites, roads and other similar public places or parts thereof in the panchayat village;

(j) fees levied by the village panchayat in pursuance of any provision of this Act or any rule or order made thereunder;

(k) income from endowments and trusts under the management of the village panchayat;

(l) the net assessment on service inams which are resumed by the Government;

(m) the proportionate share of the proceeds of the entertainments tax received by the village panchayat under section 13 of the Tamil Nadu Entertainments Tax Act, 1939; (Tamil Nadu Act X of 1939)

(n) income derived from panchayat village fisheries;

(o) income derived from ferries under the management of the village panchayat;

(p) unclaimed deposits and other forfeitures;

(q) a sum equivalent to the seigniorage fees collected by the Government every year from persons permitted to quarry for road material in the panchayat village;

(r) all income derived from porambokes the user of which is vested in the village panchayat:

(s) where the panchayat village is in a ryotwari tract, all income derived from trees standing on porombokes although the user of the porambokes is not vested in the village panchayat;

(t) income from leases of Government property obtained by the village panchayat;

(u) fines and penalties levied under this Act by the village panchayat or at the instance or on behalf of the village panchayat;

(v) all sums other than those enumerated above which arise out of , or are received in aid of or for expenditure on any institutions or services maintained or financed from the village panchayat fund or managed by the village panchayat;

(w) all other moneys received by the village panchayat].

[1][“(2) Notwithstanding anything contained in sub-section (1) , the Government may direct any village panchayat to constitute separate funds to which shall be credited such receipt as may be specified and such funds shall be applied and disposed of in such manner as may be prescribed.

(3) Subject to such general control as the village panchayat may exercise from time to time, all cheques for payment from village panchayat fund or other funds constituted under sub-section (2) shall be signed jointly by the President and Vice-President and in the

---

[1] *Added by Act. 54/1997*

absence of the President or Vice-President, as the case may be, by the Vice-President or the President and another member authorised by the Village Panchayat at a meeting in this behalf"]

189. District Panchayat (General) Fund. – (1) There shall be constituted for each district panchayat, a District Panchayat (General) Fund and the following shall form part of, or be paid into, the District Panchayat (General)Fund, namely;-

(a) The amount transferred to the District Panchayat (General) Fund by appropriation from out of the Consolidated Fund of the State:

(b) all grants, assignments, loans and contributions made by the Government;

(c) all rents from lands or other property of the district panchayat;

(d) all interest, profits and other moneys accruing by gift, grants, assignments or transfer from private individual or institutions;

(e) all proceeds of land, security and other properties sold by the district panchayat;

(f) all fees and penalties paid to or levied by or on behalf of the district panchayat under this Act;

(g) all sums received by or on behalf of the district panchayat by virtue of this Act.

(2) The Government shall make a grant to every District Panchayat (General) Fund, to cover the expenses of establishment at such scale as may be determined by it.

EXPENDITURE

190. Application of moneys received and expenditure from funds. – All moneys received by the panchayat union council and the village panchayat shall be applied and disposed of in accordance with the provisions of this Act and other laws;

Provided that the panchayat union council or the village panchayat union council or the village panchayat shall have power subject to such rules as may be prescribed to direct that the proceeds of any tax or additional tax levied under this Act shall be earmarked for the purpose of financing any specific public improvement. A separate account shall be kept of the receipts from every such tax or additional tax and the expenditure thereof.

191. Expenditure from village panchayat fund and panchayat union fund. – (1) The purposes to which the funds of he panchayat union council or of he village panchayat may be applied include all objects expressly declared obligatory or discretionary by this Act or any rules made thereunder or by any other laws or rules and the funds shall be applicable thereto within the panchayat development block or the panchayat village, as the case may be, subject to such rules or special orders as the Government may prescribe or issue and shall, subject as aforesaid be applicable to such purposes outside the panchayat development block or panchayat village if the expenditure is authorized by this Act or specially sanctioned by the Inspector.

(2) It shall be the duty of every panchayat union council and village panchayat to provide for the payment of-

(a) any amount falling due on any loans contracted by it;

(b) the salaries and allowances and the pensions, pensionary contributions and provident fund contributions of its officers and servants;

(c) sums due under any decree or order of a court; and

(d) Any other expenses rendered obligatory by or under this act or any other law.

(3) A panchayat union council or village panchayat may, with the sanction of the Government, contribute to any fund for the defence of India.

(4) A panchayat union council or village panchayat may, with the sanction of the Inspector also-

(a) contribute towards the expenses of any public exhibition, ceremony or entertainment in the panchayat development block or panchayat village;

(b) contribute to any charitable fund, or to the funds of any institution for the relief of the poor or the treatment of disease or infirmity or the reception of indisposed or infirm persons or the investigation of the causes of disease; and

(c) defray any other extraordinary charges.

192. Preparation and sanction of budgets. – (1) The executive authority of the village panchayat and the commissioner, shall in each year frame and place before the village panchayat or the panchayat union council, as the case may be, a budget showing the probable receipts and expenditure during the following year.

(2) The budget of a village panchayat or panchayat union council shall after preparation by the executive authority or the commissioner, be submitted on or before such date and to such officer as may be prescribed, and if the prescribed officer is satisfied that adequate provision has not been made therein for the performance of any necessary service or services, he shall have power to return the budget for modification in such manner as may be necessary to secure such provision.

(3) The village panchayat or the panchayat union council as the case may the, shall sanction the budget with such modification as it thinks fit. If there is a difference of opinion between the officer referred to in sub-section (2) and he village panchayat and the panchayat union council, as the case may be, the budget shall be referred to the Inspector in the case of village panchayat and the Government in the case of the panchayat union council. The Inspector or the Government as the case may be, shall have power to modify the budget in such manner as he or they may consider necessary.

(4) If in the course of a year, a village panchayat or panchayat union council finds it necessary to alter the figures shown in the budget with regard to its receipts or to the distribution of the amounts to be expended on the different services undertaken by it, a supplemental or revised budget may be framed, sanctioned, submitted and modified in the manner provided in sub-sections (1) and (2), provided that no such alteration shall be given effect to except with the consent of the prescribed officer.

(5) On or before such date in each year as may be prescribed, every commissioner shall submit to the Government through such officer and in such forms as may be prescribed a budget for the ensuing financial year showing the income and expenditure relating to the Panchayat Union (Education) Fund.

(6) The Government may pass such orders as they think fit in respect of the budget referred to in sub-section (5) and the panchayat union council concerned shall be bound to carry out all such orders.

(7) The accounts of the Panchayat Union (Education) Fund shall, be examined and audited by an auditor appointed by the Government under section 193, and the panchayat union council concerned shall carry out any instruction which the Government may issue on the audit report.

193. Appintment of auditors. – (1) The Government shall appoint auditors for the accounts of the receipts and expenditure of the funds of the panchayat. Such auditors shall be deemed to be "public servants' within the meaning of section 21 (Central Act XLV of 1860) of the Indian Penal Code.

[1][“(2) No contribution shall be recovered by the Government from the panchayat towards the pay and allowances of such auditors or towards any other expenditure involved in the audit of the accounts of the panchayat”].

194. Contribution to expenditure by other local authorities. – If the expenditure incurred by the Government or by any panchayat union council or by any village panchayat or by any other local authority in the State for any purpose authorised by or under this Act, is such as to benefit the inhabitants of the panchayat union or panchayat village, the panchayat union council or the village panchayat, as the case may be, may, with the sanction of the Inspector, and shall, if so directed by him, make a contribution towards such expenditure.

195. Recovery of loans and advances made by government. – (1) Notwithstanding anything contained in the Local Authorities Loans Act, 1914 (Central Act IX of 1914) the Government may-

(a) by order direct any person having custody of the funds of the panchayat union council or the village panchayat to pay to them in

---

[1] *Substituted by Act. 19/2001*

priority to any other charges against such fund, except charges for the service of authorised loans, any loan or advance made by them to the panchayat union council or the village panchayat for any purpose to which its funds may be applied under this Act;

(b) recover any such loan or advance by suit

(2) The person to whom the order referred to in clause (a) of sub-section (1) is addressed shall be bound to comply with such order

196. Application of certain sections of this Act to district panchayat. – The provisions of sections 190, 191, 192, 194 and 195 (both inclusive) shall, in as far as may be, apply in relation to the district panchayat as they apply in relation to village panchayat and panchayat union council

197. Certain powers and functions of district panchayat to be notified by the government. – (1) It shall be lawful for the Government from time to time to direct by notification that-

(a) any of the powers and functions of the village panchayat or panchayat union council or of the Government; or

(b) any road, bridge, channel, building or other property movable, or immovable which is vested in the village panchayat or the panchayat union council or the Government and which is situated in the district, shall with the consent of the district panchayat and subject to such exemption and conditions as the Government may make and impose, be exercised or placed under the control and administration of the district panchayat for the purposes of this Act and thereupon such powers and functions and such road, bridge, channel, building or other property, shall be under the control and administration of the district panchayat , subject to all exceptions and to all charges and liabilities affecting the same.

(2) It shall be competent for the Government by notification, to resume any of the powers and functions or property, placed under the control of the district panchayat under sub-section (1) on such terms as the Government may determine.

198. Finance commission. – (1) The Governor shall as soon as may be, after the commencement of this Act, but not later than 24th April 1994 and thereafter at the expiration of every fifth year, constitute a Finance Commission referred to in Article 243-I of the Constitution to review the financial position of the panchayats, and to make recommendations to the Governor as to

(a) the principles which should govern-

(i) the distribution between the State and panchayats of the net proceeds of the taxes, duties, tolls and fees leviable by the Government which may be divided between them and allocation between the district panchayats, panchayat union councils and village panchayats of their respective shares of such proceeds;

(ii) the determination of the taxes, duties, tolls and fees which may be assigned to or appropriated by the panchayats;

(iii) the grants-in-aid to the panchayats, from the Consolidated Fund of the State;

(b) the measures needed to improve the financial position of the panchayats;

(c) any other matter referred to the Finance Commission by the Governor in the interest of sound finance of he panchayats

(2) The Finance Commission shall consist of a chairman and four other members.

(3) The chairman and members of Finance Commission shall possess such qualifications and shall be appointed in such manner as may be prescribed.

(4) The Finance commission shall determine their procedure

(5) The chairman or a member of the Finance Commission may resign his office by writing under his hand and addressed to the Finance Secretary to the Government, but he shall continue in office until his resignation is accepted by the Governor.

(6) The casual vacancy created by the resignation of the member or chairman under sub-section (5) or for any other reasons may be filled by fresh appointment and a member or chairman so appointed, shall hold office for the remaining period for which the member or chairman in whose place he was appointed would have held office.

(7) The Finance Commission shall have the following powers in the performance of its functions, namely;-

(a) to call for any record from any officer or authority;

(b) to summon any person to give evidence or produce records; and

(c) such other powers as may be prescribed

(8) The Finance Commission shall prepare a report on the activities of he Commission and submit the same to the Government at the end of each financial year.

(9) The Governor shall cause every recommendation made by the Finance Commission under this section together with an explanatory memorandum as to the action taken thereon to be placed in the table of the Legislative Assembly.

[1][“CHAPTER IX-A
TAX ON PROFESSION, TRADE, CALLING AND EMPLOYMENT

198-A Tax on profession, trade, calling and employment. – Definitions – For the purposes of this Chapter-

(a) “employee” means a person employed on salary and includes. -

(i) a Government servant receiving pay from the revenue of the Central Government or any State Government;

---

[1] *New sections 198-A to 198-I have been inserted by Act. 55/1998*

(ii) a person in the service of a body whether incorporated or not, which is owned or controlled by the Central Government or any State Government where such body operates within the panchayat village even though its headquarters may be outside that panchayat village; and

(iii) a person engaged in any employment by an employer, not covered by sub-clauses (i) and (ii);

(b) "employer" in relation to an employee earning any salary on a regular basis under him means, the person or the officer who is responsible for disbursement of such salary and includes the head of the office or any establishment as well as the Manager or Agent of the employer;

(c) "half year" shall be from the 1st day of April to the 30th day of September and from the 1st day of October to the 31st day of March of a year;

(d) "month" means a calendar month;

(e) "person" means any person who is engaged actively or otherwise in any profession, trade, calling or employment in the State of Tamil Nadu and includes a Hindu Undivided Family, firm, company, corporation or other corporate body, any society, club, body of persons or association , so engaged, but does not include any person employed on a casual basis;

(f) "tax" means the tax on profession, trade, calling and employment levied under this chapter.

198-B. Levy of Profession Tax. – (1) There shall be levied by the village Panchayat a tax on profession, trade, calling and employment.

(2) Every company which transacts business and every person, who is engaged actively or otherwise in any profession, trade, calling or employment within the Panchayat Village on the first day of the half year for which return is filed, shall pay half yearly tax at the rates specified in the Table below in such manner as may be prescribed:-

THE TABLE

Sl. No.	Average half-yearly income		Half-yearly tax
	From	To	
(1)	(2)	(3)	(4)
1.	Upto Rs.21,000	"	Nil
2.	Rs.21,001	Rs.30,000	Rs.60
3.	Rs.30,001	Rs.45,000	Rs.150
4.	Rs.45,001	Rs.60,000	Rs.300
5.	Rs.60,001	Rs.75,000	Rs.450
6.	Rs.75,001	and above	Rs.600

(3) The rate of Tax payable under sub-section (2) shall be published by the Inspector in such manner as may be prescribed.

(4) Where a company or person proves that it or he has paid the sum due on account of the tax levied under this Chapter or any tax of

the nature of a profession tax imposed under the Cantonments Act, 1924 (Central Act II of 1924) for the same half year to any local authority or containment authority in the State of Tamil Nadu, such company or person shall not be liable, by reason, merely of change of place of business, exercise of profession, trade, calling or employment, or residence, to pay the tax to any other local authority or cantonment authority.

(5) The tax leviable from a firm, association or Hindu Undivided Family may be levied on any adult member of the firm, association or family.

(6) Where a person doing the same business in the same name in one or more places within the Panchayat Village, the income of such business in all places within the Panchayat Village shall be computed for the purpose of levy of tax and such person shall pay the tax in accordance with the provisions of this Chapter.

(7) Where any company, corporate body, society, firm, body of persons or association pays the tax under this Chapter, any director, partner or member, as the case may be, of such company, corporate body, society, firm, body of persons or association shall not be liable to pay tax under this Chapter for the income derived by such director, partner or member from such company, corporate body, society, firm, body of persons or association :

Provided that such director, partner or member shall be liable to pay tax under this Chapter for the income derived from other sources.

(8) Every person who is liable to pay tax, other than a person earning salary or wage shall furnish to the Executive Authority a return in such form for such period and within such date and in such manner as may be prescribed:

Provided that subject to the provisions of sub-sections (10) and (11), such person may make a self-assessment on the basis of average half yearly income of the previous financial year and the return filed by him shall be accepted without calling for the accounts and without any inspection.

(9) Every such return shall accompany with the proof of payment of the full amount of tax due according tot the return and a return without such proof of payment shall not be deemed to have been duly filed.

(10) Notwithstanding anything contained in the proviso to sub-section (8), the Executive Authority may select ten per cent of the total number of such assessment in such manner as may be prescribed for the purpose of detailed scrutiny regarding the correctness of the return submitted by a person in this connection and in such cases final assessment order shall be passed in accordance with the provisions of this Chapter.

(11) If no return is submitted by any person under sub-section (8) within the prescribed period or if the return submitted by him appears to the Executive Authority to be incomplete or incorrect, the Executive

Authority shall, after making such enquiry as he may consider necessary, assess such person to the best of his judgement.

Provided that before taking action under this sub-section, the person shall be given a reasonable opportunity of proving the correctness or completeness of any return submitted by him.

(12) Every person who is liable to pay tax under this section, other than a person earning salary or wage –

(a) shall be issued with a pass book containing such details relating to such payment of tax as may be prescribed and if the pass book is lost or accidentally destroyed, the Executive Authority may, on an application made by the person accompanied by such fees may be fixed by the Village Panchayat issue to such person a duplicate of the pass book;

(b) shall be allotted a permanent account number and such person shall-

(i) quote such number in all his returns to or correspondence with the Executive Authority;

(ii) quote such number in all chalans for the payment of any sum due under this Chapter.

(13) The rate of tax specified under sub-section (2) shall be revised by the Village Panchayat once in every five years and such revision of tax shall be increased not less than twenty-five per cent and not more than thirty five per cent of the tax levied immediately before the date of revision.

198-C. Employers liability to deduct and pay tax on behalf of the employees. – The tax payable by any person earning a salary or wage shall be deducted by his employer from the salary payable to such person, before such salary or wage is paid to him in such manner as may be prescribed, and such employer shall irrespective of whether such deduction has been made or not when the salary or wage is paid to such person be liable to pay tax on behalf of such person:

Provided that if the employer is an officer of the State or Central Government, the Government may, notwithstanding anything contained in this Chapter prescribe the manner in which such employer shall discharge the said liability.

198-D Filing of returns by employer. – (1) Every employer liable to pay tax under this Chapter shall file a return to the Executive Authority, in such form, for such period and by such date as may be prescribed, showing therein the salaries paid by him to the employees and the amount of tax deducted by him in respect of such employees.

(2) Every such return shall accompany with the proof of payment of the full amount of tax due according to the return and a return without such proof of payment shall not be deemed to have been duly filed.

198-E. Assessment of the employer. – (1) The Executive Authority, if satisfied that any return field by any employer under sub-section (1) of section 198-D is correct and complete, shall accept the return;

(2) Where an employer has failed to file any return under sub-section (1) of Section 198-D within the time or if the return filed by him appears to the Executive Authority to be incorrect or incomplete, the Executive Authority shall, after making such enquiry as he considers necessary, determine the tax due and assess the employer to the best of his judgement and issue a notice of demand for the tax so assessed;

Provided that before assessing the tax due, the Executive Authority shall give the employer a reasonable opportunity of being heard.

198-F. Penalty and Interest. – (1) In addition to the tax assessed under sub-section (11) of section 198-B or sub-section (2) of section 198-E, the Executive Authority shall direct the person or employer to pay by way of penalty a sum,

Which shall be, in the case of submission of incorrect or incomplete return, one hundred per cent of the difference of the tax assessed and the tax paid as per return;

Provided that no penalty under this sub-section shall be imposed after the period if three years from the date of the order of the assessment under this Chapter and unless the person affected has had a reasonable opportunity of showing cause against such imposition.

(2) On any amount remaining unpaid after the date specified for its payment, the person or employer shall pay, in addition to the amount due, interest at such rate not exceeding one per cent per mensum of such amount for the entire period of default, as may be prescribed.

198-G. Appeal. – (1) Any person or employer aggrieved by any order or decision of the Executive Authority in relation to the payment of tax (including penalty, fee and interest) may, within such time as may be prescribed, appeal to the authority prescribed under section 174.

(2) The decision of the authority referred to in sub-section (1) shall be final and shall not be questioned in any court of law:

Provided that no such decision shall be made except after giving the person affected a reasonable opportunity of being heard.

198-H. Exemptions. – Nothing contained in this Chapter shall apply to-

(a) the members of the Armed Forces of the Union serving in any part of this State, to whom the provisions of the Army Act, 1950 (Central Act XLVI, of 1950), the Air Force Act, 1950 (Central Act XLV of 1950) or the Navy Act, 1957 Central Act 62 of 1957) applies:

(b) the members of the Central Reserve Police Force to whom the Central Reserve Police Force Act, 1949 (Central Act XLVI of 1949) applies an serving in any part of this State;

(c) physically disabled persons with total disability in one or both the hands or legs, spastics, totally dumb or deaf persons or totally blind persons:

Provided that such physical disability shall be duly certified by a Registered Medical Practitioner in the service of the Government not below the rank of a Civil Surgeon.

198-I. Repeal and savings. – (1) The Tamil Nadu Tax on Professions, Trades, Callings and Employments Act, 1992 (Tamil Nadu Act 24 of 1992) (hereafter in this section referred to as the 1992 Act), in its application to the Village Panchayat is here by repealed.

(2) The repeal of the 1992 Act under sub-section (1) shall not affect; –

(i) the previous operation of the said Act or anything done or duly suffered thereunder; or

(ii) any right, privileges, obligations or liabilities acquired, accrued or incurred under the said Act; or

(iii) any penalty, forfeiture or punishment incurred in respect of any offence committed.

(3) Notwithstanding the repeal of the 1992 Act, the rates of tax of professions, trades, callings and employments specified in the Schedule to the said Act shall continue to apply for period commencing on the 1st day of April 1992 and ending with the 30th day of September 1998 for the levy and collection of such tax for the said period where the taxes due under that Act has not been paid for the said period.

(4) The provisions of this Chapter, other than the rates of tax specified in sub-section (2) of section 198-B and the provisions relating to penalty and interest, shall mutatis mutandis apply to the levy and collection of tax for the period mentioned in sub-section (3).

(5) The arrears of tax under the 1992 Act shall be paid in six equal half yearly instalments in such manner and within such period as may be prescribed].

CHAPTER – X

CONTROLLING AUTHORITIES

199. Appointment of officers to supervise panchayats. – (1) The Government may appoint such officers as may be required for the purpose of inspecting or superintending the operations of all or any of the panchayats constituted under this Act.

(2) The Government shall have power to regulate by rules made under this Act, the classifications, methods of recruitment, conditions of service, pay and allowances and discipline and conduct of the officers referred to in sub-section (1) and of the members of their establishments.

200. Powers of inspecting officers. – (1) The Inspector or the Collector or any officer appointed under section 199 or any other officer or person whom the Government or the Inspector or the Collector may empower in this behalf, may-

(a) enter on and inspect any immovable property, or any work in progress, under the control of any panchayat or any executive authority or commissioner or Secretary

(b) enter any school, dispensary, vaccination station or choultry maintained by or under the control of any panchayat or any other institution maintained by or under the control of any panchayat and inspect any records, registers or other documents kept in any such institution;

(c) enter the office of any panchayat and inspect any records, registers or other documents kept therein.

(2) Village panchayats and their presidents, executive authorities, panchayat union councils and their chairmen, commissioners, district panchayats and their chairmen, Secretaries and the officers and servants of panchayats shall be bound to afford to the officers and persons aforesaid, such access, at all reasonable times, to panchayat property or premises and to all documents as may, in the opinion of such officer or persons, subject to such rules as may be prescribed, be necessary to enable them to discharge their duties under this section.

201. Powers of officers for purpose of control. – The Inspector or any officer or person whom the Government or the Inspector, may empower in this behalf may;-

(a) direct the village panchayat or panchayat union council or the district panchayat to make provision for and to executive or provide any public work or amenity, or service of the description referred to in sections 110, 112 and 163;

(b) call for any record, register or other document in the possession, or under the control, of any panchayat or executive authority, or commissioner or Secretary;

(c) require any panchayat or executive authority or commissioner or the Secretary to furnish any return, plan, estimate, statement , account or statistics;

(d) require any panchayat or executive authority or commissioner or the Secretary to furnish any information or report on any matter connected with such panchayat;

(e) require any panchayat or executive authority or the commissioner or the Secretary to obtain his previous sanction before giving up claim or closing down any institution which is a source of income;

(f) record in writing for the consideration of any panchayat or executive authority or commissioner or the Secretary, any observations in regard to its or his proceedings or duties.

202. Power to suspend or cancel resolution, etc under the Act. – (1) The Inspector may, by order in writings-

(i) suspend or cancel any resolution passed, order issued, or licence or permission granted, or

(ii) prohibit the doing of any act which is about to be done or is being done, in pursuance or under colour of this Act, if in his opinion-

(a) such resolution, order, licence, permission or act has not been legally passed, issued, granted or authorised, or

(b) such resolution, order, licence, permission or act is in excess of the powers conferred by this Act or any other law or an abuse of such powers or is considered by the Inspector to be otherwise undesirable, or

(c) the execution of such resolution or order, or the continuance in force of such licence or permission or the doing of such act is likely to cause danger to human life, health or safety, or is likely to lead to a riot or an affray;

Provided that nothing in this sub-section shall enable the Inspector to set aside any election which has been held.

(2) The Inspector shall, before taking action on any of the grounds, referred to in clauses (a) and (b) of sub-section (1), give the authority or person concerned an opportunity for explanation.

(3) The power conferred on the Inspector under clause (c) of sub-section (1) may be exercised by the Collector in accordance with the provisions of that clause.

203. Emergency powers of Collector and Inspector. – Subject to such control as may be prescribed, the Inspector or the Collector may, in cases of emergency, direct or provide for the execution of any, work, or the doing of any act which a panchayat or executive authority or commissioner or Secretary is empowered to execute or do, and the immediate execution or doing of which is in his opinion necessary for the safety of the public, and may direct that the expenses of executing such work or doing such act shall be paid by the person having the custody of the Village Panchayat Fund or the Panchayat Union (General) Fund or the District Panchayat (General) Fund in priority to any other charges against such Fund except charges for the service of authorized loans.

204. Power to take action in default of a village panchayat, president or executive authority, etc. – (1) If any time it appears to the Inspector that a village panchayat, president or executive authority or that a panchayat union council or its chairman or commissioner or a district panchayat or its chairman or Secretary, has made default in performing any duty imposed by or under this or any other Act, he may, by order in writing, fix a period for the performance of such duty.

(2) If such duty is not performed within the period so fixed, the Inspector may appoint some person to perform it, and may direct that the expense of performing it shall be paid by the person having the custody of the Village Panchayat Fund or the Panchayat Union Fund or the District Panchayat (General) Fund as the case may be, in priority to any other charges against such Fund except charges for the service of authorised loans.

(3) If on a representation in writing made by the president, the Inspector is satisfied that due to the non-co-operation of the members with the president, the village panchayat is not able to function, the Inspector may, by notification, authorise the president to perform, subject to the control of the Inspector, such of the duties imposed upon the village panchayat by law and for such period not exceeding six months as may be specified in such notification. During the period for which the president is so authorised, there shall be no meeting of the village panchayat.

(4) If on a representation in writing made by the chairman, the Government are satisfied that due to the non-co-operation of the members with the chairman, the panchayat union council or the district panchayat, as the case may be, is not able to function, the Government may, by notification, authorise the chairman to perform, subject to the control of the Government or any officer authorised by the Government in this behalf, such of the duties imposed upon the panchayat union council or the district panchayat, as the case may be, by law and for such period not exceeding six months as may be specified in such notification. During the period for which the chairman is so authorised, there shall be no meeting of the panchayat union council or the district panchayat.

205. Removal of president. – (1) The Inspector – (a) of his own motion, or

(b) on a representation in writing signed by not less than two-thirds of the sanctioned strength of the village panchayat containing a statement of charges against the president and presented in person to the Inspector by any two of the members of the village panchayat, is satisfied that the president wilfully omits or refused to carry out or disobeys any provision of this Act, or any rule, by-law, regulation, or lawful order made or issued under this Act or abuses any power vested in him, the Inspector shall, by notice in writing, require the president to offer within a specified date, his explanation with respect to his acts of omission or commission mentioned in the notice.

(2) If the explanation is received within the specified date and the Inspector considers that the explanation is satisfactory, he may drop further action with respect to the notice. If no explanation is received within the specified date or if the explanation received is in his opinion not satisfactory, he shall forward to the Tahsildar of the taluk a copy of the notice referred to in sub-section (1) and the explanation of the president if received within the specified date with a proposal for the removal of the president for ascertaining the views of the village panchayat.

(3) The Tahsildar shall then convene a meeting for the consideration of the notice and the explanation, if any, and the proposal for the removal of the president, at the office of the village panchayat at a time appointed by the Tahsildar.

(4) A copy of the notice of the meeting shall be caused to be delivered to the president and to all the members of the village panchayat by the Tahsildar at least seven days before the date of the meeting.

(5) The Tahsildar shall preside at the meeting convened under this section and no other person shall preside thereat. If, within half an hour appointed for the meeting, the Tahsildar is not present to preside at the meeting, the meeting shall stand adjourned to a time to be appointed and notified to the members and the president by the Tahsildar under sub-section(6)

(6) If the Tahsildar is unable to preside at the meeting, he may, after recording his reasons in writing, adjourn the meeting to such other time as he may appoint. The date so appointed shall be not later than thirty days from the date so appointed for the meeting under sub-section (3), Notice of not less than seven clear days shall be given to the members and president of the time appointed for the adjourned meeting.

(7) Save as provided in sub-sections (5) and (6), a meeting convened for the purpose of considering the notice and the explanation, if any, and the proposal for the removal of the president under this section shall not for any reason, be adjourned.

(8) As soon as the meeting convened under this section is commenced, the Tahsilar, shall read to the village panchayat the notice of the Inspector and the explanation, if any, of the president [1]["and the proposal for the removal of the president"] for the consideration of which it has been convened.

[2]["(8A) There shall be no debate in any meeting under this section"]

(9) The Tahsildar shall not speak on the merits of the notice or explanation nor shall be entitled to vote at the meeting.

(10) The views of the village panchayat shall be duly recorded in the minutes of the meeting and a copy of the minutes shall forthwith on the termination of the meeting be forwarded by the Tahsildar to the Inspector.

(11) The Inspector may, after considering the views of the village panchayat in this regard, in his discretion either remove the president from office by notification with effect from a date to be specified therein or drop further action.

(12) The Government shall have power to cancel any notification issued under sub-section (11) and may, pending a decision on such cancellation, postpone the date specified in such notification.

(13) Any person in respect of whom a notification has been issued under sub-section (11) removing him from the office of president shall, unless the notification is cancelled under sub-section (12), be ineligible for election as president until the date on which notice of the next

---

[1&2] *Inserted by Act. 2/1999.*

ordinary elections to the village panchayat is published in the prescribed manner, or the expiry of one year from the date specified in such notification as postponed by the order, if any, issued under sub-section (12) whichever is earlier.

206. Removal of vice-president. – (1) If in the opinion of the Inspector, the vice-president wilfully omits or refuses to carry out or disobeys any provisions of this Act, or any rule, by-law, regulation, or lawful order made or issued under this Act or abuses any power vested in him, the Inspector shall by notice in writing, require the vice-president to offer within a specified date, his explanation with respect to his cases of omission or commission mentioned in the notice.

(2) The provisions of sub-sections (2) to (13) (both inclusive) of section 205 shall, as far as may be, apply in relation to the removal of the vice-president as they apply in relation to the removal of the president by the Inspector on his own motion.

207. Removal of chairman of Panchayat Union Council. – (1) If the Government –

(a) of their own motion, or

(b) on a representation in writing signed by not less than two-thirds of the strength of the panchayat union council containing a statement or charges against the chairman of the panchayat union council and presented in person to any officer appointed by the Government in this behalf by any two of the members of the panchayat union council,are satisfied that the chairman wilfully omits or refuses to carry out or disobeys the provisions of this Act, or any rules, by-laws, regulations or lawful orders issued thereunder or abuses the powers vested in him, the Government shall, by notice in writing, require the chairman to officer within a specified date, his explanation with respect to his acts of omission or commission mentioned in the notice.

(2) If the explanation is received within the specified date and the Government consider that the explanation is satisfactory, the Government may drop further action with respect to the notice. If no explanation is received within the specified date or if the explanation received is in their opinion not satisfactory, the Government shall forward to the Revenue Divisional Officer of the division concerned, a copy of the notice referred to in sub-section (1) and the explanation of the chairman with a proposal for the removal of the chairman form office for ascertaining the views of the panchayat union council.

(3) The Revenue Divisional Officer shall then convene a meeting for the consideration of the notice and the explanation, if any, and the proposal for the removal of the chairman at the office of the panchayat union council at a time appointed by the Revenue Divisional Officer.

(4) A copy of the notice of the meeting shall be caused to be delivered to the concerned chairman and to all the members of the panchayat union council by the Revenue Divisional Officer at least seven days before the date of the meeting.

(5) The Revenue Divisional Officer shall preside at the meeting convened under this section and no other person shall preside thereat. If within half an hour appointed for the meeting, the Revenue Divisional Officer is not present to preside at the meeting, the meeting shall stand adjourned to a time to be appointed and notified to the members by the Revenue Divisional Officer, under sub-section (6).

(6) If the Revenue Divisional Officer is unable to preside at the meeting, he may, after recording his reasons in writing, adjourn the meeting to such other time as he may appoint. The date so appointed shall be not later than thirty days from the date appointed for the meeting under sub-section (3). Notice of not less than seven clear days shall be given to the members of the time appointed for the adjourned meeting.

(7) Save as provided in sub-sections (5) and (6) a meeting convened for the purpose of considering the notice and the explanation, if any, and the proposal for the removal of the chairman under this section shall not, for any reason, be adjourned.

(8) As soon as the meeting convened under this section is commenced, the Revenue Divisional Officer shall read to the panchayat union council the notice of the Government and the explanation, if any, of the chairman [1][and the proposal for the removal of the chairman] for the consideration of which it has been convened.

(9) There shall be no debate in any meeting under this section.

(10) The Revenue Divisional Officer shall not speak on the merits of the notice or explanation nor shall he be entitled to vote at the meeting.

(11) The views of the panchayat union council shall be duly recorded in the minutes of the meeting and a copy of the minutes shall forthwith on the termination of the meeting be forwarded by the Revenue Divisional Officer to the Government.

(12) The Government may, after considering the views of the panchayat union council in this regard in their discretion either remove the chairman from office by notification with effect from a date to be specified therein or drop further action.

(13) Any person in respect of whom a notification has been issued under sub section (12) removing him from the office of chairman shall be ineligible for election as chairman and for holding any of those offices until the date on which notice of the next ordinary elections to the panchayat union council is published in the prescribed manner or the expiry of one year from the date specified in the notification whichever is earlier.

208. Removal of vice-chairman of Panchayat Union Council. – (1) If, in the opinion of the Government, the vice-chairman of the panchayat union council wilfully omits or refuses to carry out or disobeys any provisions of this Act, or any rules, by-laws, regulations

---

[1] *Inserted by Act. 2/1999.*

or lawful orders issued thereunder or abuses any power vested in him, the Government shall, by notice in writing, require the vice-chairman to offer within a specified date, his explanation with respect to his acts of omission or commission mentioned in the notice.

(2) The provisions of sub-sections (2) to (13) (both inclusive) of section 207 shall, as far as may be, apply in relation to the removal of the vice-chairman as they apply in relation to the removal of the chairman of the panchayat union council by the Government on their own motion.

209. Removal of chairman of district panchayat. – (1) If the Government – (a) of their own motion, or

(b) on a representation in writing signed by not less than two-thirds of the strength of the district panchayat containing a statement of charges against the chairman of the district panchayat and presented in person to any officer appointed by the Government in this behalf, by any two of the members of the district Panchayat, are satisfied that the chairman wilfully omits or refuses to carry out or disobeys the provisions of this Act, or any rules, by-laws, regulations or lawful orders issued thereunder or abuses the powers vested in him, the Government shall, by notice in writing, require the chairman to offer within a specified date, his explanation with respect to his acts of omission or commission mentioned in the notice.

(2) The provisions of sub-sections (2) to (13) (both inclusive) of section 207 shall, as far as may be, apply in relation to the removal of the chairman of district panchayat as they apply in relation to the removal of the chairman of panchayat union council by the Government on their own motion.

210. Removal of vice-chairman of district panchayat. – (1) If, in the opinion of the Government, the vice-chairman of district panchayat, wilfully omits or refuses to carry out or disobeys any provisions of this Act, or any rules, by-laws, regulations or lawful orders issued thereunder or abuses any power vested in him, the Government shall, by notice in writing, required the vice-chairman of district panchayat to offer within a specified date, his explanation with respect to his acts of omission or commission mentioned in the notice.

(2) The provisions of sub-section (2) to (13) (both inclusive) of section 207 shall, as far as may be, apply in relation to the removal of the vice-chairman of district panchayat, as they apply in relation to the removal of the chairman of panchayat union council, by the Government on their own motion.

211. Motion of no confidence in vice-president of panchayat. – (1) Subject to the provisions of this section, a motion expressing want of confidence in the vice-president of a village panchayat may be made in accordance with the procedure laid down herein.

(2) Written notice of intention to make the motion, signed by members of the village panchayat not less in number than one-half of the sanctioned strength of the village panchayat, together with a copy of the motion which is proposed to be made, and a written statement of the charges against the vice-president, shall be delivered in person to the Tahsildar of the taluk by any two of the members of the village panchayat signing the notice.

(3) A copy of the statement of charges along with the notice of the meeting shall be caused to be delivered to the vice-president concerned by the Tahsildar, and the vice-president shall be required to give a statement in reply to the charges within a week of the receipt of the notice by the vice-president.

(4) The Tahsildar shall, after the expiry of the period of the notice issued under sub-section (3) convene a meeting for the consideration of the motion, at the office of the village panchayat at a time appointed by him.

(5) The Tahsildar shall give to the members notice of not less than fifteen clear days of such meeting and of the time appointed therefor.

(6) The Tahsildar shall preside at the meeting convened under this section, and no other person shall preside thereat. If within half an hour after the time appointed for the meeting, the Tahsildar is not present to preside at the meeting, the meeting shall stand adjourned to a time to be appointed and notified to the members by the Tahsildar under sub-section (7)

(7) If the Tahsildar is unable to preside at the meeting, he may, after recording his reasons in writing, adjourn the meeting to such other time as he may appoint. The date so appointed shall not be later than thirty days from the date appointed for the meeting under sub-section (4). Notice of not less than seven clear days shall be given to the members, of the time appointed for the adjourned meeting.

(8) Save as provided in sub-sections (6) and (7), a meeting convened for the purpose of considering a motion under this section shall not for any reason be adjourned.

(9) As soon as the meeting convened under this section has commenced, the Tahsildar shall read to the village panchayat, the motion for the consideration of which it has been convened, the statement of charges and the written statement, if any, of the vice-president in reply to the said charges.

(10) There shall be no debate on any motion under this section.

(11) The Tahsildar shall not speak on the merits of the motion, nor shall he be entitled to vote thereon.

(12) A copy of the minutes of the meeting together with a copy of the motion and the result of the voting thereon shall forthwith on the termination of the meeting be forwarded by the Tahsildar to the Inspector.

(13) If the motion is carried with the support of not less than two-thirds of the sanctioned strength of the village panchayat, the Inspector shall, by notification, remove the vice-president of the village panchayat.

(14) If the motion is not carried by such a majority as aforesaid, or if the meeting cannot be held for want of the quorum referred to in sub-section (13), no notice of any subsequent motion expressing want of confidence in the same vice-president shall be received until after the expiry of six months from the date of the meeting.

(15) No notice of a motion under this section shall be received within six months of the assumption of office by the vice-president.

212. Motion of no confidence in [1]["chairman or vice-chairman"] of Panchayat Union Council. – (1) Subject to the provisions of this section, a motion expressing want of confidence in the [2]["Chairman or vice-chairman"] of a panchayat union council may be made in accordance with the procedure laid down herein.

(2) Written notice of intention to make the motion, signed by members of the panchayat union council not less in number than one-half of the sanctioned strength of the panchayat union council, together with a copy of the motion which is proposed to be made and a written statement of the charges against the [3]["Chairman or vice-chairman"] shall be delivered in person to the Revenue Divisional Officer of the division by any two of the members of the panchayat union council signing the notice.

(3) A copy of the a statement of charges along with the motion shall be caused to be delivered to the concerned [4]["Chairman or vice-chairman"] by the Revenue Divisional Office and the ["chairman or vice-chairman"] shall be required to give a statement in reply to the charges within a week of the receipt of the motion by the Vice-chairman.

(4) The Revenue Divisional Officer shall then convene a meeting for the consideration of the motion at the office of the panchayat union council at a time appointed by him.

(5) The Revenue Divisional Officer shall give to the members notice of not less than fifteen clear days of the meeting and of the time appointed therefor.

(6) The Revenue Divisional Officer shall preside at the meeting convened under this section, and no other person shall preside thereat. If within half an hour after the time appointed for the meeting, the Revenue Divisional Officer is not present to preside at the meeting, the meeting shall stand adjourned to a time to be appointed and notified to the members by the Revenue Divisional Officer under sub-section(7).

(7) If the Revenue Divisional Officer is unable to preside at the meeting, he may, after recording his reasons in writing adjourn the meeting to such other time as he may appoint. The date so appointed shall not be later than thirty days from the date appointed for the meeting under sub-section (4). Notice of not less than seven clear days shall be given to the members of the time appointed for the adjourned meeting.

[1,2,3] *Substituted by Act. 31/1999 for the expression "vice-chairman".*

[4] *Substituted by Act. 31/1999 for the expression "vice-chairman".*

(8) Save as otherwise provided in sub-sections (6), (7) a meeting convened for the purpose of considering a motion under this section shall not for any reason be adjourned.

(9) As soon as the meeting convened under this section has commenced, the Revenue Divisional Officer shall read to the village panchayat union council, the motion for the consideration of which it has been convened, the statement of charges and the written statement, if any, of the [1]["chairman or the vice-chairman"] in reply to the said charges.

(10) There shall be no debate on any motion under this section.

(11) The Revenue Divisional Officer shall not speak on the merits of the motion, nor shall he be entitled to vote thereon.

(12) A copy of the minutes of the meeting together with a copy of the motion and the result of the voting thereon shall forthwith on he termination of the meeting be forwarded by the Revenue Divisional Officer to the Government.

(13) If the motion is carried with the support of not less than two-thirds of the sanctioned strength of the panchayat union council, the Government shall, by notification, remove the [2]["chairman or vice-chairman"] of the panchayat union council.

(14) If the motion is not carried by such a majority as aforesaid, or if the meeting cannot be held for want of the quorum referred to in sub-section (13), no notice of any subsequent motion expressing want of confidence in the same [3]["chairman or vice-chairman"] shall be received until after the expiry of [4]["one year"] from the date of the meeting.

(15) No notice of a motion under this section shall be received within [5]["one year"] of the assumption of office by [6]["chairman or the vice-chairman"].

213. Motion of no confidence in [7]["Chairman or vice-chairman"] of district panchayat. – A motion expressing want of confidence in the [8]["chairman or vice-chairman"] of a district panchayat may be made in accordance with the procedure specified in sub-sections (2) to (15) (both inclusive) of section 212, subject to the modification that the reference to Revenue Divisional Officer in the said sub-sections shall be construed as a reference to Collector.

214. Dissolution of village panchayat. – (1) If, in the opinion of the Government, a village panchayat is not competent to perform or persistently makes default in performing the duties imposed on it by law, or exceeds or abuses its powers, they may, by notification, direct that the village panchayat be dissolved with effect from a specified date and reconstituted with effect from a specified date

---

[1, 2, 3, 4] *Substituted by Act. 31/1999 for the expression "vice-chairman".*

[5, 6, 7, 8] *Substituted by Act. 31/1999 for the expression "Vice-chairman".*

which shall be within a period of six months from the date of such dissolution.

(2) Before publishing a notification under sub-section (1), the Government shall communicate to the village panchayat, the grounds on which they propose to do so, fix a reasonable period for the village panchayat to show cause against the proposal and consider its explanations and objections if any.

(3) On the date fixed for the dissolution of a village panchayat under subsection (1) all its members as well as its president and vice-president shall forthwith be deemed to have vacated their offices as such and thereupon the provisions contained in the proviso to sub-section (2) of section 16 shall apply.

(4) In case the president of a village panchayat which is dissolved under this section is a member of a panchayat union council, he shall, with effect on and from the date of the dissolution, be deemed to have vacated his office as such member notwithstanding anything contained in section 22.

(5) On the reconstitution of the village panchayat after the dissolution, the Government may pass such orders as they deem fit as to the transfer to the village panchayat from the panchayat union council during the period of dissolution on behalf of the village panchayat and as to the discharge of the discharge of the liabilities if any, of such village panchayat relating to such assets or institutions.

(6) In the case of a village panchayat reconstituted after dissolution, the elected member including the president shall enter upon their offices on the date fixed for its reconstitution and shall hold their offices only for the remainder of the period for which the dissolved village panchayat would have continued under sub-section (1) of section 9, had it not been dissolved.

215. Dissolution of Panchayat Union Council. – (1) If, in the opinion of the Government a panchayat union council is not competent to perform or persistently makes default in performing the duties imposed on it by law or exceeds or abuses its powers, they may, by notification-

(a) dissolve the panchayat union council from a specified date; and

(b) direct that the panchayat union council be reconstituted with effect from a date which shall not be later than six months from the date of dissolution.

(2) Before publishing a notification under sub-section (1), the Government shall communicate to the panchayat union council the grounds on which they propose to do so, fix a reasonable period for the panchayat union council to show cause against the proposal and consider its explanations and objections, if any.

(3) On the date fixed for the dissolution of a panchayat union council under sub-section (1) all its members as well as its chairman and vice-chairman shall forthwith be deemed to have vacated their offices as such.

(4) During the interval between the dissolution and the reconstitution of a panchayat union council, the Inspector may appoint a persons to exercise the powers and discharge the duties of the panchayat union council and of its chairman;

Provided that any person to be appointed under the provisions of this sub-section shall be a person in the service of the Government not below the rank of a Tahsildar or a commissioner.

(5) The Government may direct that the panchayat union council be reconstituted before the date fixed for its reconstitution under clause (b) of sub-section (1).

(6) The members as well as the chairman and vice-chairman of a reconstituted panchayat union council shall enter upon their offices on the date fixed for its reconstitution and they shall hold their offices only for the remainder of the period for which the dissolved panchayat union council would have continued under sub-section (1) of section 18, had it not been dissolved.

(7) When a panchayat union council is dissolved under this section, the Government until the date of the reconstitution of the panchayat union council and the reconstituted panchayat union council thereafter shall be entitled to all the assets and be subject to all the liabilities of the panchayat union council as on the date of the reconstitution respectively.

216. Dissolution of district panchayat. – (1) If, in the opinion of the Government, a district panchayat is not competent to perform or persistently makes default in performing the duties imposed on it by law or exceeds or abuses its powers, they may, by notification –

(a) dissolve the district panchayat from a specified date; and

(b) direct that the district panchayat be reconstituted with effect from the date, which shall not be later than six months from the date of dissolution.

(2) The provisions of sub-section (2) to (7) (both inclusive) of section 215 shall, as far as may be, apply in relation to the dissolution of a district panchayat as they apply in relation to the dissolution of a panchayat union council.

217. Powers of officers acting in behalf of panchayat and liability for payment of compensation. – The Government, the Inspector or any other person lawfully taking action on behalf, or in default, of a panchayat under this Act, shall have such powers as are necessary for the purpose and shall be entitled to the same protection under this Act as the panchayat or its officers or servants whose powers are exercised; and compensation shall be recoverable from the Village Panchayat Fund or the Panchayat Union Fund or the District Panchayat (General) Fund by any person suffering damage from the exercise of such powers to the same extent, as if the action had been taken by the panchayat or their officers or servants.

218. Delegation of powers. – (1) The Government may, by notification, authorize any authority or officer not below the rank of a Collector to exercise in regard to any panchayat or any class of panchayats in any area or all panchayats in any area, any of the powers vested in them by this Act except the power to make rules and may in like manner withdraw such authority.

(2) The Inspector or the Collector may by notification authorise any officer not below the rank of a Revenue Divisional Officer to exercise in respect of any panchayat union councils or any panchayat union councils or all panchayat union councils in the area under the jurisdiction of such officer, any of the powers vested by this Act on the Inspector or the Collector as the case may be and may in like manner withdraw such authority.

(3) The Inspector or the Collector may, by notification, authorise any officer not below the rank of a commissioner to exercise in respect of any village panchayat or any class of village panchayats or all village panchayat in the panchayat development block any of the powers vested by this Act on the Inspector or the Collector as the case may be and may in like manner withdraw such authority.

(4) The exercise of any power delegated under sub-sections (1) to (3) shall be subject to such restrictions and conditions as may be prescribed or as may be specified in the notification and also to control and revision by the delegating authority, or where such authority is the Government by such officer as may be empowered by the Government in this behalf. The Government shall also have power to control and revise the acts or proceedings of any officer so empowered.

(5) The exercise of any power conferred on the Inspector or the Collector by any of the provisions of this Act including sub-sections (2) to (4) of this section shall whether such power is exercised by the Inspector or the Collector himself or by any officer to whom it has been delegated under sub-section (2) or (3) be subject to such restrictions and conditions as may be prescribed and also control by the Government or by such officer as may be empowered by them in this behalf. The Government shall also have power to control the acts or proceedings of any officer so empowered.

219. Revision. – (1) The Government may, after consulting the Inspector, Collector or such other officer or authority as they may deem fit, at any time, either *suo moto* or on application, call for and examine the record of any order passed or proceeding recorded under the provisions of this Act by-

(a) the Inspector or the Collector or any officer authorised by the Inspector or the Collector under sub-section (2) or (3) of section 218; or

(b) any officer authorised by the Government under sub-section (1) of that section or any officer empowered by them under sub-section (4) of that section; or

(c) any other authority or officer; for the purpose of satisfying themselves as the legality or propriety of such order, or as to the regularity of such proceeding and pass such order in reference thereto as they think fit.

(2) The powers of the nature referred to in sub-section (1) may also be exercised by such authority or officer as may be empowered in this behalf by the Government.

CHAPTER XI

GENERAL AND MISCELLANEOUS

LICENCES AND PERMISSIONS

220. General provisions regarding licence and permission. – (1) Save as otherwise expressly provided in or may be prescribed under this Act., every application for any licence or permission under this Act or any rule, by-law or regulation made thereunder, or for the renewal thereof, shall be made not less than thirty and not more than ninety days before the earliest date with effect from which, or the commencement of the period (being a year or such less period as is mentioned in the application) for which the licence or permission is required.

(2) Save as aforesaid, for every such licence or permission, fees may be charged on such units and at such rates as may be fixed by the panchayat, provided that the rates shall not exceed the maximum, if any, prescribed.

(3) Save as aforesaid, if orders on an application for any such licence or permission are not communicated to the applicant within thirty days or such longer period as may be prescribed in any class of cases after the receipt of the application by the executive authority of the village panchayat or the commissioner or the Secretary. The application shall be deemed to have been allowed for the period, if any, for which it would have been ordinarily allowed and subject to the law, rules, by-laws and regulations and all conditions ordinarily imposed.

(4) The acceptance of the pre-payment of the fee for any such licence or permission shall not entitle the person making such pre-payment to the licence or permission, but only to a refund of the fee in case of refusal of the licence or permission.

(5) If an act, for which any such licence or permission is necessary, is done without such licence or permission, or in a manner inconsistent with the terms of the licence or permission obtained, then-

(a) the executive authority of the village panchayat or the commissioner or the Secretary may by notice require the person so doing such act to alter, remove, or as far as practicable restore to its original state, the whole, or any part of any property, movable or immovable, public or private affected thereby, within a time to be specified in the notice; and further,

(b) if no penalty has been specially provided in this Act for so doing such act the person so doing it shall be punishable with fine not exceeding fifty rupees for such offence.

(6) Whenever any person is convicted of an offence in respect of the failure to obtain any such licence or permission, the Magistrate

shall, in addition to any fine which may be imposed, recover summarily and pay over to the panchayat the amount of the fee chargeable for the licence or permission, and may, in his discretion, also recover summarily and pay over to the panchayat such amount, if any as he may fix as the costs of the prosecution

Explanation – The recovery of the fee for a licence or permission under this sub-section shall not entitle the person convicted to the licence or permission.

221. Government and market committees not to obtain licence and permission. – Nothing in this Act or in any rule, by-law or regulation made thereunder shall be construed as requiring the taking out of any licence or the obtaining of any permission under this Act or any such rule, by-law or regulation in respect of any place in the occupation or under the control of the Central or the State Government or of a market committee established under the Tamil Nadu Agricultural Produce Marketing (Regulation) Act, 1987, (Tamil Nadu Act 27 of 1989) or in respect of any property of the Central or the State Government or of any property belonging to such market committee.

POWER TO ENFORCE NOTICES, ORDERS ETC.

222. Time for complying with notice, order etc and power to enforce in default. – (1) Whenever by any notice, requisition or order under this Act, or under any rule, bye-law or regulation made thereunder, any person is required to execute any work to take any measures or to do anything, a reasonable time shall be named in such notice, requisition or order within which the work shall be executed, the measure taken or the thing done.

(2) If such notice, requisition or order is not complied with within the time so named;-

(a) the executive authority of the village panchayat or the commissioner or the Secretary, as the case may be, may cause such work to be executed, or may take any measure or do anything which may, in his opinion, be necessary for giving due effect to the notice, requisition or order and

(b) if no penalty has been specially provided in this Act for failure to comply with such notice, requisition or order, the said person shall be punishable with fine not exceeding fifty rupees for every such offence.

POWER OF ENTRY AND INSPECTION

223. Power of Entry and Inspection. – (1) Subject to such restrictions and conditions as may be prescribed, the executive authority or the commissioner or the Secretary or any person authorised by him may enter on or into any place, building or land, with or without assistants or workmen in order

(a) to make any enquiry, inspection, test, examination, survey, measurement or valuation or to execute any other work, which is authorised by the provisions of this Act or of any rule, by-law, regulation or order made under it or which it is necessary to make or execute for any of the purposes of this Act or in pursuance of any of the said provisions, or

(b) to satisfy himself that nothing is being done in such place, building or land for which a licence or permission is required under any of the said provisions, without such licence or permission or otherwise than in conformity with the terms of the licence or permission obtained.

(2) No claim shall lie against any person for any damage or inconvenience necessarily caused by the exercise of powers under sub-section (1) or the use of any force necessary for effecting an entrance under that sub-section.

224. Testing of weights and measures. – The executive authority or the commissioner or the Secretary or any person authority by him, may examine and test the weights and measures used in the markets and shops in the panchayat village or the panchayat union or the district panchayat area as the case may be, with a view to the prevention and punishment of offences relating to such weights and measures under Chapter XIII of the Indian Penal Code (Central Act XLV of 1860).

225. Power to call for information from village administrative officer. – (1) The executive authority or the commissioner or the Secretary may, by an order in writing, require the Village Administrative Officer of any revenue village comprised within the jurisdiction of the village panchayat or panchayat union council or district panchayat to furnish him with information on any matter falling within such categories as may be prescribed in respect of such village or any part thereof or any person or property therein.

(2) The order shall specify the period within which it may be complied with but the executive authority or the commissioner or the Secretary, may, from time to time, extend such period.

LIMITATION

226. Limitation for recovery of dues. – No distraint shall be made, no suit shall be instituted and no prosecution shall be commenced in respect of any tax or other sum due to a panchayat under this Act or any rule, bye-law, regulation or order made under it after the expiration of a period of six years from the date on which distraint might first have been made, a suit might first have been instituted or prosecution might first have been commenced, as the case may be, in respect of such tax or sum.

PROSECUTIONS, SUITS, ETC.

227. Persons empowered to prosecute. – Save as otherwise expressly provided in this Act (Central Act 2 of 1974), no person shall be tried for any offence against this Act or any rule or bye-law made thereunder unless complaint is made within three months of the commission of the offence by the police, [1]["the village panchayat"], the executive authority, the panchayat union council, the commissioner, the district panchayat, the Secretary or a person expressly authorised in this behalf by the village panchayat, panchayat union council, district panchayat, executive authority or commissioner or the Secretary but nothing herein shall affect the provisions of the Code of Criminal Procedure, 1973 (Central Act.II of 1974) in regard to the power of certain Magistrates to take cognizance of offence upon information received or upon their own knowledge or suspicion:

Provided that failure to take out a licence or obtain permission under this Act shall, for the purposes of this section, be deemed to be a continuing offence until the expiration of the period , if any, for which the licence or permission is required and if no period is specified, complaint may be made at any time within twelve months from the commencement of the offence.

228. Composition of offences. – The executive authority or the commissioner or the Secretary may, subject to such restrictions and control, as may be prescribed, compound any offence against this Act or any rule or by-law made thereunder, which may by rules, be declared compoundable.

229. Prosecutions and compositions to be reported to village panchayat, panchayat union council or district panchayat. – Every prosecution instituted or offence compounded by the executive authority or the commissioner or the Secretary shall be reported by him to the village panchayat or panchayat union council or the district panchayat, as the case may be, at its next meeting.

230. Sanction of prosecution. – (1) When the president or the executive authority or the chairman or vice-chairman of a panchayat union council or district panchayat or the commissioner or the Secretary or any member is accused of any offence alleged to have been committed by him while acting or purporting to act in the discharge of his official duty, no court shall take cognizance of such offence except with the previous sanction of the Government.

(2) When according previous sanction under sub-section (1), it shall be open to the Government to direct by order that the president, executive authority, chairman, vice-chairman or commissioner or the Secretary, as the case may be, shall not discharge his duties as such until the disposal of the case.

231. Notice of action against village panchayat, etc. – (1) Subject to the provisions of section 232, no suit or other legal proceeding shall be brought against any village panchayat or its president or executive authority or any panchayat union council or its chairman or the

---

[1] *Inserted by Act. 2/1999*

commissioner or the district panchayat or its chairman or the Secretary or any member, officer or servant thereof or against any person acting under the direction of such village panchayat, president, panchayat union council or its chairman, district panchayat or its chairman, executive authority, commissioner, Secretary, member, officer or servant, in respect of any act done or purporting to be done under this Act, or in respect of any alleged neglect or default in the execution of this Act or any rule, by-law, regulation or order made under it until the expiration of two months next after notice in writing, stating the cause of action, the nature of the relief sought, the amount of compensation claimed and the name and place of residence of the intended plaintiff has been left at the office of the village panchayat or panchayat union council and if the proceeding is intended to be brought against any such president, executive authority, chairman, commissioner, chairman of district panchayat, Secretary, member, officer servant or person, also delivered to him or left at his place of residence.

(2) Every such proceeding shall, unless it is a proceeding for the recovery of immovable property or for a declaration of title thereto, be commenced within six months after the date on which the cause of action arose or in case of a continuing injury or damage, during such continuance or within six months after the ceasing thereof.

(3) If any village panchayat, panchayat union council or district panchayat or person to whom notice is given under sub-section (1), tenders amount to the plaintiff before the proceeding is commenced and if the plaintiff does not in such proceeding recover more than the amount so tendered, he shall not recover any costs incurred by him after such tender and the plaintiff shall also pay all costs incurred by the defendant after such tender.

232. Protection of chairman, president and officers acting in good faith. – No suit or other legal proceeding shall be brought against the chairman, commissioner, president, executive authority, Secretary or any member, officer or servant of a panchayat or any person acting under the direction of a panchayat or of such chairman, commissioner, president, executive authority, Secretary, member, officer or servant in respect of any act done or purporting to be done under this Act or in respect of any alleged neglect or default on his part in the execution of any act under this Act, or any rule, by law regulation or order made under it, if such act was done, or such neglect or default occurred in good faith; but any such proceeding shall, so far as it is maintainable in a court, be brought against the panchayat except in the case of suits brought under section 234.

233. Injuction not to be granted in election proceedings. – Notwithstanding anything contained in the Code of Civil Procedure, 1908, (Central Act V of 1908) or in any other law for the time being in force, no court shall grant any permanent or temporary injunction or make any interim order restraining any proceeding which is being or about to be taken under this Act for the preparation or publication of any electoral roll for the conduct of any election.

234. Liability of the president, executive authority and members, etc for loss, waste or misapplication of property. – (1) The president, executive authority and every member of a village panchayat and the chairman, commissioner and every member of a panchayat union council and the chairman, Secretary and every member of a district panchayat shall be liable for the loss, waste or misapplication of any money or other property owned by or vested in the village panchayat or panchayat union council or the district panchayat if such loss, waste or misapplication is a direct consequence of his neglect or misconduct; and a suit for compensation may be instituted against him in any court of competent jurisdiction by the panchayat or panchayat union council or the district panchayat with the previous sanction of the Inspector.

(2) Every such suit shall be commenced within three years after the date on which the cause of action arose.

235. Assessment etc not to be impeached. – (1) No assessment or demand made, and no charge imposed under the authority of this Act shall be impeached or affected by reason of any clerical error or by reason of any mistake (a) in respect of the name, residence, place of business or occupation of any person, or (b) in the description of any property or thing or (c) in respect of the amount assessed, demanded or charged, provided that the provisions of this Act have in substance and effect been complied with and no proceedings under this Act shall, merely for defect in form, be quashed or set aside by any court of law.

(2) No suit shall be brought in any court to recover any sum of money collected under the authority of this Act or to recover damages on account of assessment or collection of money made under the said authority:

Provided that the provisions of this Act have in substance and effect been complied with.

(3) No distraint or sale under this Act shall be deemed unlawful, nor shall any person making the same be deemed a tress passer, on account of any error, defect, or want of form in the bill, notice, schedule, form, summon, notice of demand, warrant of distraint, inventory, or other proceeding relating thereto, if the provisions of this Act, and of the rules and by-laws made thereunder have in substance and effect been complied with.

Provided that every person aggrieved by any irregularity may recover satisfaction for any special damage sustained by him

236. Public roads markets, wells, tanks etc to be open to all. – All roads, markets, wells, tanks, reservoirs and waterways vested in or maintained by a panchayat shall be open to the use and enjoyment of all persons, irrespective of their caste or creed.

237. Power to farm out fees. – A panchayat shall have power to farm out the collection of any fees due to it under this Act or any rule, by-law or regulation made thereunder for any period not exceeding three years at a time, on such conditions as it thinks fit.

238. Adjudication of disputes between local authorities. – (1) When a dispute exists between a village panchayat or a panchayat union council or a district panchayat and one or more other local authorities in regard to any matter arising under the provisions of this or any other Act and the Government are of opinion that the village panchayat or the panchayat union council or the district panchayat and the other local authorities concerned are unable to settle it amicably among themselves, the Government may take cognizance of the dispute, and –

(a) decide it themselves, or

(b) refer it for inquiry and report, to an arbitrator or a board of arbitrators or to a joint committee constituted for the purpose.

(2) The report referred to in clause (b) of sub-section (1) shall be submitted to the Government who shall decide the dispute in such manner, as they deem fit.

(3) Any decision given under clause (a) of sub-section (1) or under sub-section (2) may be modified from time to time by the Government in such manner as they deem fit, and any such decision with the modifications, if any made therein under this sub-section may be cancelled at any time by the Government:

Provided that any such decision or any modification therein or cancellation thereof shall be binding on the village panchayat, the panchayat union council, the district panchayat and each of the other local authorities concerned and shall not be liable to be questioned in any court of law.

(4) Where one of the local authorities concerned is a cantonment authority or the port authority of a major port, the powers of the Government under this section shall be exercisable only with the concurrence of the Central Government.

239. Tamil Nadu State Election Commission. – (1) The superintendence, direction and control of the preparation of electoral rolls for, and the conduct of all elections to the village panchayats, panchayat union councils and district panchayats shall be vested in the Tamil Nadu State Election Commission consisting of a Tamil Nadu State Election Commissioner to be appointed by the Governor under Article 243-K of the Constitution.

(2) (a) No person shall be qualified for appointment as Tamil Nadu State Election Commissioner unless he is or has been an officer of the Government not below the rank of Secretary to the Government.

(b) The Tamil Nadu State Election Commissioner shall hold office for a tem of two years and shall be eligible for reappointment for two successive terms:

Provided that no person shall hold the office of the Tamil Nadu State Election Commissioner for more than six years in the aggregate:

Provided further that a person appointed as Tamil Nadu Tamil Nadu State Election Commissioner shall retire from office if he completes the age of sixty-two years during the term of his office.

(3) Subject to the provisions of sub-section (2), the conditions of service and tenure of office of the Tamil Nadu Tamil Nadu State Election Commissioner shall be such as the Governor may by rules determine.

Provided that the Tamil Nadu State Election Commissioner shall not be removed from his office except in like manner and on the like grounds as a Judge of a High Court and conditions of service of the Tamil Nadu State Election Commissioner shall not be varied to his disadvantage after his appointment.

(4) The Governor shall, when so requested by the Tamil Nadu State Election Commission make available to the Tamil Nadu State Election Commission such staff as may be necessary for the discharge of the functions conferred on the Tamil Nadu State Election Commission by sub section (1).

240. Preparation of development plan. – (1) Every village panchayat shall prepare every year a development plan for the panchayat village and submit it to the panchayat union council before such date and in such form as may be prescribed.

(2) Every panchayat union council shall prepare every year a development plan for the panchayat union after including the development plans of the village panchayats and submit it to the district panchayat before such date and in such form as may be prescribe.

(3) Every district panchayat shall prepare every year a development plan for the district after including the development plans of the panchayat union councils and submit it to the District Planning Committee constituted under section 241.

[1][“**241. District Planning Committee.** – (1) The Government shall constitute in every district a District Planning Committee (hereinafter in this section referred to as the Committee) to consolidate the plans prepared by the district panchayats, panchayat union councils, village panchayats. [2][Town Panchayat] Municipal councils and municipal corporations in the district and to prepare a draft development plan for the district as a whole

[3][“(2) (a) The Committee shall consists of , –

[1] *The whole section 241 has been substituted for the existing section by Act. 37/1999*

[2] *Inserted by Act. 55/1997*

[3] *Sub-section (2) has been substituted by Act. 30/2000 for the sub-section (2) which was substituted by Act. 37/1997*

(i) The Chairman of the district panchayat;

(ii) the Mayor of the City Municipal Corporation in the district;

(iii) the Collector of the district;

such number of persons, not less than four-fifth of the total number of members of the Committee as may be specified by the Government, elected in the prescribed manner from amongst the members of the district panchayats, town panchayats and councilors of the municipal corporations and the municipal councils in the district, in proportion to the ratio between the population of the rural areas and of the urban areas in the district.

(b) The following persons shall be permanent special invitees of the Committee:

(i) Members of the House of the people who represent the whole or part of the district;

(ii) Members of the Council of States who are registered as electors in the district;

(iii) Members of the Tamil Nadu State Legislative Assembly whose constituencies lie within the district;

(iv) All the Chairmen of the panchayat union councils in the district;

(v) All the Chairmen of the municipal councils in the district;

(vi) All the Chairmen of the town panchayats in the district.

(c) The permanent special invitees referred to in clause (b) shall be entitled to take part in the proceedings in the meetings of the Committee.

(3) The Secretary of the District Panchayat shall be the Secretary to the Committee

[1][(4) The Chairman of the District Panchayat shall be the Chairperson of the Committee and the Collector of the District shall be the Vice-Chairman of the Committee].

(5) The Committee shall meet at such place, at such interval and at such time and observe such rules of procedure in regard to transaction of business at its meetings (including the quorum at its meetings) as may be prescribed

(6) The Committee shall consolidate the plans prepared by the district panchayat, panchayat union councils, village panchayats, town panchayats, municipal councils and the municipal corporation in the district and prepare a draft development plan for the district as a whole

(7) Every Committee shall, in preparing the draft development plan –

(a) have regard to –

(i) the matters of common interest between the district panchayats, panchayat union councils, village panchayats, town panchayats, municipal corporations and municipal councils in the district including spatial planning, sharing of water and other physical

---

[1] *Substituted by Act. 24/2000*

and natural resources, the integrated development of infrastructures and environmental conservation;

(ii) the extent and type of available resources whether financial or otherwise.

(b) consult such institutions and organisations as the Governor may, by order, specify.

(8) The chair-person of every committee shall forward the development plan, as recommended by such Committee to the Government

(9) The committee shall allocate funds to various schemes to the panchayats unions and shall monitor the implementations of the schemes.

Explanation. – For the purposes of this section "town panchayat" and "municipal council", shall mean the town panchayat and the municipal council constituted under the Tamil Nadu District Municipalities Act, 1920, and "municipal corporation" means the corporations constituted under the Madurai City Municipal Corporation Act, 1971 or the Coimbatore City Municipal Corporation Act, 1981 or the Tiruchirappalli City Municipal Corporation Act, 1994 or the Tirunelveli City Municipal Corporation Act, 1994 or the Salem City Municipal Corporation Act, 1994 or any other municipal corporation that may be constituted under any law for the time being in force as the case may be"].

RULES

242. Power of Government to make rules. – (1) The Government shall in addition to the rule making powers conferred on them by any other provision contained in this Act, have power to make rules generally to carry out the purposes of this Act

[1]["(1-A) A rule under section 188 may be made so as to have retrospective effect on and from a date not earlier than the 26th day of March 1997"].

(2) In particular, and without prejudice to the generality of the forgoing power, the Government may make rules-

(i) as to the principles to be followed in regard to the exclusion of any local area from or the inclusion of any local area in a village under subsection (2) of section 4;

(ii) providing for-

[2][(a) the adjudication of disputes arising out of election by the district judge having jurisdiction]

(b) all matters relating to electoral rolls or elections, not expressly provided for in this Act, including deposits to be made by candidates standing for election and the conditions under which such deposits may be forfeited, and the conduct of inquiries and the decision of disputes relating to electoral rolls;

(iii) as to the determination of the population for the purposes of this Act;

---

[1] *Inserted by Act. 54/1997*

[2] *Substituted by Act. 21/1996.*

(iv) as to the resignations of chairman, vice-chairman and members of panchayat union councils and district panchayats and of the presidents, vice-presidents and members of village panchayats and the date on which such resignations shall take effect;

(v) as to the interpellation of the chairman and vice-chairman by the members of a panchayat union council or the district panchayat and of the president of a village panchayat by the members of the village panchayat, and the moving of resolutions at meetings;

(vi) as to the constitution of committees of the panchayat and the inclusion of outsiders therein and the delegation of functions to such committees;

(vii) providing for the procedure to be followed at meetings of the panchayats and at committees thereof and for the conduct of business and the number of members which shall form a quorum at any meeting;

(viii) providing for the classification of resolutions of panchayats as those involving financial implications or otherwise and for laying down the proportion of the sanctioned strength of panchayats with whose support such resolution shall be carried;

(ix) as to the powers of the panchayat union council and district panchayats, its chairman and committees thereof with respect to the incurring of expenditure and the powers and duties of the commissioner and Secretary.

(x) providing for the travelling and other allowances of the chairman, vice-chairman and other members of the panchayat union council, district panchayat and of members of the committees of the panchayat union council and district panchayat;

(xi) as to the delegation of any function of a panchayat to the president, chairman, member, any officer of the panchayat or any servant of the Central or State Government;

(xii) for the lodging and investment of the moneys of the panchayats and for the manner in which such moneys may be drawn upon;

(xiii) as to the transfer of allotments entered in the sanctioned budget of a panchayat from one head to another;

(xiv) as to the estimates of receipts and expenditure, returns, statements and reports to be submitted by panchayat;

(xv) as to the preparation of plans and estimates for works and the power of panchayat and of servants of the Central or state Government to accord professional or administrative sanction to estimates;

(xvi) as to the accounts to be kept by panchayat, the audit and publication of such accounts and the conditions under which rate-payers may appear before auditors, inspect books and accounts, and take exception to items entered or omitted;

(xvii) as to the powers of auditors to disallow and surcharge items, appeals against orders of disallowance or surcharge and recovery of sums disallowed or surcharged;

(xviii) as to the powers of auditors, inspecting and superintending officers and officers authorised to hold inquiries, to summon and examine witness and to compel the production of documents, and all other matters connected with audit, inspection and superintendence;

(xix) as to the conditions on which property may be acquired by a panchayat or on which property vested in or belonging to a panchayat may be transferred by sale, mortgage, lease, exchange or otherwise;

(xx) as to the conditions on which and the mode in which contracts may be made or on behalf of panchayat.

(xxi) as to the assessment of taxes under this Act and the revision of assessments;

(xxii) as to the acceptance in lieu of any tax due under this Act of any service by way of labour, cartage or otherwise;

(xxiii) as to the realisation of any tax or other sum due to a panchayat under this Act or any other law or any rules or by-laws, whether by distraint and sale of movable property, by prosecution before a Magistrate, by a suit, or otherwise;

(xxiv) as to the realisation of fees due in respect of the use of cart-stands and the like, whether by the seizure and sale of the vehicle or animal concerned or any part of its burden or otherwise.

(xxv) as to the form and contents of licences, permissions and notices granted or issued under this Act, the manner of their issue or the method of their service, and the modification, suspension or cancellation thereof;

(xxvi) as to the powers of executive authorities, commissioners, Secretaries to call for information on any matter, to summon and examine witness, and to compel the production of documents;

(xxvii) for the use of the facsimiles of the signatures of the executive authorities, commissioners, Secretaries and officers of panchayat;

(xxviii) as to the grant to the public of copies of any proceeding or record of the panchayat not relating to any matter classified as confidential by the Government or any authority empowered by them, and the fees to be levied for the grant of such copies;

(xxix) as to the opening, maintenance, management and supervision of elementary schools;

(xxx) regulating contracts between the panchayat and the owners or occupiers of private premises for the removal there from of rubbish or filth, or any kind of rubbish or filth;

(xxxi) as to the provision of burial and burning grounds; the licensing of private burial and burning grounds; the regulation of the use of all grounds so provided or licensed; the closing of any such grounds; and the prohibition of the disposal of corpses except in such grounds or other permitted places;

(xxxii) as to the licensing of pigs and dogs and the destruction of unlicensed pigs and dogs;

(xxxiii) as to the regulation or restriction of building and the use of sites for building;

(xxxiv) for the removal of encroachments of any description from public roads vesting in panchayat and the repair of any damage caused to such roads by the person causing the damage or at his expense;

(xxxv) for the determination of any claim to trees growing on public roads or other property vesting in or belonging to panchayat or on porambokes or on lands the use of which is regulated by them under section 134 or 135; and for the presumptions to be drawn as regards the ownership of such trees;

(xxxvi) as to the imposition and recovery of penalties for the unauthorised occupation of public roads or other land vesting in or belonging to panchayat and the assessment and recovery of compensation for, and damage caused by, such occupation.

(xxxvii) as to the powers which may be exercised by the panchayat or the executive authority or the commissioner or the Secretary office in respect of any public or private market or the user thereof, and the enforcement of any order issued in pursuance of such powers;

(xxxviii) for compelling owners of cattle to stall them in cattle-sheds provided by the panchayat and the fees leviable in respect thereof;

(xxxix) as to the disposal of household and farmyard waste in the village, the acquisition of land by the panchayat or laying out plots for digging pits in which such waste may be thrown, the assignment or those plots to persons in the village, and the conditions subject to which such assignment may be make, including the rent to be charged;

(xl) as to the duties to be discharged by officers in relation to panchayats and their executive authorities their chairmen, commissioners and Secretaries;

(xli) as to appeals against orders (including orders granting or refusing licences or permissions) passed under this Act, and the time within which appeals whether allowed by this Act or by rules or otherwise should presented:

(xlii) as to the classification of public roads and fairs and festivals as appertaining to the panchayat;

(xliii) for regulating the sharing between local authorities in the State of the proceeds of any tax or income levied or obtained under this or any other Act;

(xliv) for decision of disputes between two or more local authorities of which one is a panchayat;

(xlv) regulating the principles in accordance with which grant and contribution may be paid by the Government to the panchayat;

(xlvi) as to the accounts to be kept by owners, occupiers and farmers of private markets and the audit and inspection of such accounts;

(xlvii) as to the manner of publication of notifications or notices to the public under this Act.

CHAPTER XII
PENALTIES

243. Penalties for breach of rules. – In making any rule under this Act, the Government may provide that a breach thereof shall be punishable with fine which may extend to one hundred rupees, or in case of a continuing breach, with fine not exceeding fifteen rupees for every day during which the breach continues after conviction for the first breach.

244. By Laws and penalties for their breach. – (1) Subject to the provisions of this Act and of any other law and to such rules as may be prescribed, a Panchayat may, with the approval of the Inspector, make by-laws for carrying out any of the purposes for which it is constituted.

(2) In making a by-law, the Panchayat may provide that any person who commits a breach thereof shall be liable to pay by way of penalty such sum as may be fixed by the Panchayat not exceeding fifteen rupees or, in case of a continuing breach, not exceeding five rupees for every day during which the breach continues after a penalty has been levied for the first breach.

(3) The Government shall have power to make rules regarding the procedure for the making of by-laws, the publication thereof, and the date on which they shall come into effect.

245. General provisions regarding penalties specified in the schedules. – (1) Whoever – (a) contravenes any of the provisions of this Act specified in the first and second columns of Schedule II; or

(b) contravenes any rule or order made under any of the provisions so specified or

(c) fails to comply with any directions lawfully given to him, or any requisition lawfully made upon him under or in pursuance of any of the said provisions shall be punishable with fine which may extend to the amount mentioned in that behalf in the fourth column of the said Schedule.

(2) Whoever after having been convicted of-

(a) contravening any of the provisions of this Act specified in the first and second columns of Schedule III, or

(b) contravening any rule or order made under any of the provisions so specified or

(c) failing to comply with any direction lawfully given to him or any requisition lawfully made upon him under or in pursuance of any of the said provisions, or continues to contravene the Said provision or the said rule or order fail to comply with the said direction or requisition.

shall be punishable for each day after the previous date conviction during which he continues so to offend, with fine which may extend to the amount mentioned in that behalf in the fourth column of the said Schedule.

Explanation. – The entries in the third column of Schedules II and III headed "subject" are not intended as definitions of the offences described in the provisions specified in the first and second columns thereof, or even as abstracts of those provisions, but are intended merely as references to the subject dealt with therein.

246. Penalty for acting as member president or vice-president of a village panchayat or as member chairman or vice-chairman of a Panchayat Union Council or district panchayat when disqualified. –

(1) Whoever acts as a member of a Panchayat or Panchayat Union council or district Panchayat knowing that, under this Act or the rules made there under, he is not entitled or has ceased to be entitled to hold office as such, shall be punishable with fine not exceeding two hundred rupees for every such offence.

(2) Whoever acts as the president, temporary president or vice-president of a Village Panchayat, or exercises any of his functions including where he is also the executive authority, any of his functions as such and whoever acts as the chairman, temporary chairman or vice-chairman of a Panchayat Union Council or district Panchayat or as Commissioner or Secretary or exercise any of his functions as such knowing that, under this Act or the rules made thereunder, he is not entitled or has ceased to be entitled to hold office as such, or to exercise such functions, shall be punishable with fine not exceeding one thousand rupees for every such offence.

(3) Any person who having been the president, temporary president or vice-president of a village Panchayat, or the Chairman, temporary Chairman or Vice-chairman of a Panchayat Union council or district Panchayat fails to hand over any documents of, or any moneys or other properties vested in or belonging to the village Panchayat or Panchayat Union council or district Panchayat which are in or have come into his possession or control, to his successor in office or other prescribed authority-.

(a) in very case as soon as his term of office as such president, temporary president or vice-chairman or as such chairman, temporary chairman or vice-chairman expires.

(b) in the case of a person who was the vice-president also on demand by the president ;and

(c) in the case of a person who was the vice-chairman also on demand by the Chairman.

Shall be punishable with fine not exceeding one thousand rupees for every such offence.

247. Penalty for acquisition by an officer or servant of interest in contract work. – If any officer or servant of a Panchayat knowingly acquires, directly or indirectly by himself or by a partner, employer or servant, any personal share or interest in any contract or employment with, by or on behalf of, the Panchayat, he shall be deemed to have committed an offence under section 168 of the Indian Penal Code. (Central Act XLV of 1860).

Provided that no person shall, by reason of being a shareholder in, or member of, any company, be held to be interested in any contract entered into between such company and the Panchayat unless he is a director of such company.

248. Wrongful restraint of executive authority or Commissioner or Secretary or his delegates. – Any person who prevents the executive authority or the commissioner or the Secretary or any person to whom the executive authority or the Commissioner or the Secretary has lawfully delegated his powers of entering on or into any place, building or land from exercising his lawful power of entering thereon or there into shall be deemed to have committed an offence under section 341 of the Indian Penal Code. (Central Act XLV of 1860)

249. Prohibition against obstruction of panchayat. – Any person obstructing or molesting the president, or the executive authority or the Chairman or the Secretary or a member of the Panchayat, or any person employed by the Panchayat or any person with whom a contract has been entered into by or on behalf of the Panchayat in the discharge of their duty or of anything which they are empowered or required to do by virtue or in consequence of this Act or of any rule, by-law, regulation or order made thereunder, shall be punished with fine which may extend to fifty rupees.

250. Prohibition against removal of obliteration of notice. – Any person who, without authority in that behalf removes, destroys, defaces or otherwise obliterates any notice exhibited or any sign or mark erected by, or under the orders of, a Panchayat or its executive authority, or by the Commissioner or by the Secretary shall be punishable with fine which may extend to fifty rupees.

251. Penalty for not giving information or giving false information. – Any person required by this Act or by any notice or other proceedings issued thereunder to furnish any information, who omits to furnish such information, or knowingly furnishes false information, shall be punishable with fine not exceeding one hundred rupees.

CHAPTER XIII
MISCELLANEOUS

252. Construction or reference to a panchayat etc. – In the application of any law, rule, by-law, regulation, notification, Scheme, form or order to any area, in the absence of an intention to the contrary appearing in this Act and unless the Government otherwise direct, any reference to a "Panchayat" or a Union Council" or a "Panchayat Village" or a "Panchayat Union" shall be deemed to include also a reference to the Village Panchayat or a Panchayat Union council or a district Panchayat or a Panchayat Village or a Panchayat Union constituted under this Act.

253. Special provisions relating to newly constituted panchayat. – (1) The provisions of this section shall apply when a Panchayat is constituted for the first time under this Act.

(2) When a Panchayat is newly constituted under this section, the Tamil Nadu State Election Commissioner shall make arrangements for the election of members and of the President or the Chairman, as the case may be, so that the member and the president or the Chairman, may come into office on the date specified in the notification issued for the constitution of such Panchayat.

(3) When a Panchayat is constituted under this section, the Government may appoint a special Officer not below the rank of a Tahsildar, for such period not exceeding six months as the Government may, by order, specify, to exercise the powers, discharge the duties perform the functions of the Panchayat, its president or chairman as the case may be. (Tamil Nadu Act 44 of 1999)

[1]["(3A) Notwithstanding anything contained in sub-section (3), the special officers appointed under that sub-section in respect of the village panchayats and panchayat union specified in Schedule IV-A shall hold office upto the 31st day of March, 2000 or such shorter period as the Government may by notification, specify in this behalf."].

(4) The special officer shall exercise the powers, discharge the duties and perform the functions of the Panchayat, its president or Chairman, until the members of the Panchayat have come into office and a president or chairman has been elected.

254. Construction or reference to "local boards" Madras Local Boards Act 1920 etc. – In the application of any law, rule, by law, regulation, notification, scheme form or order to any Panchayat after the constitution of a Panchayat under this Act, in the absence of an intention to the contrary appearing in this Act and unless the Government otherwise direct-

(i) any reference to a village or local area shall be deemed to be reference to a Panchayat village, Panchayat development block or a Panchayat union or Panchayat district as the circumstances may require; Tamil Nadu Act XIV of 1920 Tamil Nadu Act X of 1950 Tamil Nadu XXXV of 1958.

(ii) any reference to local boards shall bedeemed to be a reference to district Panchayats, Panchayat Union Councils or village Panchayats as the case may be.

(iii) any reference to the Madras Local Boards Act, 1920 shall be deemed to be a reference to the Tamil Nadu District Boards Act, 1920 (TN Act. XIV of 1920), the Tamil Nadu Village Panchayats Act, 1950

---

[1] *Inserted by Act. 44/1999*

(TN Act. X of 1950), the Tamil Nadu Panchayats Act 1958 (TN Act. XXXV of 1958) and the Tamil Nadu Panchayats Act 1994.

(iv) any reference to the Tamil Nadu District Boards Act, 1920 (Tamil Nadu Act XIV of 1920) or the Tamil Nadu Village Panchayats Act 1950 (Tamil Nadu Act X of 1950) or the Tamil Nadu Panchayats Act, 1958 (TN Act. XXXV of 1958), shall be deemed to be a reference to the Tamil Nadu Panchayats Act 1994 and

(v) any reference to district boards or its president shall be deemed to be a reference to the Panchayat Union council having jurisdiction or its Chairman, as the case may be.

255. Repeal and savings. – (1) The Tamil Nadu Panchayats Act, 1958 (Tamil Nadu Act. XXXV of 1958), (hereinafter referred to in this section as the said Act) is hereby repealed.

(2) The repeal, by sub-section (1) of the said Act shall not affect-

(a) the previous operation of the said Act or anything done or duly suffered thereunder, or

(b) any right, privilege, obligation or liability acquired, accrued or incurred under the said Act; or

(c) any penalty, forfeiture, or punishment incurred in respect of any offences committed against the said Act; or

(d) any investigation, legal proceedings or remedy in respect of any such right, privilege, obligation, liability, penalty, forfeiture or punishment as aforesaid and any such investigation, legal proceedings or remedy may be instituted, continued or enforced and any such penalty, forfeiture or punishment may be imposed as if this Act had not been passed.

(3) Subject to the provisions of sub-section (2) anything done or any action taken, including any appointment, or delegation mad, notification, order, instruction or direction issued, or any rule, regulation or form framed, certificate granted or registration effected, under the said Act shall be deemed to have been done or taken under this Act and shall continue to have effect accordingly, unless and until superseded by anything done any action taken under this Act.

256. Power to remove difficulties. – (1) If any difficulty arises in giving effect to the provisions of this Act, the Government may, by order published in the Tamil Nadu Government Gazette, make such provisions, not inconsistent with the provisions of this Act and to be in conformity with the provisions of the Constitution (Seventy-third Amendment) Act 1992 as appear to it to be necessary or expedient for removing the difficulty.

Provided that no such order shall be made after the expiry of a period of two years from the date of commencement of this Act.

(2) Every order made under this section, shall, as soon as may be, after it is made, be placed on the table of the Legislative Assembly.

257. Power, authority and responsibilities of panchayats. – Save as otherwise provided in this Act, the Government may, by notification and subject to such conditions and restrictions as may be specified therein, entrust to a Panchayat or any other committee constituted under this Act with such powers and responsibilities with respect to the preparation of plans for economic development and social justice and also with such powers and authority as may be necessary to enable them to carry out the responsibilities conferred upon them including those in relation to the matters listed in Schedule-IV.

DISPUTES REGARDING ELECTIONS

258. Election Petitions. – (1) No election of a president or a chairman or a member shall be called in question except by an election petition presented to the district judge of the district in which the Panchayat is situated, within [1]["forty five days"] from the date of the publication of the result of the election under this Act.

(2) An election petition calling in question any such election may be presented on one or more of the grounds specified in section 259 by any candidate at such election, by any elector of the ward concerned or by any member.

(3) A petitioner shall join as respondents to his petition all the candidates at the election.

(4) an election petition –

(a) shall contain a concise statement of the material facts on which the petitioner relies:

(b) shall, with sufficient particulars, set forth the ground or grounds on which the election is called in question; and

(c) shall be signed by the petitioner and verified in the manner laid down in the Code of Civil Procedure, 1908 (Central Acts V of 1908) for the verification pleadings.

[2]["(5) The trial of an election petition shall, so far as is practicable consistently with the interest of justice in respect of the trial, be continued from day-to-day until its conclusion, unless the district judge finds the adjournment of the trial beyond the following day to be necessary for reasons to be recorded.

(6) Every elevation petition shall be tried as expeditiously as possible and endeavor shall be made to conclude the trial within six months from the date on which the election petition is presented to the district judge for trial"].

259. Grounds for declaring election to be void. – (1) Subject the provisions of sub-section (2), if the District Judge is of opinion-

(a) that on the date of his election returned candidate was not qualified or was qualified, to be chosen as a member under this Act. or

---

[1] *Substituted by Act. 18/2001 for the expression "fifteen days"*

[2] *Added by Act. 1/2001*

(b) that any corrupt practice has been committed by a returned candidate or his agent or by any other person with the consent of a returned candidate or his agent, or

(c) that any nomination paper has been improperly rejected, or

(d) that the result of the election in so far as it concerns a returned candidate has been materially affected:

(i) by the improper acceptance of any nomination, or

(ii) by any corrupt practice committed in the interests of the returned candidate by a person other than that candidate or his agent or a person acting with the consent of such candidate or agent or

(iii) by the improper acceptance or refusal of any vote or reception of any vote which is void; or

(iv) by the non-compliance with the provisions of this Act or of any rules or orders made thereunder, the court shall declare the election of the returned candidate to void.

(2) If in the opinion of the Court, a returned candidate has been guilty by an agent of any corrupt practice, but the court is satisfied-

(a) that no such corrupt practice was committed at the election by the candidate, and every such corrupt practice was committed contrary to the orders, and without the consent of the candidate.

(b) that the candidate took all reasonable means for preventing the commission of corrupt practice at the election; and

(c) that in all other respects the election was free from any corrupt practice on the part of the candidate or any of his agents, then, the court may decide that the election of the returned candidate is not void.

260. Corrupt practices. – The following shall be deemed to be corrupt practice for the purposes of this Act: – (1) Bribery as defined in clause (1) of section 123 of the Representation of the People Act 1951. (Central Act XLIII of 1951)

(2) Undue influence as defined in clause (2) of the said section.

(3) The systematic appeal by a candidate or his agent or by any other person to vote or refrain from voting on grounds of caste, race, community or religion or the use of or appeal to, religious symbols, or, the use of or appeal to, national symbols such as the national flag or the national emblem, for the furtherance of the prospects of the candidate's election.

(4) The publication by a candidate or his agent or by any other person of any statement of fact which is false, and which he either believes to be false or does not believe to be true, in relation to the personal character or conduct of any candidate, or in relation to the candidate, or withdrawal from [1]["contest"] of any candidate, or statement reasonable calculated to prejudice the prospects of that candidate's election.

(5) The hiring or procuring whether on payment otherwise of any vehicle or vessel by a candidate or his agent or by any other person for

---

[1] *Substituted by Act. 2/1999 for the word "contact"*

conveyance of any elector (other than the candidate himself, and the members of his family or his agent) to or from any polling station provided in accordance with the rules made under this Act.

Provided that the hiring of a vehicle or vessel by an elector or by several electors at their joint costs for the purpose of conveying him or them to or for any such polling station shall not be deemed to be a corrupt practice under this clause if the vehicle or vessel so hired is a vehicle or vessel not propelled by mechanical power.

Provided further that the use of any public transport vehicle or vessel or any tram, car or railway carriage by an elector at his own cost for the purpose of going to or coming from any such polling station shall not be deemed to be corrupt practice under this clause.

Explanation. – In this clause the expression "vehicle" means any vehicle used or capable of being used for the purpose of road transport whether propelled by mechanical power or otherwise and whether used for drawing other vehicles or otherwise.

(6) The holding of any meeting in which intoxicating liquors are served.

(7) The issuing of any circular, play-card or poster having a reference to election which does not bear the name and address of the printer and publisher thereof.

(8) Any other practice which the Government may by rules, specify to be corrupt practice.

261. Transitory provision. – (1) Notwithstanding anything contained in this Act, or in any other law for the time being in force, the Government may, by notification, if necessary, appoint special officers to exercise the powers and discharge the functions of the Village Panchayats, the Panchayat Union councils, or the district Panchayats, as the case may be, until the day on which the first meetings of the village Panchayats, Panchayat Union Councils, or the district Panchayats as the case may be, are held after ordinary elections to the said panchayats after commencement of this Act.

[1]["(2) The special officers appointed under sub-section (1) in respect of the village panchayats and panchayat union councils specified in the schedule V shall hold office upto 24th day of October, 2002 or for such shorter period as a Government may by notification specified in this behalf"].

---

[1] *The original sub-section (2) in the parent Act.21/1994 contained a period of nine months from the date of commencement of the parent Act. 21/1994 (viz.,22.04.1994). This date was extended to 31.12.1995 in Act. 51/1994, to 30.06.1996 in Act. 45/1995 and to 31.12.1996 in Act. 14/1996. Then the whole sub-section(2) was substituted by Act. 10/1997 in the present form given above the except the period mentioned therein, viz., upto 30.06.1997. This sub-section (2) was periodically substituted by Act.55/1997, Act.5/1998, Act.53/1998, Act.46/1999, Act. 5/2000, extending the dates suitably and lastly by Act.8/2002 prescribing the date as mentioned above.*

262. Rules, notifications and orders to be placed before the Legislative Assembly. – (1) All rules, notifications and orders made or issued under this Act except the notifications issued under sections 3,5,7 read with section 4, 11, 12, 20, 21 and 32 shall be published in the Tamil Nadu Government Gazette and unless they are expressed to come into force on a particular day, shall come into force on the day on which they are so published.

(2) All notifications issued under sections 3,5,7 read with section 4, 11, 12, 20, 21 and 32 shall be published in the District Gazette concerned and unless they are expressed to come into force on a particular day, shall come into force on the day on which they are so published.

(3) Every rule, notification or order made or issued by the Government under this Act shall, as soon as possible after it is made or issued, be placed on the table of the Legislative Assembly, and if before the expiry of the session in which it is so placed or the next session, the Legislative Assembly agrees in making any modification in any such rule, notification or order, or legislative assembly agrees that the rule notification or order should not be made or issued, the rule, notification or order shall, thereafter have effect only in such modified form or be of no effect, as the case may be, so, however, that any such modification or annulment shall be without prejudice to the validity of anything previously done under that rule, notification or order.

SCHEDULE I

(See Section 172(1))

Sl. No	Classification (1)		If the tax is levied every half year (2)				If the tax is levied every year (3)		
			Minimum rate per half year (i)		Maximum rate per half year (ii)		Minimum rate per year (iii)		Maximum rate per year (iv)
		Rs.Ps		Rs.Ps		Rs.Ps		Rs.Ps	
(i)	Concrete houses, Madras terraced houses storied houses	0.25	Per 9.29 square decimetres of the plinth area	0.50	Per 9.29 square decimetres of the plinth area	0.50	Per 9.29 square decimetres of the plinth area	1.00	Per 9.29 square decimetres of the plinth area
(ii)	Tiled houses	0.15	Per 9.29 square decimetres of the plinth area	0.30	Per 9.29 square decimetres of the plinth area	0.50	Per 9.29 square decimetres of the plinth area	0.60	Per 9.29 square decimetres of the plinth area
(iii)	Thatched houses 20 square metres and above	1.10	Per 9.29 square decimetres of the plinth area	0.20	Per 9.29 square decimetres of the plinth area	0.20	Per 9.29 square decimetres of the plinth area	0.40	Per 9.29 square decimetres of the plinth area
(iv)	Thatched houses below 20 square metres	0.20	For every 9.29 square metres or part thereof plinth area.	0.50	For every 9.29 square metres or part thereof plinth area.	0.40	For every 9.29 square metres or part thereof plinth area.	1.00	For every 9.29 square metres or part thereof plinth area.

Explanation I. – In respect of buildings which are partly concrete, terraced, tiled or thatched, the rates applicable to the respective categories as above shall be applicable for the portions covered by each kind:

Provided that in respect of buildings the plinth area of which does not exceed 18.58 square metres and which are fully concrete, terraced or tiled, or partly concrete, terraced or tiled, house tax shall be levied at a flat rate of rupees twenty per half year.

Explanation II. – The use of the building may be classified and surcharge shall be levied on the levy of house tax at the rates specified below:

	Class of usage		Rate of surcharge
i)	Purely residential	Village Panchayats	Nil
ii)	Simple commercial like petty shops and other small commercial establishments	Village Panchayats	20%
iii)	Largely commercial, industrial and business establishments, Cinema theatres, Hostels, Lodges etc.	Village Panchayats	60%

Provided that in respect of buildings used partly as residential and partly as commercial, industrial, etc, purposes, the rate of surcharge applicable to the respective categories as above shall be applicable for the portions covered by each class of usage.

Provided further that Educational institutions (not commercial in nature) exempted from levy of house tax immediately before the commencement of this Act shall continue to be exempted under this Act.

SCHEDULE II

ORDINARY PENALTIES

(See Section 245 (1)

Section (1)	Sub-section or clause (2)	Subject (3)	Fine which may be imposed. (4)
128	(1)	Failure to obey requisition to fence off, take down, secure or repair dangerous structure	Five hundred rupees
129	(1)	Failure to obey requisition to secure, lop or cut down dangerous trees	Fifty rupees
130		Failure to obey requisition to fence building or land or trim, prune or cut hedges and trees or lower an enclosing wall.	Fifty rupees
131	(1) (a)	Unlawful building of wall or erecting of fence, etc, in or over public road	One hundred rupees
131	(1)(b)	Unlawful making of hole or depositing of matter in or upon public road	Fifty rupees

Section (1)	Sub-section or clause (2)	Subject (3)	Fine which may be imposed. (4)
131	(1) (c)	Unlawful quarrying in any place near public road etc.	Fifty rupees
131	(1) (d)	Unlawful erection of building over drain	Two hundred rupees
131	(1) (e)	Planting of trees without permission on any public road or other property vested in a Panchayat or Panchayat Union Council	Two hundred rupees
131	(1) (f)	Felling, etc. without permission of trees growing on public road or other property vested in a Panchayat or on poramboke or land the use of which is regulated by it under section 134 or section 135	Two hundred rupees
139		Failure to close place of public entertainment	Two hundred rupees
140		Sending infected child to school	Fifty rupees
142		Failure to give information of small pox	Fifty rupees
143	(1)	Failure to obey requisition to fill in, etc. tank or other place dangerous to public health or safety.	Fifty rupees
144	(1)	Failure to obey requisition to clear or cleanse etc. building or land in filthy state or overgrown with noxious vegetation	Fifty rupees
148	(1)	Opening a new private market or continuing to keep open a private market without licence or contrary to licence.	Five hundred rupees
148	(3)	Levy of fees in private market without a Certificate.	One hundred rupees
150		Sale or exposure for sale in public or private market of any animal or article without permission.	Twenty rupees
151		Sale, etc. of articles in public roads or places after	Ten rupees

Sec-tion (1)	Sub-section or clause (2)	Subject (3)	Fine which may be imposed. (4)
		prohibition or without licence or contrary to regulations.	
154	(b)	Using any public place or road side as a landing or halting place or as a cart-stand without prohibited distance.	Fifty rupees
155	(1)	Opening a private cart-stand or continuing to keep open a private cart-stand without licence or contrary licence.	Two hundred rupees
157	(a)	Slaughtering, cutting up or skinning etc. of animals outside public slaughter-houses in contravention of rules.	Two hundred rupees
157	(b)	Slaughtering animals for purposes of sale without licence or contrary to licence.	Twenty rupees
158	(3)	Unlawful destruction etc. of number affixed of buildings	Five rupees
158	(4)	Failure to replace number when required to do so	Twenty rupees
159		Using a place for offensive or dangerous trade without licence or contrary to licence.	Five hundred rupees
160		Unlawful erection of factory, workshop etc.	One thousand rupees.
236		Obstructing a person in the use or enjoyment of a public road market, well, tank etc.	Five hundred rupees

SCHEDULE III

PENALITIES FOR CONTINUING BREACHES

[See Section 245 (2)]

Sec-tion (1)	Sub-section or clause (2)	Subject (3)	Fine which may be imposed. (4)
128	(1)	Failure to obey requisition to fence off, take down, secure or repair dangerous structure	Fifty rupees

Section (1)	Sub-section or clause (2)	Subject (3)	Fine which may be imposed. (4)
129	(1)	Failure to obey requisition to secure, lop or cut down dangerous trees	Ten rupees
130		Failure to obey requisition to fence building or land or trim, prune or cut hedges and trees or lower an enclosing wall.	Ten rupees
131	(1) (a)	Unlawful building of wall or erecting of fence, etc, in or over public road	Twenty rupees
131	(1)(b)	Unlawful making of hole or depositing of matter in or upon public road	Ten rupees
131	(1) (c)	Unlawful quarrying in any place near public road etc.	Ten rupees
131	(1) (d)	Unlawful erection of building over drain	Fifty rupees
139		Failure to close place of public entertainment	One hundred rupees
143	(1)	Failure to obey requisition to fill in, etc. tank or other place dangerous to public health or safety.	Ten rupees
144	(1)	Failure to obey requisition to clear or cleanse etc. building or land in filthy state or overgrown with noxious vegetation	Ten rupees
148	(1)	Keeping open a private market without licence or contrary to licence.	One hundred rupees
148	(3)	Levy of fees in private market without a Certificate.	Fifty rupees
150		Sale or exposure for sale in public or private market of any animal or article without permission.	Ten rupees
155	(1)	Keeping open a private cart-stand without licence or contrary to licence.	Twenty rupees

Section (1)	Sub-section or clause (2)	Subject (3)	Fine which may be imposed. (4)
159		Using a place for offensive or dangerous trade without licence or contrary to licence.	Twenty rupees
160		Unlawful erection of factory, workshop etc.	One hundred rupees

SCHEDULE – IV

(See Section 257)

1. Agriculture, including agricultural extension
2. Land improvement, implementation of land reforms, land consolidation and soil conservation.
3. Minor irrigation, water management and watershed development.
4. Animal husbandry, dairying and poultry
5. Fisheries
6. Social forestry and farm forestry
7. Minor forest produce
8. Small scale industries, including food processing industries
9. Khadi, Village and cottage industries
10. Rural housing
11. Drinking water
12. Fuel and fodder
13. Roads, culverts, bridges, Water ways and other means of communication
14. Rural electrification, including distribution of electricity
15. Non-conventional energy sources
16. Poverty alleviation programme
17. Education, including primary and secondary schools
18. Technical training and vocational education
19. Adult and non formal education
20. Libraries
21. Cultural activities
22. Market and fairs
23. Health and sanitation, including hospitals, primary health centres and dispensaries.
24. Family welfare
25. Women and child development.
26. Social Welfare, including welfare of the handicapped and mentally retarded
27. Welfare of the weaker sections, and in particular, of the Scheduled Castes and Scheduled Tribes.
28. Public distribution system
29. Maintenance of community assets.

[1]["SCHEDULE – IV – A

[See Section 253 (3-A)]

Serial Number	Name of the Village Panchayats	Serial Number	Name of the Village Panchayats
(1)	(2)	(1)	(2)
1	Yercaud	6	Semmanatham
2	Manjakuttai	7	Valavanthi
3	Vellakkadai	8	Thalaisholai
4	Velur	9	Maramangalam
5	Nagalur		

PART – B

"Yercaud Panchayat Union".]

---

[1] *Inserted by Act. 44/1999*

SCHEDULE – V

[(See Section 261 (2)]

Serial Number	Name of the Village Panchayats
1	Keeripatti
2	Pappapatti

This schedule was added by Act. 10/1997 containing six village panchayats namely: 1.S.Malayandipattinam, 2.Kottakatchiyendal, 3. Keeripatti, 4.Pappapatti, 5.Marudhangudi and 6.Thandanur. The village panchayat namely: Maruthangudi was deleted in Act.46/1999 and the village panchayats S.Malayandipattinam, Kottakatchiyendal, and Thandanur were deleted by Act.53/1998 leaving only two village panchayats namely Keeripatti and Pappapatti in the schedule now.

SCHEDULE – VI

[(See Section 9-A (1)]

Serial Number	Name of the Village Panchayats
1	Kottkatchiyendal
2	Nattarmangalam

This schedule was originally added by Act. 3/2002 containing three village panchayats namely: Kottakatchiyendal, Melasathambur and Nattarmangalam and was later substituted by Act.8/2002 by deleting the village panchayat "Melasathambur" from the original list of three village panchayats mentioned in the schedule added by Act.3/2002, leaving only two village panchayats mentioned above.

LIST OF AMENDMENT ACTS OF TAMIL NADU PANCHAYATS ACT, 1994 (T.N. Act 21 of 1994)

1. Tamil Nadu Panchayats (Amendment) Act. 1994 (T.N.Act No.51 of 1994).
2. Tamil Nadu Panchayats (Amendment) Act. 1995 (T.N.Act No.29 of 1995).
3. Tamil Nadu Panchayats (Second Amendment) Act. 1995 (T.N.Act No.30 of 1995)
4. Tamil Nadu Panchayats (Third Amendment) Act. 1995 (T.N.Act No45 of 1995).
5. Tamil Nadu Panchayats (Amendment) Act. 1996 (T.N.Act No.14 of 1996).
6. Tamil Nadu Panchayats (second Amendment) Act. 1996 (T.N.Act No15 of 1996)
7. Tamil Nadu Panchayats (Third Amendment) Act. 1996 (T.N.Act No21 of 1996)
8. Tamil Nadu Panchayats (Amendment) Act. 1997 (T.N.Act No.10 of 1997).
9. Tamil Nadu Panchayats (Second Amendment) Act. 1997 (T.N.Act No37 of 1997).
10. Tamil Nadu Panchayats (Third Amendment) Act. 1997 (T.N.Act No.54 of 1997)
11. Tamil Nadu Panchayats (Fourth Amendment) Act. 1997 (T.N.Act No.55 of 1997)
12. Tamil Nadu Panchayats (Amendment) Act. 1998 (T.N.Act No.4 of 1998)
13. Tamil Nadu Panchayats (Second Amendment) Act. 1998 (T.N.Act No.5 of 1998)
14. Tamil Nadu Panchayats (Third Amendment) Act. 1998 (T.N.Act No.28 of 1998)
15. Tamil Nadu Panchayats (Fourth Amendment) Act. 1998 (T.N.Act No.29 of 1998)
16. Tamil Nadu Panchayats (Fifth Amendment) Act. 1998 (T.N.Act No.53 of 1998)
17. Tamil Nadu Panchayats (Sixth Amendment) Act. 1998 (T.N.Act No.54 of 1998)
18. Tamil Nadu Panchayats (Seventh Amendment) Act.1998 (T.N.Act No.55 of 1998)
19. Tamil Nadu Panchayats (Amendment) Act. 1999 (T.N.Act No.2 of 1999).
20. Tamil Nadu Panchayats (Second Amendment) Act. 1999 (T.N.Act No.19 of 1999)
21. Tamil Nadu Panchayats (Third Amendment) Act. 1999 (T.N.Act No.29 of 1999)
22. Tamil Nadu Panchayats (Fourth Amendment) Act. 1999 (T.N.Act No.30 of 1999.

23. Tamil Nadu Panchayats (Fifth Amendment) Act. 1999 (T.N.Act No. 31 of 1999).
24. Tamil Nadu Panchayats (Sixth Amendment) Act. 1999 (T.N.Act No.32 of 1999)
25. Tamil Nadu Panchayats (Seventh Amendment) Act1999 (T.N.Act No.44 of 1999)
26. Tamil Nadu Panchayats (Eighth Amendment) Act. 1999 (T.N.Act No.46 of1999)
27. Tamil Nadu Panchayats (Amendment) Act. 2000 (T.N.Act No. 5 of 2000)
28. Tamil Nadu Panchayats (Second Amendment) Act 2000 (T.N.ActNo.23 of 2000)
29. Tamil Nadu Panchayats (Fifth Amendment) Act. 2000 (T.N.Act No.24 of 2000).
30. Tamil Nadu Panchayats (Third Amendment) Act. 2000 (T.N.Act No.27 of 2000)
31. Tamil Nadu Panchayats (Sixth Amendment) Act. 2000 (T.N.Act No.30 of 2000)
32. Tamil Nadu Panchayats (Fourth Amendment) Act. 2000 (T.N.Act No.1 of 2001)
33. Tamil Nadu Panchayats (Amendment) Act. 2001 (T.N.Act No.18 of 2001)
34. Tamil Nadu Panchayats (Second Amendment) Act. 2001 (T.N.Act No.19 of 2001)
35. Tamil Nadu Panchayats (Amendment) Act. 2002 (T.N.Act No.3 of 2002)
36. Tamil Nadu Panchayats (Third Amendment) Act. 2002 (T.N.Act No.8 of 2002)
37. Tamil Nadu Panchayats (Second Amendment) Act. 2002 (T.N.Act No.28 of 2002).

INDEX